British Regionalism and Devolution

Regional Policy and Development Series

Series Editor: Ron Martin, Department of Geography, University of Cambridge

Throughout the industrialised world, widespread economic restructuring, rapid technological change, the reconfiguration of State intervention, and increasing globalisation are giving greater prominence to the nature and performance of individual regional and local economies within nations. The old patterns and processes of regional development that characterised the post-war period are being fundamentally redrawn, creating new problems of uneven development and new theoretical and policy challenges. Whatever interpretation of this contemporary transformation is adopted, regions and localities are back on the academic and political agenda. *Regional Policy and Development* is an international series which aims to provide authoritative analyses of this new regional political economy. It seeks to combine fresh theoretical insights with detailed empirical enquiry and constructive policy debate to produce a comprehensive set of conceptual, practical and topical studies in this field. The series is not intended as a collection of synthetic reviews, but rather as original contributions to understanding the processes, problems and policies of regional and local economic development in today's changing world.

British Regionalism and Devolution

The Challenges of State Reform and European Integration

Edited by Jonathan Bradbury and John Mawson

Regional Policy and Development Series 16

Jessica Kingsley Publishers
London and Bristol, Pennsylvania

Regional Studies Association
London

First published in the United Kingdom in 1997 by
Jessica Kingsley Publishers Ltd
116 Pentonville Road
London N1 9JB, England
and
1900 Frost Road, Suite 101
Bristol, PA 19007, U S A

with

the Regional Studies Association
Registered Charity 252269

Library of Congress Cataloguing in Publication Data
A CIP catalogue record for this book is available from the Library of Congress

British Library Cataloguing in Publication Data
Bristish Regionalism and Devolution: the challenges of state reform and European integration. – (Regional Policy and Development; 16)
1. Regionalism – Great Britain 2. Great Britain – Politics and government – 1979–
I. Bradbury, Jonathan II. Mawson, John

ISBN 1 85302 370 1

Printed and Bound in Great Britain by
Athenæum Press, Gateshead, Tyne and Wear

Contents

Part III: Local Government, European Union and British Regionalism

List of Tables

List of Figures

Preface

Many of the essays in this book were originally presented as papers for a seminar group on British Regionalism and Devolution in a Single Europe. The group was supported by the Economic and Social Research Council and was convened by Michael Hebbert, Eleonore Koffinan and Jack Brand. Seminars were held at the London School of Economics, Strathclyde University, Nottingham Trent University and Birmingham University between 1993 and 1995. The inspiration for the group was a desire to consider the pressures for devolution and regional reforms which had emerged before the 1992 British General Election and seemed destined to continue thereafter. The seminars highlighted the persistence of these pressures and their significance in terms of the constitutional debate and of governance and policy making more generally. It was evident that these developments were strongly influenced by the changing nature of the British State following the Thatcher reforms, as well as European integration after the 1986 Single European Act. A number of papers from the seminars were published in journals, and further papers inspired by the work of the group were published in the Policy Review Section of the *Regional Studies* journal, focusing in particular on New Labour and Devolution (vol.30, no.6, 1996 and vol.30, no. 7,1996). The collection of revised and updated papers from the seminars offered here represents an attempt to provide a more general overview of developments in the practice of British regionalism and the debates surrounding devolution and territorial management in the period from the mid 1980s to the mid 1990s. For the sake of completeness the papers cover the story up to the end of the second Major government, taking Christmas 1996 as the end point. To reflect this focus of analysis the phrasing of the text is largely kept in the past tense. As a general record of this period the book seeks to identify the key issues, and to present a challenging perspective on these important trends and developments. The book is intended to present more than a historical record. Given the likely continued saliency of regionalism and the debate surrounding devolution, the book is intended to be a source of information and insights which will be of continuing practical value. On this basis it is hoped that the book may prove to be a valuable source for practitioners, act as a key text for students, and be informative for the general reader seeking to understand the issues surrounding this complex subject.

As editors we are grateful to the conveners of the seminar group for asking us to bring the book together, and to the contributors for their responsiveness to the needs of making the book cohesive and hopefully greater than the sum of its parts. Several chapters draw upon the findings of a research project undertaken by Ken Spencer and John Mawson entitled 'Whitehall and the Reorganisation of Regional Offices in England'. The authors gratefully acknowledge the support forthcoming from the ESRC Whitehall Programme without which this work could not have been undertaken. We would also like to thank Kate Stephenson for her assistance in helping to prepare the book on computer, and Anne Mather (Dundee), and Ann Burton-Davies and Christine Roberts (Swansea) for their secretarial assistance. Finally we would like to thank Jessica Kingsley for her co-operation and support in publishing the book.

Jonathan Bradbury and John Mawson
January 1997

CHAPTER 1

Introduction

Jonathan Bradbury

During the early to mid 1990s an important debate emerged regarding the government of Scotland, Wales and the English regions within the British state. The Major governments maintained support for a traditional constitutional approach. This asserted rule according to laws determined in the Westminster parliament, and implemented through the administrative machinery of central government, including the Scottish and Welsh Offices and the English field administration of central departments. In contrast, all other parties called for change. The Scottish National Party (SNP) and Plaid Cymru questioned the right of British rule altogether; the Liberal Democrats campaigned for the creation of a federal Britain. Most attention, however, focused on the position of the Labour Party, the principal alternative to the Conservatives in forming a government. Labour made commitments to introduce devolution, involving the transfer of powers from Westminster to Scottish and Welsh elected assemblies, albeit under the continuing supremacy of the Westminster parliament. These assemblies would take over the roles and resources of the Scottish and Welsh Offices. In addition Labour advocated decentralisation of certain central government powers to new regional chambers in England. In response to these proposals, the Major governments carried out initiatives which they claimed further enhanced governmental effectiveness within a Westminster-based approach. These included reform of the Scottish and Welsh Offices and parliamentary business; the reform of central field administration in England through the establishment of ten Government Offices of the Regions; and reform of local government structure throughout Scotland, Wales and England. Labour derided these initiatives as minimalist tinkering, whilst reasserting and refining its own proposals.

The divide between the parties remained comparatively low key until December 1994 when John Major personally criticised Labour's proposals as, 'one of the most dangerous propositions ever put to the British nation'. He suggested that devolution and regional reform would damage the economic interests of Scotland, Wales and the English regions, and that the new assemblies would destabilise British government generally by creating conflict with Westminster. Indeed, by encouraging the idea of self-government he believed that devolution could lead ultimately to the break-up of the state. He accused the Labour leader, Tony Blair, of 'a sort of teenage madness' (White1994). Blair refuted such criticisms, arguing that it was the government, by its abuse of central power, which had undermined democracy and governmental effectiveness and damaged economic interests, thereby eroding allegiance in Scotland and Wales to the British state. It was the continuation of the Major governments' approach, Labour argued, which would lead to political instability and the hardening of anti-British attitudes, which in turn might lead to the break-up of the state. In this context, Blair suggested that it was devolution and regional reform which would preserve the British Union. It needed to be seen as a wise revision of constitutional arrangements which, whilst diluting some Westminster power, would improve the nature of government and rebuild allegiance. The comparable firmness of conviction shown by both Mr Major and Mr Blair drew considerable political and media attention. Consequently, the debate over how best to develop government in Scotland, Wales and the English regions was thrust firmly up the political agenda, making it a key issue for the 1997 general election campaign. Indeed it was clear that the debate would remain highly politically salient, as it was on matters of the constitution that the main parties were most divided.

This policy debate occurred against a background of complex institutional and political change within Scotland, Wales and the English regions. At first glance these underlying forces appeared to underpin the logic of the policies of the opposition parties. For there was a decline in Conservative Party fortunes in all forms of election in Scotland and Wales against parties offering more political autonomy. In Scotland a constitutional convention was established in 1989 to campaign for a Scottish parliament. In England a campaign for a Northern assembly was launched in 1992 to pursue change along similar lines. Increasingly local government operated on a collaborative basis to try and promote shared Scottish and Welsh interests, and in England local government networks operating at a regional level became accepted practice across a wide range of policy areas. Moreover, a large number of quasi-public authorities and private sector bodies began to work at the regional level, and inspired a debate about the need for co-ordination, particularly in the spheres of economic development and regeneration. This dynamism within British regionalism – using the term in a comparative sense to refer to developments in any meso level sub-state territory and the pressures they inspire for reform – was less publicised, but was no less dramatic for being so.

Britain, of course, had seen the emergence of similar developments and policy debates before. Home rule as a major political issue dated back to the late nineteenth century, and as recently as the 1960s and 1970s, the relationship between the British state and government in Scotland, Wales and the English regions had been a key issue in British politics. In the latter era devolution received extensive debate, only to fail after referenda in 1979. The traditional Westminster-based approach to government was sustained and the only reforms of lasting significance ultimately focused on enhancing governmental effectiveness within this approach. On the basis of historical experience, it was tempting, therefore, to suggest that the significance of the developments in the early to mid 1990s should be treated with similar scepticism; that yet again the pressures for radical change in the regions and the case for devolution in the national policy debate were probably less compelling than at first appearance. However, it was also apparent that after the 1970s domestic state reform and developments in European integration both had the potential to change the long-standing order of political authority in Britain and, therefore, the existing relationships between government at the centre and government at the regional and local levels (Keating 1988; Keating and Jones 1985). They offered new challenges whose implications for the nature of British regionalism and the policy debate over devolution were frequently judged to be profound and needed to be explored. Consequently, this book addresses the question: were there novel developments and policy issues to be understood which arose from these challenges in the early to mid 1990s or was there largely a repetition of earlier trends and problems?

Informed by original research, the book sets out a number of perspectives on British regionalism, devolution debates and Conservative government policy in the early-mid 1990s which attempt to answer this question. It should be noted, however, that from the beginning contributors to the book, in limiting themselves to this focus, excluded explicit attention to several allied concerns. First, it might be considered relevant to extend such a study to include analysis of Northern Ireland. The view taken here, however, was that Northern Ireland was a subject worthy of separate treatment and, as a result, should not be specifically addressed. Second, some readers might be interested in the changing nature of separatist nationalist politics within the British periphery. This is of substantial interest, but again it was decided that the changing nature of regionalist politics was quite sufficient a focus, and that an assessment of separatist nationalism would be capable of generating a book-length study by itself. Consequently, whilst separatist nationalism and the politics of Plaid Cymru and the SNP were often considered for their effect on debates about the reform of government in Wales and Scotland within the context of the British state, they were not of themselves a central concern. Third, it might be considered desirable for the authors to have engaged in a normative discussion of the rights and wrongs of developments in British regionalism or in the debate over devolution. The view was taken, however, that analysis of such subjects is too often blighted by the exploration of explicitly stated partisan perspectives and that the book instead should set out as rigorously as possible to describe and analyse the full complexity of developments in British regionalism and those factors that affected central policy. Finally, whilst all writers subscribed to a general understanding of regionalism as outlined above (p.5), they recognised that political scientists, planners and geographers define the term specifically in different ways. Consequently, the view was taken that rather than developing a single prescriptive understanding of regionalism, the book should attempt to provide an appreciation of the complexity of regionalism in modern Britain. At the same time it was recognised that for political scientists in particular, use of the language of nationalism, albeit of a non-separatist kind, in relation to Scotland and Wales is still often more appropriate than that of regionalism.

As a prelude to the chapters which develop perspectives on regionalism and policy developments in the early-mid 1990s, the rest of this chapter addresses three issues which require fuller preliminary discussion. Section one discusses the development of the traditional British constitutional approach to the government of Scotland, Wales and the English regions. Section two analyses previous pressures for reform, focusing on the devolution debate in the 1960s and 1970s, and the results that followed. These two sections taken together establish a historical record of constitutional development, regionalism and reform, providing a basis against which developments in British regionalism, arguments for devolution and government policy in the 1980s and early–mid 1990s can be compared. Section three then discusses state reform and European integration after the 1970s and their potential for stimulating novel dimensions for these latter developments. Finally, the chapter sets out the approach which the book takes in seeking to make a contribution to current understanding.

Constitutional traditions

In establishing the nature of the traditional British constitutional approach, one is immediately struck by the fact that from the seventeenth century it developed primarily in accord with a unitary tradition, allowing for uniform government from the centre. This derived ultimately from acceptance of the legislative and fiscal sovereignty of parliament over all of its territory. In this tradition, no aspect of government had a constitutional legitimacy other than that lent to it by parliament. The conventions of parliament were reinforced by the unitary nature of British politics. From the nineteenth century the adversarial party system encouraged the framing of political debate, both in elections and within parliament, on a Britain-wide basis. Moreover, the 'first past the post' voting system had a tendency to result in single-party majorities in parliament. This, combined with strong party whipping, meant that the power of parliament generally accrued to a single-party elected government, allowing a unitary approach to government in practice. For much of the twentieth century both the Conservative and Labour Parties were committed to this supremacy of the centre. In the country at large this concentration of power was also legitimised through a whiggish theory of history which associated such arrangements with economic and imperial success in the nineteenth and early twentieth centuries, and upon a broader acceptance of the centralisation of power, reflecting London's economic and cultural significance within Britain as a whole (Garside and Hebbert 1989; Keating and Jones 1991).

In England there was little effective opposition to the unitary tradition. England has long been a unified kingdom, and in the nineteenth and for much of the twentieth century experienced no strong countervailing regionalism. As the role of the state expanded central government became more reliant on a range of sub-national authorities, but the basis of power remained at the centre. Regional offices of central government departments and public authorities which developed after 1945, such as the National Health Service, represented an outgrowth of central government, funded by the national exchequer. They did not serve regional political communities, a fact borne out by the general lack of regional political movements in England. Nor did they constitute a coherent regional system of government, their inter-relationships being more marked by complexity and diversity (Harvie 1991; Hogwood 1982; Hogwood and Lindley 1982).

Following the local government acts of 1888–94, elected local government – focused increasingly on county and county borough councils – took on a number of major state services, such as housing and education. Again, however, local government could not act outside the powers bestowed by parliament, and the option was always open to central government to pressurise local authorities to implement national policies, standardise service provision and bow to central financial controls. Indeed, it was commonplace for defenders of local self-government to complain of the readiness of government to impose central controls whenever it really mattered (Loughlin,

Gelfand and Young 1985). However, it should be recognised that the unitary potential for power was not always used. A tradition of local self-government was established prior to the nineteenth century which asserted the rights of autonomy over local affairs, one which was also applied in the twentieth century. Most analysts now accept that in England between the 1920s and 1960s, in order to gain freedom to concentrate on the high politics of economic and foreign policy, central government granted considerable autonomy to local government (Bulpitt 1983). This dual polity, whilst containing an overall national framework for public administration and granting local autonomy only on a discretionary basis and on the assumption that local government was in 'reliable' hands, nevertheless sustained the convention of respect for local self-government.

The unitary tradition also had a major bearing on government in Scotland and Wales. The system of government in Scotland until the late nineteenth century, and in Wales until the twentieth century, amounted mainly to the administrative apparatus of British central government, with the same potential for central control. The party system in Scotland and Wales, too, was dominated by Britain-wide parties. Here, however, there were more pressing features of political development which ensured the need to compromise on a unitary approach to government. As Rokkan and Urwin (1982, p.11) have argued, in some states the manner in which they are unified out of prior territories may entail the survival of pre-Union rights and institutional infrastructures which preserve a degree of autonomy for those prior territories and serve as agencies of indigenous elite recruitment. In the case of British state formation such special rights and institutional distinctiveness were claimed with success in Scotland and to a lesser extent in Wales. Consequently, the British constitutional state also developed in accord with what Rokkan and Urwin would define as a union-state tradition, giving rise to an increased complexity in British state development in terms of Scottish and Welsh government (Urwin 1982). The details of this complexity deserve emphasis.

Scotland's special treatment derived initially from its position in the British state resting on a voluntary union of the English and Scottish crowns, which was completed by treaty in 1707. The treaty ensured that Scotland retained separate legal, local government and education systems, as well as its own established Presbyterian Church of Scotland. A separate legal system then meant that distinctive Scottish legislation had to be passed in parliament, and led in the 1880s to the creation of special House of Commons committees to debate Scottish bills. In addition, from 1907 there was a standing Scottish Grand Committee within the House of Commons to debate matters purely affecting Scotland. Scotland also continued to have its own bank notes, sporting teams and anthems, and diverse national daily press. As a natural concomitant to such differences there also developed a separate Scottish organisation for the Confederation of British Industry, major trade unions, and the Conservative and Labour Parties (Kellas 1989).

Moreover, as Mitchell (1995) suggests, until the 1980s most politicians in Westminster, and notably Conservative Party members, had an understanding of the British state as a union-state, which underpinned a willingness to treat Scotland as a special case, particularly during periods of nationalist popularity. This had several important implications. First, from 1922 Scotland received an allocation of House of Commons seats higher than would have been the case had the English ratio of votes to seats been followed. By 1974 Scotland was over-represented in the House of Commons by just over 20 per cent (Mclean 1995). Second, in 1885 a Scottish Office was created, with the post of Scottish Secretary being elevated to cabinet status in 1926. The Scottish Office was consistent with the unitary tradition in the sense that it was part of British central government, and not all central government functions in Scotland were placed with the Scottish Office. However, the Scottish Office did gradually accrue a wide range of services, including health, law and order, police, prisons and specific regional aid initiatives. The Secretary of State, conventionally a Scottish MP, was also seen from the start as the champion of Scottish interests in London. In turn, within Scotland, the Secretary of State was treated as the Scottish Prime Minister, and the Scottish Office, located in Edinburgh, became the focus of local government and pressure group politics, at the heart of what Kellas calls the Scottish political system. In such ways the creation and development of the Scottish Office became the focus of a considerable measure of administrative devolution, not seen in English regions (Kellas 1989). In addition, the presence of the Scottish Office gave rise to the creation of a Scottish Affairs Select Committee in 1979. Like the other select committees this was intended to review the operations of a single government department, but as well as focusing on the work of the Scottish Office it became another vehicle for discussing specifically Scottish concerns.

Finally, Scotland was granted additional fiscal subsidies from the late nineteenth century onwards which were over and above those enjoyed in England. This was initially based on the creation and working of prejudicial formulae for public expenditure in response to Scottish Secretaries voicing the Scottish grievance over subjugation within the British state. After the Second World War it also arose from the more than proportionate impact of state intervention in Scottish interests. By this time the state's role embraced a commitment to full employment, an extensive public sector in a mixed economy, regulation of the private sector and a universalist welfare state.

Given the greater emphasis on government support for industry, the prevalence of public sector employment and consumer use of public services in Scotland, the era of the so-called post-war consensus also represented a significant contribution to territorial consensus. According to official statistics, Scotland benefited from some 20 per cent higher per capita public expenditure than England in the post-war period (Keating and Jones 1995).

Respect for Welsh political sensitivities prior to recent times was much less dramatic. This derived from the fact that Wales had no unified government prior to English expansion into Wales in the twelfth and thirteenth centuries, and from the formal act of union in 1536 was ruled as part of a common political, administrative and legal system with England. Wales did not sustain the separate civic institutions which could underpin the idea of self-government, as pertained in Scotland. Indeed, from the late nineteenth century Wales developed more strongly the Anglo-Welsh face of south-east Wales as industrialisation and urbanisation progressed. Working-class dissent was channelled into class politics and social reform, a trend accentuated by the inter-war recession. Support for home rule and the disestablishment of the Church of England flowered in the late nineteenth century as Wales became a preserve of Gladstonian Liberalism, but the predominance of Labour Party politics took over during the twentieth century. Instead Welshness came to be expressed primarily in a cultural sense through religious non-conformism and the Welsh language. It was predominantly as a movement of cultural defence that Plaid Cymru was created in 1925.

Wales was over-represented in the House of Commons from 1922, and by 1974 had around 17 per cent more seats than would have been the case had the English ratio of voters to seats been followed (Mclean 1995). Otherwise, it was only after the Second World War that Wales began to receive similar treatment to that of Scotland. Following the creation in 1948 of an advisory council for Wales and Monmouthshire, and its recommendations of 1957, the Welsh Office was finally established in 1964. Concern for the need to respond to distinctive Welsh concerns in this era also yielded the creation of the Welsh Grand Committee to debate Welsh matters in parliament. This was first set up in 1960, becoming a standing committee of the House of Commons in 1969. In addition, in 1979 as part of the general process of creating select committees to review the work of government departments, the Welsh Affairs Select Committee was established. Finally, Wales also came to enjoy more than proportionately the fruits of post-war state intervention. This derived from the fact that the industrial strength of the Welsh economy was mainly based on the nationalised coal and steel industries, and the commitment to full employment which helped to maintain their size and importance (Foulkes, Jones and Wilford 1983;

Mackintosh 1968). There was still, nevertheless, less distinctive treatment for Wales than for Scotland, for example in terms of parliamentary review of legislation. The fact that there was no separate body of Welsh law meant that there were no standing committees of the House of Commons along the lines of those established in the 1880s for Scotland.

Variations in government for Scotland and Wales reflected the complexity of state development in accord with the union-state tradition. Of course, further sophistication was often suggested in terms of applying the concept of devolution. As Bogdanor has reminded us, this is a peculiarly British concept of how power can be divided territorially within a state. A distinction is normally drawn between unitary and federal states: in the former a single parliament has supreme authority; in the latter there is an entrenched division of powers between a parliament and various provincial bodies. By contrast, devolution creates elected provincial bodies and gives them legislative and/or executive powers divided from the state parliament. These are not, however, entrenched powers, and the ultimate power of override formally remains with the parliament. It could be argued that devolution is consistent with the union-state tradition in that it is a further mechanism for developing a state which remains essentially unitary and centralised but not dogmatically so (Bogdanor 1979, pp.2–9). However, historically, the union-state tradition in British constitutional thought did not provide much support for the idea of devolution to elected assemblies in Scotland and Wales. Nor indeed did the discretionary granting of local autonomy in England provide much basis for reform which might lead to something similar for the English regions. For, at root, the British state was seen as one which was still based on the central convention of the unitary concept of parliamentary sovereignty. Whilst civic autonomy and administrative devolution on different bases for different parts of the state were considered at Westminster to be compatible with the unitary concept of parliamentary sovereignty, political devolution, involving the creation of potential multiple sovereignty, was not. Historically, majority opinion concurred with Urwin's comment on proposals for devolution that, 'their attractiveness has been limited, their costs high and their outcomes uncertain'. Indeed, in that devolution was often seen as quasi-federal in its practical implications, it was generally thought that devolution 'would require a fundamental reformulation of the State' (Urwin 1982, p.68). In this context the granting of devolution to Northern Ireland between 1921 and 1972 should be seen as a special case, determined by the sectarian politics of the province and the historical peculiarities of the creation of a separate Irish state. In the rest of the United Kingdom, by contrast, the primacy of the unitary tradition in the historical development of the state placed fundamental constraints on adaptation to incorporate devolution

(Keating and Jones 1991). A cautious response to territorial and political differences exemplified in concessions to local autonomy and governing according to a union-state tradition was about as far as constitutional development allowed. This framework of constitutional development remained the dominant historical context for understanding the nature of government of Scotland, Wales and the English regions as Britain entered the 1990s.

Reform debates

As is the case in many other areas of British constitutional development, the apparently steady evolution of the practice of government in Scotland, Wales and England occurred against a background of controversy. Whilst devolution was ultimately rejected, on several occasions between the 1880s and the 1920s it was raised as a possibility or as a firm policy commitment by major political parties. Devolution for Scotland, Wales and England was first raised in the context of the debate over devolution for Ireland, in particular by Joseph Chamberlain around the time of the first Irish Home Rule Bill in 1886. It also appeared in a draft of the 1912 Irish Home Rule Bill. The attractiveness of devolution lay partly in its capacity to act as a response to Scottish grievance against British rule, but more in its ability to make Irish home rule constitutionally defensible. Uniform devolution across the nations of Britain was seen as a way of solving the problems involved in just granting devolution to Ireland, relating particularly to representation in the House of Commons and the distribution of fiscal powers. Uniform devolution was raised again immediately after the First World War as a possible solution to the problems of an overloaded Westminster parliament (Bogdanor 1979, pp.35–41). These cases for devolution for the sake of helping to stabilise the British state or improve the effectiveness of government were not, however, terribly robust. Pressures for reform in the periphery were slight or, in the case of England, non-existent. Moreover, as we have seen, British constitutional thought at the centre erred towards seeing devolution as a threat to constitutional stability.

Another case for devolution emerged in the 1960s and 1970s, and although it failed again, it would be fair to say that by this period factors influencing the debate about government in Scotland, Wales and England had changed in character: pressures for reform appeared more substantial; and the debate at the centre over whether devolution was a necessary adaptation for overall constitutional stability had become part of mainstream politics. Given these developments, this period is worthy of more detailed consideration.

The pressures for radical change in the 1960s and 1970s emerged because of nationalist dissent in Scotland and Wales. The secessionist SNP argued that the Scottish people had to take charge of their own affairs, especially in order to safeguard their economic interests given the relative decline of the British economy. They argued that Scotland subsidised the English economy whilst being governed by remote plummy-voiced Englishmen. The wider appeal of this argument found telling expression in the SNP victory over the Labour Party in the 1967 Hamilton by-election and subsequent successes in the 1968 local elections. Studies showed that some 65 per cent of the voters who supported the SNP at this time supported more autonomy for Scotland within the British state rather than independence. Hence the rise of the SNP, to peak at 30 per cent of the Scottish vote in 1974, was taken as representing both a pressure for the creation of more Scottish political autonomy within the British state and a warning of a growth in support for independence if this did not come to pass (Mackintosh 1968).

In Wales Plaid Cymru also made a breakthrough. The party changed its character to become more politically engaged, a result of perceptions of the neglect of the Welsh economy. There was also anger at Welsh water being piped to English cities and growing doubts about the Labour Party's ability in national government to serve Welsh interests. Evidence too of Plaid Cymru's wider appeal came in the victory in the Carmarthen by-election in 1966, although the party peaked at the lower figure of 11.5 per cent of the Welsh vote in 1970. Plaid Cymru was rather less overtly pro-independence than the SNP at this time, but its growth in support left little doubt about the increasing desire for more political autonomy among a significant minority (Keating and Jones 1991). At the same time the Labour Party in Wales moved in favour of an elected Welsh assembly. Back in the 1950s some Welsh Labour MPs had joined in an all-party devolution campaign, and as early as 1965, before Plaid Cymru's breakthrough, the executive committee of the Welsh Council of Labour had advocated a Welsh assembly with legislative powers to form the upper tier of a two-tier Welsh local government system. The idea was that it would take control of the quangos which had grown so markedly under Conservative governments between 1951 and 1964 (Bogdanor 1979, pp. 131–144).

Pressure for regionalisation across Britain also drew inspiration from the rationalist-functionalist arguments of the regional planning movement, which was concerned with the organisational deficiencies of state intervention. Regionalists believed that government in the post-war period had become over-centralised, resulting in poor decision-making and an unequal distribution of economic and social development across the state. However, they also took the view that the local government structure provided too limited a basis for the effective provision of strategic services such as transport, economic development and planning. Hence the development of a regional structure was thought logical. Such views had a particular importance for the development of English regionalism, where popular regional identities were perceived as weak. Indeed it was arguments surrounding planning and strategic service provision that had led geographers and planners such as Fawcett and Geddes, and Fabian political analysts such as Cole and Robson, to advocate regional government since the turn of the century. In the 1960s and 1970s new advocates, such as Peter Self, restated the regionalist case in the context of the need to integrate land use and economic planning and address the major urban change which had occurred since the Second World War (Garside and Hebbert 1989; Keating 1982; Smith 1964, 1965; Thornhill 1972).

Whilst Scottish and Welsh territories were well defined, there remained, nevertheless, differences over the geographical definition of a regional structure in England. Here Cole's discussion of reform is instructive. He recognised that different structures would result depending on the methodology used. If, for example, the initiative was taken from the bottom up to rationalise the activities of small-scale local authorities and address the planning of city regions, then there would be more smaller regions with a greater premium on democratic representation. If it was taken from the top-down to split up central administration, there would be fewer larger regions with a greater premium on bureaucratic coherence, involving a key role for a single senior civil servant. Plans for both types of regional reform were considered in the period. For example, Derek Senior's proposals in the minority report of the Royal Commission on Local Government in 1969 developed the city region idea, producing a regional map of over 40 regions. By contrast, others of a more centralist disposition still had in mind C.B. Fawcett's 1942 proposals, which divided central administration into 11 English regions (Cole 1947; Garside and Hebbert 1989).

There were similar pressures for sub-national political autonomy and regional planning administration across Europe at this time, resulting in a general trend of regionalisation. This characteristically involved the development of large-scale sub-state authorities, for which there was a significant policy competence, often derived from a transfer of responsibilities from central government. Some went on to become popularly elected authorities, with a legislative function and independent budgetary powers. Broadly, the development of regionalisation, however, took two forms: in some countries it involved the insertion of a new, separately elected, tier of regional government; in others it involved the simple merging and strengthening of local government, focusing on the refurbishing of the county level (Hebbert

1989; Sharpe 1993). In Britain, initially at least, there was an apparent political consensus that regionalisation of the more radical former variety should be considered seriously. In 1968 the Conservative Party under Edward Heath adopted in the Perth declaration the policy of favouring a directly elected assembly for Scotland. At the same time, the Labour government under Harold Wilson set up a Royal Commission on the constitution, under Lord Kilbrandon, to consider devolution more thoroughly. The Kilbrandon Commission, which finally reported in 1973, came out cautiously in favour of devolution to directly elected legislative assemblies in Scotland and Wales and to advisory English regional councils which might become directly elected in due course. A minority memorandum to the Kilbrandon Report, written by Lord Crowther Hunt and Professor Alan Peacock, advocated the bolder approach of home rule all round, including English provincial authorities to match those for Scotland and Wales.

The devolution bandwagon, however, slowed down and came to an eventual stop in the late 1970s. First, the Conservative Party in office between 1970 and 1974 let the matter drift. Although promising devolution in the 1970 election manifesto, the Heath government effectively shelved the issue until after the Kilbrandon Commission had reported. By then the government's efforts had gone into local government reform in Scotland as well as in England and Wales. The Heath government then responded unenthusiastically to the Kilbrandon Report, its attentions focused on the more pressing matters of economic and industrial relations strife which ultimately led to its downfall in 1974. Second, the Labour Party, even though formally committed, failed to deliver devolution during its period of office between 1974 and 1979. They came to it, in any case, with reluctance. The Labour Party leadership in reality remained wedded to an agenda of social democratic policies that assumed delivery upon a basis of centralised power, and in the February 1974 election did not support devolution either in Scotland or in Wales. The party in Scotland was also largely opposed to devolution, asserting the necessity of centralised power to deliver socialism, and the party in Wales was split. In this context, the decisive influence on Labour policy appeared to be the February 1974 election result, which showed Labour's reliance on Scottish seats to form a government, and the vulnerability of those seats to an SNP challenge. Hence in the October 1974 election, Labour went pro-devolution for pragmatic electoral purposes to see off the nationalist threat. The Scottish party had to be coerced into support.

In office the Labour government's efforts to carry through devolution floundered. From the start there were cabinet members who were sceptical given the conflict between devolution and the centralisation thought necessary to implement policy aims. Wilson, Prime Minister again between 1974 and 1976, insisted upon devolution, but the approach even so was cautious. By 1975, reform in England had been shelved on the basis that consideration should await the results of reform in Scotland and Wales. The reforms proposed for Scotland and Wales then reflected the need to bridge a wide diversity of opinion within the party, which meant that they were both limited and different. It was intended that Scotland should have an assembly, elected on the 'first past the post' method, with legislative powers on a number of specified matters. These covered a broad range of social and infrastructural policy concerns, local government and the Scottish Development Agency. However, they did not cover all Scottish Office concerns, and it was proposed that the assembly would be funded by block grant and have no independent tax-raising powers. Parliamentary supremacy at Westminster was to be maintained by reserving the formal right to legislate on any matter that was to be devolved, and by means of the Secretary of State acting in a vice-regal capacity to recommend to parliament its response to any Scottish assembly legislation. The Scottish Office would also remain as the instrument of implementing public policy, meaning that the Secretary of State still had significant executive power. The judicial committee of the privy council was to have ultimate say over interpretation of powers between the assembly and parliament. An assembly, elected on the 'first past the post' basis, and subject to the Westminster constraints was also envisaged for Wales. However, its powers were to be even more limited: it was not to be granted legislative powers, merely executive powers. These would cover rather fewer policy areas than the Scottish assembly. Moreover, while the Scottish assembly would operate on a cabinet-style executive system, it was intended that the Welsh assembly would operate on a local government-style committee system. Despite the differences in the proposals for Scotland and Wales and the absence of any devolution for England, it was envisaged that parliamentary representation in Westminster would not be changed.

These proposals were first put in one combined Scotland and Wales Bill, which passed its second reading in December 1976. However, it faced opposition from the Conservative Party which under Mrs Thatcher moved staunchly in favour of Westminster power and an unreformed union. In addition, Welsh Labour MPs continued to be divided over the merits of devolution and a number of Northern English Labour MPs were hostile to a Scottish assembly for the preferential treatment this gave Scotland over the North. The Scottish party, whilst generally coming round in favour of devolution, also had many dissidents. They posed constitutional questions, notably the West Lothian question, so called after Tam Dalyell, the Labour MP for West Lothian. He questioned the logic that, following the creation of a Scottish assembly, he could come down to Westminster and continue to vote on legislation for England on issues which in Scotland would have been transferred to the Scottish assembly and over which English MPs would have no say. Behind the asking of this question lay an underlying Labour commitment to Britain's historic constitutional arrangements and to the winner takes all game at the Westminster level. Such Labour opposition was significant because the government had a vulnerable parliamentary position. Following a series of cogent attacks on the Bill, poorly defended by the government, a guillotine motion to speed up the Scotland and Wales Bill was lost in February 1977, meaning that the Bill was effectively defeated.

However, the Labour government could not afford to abandon the devolution question. Faced with plummeting public opinion poll ratings, particularly in Scotland where the SNP benefited, the government under James Callaghan tried again with separate Bills for Scotland and Wales. These essentially contained the same proposals as the earlier Bill, but with more effective parliamentary management and the help of Liberal support, were enacted in 1978. Even so, they both contained the so-called Cunningham amendment that devolution had to be supported in referenda in Wales and Scotland by 40 per cent of the registered electorate. It was this that allowed sceptical Labour backbench MPs to vote for the legislation, and therefore back the government, safe in the knowledge that the referenda would give them a chance to campaign to defeat the legislation in practice. In addition, a House of Lords amendment to the Scotland Act, tabled by Lord Ferrers, stipulated that following devolution there would need to be a second House of Commons vote on any matter specifically affecting England and Wales which had been passed on the votes of Scottish MPs. This raised the possibility of a convention governing the House of Commons which would answer the West Lothian question, namely that Scottish MPs simply would not vote on English–Welsh matters. In such a situation a scenario could be envisaged whereby a future Labour government, relying on Scottish MPs, could lose its parliamentary majority on exclusively English–Welsh matters; a position known as a bifurcated executive and a recipe for political chaos (Bogdanor 1979; Keating 1989).

As it turned out, the Ferrers amendment was not put to the test. The devolution referenda were held on 1 March 1979. In Scotland 51.6 per cent voted yes, 48.4 per cent voted no, and there was a 63 per cent turnout. The 'yes' vote represented only 32.8 per cent of the electorate. In Wales only 20.3 per cent voted 'yes' on a 58.3 per cent turnout. The 40 per cent threshold of electoral support was not passed in either case, leading the Labour government to drop plans for the new assemblies. The reasons for the failure of the devolution initiative were many and varied, but included criticisms from people, who might otherwise have supported devolution, of the limited devolution that was actually being proposed. Overall, however, it was always going to be difficult to gather the support to clear the 40 per cent threshold. In both Scotland and Wales, the Labour Party was split, significant sections of the trade union movement and local government were opposed, and business was hostile. The general public had doubts over the benefits of devolution and were concerned over what they saw as economically going it alone from England. Consequently, they were open to persuasion by the 'no' campaigns in both Wales and Scotland, led by the Conservative Party and funded by business, which concentrated on portraying the dire economic consequences of devolution, extra fiscal costs that would arise and the possibility of devolution leading to the break-up of the British state. In Wales there were also particular concerns that an assembly would become a vehicle for the promotion of the Welsh language and discrimination against non-Welsh speakers. Finally, the Labour government was widely seen as pursuing devolution for cynical reasons, in that it would help negate competition from the SNP for Westminster seats in Scotland (Bochel, Denver and Macartney 1981; Foulkes *et al.* 1983). Unfortunately for reformers, the failure of the devolution legislation led the SNP to table a motion of no confidence which led to the government's downfall on 28 March 1979. The general election of 1979, of course, returned the Thatcher-led Conservative government which was implacably opposed to considering devolution again.

Whilst the battles over political devolution captured the headlines, the case for regional reform was also being pursued by advocates of regional policy and planning. To this both Labour and Conservative governments of the 1960s and 1970s responded somewhat more positively. In part this enthusiasm was linked to a fear of peripheral dissent. For example, Macmillan's Toothill Committee and the Central Scotland Plan 1960–63, and the establishment of the Highlands and Islands Development Board (1965) and the Scottish Development Agency (1975) were all attempts to reassure Scottish concerns about declining economic prospects. Otherwise regional planning reform was linked more strongly to rationalist-functionalist arguments. The main initiative came in 1965 when the Wilson Labour government established regional economic planning councils for Scotland and Wales and for eight English regions as part of the structure for implementing Wilson's national economic plan. The councils were made up of nominated representatives from organisations such as the regional CBI, regional TUC, local universities and local government. The boundaries of the regional planning councils provided the basis for the standard planning regions which broadly followed Fawcett's prescription, and influenced the collection of public statistics thereafter. They also introduced into Britain the idea of indicative planning, on the French model, by which planning, it was argued, should be carried out with public consultation according to different territorial needs rather than determined solely at the centre on a fragmented policy basis. The direct influence of the regional planning movement did not, however, out-live the end of the Labour government in 1979. Regional planning was an anathema to the anti-planning, free market principles of the Thatcher governments, and Wilson's regional economic planning councils were rapidly disbanded with little public mourning (Garside and Hebbert 1989; Keating 1982).

Britain, therefore, flirted with, but ultimately shied away from, a dramatic embrace with the regional agenda. Constitutional conservatism certainly had much to do with the sceptical responses that many at Westminster displayed towards devolution as well as ultimately towards regional planning. Subsequently, however, commentators also explained the failure of devolution in terms of the weakness in the pressures for reform compared with those against. For example, Birch (1989) emphasised the historic forces of integration within the British state, involving the incorporation of Welsh and Scottish elites into Westminster politics, economic integration, inter-marriage and cultural exchange. Whilst he conceded that strong Scottish and Welsh national identities had continued to exist, he argued that only for a minority had identity been politicised and generally a strong cultural Scottish/Welsh identity was accompanied by a strong British political identity. Scottish and Welsh elites still prioritised their careers at Westminster and aspired to political projects that required centralised power. Bulpitt (1983) further interpreted the still relatively high levels of compliance in Scotland and Wales to rule from Westminster as resulting from central territorial management which had made concessions to territorial interests when necessary. Large sections of the Scottish and Welsh political classes had been enlisted as elite collaborators in return for some autonomy in running administratively devolved structures. Others agree that sensitivity to the union-state tradition, in which sympathy has been shown to Scottish and Welsh interests during the twentieth century, paid handsome political dividends in support for the status quo in 1979 (Sharpe 1993).

At the same time, at Westminster it should be noted that the Conservative Party had only temporarily committed itself to devolution. Even the Labour government of the 1970s which sought to legislate for devolution can be accused of lacking genuine commitment; that in reality it was driven to the commitment as an electoral ploy rather than through conviction. There was also an absence of detailed planning, a serious flaw given the constitutional complexities. The result was that the devolution legislation was itself full of holes. For example, Bogdanor (1979) concluded that it did not provide for clear decentralisation or democratisation; it did not offer clarity as to the precise relationships between Westminster and the proposed assemblies; nor did it ensure legitimisation of the proposed assemblies as a safeguard against either re-centralisation or separatist pressures. This resulted from five key problems present within the devolution proposals: first, the legislative competence available to the new assemblies was too limited; second, the assemblies were denied the right to raise their own revenues; third, where powers were given, Westminster retained the right to override decisions; fourth, election on the 'first past the post' basis denied broad party representation; and fifth, the referenda asked no second question on independence, thus foregoing the chance to have a 'no to independence' vote with which to see off future nationalist aspirations. In addition, Labour's plans provided for an asymmetrical approach to devolution – legislative in Scotland, executive in Wales and none in England – which quite naturally aroused constitutional and English opposition. The decision not to try to defend this asymmetry or compensate for it, for example by changing the relative numbers of Scottish, Welsh and English MPs, proved to be a serious mistake. Labour neither succeeded in convincingly arguing that devolution was an adaptation of the British constitutional tradition within the union-state tradition, nor did it promote devolution as a step towards a beneficial reformulation of the British constitution on quasi-federal grounds.

Following the failure to regionalise via the insertion of new regional assemblies, regionalisation in Britain took the less radical form of the refurbishment of local government at the county level, based upon the 1972 Local Government Act carried by the Conservative government of Edward Heath. This resulted from a separate strand of the 1960s debate about the need for more rational and efficient sub-national government to ensure improved provision of strategic services and infrastructure, which came to a head in the Redcliffe Maud Royal Commission on local government in the late 1960s. The 1972 Act created a two-tier metropolitan structure for the big cities and their hinterlands on the model of Greater London, and a parallel two-tier shire county structure in England and Wales. In Scotland a new structure of regional and district councils was created in 1973. In the absence of Scottish and Welsh devolution or the establishment of regional assemblies in England, local government reform became the only lasting territorial reform of significance arising from this period (Keating 1982). In terms of the development of the British state, it represented an entirely orthodox adaptation of government to economic and social change within the unitary tradition, with separate local government arrangements for Scotland also showing respect for the union-state tradition. Whilst peripheral dissent and the regional planning movement had threatened a new era in

British regionalism, the British polity instead experienced a different form of regionalisation based upon local government which was entirely consistent with the existing unitary and union-state traditions. Orthodoxy in constitutional state development was thus preserved, leaving only bitter memories for the reformers who had lost of the weakness of their case and support, and of the mistakes they had made in attempting to reform permanently Britain's constitution and approach to regional government.

The challenges of state reform and European integration

State reform

Following the 1979 referenda, support for the nationalist parties in Wales and Scotland and peripheral pressures for constitutional reform receded. Similarly, the first two Thatcher governments from 1979 to 1987 appeared to have no novel explicit policy on government at the regional level. Only the abolition in 1986 of the English metropolitan county councils, a major part of the refurbishment of local government which constituted British regionalisation in the 1970s, appeared to broach the issue. Even then this was seen as merely an attack on Labour local government power, as the services of metropolitan counties were continued through other bodies working at the metropolitan level or through joint arrangements. Elsewhere, in Scotland, Wales and England, the Thatcher governments preferred to conduct policy within the framework of existing institutions, as reformed in the 1970s. The Labour Party in turn at a national level dropped its interest in devolution. Nevertheless, domestic politics and policy in the 1980s clearly did have some sort of impact on how Scotland, Wales and the English regions were governed. The focus of this was the state reforms, initiated by the early Thatcher governments and continued, albeit in changing circumstances, during the final Thatcher administration. Clearly we need to understand the nature of these reforms, how they affected Scotland, Wales and England and the questions they raised in relation to subsequent developments in British regionalism and policy debate.

It is important to recognise that the Thatcher reforms represented a serious attempt to alter the course of British state development. They were based upon a New Right critique that British relative decline had been caused by excessive regulation and state intervention. From this perspective the post-war welfare state settlement and the development since the 1960s of corporatist styles of policy-making were clear indications that the British political class was intent on no higher an ambition than the steady management of decline. Consequently, after a century of state expansion the Thatcher reforms focused upon hauling back the frontiers of the state and breaking the vested interests in continued statism. First, there was an attempt to change the priority in economic management from that of the promotion of full employment to that of the control of inflation. Second, the Thatcher governments sought to reduce the direct role of the state as an employer, producer and provider of services. This was done principally through the privatisation of state-owned utilities and companies, and the introduction of market mechanisms into the management and provision of public services. Third, there was a drive to reduce state controls over the private sector by freeing up the use of capital, land and labour in the market-place and encouraging entrepreneurship. Fourth, the Thatcher governments sought to erode what they saw as welfare dependency by encouraging self-reliance, reforming welfare provision and, where possible, privatising welfare functions. Finally, there was a move to reassert the powers of the traditional institutions of the unitary state, based in Westminster, in the process ejecting pressure groups from an extensive influence on the policy-making process. Overall the aim was to diminish and revise the state's role and promote a successful market economy, carrying necessary policies uncompromisingly against all other interests (Gamble 1988; Kavanagh 1987).

Much of this attempted state transformation implicitly challenged the existing relationship between the state and government in Scotland and Wales. As the final aim suggests, the renewed assertion of the primacy of Westminster offered a symbolic challenge to the convention of giving special treatment to Scottish and Welsh political and economic interests. Indeed the desire to impose a uniform reform of the state's role meant that in a wide range of matters, respect for the union-state tradition in the British state could no longer be taken for granted. For example, policies on the state and the economy presented a threat to levels of employment in both Scotland and Wales, where there was a heavy reliance on public sector jobs and on state-aided industries, notably coal, steel and shipbuilding. Similarly, welfare policies also posed a more than proportionate threat, given the heavy dependence of Scotland and Wales on state support. For example, changes in council housing policy potentially had a much more marked effect on the meeting of housing needs in Scotland, given that a much higher proportion of people lived in council housing than in England (Keating and Jones 1991).

The uniformity of the Thatcher project also appeared to offer little respect for local government autonomy across Britain. Policy initiatives affecting local government involved the application of controls that had always been at central government's disposal. The treatment of Britain as a centralised as well as unitary state became synonymous with Thatcherism. In England perceived attacks on local government were interpreted as an erosion of the only facility through which sub-national interests could be pursued. Given that market-orientated policies favoured the South and opened up the prospect of a North–South divide as well as lesser regional disadvantages, this was a serious development. At the same time, reforms in individual policy areas led to a flood of new quasi-public agencies operating at both the local and regional level which critics argued often had little relationship or accountability to local democratic institutions. Training and Enterprise Councils, hospital trusts, Next Step agencies with their various regional structures, housing action trusts, urban development corporations and grant maintained schools all emerged under the late Thatcher and Major administrations. Each appeared to represent further examples of central control and confusion for effective responses to regional and local needs.

Of course, there has been considerable dispute over whether the rhetoric of Thatcherism was actually matched by its reality. However, there was certainly a widely held perception that a zealous assertion of unitary and central power adversely affected Scottish, Welsh and particular English regional interest in significant respects. It is not surprising that this was linked to the re-emergence of a regional agenda in the 1990s. From this a series of specific questions can be isolated. First, did state reform sow the seeds of more serious problems for constitutional conservatives than in the 1960s/70s? Did it affect patterns of government and political opinion in ways which changed the nature of the movements for devolution or strengthened their potential appeal? Did it lead to the kind of local authority regionalism which in other states has been seen as the classic precursor of regionalism and reform? Second, what was the legacy of Thatcherism for the Major government's approach to the new regional agenda? How could the Major government's explicit attention to the nature of government in Scotland, Wales and England and the consequent reforms, especially after the 1992 election, be broadly characterised? Did it reveal a changed approach in Conservative policy to British regionalism since the 1970s, and if so how? What were the prospects of the Major government's approach for affecting support for regionalist prescriptions, and for offering a successful further adaptation of British government within the historic conventions of the British constitutional state? Finally, how did the experience of Thatcherism and state reform affect the level of Labour Party commitment to pursuing devolution and regional reform in the event of office? How did the failures of the 1970s and the experience of opposition affect the contents of Labour's proposals? Was the re-modelled Labour Party more clearly in possession of plans which could provide for the successful implementation of devolution in practice?

European integration

Back in the 1970s it was hard to envisage that Britain's membership of the EC would be of any importance to the development of British regionalism and the debate between orthodox approaches to government and devolution. Indeed, as Keating and Jones (1991) comment, the EC was seen as a limited organisation which primarily acted as a prop to the authority of the existing British state. However, in the late 1980s and early 1990s European integration developed in rather different ways, and as a result analysts as well as suggesting links between domestic state reform and the re-emergence of a British regional agenda, suggested links between a developing European Union and this phenomenon. Such links were rooted at a general level in the fact that the EC/EU had become a major internationalising force in the British economy. The pursuit of a Single European Market (SEM) following the 1986 Single European Act was a microcosm of growing economic interdependence in which capital had spread across state frontiers and production methods had entered an age of flexible specialisation suited to many diverse markets. The moves towards economic and monetary union after the Treaty on European Union in 1992 only exacerbated such trends. In these circumstances the state lost its purchase as sole defender of economic interests. In economic competition spreading across as well as within state boundaries, regions instead often became primary agents for trying to cope with the site-specific impacts of economic change. This was recognised no less in Britain than in any other state, notably by business as well as public sector organisations and civic bodies (Keating 1995; Kellas 1991). In assessing the relationships between this process of internationalisation and British regionalism, attention has focused more specifically on the policy and institutional developments within the EC/EU and the questions they raised in relation to developments in British regionalism and arguments for devolution, and Conservative government policy.

European regional policy developments emerged because of the considerable interest in addressing the needs of regional economies generated by the development of the SEM and the moves towards economic and monetary union. From the start economists predicted that there would be at least greater regional inequalities in the SEM, and some economists predicted an absolute decline of some regions. This was deemed economically dysfunctional and unacceptable in terms of broader arguments for social cohesion within the EC/EU. With economic and monetary union it was further accepted that having mechanisms to correct regional inequalities would become even more of a political necessity, although, as the Werner Committee showed, it was improbable that the EU would make the commitment of devoting the equivalent of the 8 per cent tax on EU GDP, needed to correct inequalities. In practice, greater interest at the EC level in developing assistance to regional economies led to the merging of the EC structural funds for regional and social aid and significant increases in their amount in 1988 and 1992, to the point at which they became in the mid 1990s equivalent to a *c.* 1.3 per cent tax on EU GDP. In addition, where previously EC regional aid had been merely a top-up of state regional aid programmes, after 1988 the Commission took a much greater role in defining the regions requiring aid. At the same time regional authorities were drawn in to the planning of structural funds programmes and projects, an initiative developed in 1992 by means of the stress on the involvement of sub-national partnerships in EC structural funds policy. This development had particular importance for Britain as she was a major recipient of structural funds, both for Scotland and Wales and for designated regions in England. Meanwhile, in the absence of separately elected regional authorities in Britain, both central and local government were drawn into working more at the regional level. There was, therefore, a direct financial and institutional stimulus given to the development of new political forms in Britain's regions (Armstrong 1995).

Such a stimulus was complemented by the proliferation of specific assistance funds for areas with special needs, for example with regard to traditional industries or the motor industry, which provided a further basis for networks of sub-state authorities participating in EC politics. In addition, there was a general need for local authorities and other organisations to gear themselves up for Europe as a result of the broader transfer of state policy competencies to the EC/EU level, particularly as a result of the 1986 Single European Act. The potential response of sub-state authorities to EC/EU developments was also heightened by its coincidence with the apparent end of special treatment for Scotland and Wales and disadvantaged regions in Britain at the domestic level as a result of the Thatcher reforms. While such developments undoubtedly provided additional avenues for the development of Scottish and Welsh political forms, potentially the biggest spur was given to the development of local authority and regional working in England, and complex forms of inter-governmental relations which inspired consideration of whether Britain needed structural reform to allow Britain's regions a better voice in Europe (Goldsmith 1993).

Institutional developments flowed from the parallel emergence of the concept of a Europe of the Regions as a key ideal in European Union. This concept derives from the writings of de Rougemont and Heraud and envisages a Europe of the Regions replacing a Europe of the States. In the 1990s its advocacy was linked to the EC/EU's need to develop a political legitimacy that was deeper than that leant to it by its constituent member states. It also gained support from regionalist movements and democratic theorists who saw in the development of regional autonomy the decentralisation which has long been seen as a measure of democratic maturation. The prospect of a Europe of Regions still seemed remote but a move towards a Europe of the states and regions had more validity. In the late 1980s the Council of European Regions was advocating the development of a senate of the regions as a second legislative chamber to the European parliament in the EC, and in this ambition received support from the parliament. As a step towards this goal, in the 1992 Treaty on European Union, provision was made for a committee of the regions, composed of elected representatives of regional authorities and in some countries by necessity local authorities, to act as a consultative body within the EC/EU decision-making structure. At the same time, with the devolution of power in other member states, regional representatives on certain issues also started to take the place of state representatives on the Council of Ministers. In addition, subsidiarity, by which it was intended that the lowest level of government appropriate be given responsibility for the making of each policy, became a working assumption of the EU (Hebbert 1989, 1993). Such institutional developments at the EU level potentially further encouraged developments in British regionalism.

There is a clear case, then, that suggests that European integration in the early–mid 1990s affected the nature of British regional politics and policy in ways previously not considered. As a result a second series of questions can be raised. First, like state reform, did European integration have such an impact as to mean that British regionalism represented a stronger challenge to the status quo than in the 1960s and 1970s? Second, in looking at the Major government's policies on government in Scotland, Wales and the English regions, what role did the changing EC/EU context play in their development? Finally, what impact did the changing context of European integration have on the Labour Party's commitment to devolution, its detailed proposals for legislation, and its approach to developing devolution and regionalism in practice? Overall, what was the impact of the novel external dimension of European integration on the regional policy debate which made it anyway notably different from the policy debate of the 1960s and 1970s?

State reform and European integration, therefore, offered new challenges which had the potential to transform the importance of developments in British regionalism and central policy on regional government in the early–mid 1990s relative to those of the 1960s/1970s era. The general question which this book addresses is how much actually changed in practice. Was it '*plus ca change, plus c'est la meme chose*', or the dawn of a new era in British regionalism?

The organisation of the book

The collection of essays that follows represents the fruits of a considerable amount of research. Like most collections there is a reign of many minds and an eclecticism of approaches and interests. As a result it does not provide an entirely comprehensive survey of developments in British regionalism and policy development in the early-mid 1990s; nor does it consistently develop one set of arguments. Nevertheless, the book is clearly structured in three parts. They consider in turn developments in relation to Scotland and Wales, England, and related local government and inter-governmental issues. The first of these foci will be no surprise. The other two foci are chosen because they have also become dominant areas of research which inform academic debate. In each part of the book, essays address key developments, assessing pressures for change, both in terms of approaches to constitutional arrangements and regional policy, as well as the policy responses of central government. The chapters in each part also provide both general and case study discussions of the issues in hand. On this basis, the interaction between the bottom-up developments of British regionalism and the top-down Conservative approaches to developing the regional level may be explored. Let us now clarify the contents of each part.

The analysis of Scotland and Wales in Part 1 begins with James Mitchell and Jack Brand assessing Scottish popular politics and the movement for home rule. They assume an understanding of the broader trends of change in Scottish politics after the early 1980s, well documented in other work (see Mazey and Mitchell 1993; Midwinter, Keating and Mitchell 1991) and concentrate on a detailed analysis of elite and public opinion, and the politics of the devolution campaign after 1988. Barry Jones continues the bottom-up focus in his chapter on Wales. The changing nature of Welsh politics after the early 1980s is much less well understood and the chapter is concerned to dissect patterns of broad change. It then focuses on the nature of support for political autonomy and the politics of reform proposals, of which those of the Labour Party after 1992 were of prime interest. Part 1 then turns the focus on to central government policy in respect of the government of Scotland and Wales. The chapter by Jonathan Bradbury assesses the aims of Conservative governments from the mid 1980s in developing and reforming Scottish and Welsh government, focusing in particular on the political objectives of managing territorial dissent. A final chapter by Ronan Paddison provides a case study analysis which further assesses the aims and effects of the Major governments in reforming government within a traditional constitutional framework. He addresses the key issue of local government reorganisation, taking the Scottish experience as his focus.

Discussion of developments in England in Part 2 begins with a chapter by Jim Sharpe, which seeks to develop further an understanding of English regionalism in terms of the historical development of regionalism both more broadly in Britain and in Europe. On this basis the experiments of the 1960s and 1970s, the general absence of a regional dimension to English politics and policy in the 1980s, and the apparent limitations of opposition party ideas of English regional reform in the early–mid 1990s are assessed. Murray Stewart then provides an overarching framework for understanding developments at the regional level from a variety of perspectives, concluding upon the weakness of early local authority regionalism and the key importance for English regionalism, therefore, of the reforms carried out by the Major governments. He discusses in particular the implications of local government restructuring in England on regional capacity. John Mawson and Ken Spencer assess the aims and impact of the Major governments' other key initiative, the Government Offices of the Regions, in more detail, as a case study of how successfully government at the regional level in England was reformed within the traditional constitutional framework. Finally, John Mawson explores the pressures for alternative English regional reform with particular reference to the policy debate in the Labour Party and a wide range of other institutions prior to the 1997 general election, and developments in local authority regionalism which both pre-dated and followed the Major government initiatives.

The final part of the book looks at how local government, in its responses to European integration and other pressures, and in its dealings with other sub-national agencies and central government, developed new forms of regional working based on networks and partnerships. Chapters consider the extent to which this provided an impetus to regional reform in England, and how the increasing involvement of local government in EC/EU-related matters affected the debate over the need for elected assemblies in Scotland and Wales. This focus, whilst assessing generally the changing institutional relationships at the regional level across Britain, also fleshes out our understanding of regional developments with reference to case studies of particular regions. The chapter by Mike Goldsmith assesses the experience of British local government in accessing European funding, in lobbying to influence EC/EU policies and in the development of networks to facilitate such activities. He exemplifies this experience with reference to four institutional and area case studies. Peter John then explores in greater detail the development of sub-national partnerships between British local authorities and other public, private and voluntary sector organisations. His discussion is developed through a case study of the emergence of regional networking in London and the South East, where some of the greatest difficulties for this type of activity are to be found. Finally, Peter Roberts assesses the ability of local government to act in lieu of elected regional authorities both in terms of regional policy capacity and as the main vehicle for Scottish, Welsh and English representation in European institutions, notably the EU Committee of the Regions. The attitudes of British central government to this local government activity are also reviewed as a prelude to assessing the functional needs of Britain for regional level representation in the EU and other European forums.

A concluding chapter then draws together arguments on regionalist pressures, the nature of Conservative government policy at the regional level, and the approach whilst in opposition of the Labour Party. Broad conclusions are offered highlighting the novel developments in each of these areas, but a theme running throughout the book is that the re-emergence of the regional agenda in the early to mid 1990s was as much marked by continuity as change from trends and problems of the 1960s/1970s. Similarly, the processes of state reform and European integration clearly bore considerable responsibility for the changing nature of the regional agenda, but such processes had still to run their course. Inevitably, we provide as many questions as answers.

References

Armstrong, H. (1995) 'The role and evolution of European Community regional policy.' In B. Jones and M. Keating (eds) *The European Union and the Regions.* Oxford: Clarendon.

Birch, A.H. (1989) *Nationalism and National Integration.* London: Unwin Hyman.

Bochel, J., Denver, D. and Macartney, A. (1981) (eds) *The Referendum Experience, Scotland 1979.* Aberdeen: Aberdeen University Press.

Bogdanor, V. (1979) *Devolution.* Oxford: Oxford University Press.

Bulpitt, J. (1983) *Territory and Power in the United Kingdom: An Interpertation.* Manchester: Manchester University Press.

Cole, G.D.H. (1947) *Local and Regional Government.* London: Cassell.

Foulkes, D., Jones, B. and Wilford, R. (eds) (1983) *The Welsh Veto, the Wales Act 1978 and the Referendum.* Cardiff: University of Wales Press.

Gamble, A. (1988) *The Free Economy and the Strong State.* London: Macmillan.

Garside, P. and Hebbert, M. (1989) 'Introduction.' In P. Garside and M. Hebbert (eds) *British Regionalism 1900–2000.* London: Mansell.

Goldsmith, M. (1993) 'The Europeanisation of local government.' *Urban Studies 30,* 4/5, 683–699.

Harvie, C. (1991) 'English regionalism: the dog that never barked.' In B. Crick (ed) *National Identities, the Constitution of the UK.* Oxford: Blackwell.

Hebbert, M. (1989) 'Britain in a Europe of Regions.' In P. Garside and M. Hebbert (eds) *British Regionalism 1900–2000.* London: Mansell.

Hebbert, M. (1993) '1992: myth and aftermath.' *Regional Studies 27,* 8, 709–718.

Hogwood, B. (1982) 'Introduction.' In B. Hogwood and M. Keating (eds) *Regional Government in England.* Oxford: Clarendon.

Hogwood, B. and Lindley, P. (1982) 'Variations in regional boundaries.' In B. Hogwood and M. Keating (eds) *Regional Government in England.* Oxford: Clarendon.

Kavanagh, D. (1987) *Thatcherism and British Politics: The End of Consensus?* Oxford: Oxford University Press.

Keating, M. (1982) 'The debate on regional reform.' In B. Hogwood and M. Keating (eds) *Regional Government in England.* Oxford: Clarendon.

Keating, M. (1988) *State and Regional Nationalism, Territorial Politics and the European State.* London: Harvester Wheatsheaf.

Keating, M. (1989) 'Regionalism, devolution and the state 1969–1989.' In P. Garside and M. Hebbert (eds) *British Regionalism 1900–2000.* London: Mansell.

Keating, M. (1995) 'Europeanism and Regionalism.' In B. Jones and M. Keating (eds) *The European Union and the Regions.* Oxford: Clarendon.

Keating, M. and Jones, B. (1985) (eds) *Regions in the European Community.* Oxford: Clarendon Press.

Keating, M. and Jones, B. (1991) 'Scotland and Wales: peripheral assertion and European integration.' *Parliamentary Affairs 44,* 311–324.

Keating, M. and Jones, B. (1995) 'Nations, regions and Europe: the UK experience.' In B. Jones and M. Keating (eds) *The European Union and the Regions.* Oxford: Clarendon.

Kellas, J. (1989) 'Prospects for a new Scottish political system.' *Parliamentary Affairs* 519–532.

Kellas, J. (1991) 'European integration and the regions.' *Parliamentary Affairs 44,* 2, 226–239.

Loughlin, M., Gelfand, M. and Young, K. (1985) *Half a Century of Municipal Decline 1935–1985.* London: Allen and Unwin.

Mackintosh, J. (1968) *The Devolution of Power.* Middlesex: Penguin.

Mazey, S. and Mitchell, J. (1993) 'Europe of the regions: territorial interests and European integration: the Scottish experience.' In S. Mazey and J.J. Richardson (eds) *Lobbying in the European Community.* Oxford: Oxford University Press.

Mclean, I. (1995) 'Are Scotland and Wales over-represented in the House of Commons?' *Political Quarterly 66,* 250–268.

Midwinter, A., Keating, M. and Mitchell, J. (1991) *Politics and Public Policy in Scotland.* London: Macmillan.

Mitchell, J. (1995) 'Unionism, assimilation and the Conservatives.' In J. Lovenduski and J. Stanyer (eds) *Contemporary Political Studies 1995 Volume 3.* Belfast: Political Studies Association.

Rokkan, S. and Urwin, D. (1982) 'Introduction: centres and peripheries in western Europe.' In S. Rokkan and D. Urwin (eds) *The Politics of Territorial Identity, Studies in European Regionalism.* London: Sage.

Sharpe, L.J. (1993) 'The European meso: an appraisal.' In L.J. Sharpe (ed) *The Rise of Meso Government in Europe.* London: Sage.

Smith, B. (1964) *Regionalism in England 1: Regional Institutions – A Guide.* London: Acton Society Trust.

Smith, B. (1965) *Regionalism in England 2: Its Nature and Purpose 1905–1965.* London: Acton Society Trust.

Thornhill, W. (1972) (ed) *The Case for Regional Reform.* London: Nelson.

Urwin, D. (1982) 'Territorial structures and political developments in the United Kingdom.' In S. Rokkan and D. Urwin (eds) *The Politics of Territorial Identity, Studies in European Regionalism.* London: Sage.

White, M. (1994) 'PM scorns 'mad teenager' Blair.' *The Guardian,* 3 December 1994, p.8.

PART I

Perspectives on Scotland and Wales

CHAPTER 2

Home Rule in Scotland

The Politics and Bases of a Movement

Jack Brand and James Mitchell

Introduction

By the time the Scottish constitutional convention had produced its final set of proposals for a Scottish parliament in 1995, debate about home rule had been at the heart of Scottish politics for a quarter of a century. Indeed, supporters offered the most serious attempt to establish regional government within Britain in the 1970s, and in the first half of the 1990s made their demands a central issue in the wider arena of British politics. Yet in 1979 support failed to be sufficient to gain the necessary majority in a referendum on a Scottish assembly, and subsequently there remained a question mark over the extent and nature of support for Scottish home rule. In reviewing Scotland in the early to mid 1990s, the situation clearly was different from that elsewhere in Britain. The interest in constitutional change, as in the 1970s, was fuelled by a form of nationalism, unlike the regionalism which fostered debate in parts of England. This had implications for the prospects of success for the movement. Consequently, this chapter concentrates on addressing the issues surrounding the political importance of Scottish identity and the extent to which these issues changed between the 1970s and the 1990s.

Before we proceed further, it is necessary to say something about the terminology used. In the mid to late 1970s 'devolution' was the term used to describe plans for establishing a Scottish parliament or assembly which would exercise a limited range of central government powers principally affecting Scotland. Other powers would remain within the competence of Westminster, which would retain overall control. There was a great deal of controversy over the distribution of powers and over the status of the assembly: whether for example, it should be part of a federal scheme. In general, devolution was strictly distinguished from independence, where a government of Scotland would be responsible for everything which affected the country, since Scotland would have separated from Britain. In this chapter, however, we shall use the term 'home rule' to cover roughly the same relationships as 'devolution', because, first of all 'home rule' became in the 1990s the fashionable term, and second to draw attention to a certain fuzziness between support for Scottish control over limited powers and support for complete independence. The federal option, for example, is short of independence, but far beyond the devolution model of the 1970s. The possibility of Scotland being a partner with England and the other European Community countries became more important in the 1980s, and complicated the situation yet further. It has also been recognised that voters might support Scottish autonomy short of independence as a prelude to independence. 'Home rule' therefore means all degrees of power-holding short of independence from England, either inside or outwith the European Community. This chapter will be only incidentally concerned with support for independence.

The initial premise of the chapter's argument is that the movement for home rule in the 1980s and early to mid 1990s was based on nationalism. However, it is necessary to be careful as to what is meant by such an interpretation. Contrary to many analyses of nationalist movements, support for Scottish home rule was elite-led, not mass-based. It depended on a strong popular sentiment of Scottishness, but one which was not mainly political. Subsequent to the origins of the modern Scottish home-rule movement in the 1960s, this sentiment was partially politicised only from time to time, by the activities of certain Scottish elites. At the same time it is important to note that popular support for home rule depended on identity; there is no evidence that the majority of electors supported home-rule on the basis of 'rational' calculation (Bennie *et al.* 1997, pp.120–130). The existence of this national identification, to some extent competing with the class or party identity which was the basis of Labour's hegemony in Scotland, clearly posed a threat to the future of this hegemony.

In suggesting that the politicisation of a popular Scottish identity was sporadic, we also need to draw attention to the importance of context. For example, in one context we may feel that we are Catholics rather than Scots; in another we are British in opposition to the exigencies of the Commission in Brussels. Thus Scottish identity may take on a political meaning only when there are features in the environment which make that political meaning important. Such an occasion occurred following the imposition of the community charge by what was perceived to be an 'English' government. Another trigger of politicisation may be the existence of an institution – a party, perhaps – which draws attention to the political dimension of Scottish identity. In any case, the nature of what an actor considers to be his or her identity or his or her rational interest even is not stable. It remains heavily dependent on perceptions of that condition, and this in turn is structured in various ways by various agencies.

In developing further our analysis of the Scottish movement for home rule, we shall discuss first the development of popular support as shown by data from the 1979 and 1992 Election Surveys; second, the nature of elite support and the re-emergence of an organised movement for home rule in the late 1980s; third, the campaign forged by the Scottish constitutional convention in the early to mid 1990s; and finally the reasons which explain greater Labour Party commitment in this period. Overall, the chapter provides qualified grounds for believing that the movement for home rule clearly developed a stronger impetus during the early to mid 1990s compared to that of earlier periods.

Popular support for home rule and the importance of Scottish identity[1]

About three-quarters of Scottish voters supported home rule or independence at the time of the first recorded polling on the subject in 1947. It is interesting that this proportion did not materially change, even during the days of the SNP's greatest successes, although, it should be noted that the level of support specifically for independence did change. Under one-fifth supported independence until the mid 1980s, when the figure rose. Of course, it should be recognised that there is a problem in interpreting levels of support over time because the questions used also differed over time. Even with the same wording, the questions would have been taken to refer to contemporary proposals, which also changed over time. For example, the meaning of independence changed as approaches to the European Community developed. In the 1979 Scottish Election Survey, respondents were asked to choose one of a number of options (with proportional support shown in brackets):

1. No devolution (13%)
2. Ad hoc parliamentary committees in Scotland (16%)
3. A Scottish assembly with control over some Scottish affairs (32%)
4. A completely independent Scotland (8%)

1. Unless otherwise stated, the data used in this chapter have drawn from the Scottish Election Studies in 1979 and 1992. The 1992 study was co-directed by the authors and was funded by the ESRC (award number R000232960).

The drop in those who were in favour of independence from the normal figure of around 20 per cent suggested that minds had been concentrated by the referendum. The question in the 1992 Election Survey provided four choices, and produced the following levels of proportional support:

1. No change (24%)
2. An assembly (52%)
3. Scotland independent of Britain but within Europe (18%)
4. Scotland independent of Britain and Europe (6%)

This latter formulation was a much better reflection of the options actually on offer, but it is impossible to make any but the vaguest comparisons. It can only be said that it appears that the proportions in favour of either 'no change' or 'independence' went up. Even so, looking at either set of results, the important point is that the evidence supports the view that there was consistently a massive majority for constitutional change in the direction of home rule of some sort between the 1970s and early 1990s. It should also be pointed out that these opinions were expressed in terms of relatively specific proposals for change. This is quite different from the questions in several enquiries in England which elicited quite extensive support for more power for 'their part of Britain' or some other phrase. In the latter case it was unclear what the respondent took as a referent, either to the region or to the sorts of power which were meant. In terms of research methodology, the questions asked in Scotland and England were not comparable.

However, evidence of a very large majority in favour of a particular course of action still must be considered critically. Governments have to implement many policies of differing importance both to the politicians and the public. When respondents in 1979 were asked about the importance of the Scotland Act on their vote, 22 per cent said that it was extremely important, 37 per cent said that it was fairly important, and 41 per cent said that it was not important at all. Unfortunately there was no question on this in the 1992 questionnaire, but the results in 1979 were consistent with relatively low priorities placed on home rule in other subsequent polls. We thus conclude that there was in the early 1990s widespread support for some sort of Scottish responsible assembly, but that it was not an item of the first importance. Such a conclusion needs to be related to an understanding of the origins of popular Scottish support for home rule.

At the beginning of this chapter, it was suggested that the identity model seemed to show a more likely explanation of support for home rule than did rational choice. Although Nationalist politicians constantly have promised that life in an independent Scotland would be better, there is evidence that many of those who have supported them have not done so as rational actors concerned for their personal betterment, economically or in other ways. Considerations of personal (egocentric) or community (sociotropic) profit may be important along with perceiving a certain identity, but they seem to be secondary.

One datum which is consistent with this argument is that such a large proportion of those supporting an assembly or Scottish Parliament in the 1979 and 1992 surveys did not believe that it would improve Scotland's economy, as noted on page 36. Only 30 per cent mentioned economic improvement as an advantage of having such a legislature. The other 70 per cent mentioned the chance for Scottish people to solve their own problems (57%), or that it was a nation's right (10%), and 3 per cent thought that there would be no advantage at all.

The importance of identity emerges when we compare the relationship between Scottish identity and support for a Scottish Parliament or independence. If the model were appropriate for these data, we should expect that those who felt most strongly Scottish would be more likely to support independence or the assembly, as compared with those who felt more British. Our preliminary work on the effect and nature of identity has already been reported (Brand, Mitchell and Surridge 1992), but it is important to draw attention to the nature of the question. Following comments made by John Mackintosh (Drucker 1982), in the 1992 survey we used a question which recognised that people might hold more than one national identity at a time. They might feel only Scottish, Scottish more than British, equally Scottish and British, more British than Scottish, or British only. The relationship between national feeling and support for different types of home rule is shown in Table 2.1.

Table 2.1: National identity and support for Scottish home rule

	Scottish not British	*Scottish more than British*	*Equally Scottish and British*	*British more than Scottish*	*British not Scottish*
Independence from Britain and Europe	14	6	2	3	4
Independence from Britain in Europe	29	19	10	6	–
Assembly	40	57	48	38	50
No Change	12	17	37	50	39
Other	5	1	4	3	8
Total	**100**	**100**	**101**	**100**	**101**

There was a clear relationship between the importance of Scottish identity as opposed to British and support for independence. The relationship between a sense of Scottish identity and support for an assembly or parliament with limited powers was less pronounced, but can still be seen. The 50 per cent among those who felt only British but nevertheless supported an assembly should be discounted because of the small numbers in this category of identity. Leaving aside the last column, the strong relationship between Scottish identity and support for constitutional change can also be seen by noting how support for no change increased as the importance of British identity increased. We might be inclined to conclude from Table 2.1 that, in the context of high consciousness of Scottish identity, support for home rule would become irresistible. We should be cautious of this line of argument.

One reason for caution is the unexplored meaning of Scottish identity. To claim that one is only Scottish and not British at all is almost certainly a political statement. Most non-nationalist Scots are bound to experience a feeling of Britishness. We asked respondents about what made them most proud of being Scottish and of being British. As Table 2.2 shows, the British sources of pride tended to be largely political or public characteristics; respondents were proud of Scotland because of general perceptions of the people or the landscape.

Table 2.2: The meaning of Scottish national identity
What makes you most proud of Scotland/Britain?

	Proud of Scotland	*Proud of Britain*
Countryside, scenery	31	14
People	35	22
History	10	13
Sport	1	4
Art, music, literature	2	3
Education	10	6
Legal system	3	7
Democratic tradition	6	21
Other	–	–

In a population which was strongly nationalist, one would expect pride in history or the achievements of the people to be mentioned. These are the sorts of values which nationalists fight for. The survey showed that pride in Scotland was widespread and strong, but that it was not principally about politics for the vast majority of Scottish electors. Hence, in addition, we conclude that feelings of Scottish identity were strongly present in 1992, but that they did not have obvious implications for political action for the vast majority of Scots.

The political class and home rule

Despite their apparently high levels of support for home rule, if voters rated it so far down the political agenda and approached the issue out of a relatively unpoliticised sense of Scottish identity, one would have expected the campaign for home rule to disappear. Nevertheless, home rule remained a matter of considerable importance to the Scottish political class. The history of the campaign for Scottish home rule is well known (Brand 1978; Hanham 1969; Mitchell 1995); here we shall outline it only and draw attention to the ways in which political elites have kept reviving it, thus making Scottish identity an issue in British politics.

To begin with, it is worthwhile pointing out that the situation of Scotland is very different from that of the English regions. Non-Scottish readers are prone to gloss over the differences. The crucial factor is that Scotland was a separate kingdom until 1707 when it joined in a union with England. More than that, Scottish history before the Union had been a constant struggle with England; among the most powerful myths are those of the Wars of Independence from the thirteenth to the sixteenth centuries. They were so savage and continuous that it is difficult to believe that the distinction between the two nations was not very clear to the most ordinary Scottish peasant. The deal struck in the Act of Union was that Scotland would be left with her major institutions untouched: these included the Church, the legal system, the educational system at all levels, and local government. Although their degree of separateness from England now varies, these and other institutions still provide a substantive basis for believing in Scottish political autonomy. In addition, in modern times it is perhaps as important that a specific network of television and newspapers has provided good and pervasive communications which have been specifically Scottish. During the early to mid 1990s, the topic of home rule was seldom out of the front pages of the *Herald* or *Scotsman* and it was also a major topic on the Scottish television networks. The sympathies of the newspapers were quite clearly in favour of home rule, and it was not difficult to work out similar attitudes among major television commentators. For these reasons and others, including a vibrant and distinctive Scottish popular culture, which started with Burns and Scott and has been maintained in various forms until the present day, Scottish identity is well defined. The country's political, economic and cultural history has ensured the existence of a 'community of fate' (Anderson

1983). We have seen already that this did not push national self-government anywhere near the top of the agenda for the majority of Scottish voters, but it did sustain the interest of the Scottish political class for over a century.

The Scottish Home Rule Association (SHRA) was founded in 1886, in reality as an off-shoot of the Liberal Party and as part of the movement for 'home rule all round'. It was re-founded after the First World War, still with Liberal members but principally supported by the Labour Party in Scotland. Neither the earlier nor the later organisations had large popular memberships; they consisted of Labour MPs, clergymen, trade union officials and councillors. Their interest in Scotland was political, where the interest of ordinary Scottish people was more general. Interest in the SHRA waned as Scottish Labour MPs became more embroiled in the struggles of the party at a British level. Enraged by this, several SHRA members broke away and formed a nationalist party which became the SNP, but it was never a serious threat to Labour until the 1960s. Labour interest was revived then because the Nationalists started to win seats. After a period during which the call for constitutional change was rejected, both the Conservative and Labour Parties drew up plans for devolution. Labour in government between 1974 and 1979 maintained its campaign for devolution because it feared that otherwise it might lose votes to the SNP. Devolution became a recognisably Labour policy, although the party leadership in London was markedly more insistent on the policy of devolution out of electoral pragmatism than the party in Scotland, and even then there were opponents within ministerial ranks. The party produced two measures: the Scotland and Wales Bill and, after that was defeated, the Scotland Bill. The latter was the subject of a referendum in which, for practicable purposes, it was defeated. Only 47 per cent of Labour voters voted 'yes', despite an unequivocal official stance by the party. The Tories fought the referendum on the basis that they would later produce a better plan for devolution, and thus the Labour plan should be rejected.

It was rejected. There were many defections on the Labour side and it was also striking that, in contrast to one strong organisation on the 'no' side, those who favoured the measure were divided between one campaign fought by the Labour Party and some Liberals, another led by the SNP and yet another which attracted other electors. There were, in fact, yet more smaller organisations on the 'yes' side. These bodies refused to co-operate with one another, largely on the basis that the Nationalists did not trust the others, and the others felt that the Nationalists were only supporting the Bill as a step towards full independence. The Bill's supporters were devastated by the result. After a period of mourning, breached by yet another disaster at the 1979 general election when Labour was thrown out of office and the eleven

Nationalist MPs were reduced to two, the whole issue of devolution appeared to be dead. The Campaign for a Scottish Assembly (CSA), established in 1980 to achieve cross-party unity in the campaign for a Scottish legislature, tried hard to raise popular interest in the form of rallies, fêtes, conferences and bunfights all over Scotland, but attendances were very small.

The corpse did not revive until the late 1980s. In the intervening years, important organisations such as the Scottish Trades Union Congress and the Churches became more actively supportive of the CSA, but Labour and the Liberals were cautious. The crucial change came with the revival of Labour Party interest in home rule from the late 1980s. Undoubtedly this was related to the fact that the SNP had again been (or had been perceived to be) the major challenger to Labour in Scotland. In the 1992 general election, the SNP (with 21.4 % of the vote), was only four points behind the Conservatives. In the May 1994 Scottish local government elections, the SNP came second only to Labour and forced the Conservatives into fourth place. It could be argued that were it not for this threat, home rule would not have been an issue at all. All the schemes for a Scottish Parliament or assembly could be seen as methods for drawing the dragon's teeth. Despite their political successes, however, it should be noted that the SNP failed to translate significant electoral support into parliamentary representation. Following the 1992 election they had only three MPs, with an additional member elected at a by-election in 1995, as compared with 11 MPs in the 1974–79 parliament. It may be that the Labour Party was wrong to fear them.

The revival of the home-rule movement focused on the creation of a constitutional convention. The idea of setting up a constitutional convention had first been put forward in the years following the referendum on Labour's Scottish devolution measure in 1979. Gordon Wilson, the SNP leader, proposed a Bill establishing a constitutional convention in parliament in 1980 which received little support. Even his own party was hostile. Over the following years, Wilson worked to convince his party of the merits of a directly elected convention. By 1987 the SNP was officially committed to participation in an elected constitutional convention. At the same time, a debate on the merits of a constitutional convention was taking place within the CSA. The debates both inside the SNP and the CSA were elite affairs which had little, if any, impact on the wider Scottish electorate. Labour was hostile to the idea for most of the 1980s.

However, the idea came to the fore following the 1987 general election when the Conservatives were reduced to ten seats. Legislation introducing the poll tax in Scotland, but not elsewhere in Britain at that time, had been passed in the final days of the old parliament. Before the election there had been talk amongst the opposition parties of challenging the Conservatives' right to rule Scotland in the event of the 'Doomsday scenario', that is, the Conservatives winning again but with only minority support in Scotland. The poll tax had provided a focus for the claims that the Tories had no mandate in Scotland. This popular backdrop to the launch of the Constitutional Convention was important.

The CSA set up a committee of 'prominent Scots' chaired by Sir Robert Grieve, a retired senior Scottish public servant, to draw up a plan for a constitutional convention. Three of its members were then members of the SNP, but each was on the pragmatic/gradualist wing of the party. The document it produced was largely the work of Jim Ross, who had been the civil servant in charge of devolution in the Scottish Office a decade before. The committee reported in July 1988 with the *Claim of Right for Scotland* (see Edwards 1989). The *Claim* offered a critique of the existing arrangements for the government of Scotland, argued the case for a Scottish Parliament whilst being careful not to offend those who supported independence and those wishing a parliament within the United Kingdom, and considered different options for establishing a convention (see Bennie *et al.* 1997).

The *Claim* stressed the need to, 'achieve acceptance by those on whose behalf it presumes to speak and act' and accepted that ideally an elected convention would be necessary to achieve this (Constitutional Convention 1990, p.13). However, the practical difficulties involved in establishing an elected convention led to proposals for an alternative basis for the convention. The cost of an elected convention was felt to be prohibitive, and special efforts to raise money would be better devoted to financing a referendum than financing elections to a constitutional convention. A convention which was largely based on existing elected representatives was proposed, but the *Claim* maintained that the weaknesses in the 'first past the post' system made topping-up necessary. In fact, within the committee it was acknowledged that there would be problems in gaining widespread support if the convention were entirely based on elected members who would predominantly be Labour Party members. A balancing act was necessary to ensure a broad base of support.

The aims of the Convention were set out in the *Claim* under three broad headings: drawing up a scheme for a Scottish assembly; mobilising Scottish opinion behind the scheme; and dealing with the government in securing approval of the scheme or an acceptable modification of it. The last objective was recognised to be the Convention's most important and the organisation of a referendum was repeatedly referred to in the *Claim*. Despite this, the objectives of the Constitutional Convention were not always clear, and different participants saw the Convention as offering different means of solving quite different problems.

Little public excitement surrounded the launch of the *Claim*, but a series of events pushed the Convention further up the political agenda. The Labour Party was initially cool towards the idea, fearing that a cross-party body would result in it losing control of the constitutional agenda, but Labour soon realised that under the proposals it would have a clear overall majority in the Convention. This had been intentional as Labour's involvement without this would have proved impossible. The criticism of the lack of proportionality in the electoral system made in the *Claim* was to have little influence on the composition of the Convention. Donald Dewar, Labour Shadow Scottish Secretary, announced in late October 1988 that his party would participate. In part, Labour was reacting to pressure from the SNP. The Nationalists were on the offensive, particularly over the poll tax, and a by-election in Govan had been called.

The Convention hardly featured in the Govan by-election. The SNP had launched its 'independence in Europe' campaign, articulated by their candidate in Govan, former Labour MP Jim Sillars, and overturned a huge Labour majority to win the seat. The SNP victory was double-edged for supporters of the Convention. It forced the constitutional question to the fore, but the battle for votes between the SNP and Labour was bitter and made co-operation almost impossible. Early in 1989 discussions were held on the composition of the Convention, and it became clear to the SNP, as it had already to Labour, that Labour would dominate the Convention. With European elections pending in June and a by-election in Glasgow Central (neighbouring Govan), the SNP feared that Labour would use the Convention to attack its policies and try to force the SNP to support devolution. The SNP decided not to participate. The Scottish media, overwhelmingly sympathetic to a convention, attacked the Nationalists and the honeymoon period for the SNP, which had followed their Govan victory, was over.

From Labour's point of view, the SNP decision not to participate allowed them to portray the Nationalists as narrow and sectarian. It also made agreement in the Convention easier. There was a ceremonial launch of the Convention in March 1989. Delegates attending the launch signed a 'Claim of Right':

> We, gathered as the Scottish Constitutional Convention, do hereby acknowledge the sovereign right of the Scottish people to determine the form of Government best suited to their needs, and do hereby declare and pledge that in all our actions and deliberations their interest shall be paramount.

> We further declare and pledge that our actions and deliberations shall be directed to the following ends:
>
> To agree a scheme for an Assembly or Parliament for Scotland;
>
> To mobilise Scottish opinion and ensure the approval of the Scottish people for that scheme; and
>
> To assert the right of the Scottish people to secure the implementation of that scheme.

Almost all those present signed the declaration. Tam Dalyell, opponent of devolution in the 1970s, had attended the meeting along with all other Scottish Labour MPs, but admitted after the 1992 election that he had not signed it. Dalyell remained implacably opposed to devolution, even though he managed to give an impression of going along with it before the 1992 election. The need for party unity hid the true extent of opposition within the Labour Party.

The Scottish Constitutional Convention and proposals for a Scottish Parliament

Over the next few years, in the lead-up to the 1992 general election, the Convention held a series of meetings. Committees met in private to discuss the details of a scheme for a devolved parliament. Dates for the publication of its conclusions were continually put back, leaving an impression that the Convention was being used as a stalling device. If an agreed scheme was in place before the general election then the Convention would have had to turn its attention to the second and third of its stated objectives: mobilising Scottish opinion behind the scheme and dealing with the government in securing approval of the scheme or an acceptable modification of it. This was not something the Labour leadership would have welcomed. Scotland's Claim of Right was bound to be unacceptable to the Conservatives, and confrontation was inevitable if the Convention took its third objective seriously. Radical rhetoric surrounded the activities of the Convention, but it was an intensely conservative body in practice (see Kellas 1992).

In 1990 the Convention produced *Towards Scotland's Parliament*, outlining its proposals for a Scottish Parliament. This was followed in 1995 by *Key Proposals for Scotland's Parliament* and *Scotland's Parliament. Scotland's Right* on St Andrew's day 1995. The launch and re-launches of what were essentially the same proposals gave an impression that the Convention had run out of steam and did not know what to do next. The problem for the Convention was that the first of its objectives had proved easier to achieve, though even then drawing up a scheme for a Scottish Parliament proved difficult and many crucial matters were ignored. Translating the latent support for constitutional change into an effective campaign was beyond the Convention. By 1995, the rhetoric surrounding the launch and early work of the Convention – Scottish 'popular sovereignty' having precedence over parliamentary sovereignty – had given way to tacit acceptance that the scheme would only be implemented if and when Westminster permitted.

Debate within the Constitutional Convention concentrated on a limited range of issues. The basis of the scheme adopted in 1995 was the 1978 Scotland Act. It was envisaged that a shorter Act would be passed than the Scotland Act 1978 and, as in 1978, that it would list the devolved functions rather than list powers retained at Westminster. The list of responsibilities would be wider, though expressed in more general terms, than those proposed in 1978. The Scottish universities, the administration of social security (though not policy-making in this field), industrial development, and vocational training and retraining, would all come under the Scottish Parliament. A symbolic change from the 1970s was in the term used to describe the proposed Scottish legislature: the Convention talked of a parliament whereas the 1978 Act referred to an assembly.

Much debate surrounded the size and composition of the parliament. Three issues had to be resolved: the electoral system, the representation of women, and the number of Members of the Scottish Parliament (MSPs). The Liberal Democrats argued for the single transferable vote system but this was resisted by the Labour Party. In the end agreement was reached that an additional member system would be adopted. There would be 73 seats – consisting of the existing Westminster constituencies with Orkney and Shetland each having an MP – plus seven additional members drawn from each of the eight Scottish Euro-constituencies (56 additional members in total). The additional members would be drawn from lists provided by the political parties. Crucially, the votes cast for each party would be counted in each of the Euro-constituencies and the seven seats would be allocated so that the total representation from the area – including MSPs returned for individual constituencies – would correspond as closely as possible with the share of the vote cast for each party in the area. This would be a more proportional system than 'first past the post'. The voting system would have to be reviewed periodically, especially as Westminster constituencies and European constituencies would be reviewed too. At the same time the work of the Boundary Commission for Scotland would in future have to take account of the implications for the Scottish Parliament of its revisions. It would be necessary to ensure that Westminster/Scottish Parliament constituencies corresponded with Euro-constituencies to ensure that the additional member system worked.

Pressure for equal representation of men and women – '50–50' as it became known – came from the Labour movement and efforts were made to ensure that provision for a significantly larger proportion of women being elected to the parliament than had been the case with Westminster. The Liberal Democrats in particular were opposed to setting a quota, and a compromise was agreed that the parties involved in the Convention would strive to ensure gender balance. The size of the Scottish Parliament was also debated, with the more radical members and those supporting a greater degree of proportionality arguing for a larger parliament. The compromise figure of 129 was agreed, despite strong representation from the Scottish Trades Union Congress and others arguing for a larger body.

One area that created difficulties was the future role of the Secretary of State for Scotland. Under the terms of the Scotland Act 1978, the office of Scottish Secretary was to be retained. The Labour Party still saw a role for the Scottish Secretary but the Liberal Democrats did not. No agreement could be arrived at and the Convention side-stepped the question. Indeed the crucial area of Scotland's relations with Westminster/Whitehall was largely ignored by the Convention. There was little in any of the documents on how disputes between the Scottish Parliament and London would be resolved, how the grant settlement would be agreed and nothing on the 'West Lothian question' (see Chapter 1).

Financing the assembly proved a difficult matter in the late 1970s, and the Labour government's measure proposed that the devolution would be financed entirely by block grant. In the 1980s, Labour policy changed and it was agreed that a future Scottish Parliament would have tax-raising powers. This was partly a reaction to criticism in the 1970s that the assembly then on offer would be irresponsible as it had no such powers and partly an attempt to show that Labour was intent on creating a more powerful legislature. The 1990 proposals included assigning certain revenues to the Scottish Parliament plus a grant from London. It was claimed that this would 'underline the independence of the Parliament' (Constitutional Convention 1990, p.10). The summary proposals attempted to give the parliament financial autonomy within the context of a United Kingdom:

1. There would be the assignation of all Scottish income tax to Scotland's parliament and if possible the assignation of all Scottish VAT. If this was not possible, the best estimate of Scottish VAT would be found and then be assigned.
2. There would also be a power for Scotland's parliament to vary the income tax rate, but there would be some range defined so that the variation in income tax up or down could not be misunderstood as being a wide margin.

3. Equalisation would continue to be based on needs assessment starting from the prevailing formula basis.
4. It would be necessary to review these arrangements on a regular basis. The initial review of needs would take place as soon as possible after the establishment of Scotland's parliament. More general reviews would follow.

'New' Labour's fears that it might be branded a high tax party and criticisms of the 1990 proposals led to changes over the next few years. The 1995 document removed some of the tax-raising powers. The parliament would now be largely funded by grant. It would have the power to vary income tax by a maximum of 3 pence in the pound. The Liberal Democrats announced that they would seek to use this power to raise money to increase educational expenditure. However, Tony Blair, Labour's British leader, announced that although the power to raise or lower taxes would be given to the parliament, it would not be used, leading to the accusation that he was dictating Labour policy in Scotland. The tax-raising powers were added in order to give an impression that the parliament would have greater autonomy and be more responsible than that envisaged in the 1970s. By 1995, however, they had proved a gift to Labour's opposition. Michael Forsyth, the Conservative Secretary of State appointed in July 1995, branded the proposals 'Labour's tartan tax'.

Following this, Blair further angered the Scottish Labour Party in June 1996 by announcing that there would be a pre-legislative referendum on both the desirability of a Scottish Parliament and specifically whether it should have tax-raising powers. The referendum pledge was clearly designed to neutralise Conservative opposition. This revision of policy came at the same time as the publication of an important report on devolution by a group of former civil servants (Constitution Unit 1996) concerned about the legislative difficulties which Labour might face without a clear mandate for reforms. Hence the revision of policy was apparently also designed to ensure better prospects for reform in practice than in the 1970s, the view being that anti-devolutionists would find it harder to wreck legislation if the people had already given their assent in principle. The referendum pledge nevertheless seriously angered many in the Scottish party, fearful that it meant the start of a leadership retreat from commitment to devolution.

Probably one of the most difficult issues in the 1970s was the representation of Scottish MPs at Westminster. The so-called 'West Lothian question' was raised with typical persistence by Tam Dalyell, Labour MP for West Lothian. It had been the same intractable problem which had defeated Gladstone when he proposed Irish home rule in the nineteenth century. Would Scottish MPs be allowed to vote on devolved matters affecting

England? The Convention simply avoided this subject, though it is bound to dominate the debate in parliament whenever a devolution bill is presented. Other areas which were not addressed fully by the Convention were the institutional mechanisms and procedures governing relations between the Scottish Parliament and Westminster/Whitehall and between the parliament and Scottish local government. Many of these practical and more detailed considerations were highlighted in the report of the Constitution Unit (1996).

Overall, while much effort went into the Convention and novel proposals were made, the actual scheme proposed by the Convention was largely the same as that proposed in the Scotland Act of 1978. Key issues which caused so many problems in the 1970s remained to be addressed, leaving the potential for the defeat of home rule again. In addition, the proposals faced the problem of a lack of public response. In the early 1990s, there were rallies in Glasgow's George Square and on the Calton Hill in Edinburgh, even marches down Princes Street and round the clock vigils outside the building intended for the assembly, but this was not sustained beyond 1992. Activity from 1993 onwards reverted to elite politics. Cross-party co-operation through organisations such as Scotland United, set up immediately after the 1992 election result, faded as the leaderships of the main opposition parties fought one another and prevented any prospect of co-operation. To say this is not to say that there was no prospect of home rule being implemented. Measures of great value have been campaigned for and won by small groups of insiders. To achieve a constitutional change of this significance, however, it was clear that politicians would require legitimation and pressure in terms of a threat to their votes. If there was no pressure, ultimately they would find other, less difficult, things to do.

The Labour Party and support for home rule

In this context, the key change by the mid 1990s was the degree of commitment in the Labour Party to devolution. Though some opposition still existed in Scottish Labour and in certain sections of the party in England, Scottish Labour had become overwhelmingly in favour of change. Why was this the case? For one might have thought that two rattling defeats for Labour in 1979 and 1992 might have opened its eyes to the peripheral nature of the support for constitutional change. Fear of the potential appeal of the SNP remained the most significant influence on Labour opinion. However, two further influences need to be noted to explain the deepening of Labour support. First, the number of public dissidents on home rule in the Scottish Labour Party diminished and a growing number of members became enthusiasts for the idea, even for independence. Indeed a home rule pressure group within the Scottish Labour Party calling itself Scottish Labour Action was set up in 1988. In 1992, 20 per cent of Labour voters actually supported independence, an advance from 8 per cent in 1979. Second, the issue of home rule became strongly associated with the Labour Party, meaning that the party in Scotland could not be seen to drop the issue. The importance of support for home rule as an aspect of Labour Party identification among voters deserves further explanation.

It needs to be noted that over the years proposals for home rule changed in their meaning. Up to the decision by Labour to re-adopt the policy in 1974, home rule was associated with the SNP, which was a shrill, unimportant political sect. Subsequently, the SNP became a major player in Scottish politics. Most voters in 1992 obviously did not support independence, but the proportion was up from 1987 and a majority of its advocates identified with the SNP; in contrast, home rule or devolution had become more and more associated with Labour.

Table 2.3: Party and support for Scottish home rule (1992)

	Con.	*Lab.*	*Lib. Dem.*	*SNP*
Independence from Britain and Europe	1	6	1	14
Independence from Britain in Europe	4	14	9	43
Assembly	37	62	65	38
No change	55	15	25	4
Other/don't know	4	3	[–]	1
Total	**101**	**100**	**100**	**100**

Table 2.3 shows a strong relationship between both Labour and Liberal voting on the one hand, and support for an assembly or home rule on the other, at the 1992 general election. It should be noticed that the proportion of Labour voters in this category was (marginally) lower than that for the Liberals because a higher proportion of Labour voters supported independence. In any case, Labour, as by far the larger party, still became more prominent in the campaign and dominated the media in its support for home rule.

Thus even though pride in Scotland was not sparked off by political features, and though it was not among the most important policies for voters, in the 1992 general election it was clearly associated in Labour voters' minds with their own party. Table 2.4 furthermore shows that the proportion of Labour voters perceiving that Labour supported an assembly did not change between 1979 and 1992, but a lower percentage in 1992 believed that Labour supported the status quo and a higher percentage believed that Labour supported independence. Although there are no data directly upon this, one might guess that the public association was made in electors' minds at the time of the 1979 referendum and that it remained, perhaps boosted by Labour's support for the Constitutional Convention.

Table 2.4: Labour voters' perception of Labour's views on Scottish home rule in 1979 and 1992

	1979		*1992*
Independence	4	Independence in or out of Europe	15
Assembly	72	Assembly	73
No change	23	No change	14

It is consistent with this and with the previously discussed data that voters supported devolution in the 1992 survey at least partly because it was a Labour policy and not because they felt particularly strongly about it. Again the identity model of policy choice seems to have been influential here. This would, for example, explain the consistent support by Labour voters, but not with particular enthusiasm.

Conclusion

This chapter emphasises the growing importance between the 1970s and early 1990s of support for home rule at the level of party elites. Support derived initially from the fact that Labour, and the Liberals, first got into the game of home rule because the SNP started to attract votes which threatened Labour and Liberal votes. The performance of the Nationalists at elections up to 1992 was patchy, but the fact is that a large proportion of Scottish electors voted for them regularly. Over half of all Scottish electors, irrespective of who they voted for or their views on the constitutional issue, said in 1974, 1979 and 1992 that they believed that the SNP had been good for Scotland. This suggests that awareness of Scottish identity played a key role. Even though the political element of Scottish feeling was, as we have seen, not always prominent, there was a feeling that Scotland did have interests which were not always given their weight. If electors had wanted to register a protest, they could have voted for the Liberals or Workers' Revolutionary Party, but they voted SNP, which suggests that a sizeable number felt that Scottishness was an alternative basis of political identity and action. Hence the existence of the SNP forced Labour and the Liberals to pay attention to

Scottish matters. Its very existence made this important for ordinary Scottish voters. By reacting to the threat of the Nationalists, the Labour Party especially made the political aspect of Scottish identity even more prominent.

However, at the beginning of the chapter, we suggested that identity was contextual. One of the most important aspects of any social context is the institutions which structure the situation for the individual. For party supporters the party will be very important, but it does not explain everything. Before 1974, the Labour Party was opposed to devolution, and yet, as we pointed out at the beginning of the chapter, the level of support for devolution or home rule had been at the level of 75 per cent from as far back as 1947. However, we do suggest that the important feature of the situation in the period up to the 1992 election was that the Labour Party structured home rule as a possible line of development, and as part of a mainstream political programme, which it did not do prior to 1974. Labour's continuing commitment to the policy in the Constitutional Convention reinforced this trend. This did not seem to increase the level of popular enthusiasm, although one would expect rather fewer Labour voters to reject the parliament in a referendum than did in 1979. More obviously, though, it brought in elites from pressure groups and other public bodies.

None of the foregoing necessarily points to an inevitable trend of the intensification of popular feelings of a Scottish political identity. Hopes for such a trend suffered setbacks at the elections of 1979 and 1992, providing grounds for future pessimism. Analysis of the period 1979–92 does suggest, however, that Scottish political identity did not go away because structural features built it into the political discourse. Scottish voters did not take this to mean that home rule should be high on their collective agenda, but the conditions which we have outlined show how other developments occasionally precipitate the voters in this direction. Incidents such as the imposition of the poll tax or water privatisation, for example, easily performed this function. In the event of a Labour government holding a referendum on whether or not to have home rule, it was evident that the ability of elites to politicise popular feelings of Scottish identity would, of course, face its ultimate test.

References

Anderson, B. (1983) *Imagined Communities: Reflections on the Origin and Spread of Nationalism.* London: Verso.

Bernie, L., Brand, J. and Mitchell, J. (1997) *How Scotland Votes.* Manchester: Manchester University Press.

Brand, J. (1978) *The National Movement in Scotland.* London: Routledge and Kegan Paul.

Brand, J., Mitchell, J. and Surridge, P. (1993) 'Identity and the vote.' In P. Norris *et al.* *Elections, Parties and Public Opinion Yearbook.* London: Harvester Wheatsheaf.

Constitution Unit (1996) *Scotland's Parliament, Fundamentals for a New Scotland Act.* London: The Constitution Unit.

Constitutional Convention (1990) *Towards Scotland's Parliament.* Edinburgh: The Scottish Constitutional Convention.

Constitutional Convention (1995) *Scotland's Parliament. Scotland's Right.* Edinburgh: The Scottish Constitutional Convention.

Drucker, H. (ed) (1982) *John P. Mackintosh on Scotland.* London: Longman.

Edwards, O.D. (1989) *A Claim of Right for Scotland.* Edinburgh: Polygon.

Hanham, H.J. (1969) *Scottish Nationalism.* London: Faber.

Kellas, J.G. (1992) 'The Scottish constitutional convention.' In L. Paterson and D. McCrone (eds) *The Scottish Government Yearbook 1992.* Edinburgh: Unit for the Study of Government in Scotland.

Mitchell, J. (1995) *Strategies for Self-Government.* Edinburgh: Polygon.

CHAPTER 3

Welsh Politics and Changing British and European Contexts

Barry Jones

Introduction

Despite the overwhelming failure of the devolution referendum in 1979 the territorial management of Wales continued to pose problems for the British state. The political legitimacy of subsequent Conservative governments' mandate in Wales was called into question and by the early 1990s support for devolution had grown. In response, the Labour Party in opposition under Tony Blair saw fit to resurrect its commitment to introduce legislation setting up a devolved Welsh assembly in Cardiff, subject to the attainment of a simple majority in a pre-legislative referendum. These developments raised two key questions: why did the devolution debate resurface again in the early to mid 1990s; and how did its origins and general perception of its likely outcome compare with the 1970s? In this chapter it is argued that the revival of the devolution debate was a result of the changing face of Welsh politics during the 1980s and 1990s. Such changes focused not so much on developments in nationalism, as was often held to be the case in the 1970s, as developments in Wales' economic base, changes to the administrative structure, the difficulties of territorial management by a parliamentary state with an asymmetrical party system, and the growing importance of the European connection. The chapter examines each of these developments in turn and then addresses directly the nature of the revived devolution debate in Wales. Overall, the chapter suggests that the pressures in favour of reform in the early to mid 1990s were both different to, and more substantial than, those in the 1970s. First, however, we need to understand the nature of Welsh nationalism, and the marginal influence of separatist politics in the 1990s.

Nationalism's track record

A basic difficulty in examining Welsh politics lies in assessing the significance and impact of Welsh nationalism upon political events. While there is no doubt that the ideology of nationalism should never be underestimated, it is one of the most ambiguous concepts in the vocabulary of political science (Alter 1989). It can be argued that each nationalism is unique; the product of an unrepeatable conjunction of historical events and economic circumstances. The confusion is only partly eased by constructing typologies of various nationalisms. In this context Welsh nationalism would be regarded as a 'separation nationalism'. According to this categorisation, such nationalist movements disintegrate the existing sovereign state and establish new nation states. But it is too early to place Welsh nationalism definitively in this category. There is no guarantee that it will achieve its aspirations; on the contrary it might well be satisfied with a series of administrative, economic and political concessions within the existing framework of the United Kingdom. Such a proposition is rendered more convincing by the continuing inability of Plaid Cymru (the Welsh nationalist party) to threaten seriously the hegemony of British political parties in Wales.

The track record of Plaid Cymru is less convincing than that of the Scottish National Party (SNP), and yet at one level both parties' nationalisms appear very similar. Both are part of the Celtic periphery, explicable in terms of the internal colonialism thesis and share similar experiences of uneven economic development and cultural exploitation. Each nationalist party achieved an electoral breakthrough in the late 1960s after decades in the political doldrums and have subscribed to a common critique of the British state; that it has become increasingly centralised and insensitive to the needs of the periphery and that the party system no longer serves the needs of the periphery because the Conservatives are irredeemably unionist and Labour, traditionally the party of the periphery, has become increasingly identified with economic planning and a centralised state. It was this analysis which enabled the Scottish and Welsh nationalists to threaten Labour's industrial working-class heartlands in central Scotland and south Wales. Furthermore, it is a measure of the parallels between the two nationalist movements that they obtained virtually the same percentage vote in the 1970 general election: the SNP 11.4 per cent of the Scottish vote and Plaid Cymru 11.5 per cent of the Welsh vote.

However, at this point the similarities end. From the early 1970s the political fortunes of Welsh nationalism developed differently from those of Scottish nationalism because of five significant factors. First, Plaid Cymru failed to make a significant electoral breakthrough in Wales. Between the 1970 and 1987 general elections its vote fell steadily, from 11.5 per cent in

1970 to 7.3 per cent in 1987. Its success in the 1992 general election in increasing its vote to 9 per cent still left it on the margins of Welsh politics. Nor was Plaid Cymru able to break into Labour's industrial heartland in south Wales. In 1992 the party averaged 5 per cent of the vote in the industrial and English-speaking valleys compared with an average of 15.3 per cent of the vote in agricultural and largely Welsh-speaking Wales. Plaid's heavy dependence upon the language factor was emphasised by the location of the four parliamentary constituencies which it won in 1992. All ran along the western seaboard where the proportion of the population speaking Welsh ranged between 65 per cent and 87 per cent (Aitchison and Carter 1993).

Second, the Welsh language remained a potent political force disproportionate both to the number of Welsh-speakers and Plaid Cymru MPs. Direct action by Welsh language activists (Cymdeithas yr Iaith Cymraeg) resulted in bilingual signs in most parts of Wales and the use of bilingual forms by virtually all government documents. The establishment of the Welsh language TV channel (S4C) by the Conservatives in 1982 came about after Gwynfor Evans (a past President of Plaid Cymru) threatened a fast to death unless the government honoured its manifesto commitment. The channel's annual subsidy rose to £57.9 million per year within a decade, the highest level of subsidy per viewer of any TV station in Europe (S4C 1994).

Third, Wales continued to lack a valuable natural resource. The expectation that substantial reserves of oil would be discovered off the Welsh coast was not realised. Although natural gas in Liverpool Bay began to be brought on shore in Clwyd for processing, by the mid 1990s it still represented a very small item in the Welsh economy and coal, once Wales' most important natural resource, had become a minor industrial activity.

Fourth, Welsh nationalism continued to suffer from the fact that historically Wales had never enjoyed the status of an independent state: since the Act of Union in 1536 Wales had been progressively incorporated politically, economically and culturally into southern Britain. The manufacturing centres of the Midlands and south-east England were powerful magnets for the Welsh unemployed during periods of recession in the basic industries of coal, iron and steel; and the Welsh social elite had long looked to England for advantage and advancement (Foulkes, Jones and Wilford 1983).

Fifth, the Labour Party in Wales was ambivalent about devolution during the 1960s and 1970s. In the 1979 referendum campaign, large numbers of Labour activists were opposed to the party's devolution proposals. The so-called 'Gang of Six' Welsh Labour backbenchers, which included Neil Kinnock, fought a vigorous and successful 'no' campaign both in parliament and in the country. The close industrial links between Wales and adjacent English industrial centres encouraged Welsh Labour supporters to subscribe to the notion of a 'British working-class movement' which would be fatally divided by any move towards political devolution (Foulkes *et al.* 1983).

For all these reasons, Welsh nationalism posed a more limited threat to the political establishment in Wales than its counterpart in Scotland. Paradoxically, the emotive force of the language issue produced more significant concessions from government than one would expect with Plaid Cymru's electoral record. Given appropriate circumstances, for example in the case of the establishment of S4C, Plaid Cymru and Cymdeithas yr Iaith Cymraeg (the Welsh Language Society) were able to exert effective pressure on the policy-making process. This reflected the fact that the danger of inflaming nationalist sentiments on issues relating to the status of the Welsh language has always produced a prudently sensitive response.

In the late 1980s, and particularly in the 1992 general election, Plaid Cymru emerged as a more credible political force willing and able to act more pragmatically. First, it identified its Welsh language heartland (Y Fro Cymraeg) as a positive electoral bonus and consolidated its electoral strategy to secure this electoral beachhead from which it might threaten constituencies in English-speaking Wales. Furthermore, the party adopted a more pragmatic approach, agreeing a joint parliamentary candidate with the Greens in Ceredigion for the 1992 general election, and exhibiting a willingness to exploit the government's slim Commons majority during the Maastricht debate, as a result of which the Conservative government agreed that one of the three Welsh nominees to the Committee of the Regions should be a Plaid Cymru representative.

Morale in the nationalist movement was also raised by the 1991 census data which indicated that the fall in the number of Welsh language-speakers had been arrested and that, in certain parts of English-speaking Wales where Welsh-medium schools had been introduced, the number of young Welsh-speakers had actually increased. In 1992 a Broadcasting Audience Research Board (BARB) survey for S4C indicated that while only approximately 20 per cent could speak the language fluently, up to 27 per cent could speak Welsh with varying degrees of skill. Equally significantly, BARB figures suggested that there was a Welsh language Diaspora of 362,000 in England (RSMB for S4C 1993).

However, the relatively good news about the language highlighted a basic ambiguity in Welsh nationalism: whether its main concern was with preserving traditional cultural values which might well be accommodated within the structure of the British state; or whether it was really committed to political independence, the attainment of which would hand political power to the English-speaking majority in Wales. On this basis separatist nationalism in Wales was clearly not the influential political force it was in Scotland,

and as a result one cannot explain the changes in Welsh politics by the mid 1990s simply in the context of developments in nationalism. We must look to other issues for a more convincing explanation.

The transformation of the economic base

At the time of the 1979 referendum on devolution, the Welsh economy was still dependent upon heavy traditional industries. It was also dominated by the public sector, which employed 43 per cent of the workforce. In the campaign, the business and managerial classes, concerned about Welsh economic interests primarily in a British context, voted 'no'. In this context the 'yes' campaign made appeals to the traditional icons of Welsh radicalism, old liberal sentiments, a non-conformist conscience and the working-class movement. But the result of the referendum suggested that they no longer represented significant forces in Welsh life and that Welsh society was passing through a period of profound change. The economic and social base did not provide much ground for optimism amongst pro-devolutionists.

During the 1980s the policies of privatisation and reduced regional aid transformed the situation. The Welsh steel industry contracted from 70,000 to 18,000 workers, and coal, upon which the modern Welsh political identity had been virtually built, was almost eliminated. Whereas 43,000 had been employed in Welsh mines in 1979, there were by 1995 fewer than 2000 miners with two deep mines and one, Tower Colliery, owned and worked by a company owned by the miners (Balsom and Jones 1984). The central pillars of the traditional Welsh working-class movement had been largely removed. The justification for the government's policy was the emergence of a global economy with the relatively free movement of capital and an increasing level of competition. In this new economic environment, with a government intent upon rolling back the frontiers of the state and reducing subsidies to ailing industries, the implication was that Wales (and other peripheral regions) should no longer look to the political centre but adopt a more proactive role in attracting inward investment.

The focus of a new proactive approach became the Welsh Development Agency (WDA), which had been set up by a Labour government in 1975 and curiously was not abolished by the first Thatcher government despite an ideology hostile to such institutions. The WDA's inward investment arm, Welsh Development International (WDI) emerged during the 1980s as a significant force in the modernisation of the Welsh economy. The WDI established offices around the world and provided 'package deals' for potential investors including site location, planning procedures, labour training and employee housing. The provision of a 'one-stop' service proved to be very attractive and helped give Wales a competitive edge over other parts of the UK in attracting investment. During the 1980s and early 1990s over 300 overseas companies set up operations in Wales, of which approximately 130 were from mainland Europe. By 1995 Wales had the largest concentration of Japanese investment in Europe. The foreign firms were not simply attracted by the administrative facilities provided by the WDI; affordable land, proximity to markets, good labour relations and, not least, relatively cheap labour all contributed to the attraction of inward investment (Owen 1990).

It would be misleading to exaggerate the degree to which the Welsh economy was modernised after 1979. Deep pockets of high employment remained, particularly in the 'post-industrial' valleys. Many of the new light industries provided female employment opportunities, leaving male unemployment figures depressingly high with the inevitable social consequences. But these considerations do not invalidate the point that Welsh society did change, that the Welsh economy developed a more balanced industrial base and that the scale of inward investment enabled Wales to become more aware of Europe and the wider world beyond.

This trend almost certainly had an advantageous effect on support for devolution in comparison with 1979, for economic change created a new entrepreneurial class concerned that Wales had the political structures most favourable to its economic interests in a more European and global context. Frustrations with existing British-based structures to promote economic interests in the new context frequently had the potential to neutralise, or even reverse, hostility to change involving the advent of a Welsh assembly, which was claimed by many to promise benefits in promoting Wales abroad. This in turn had the potential for giving a new lead to deferential working-class voters. Ironically, those marginalised through economic change also provided a new radical base for arguments for self-government.

Changes in the administrative structure

Although Conservative governments under Mrs Thatcher and John Major remained consistently hostile to political devolution to Wales, their incremental changes to the Welsh administrative system also strengthened the case for devolution. First, the Conservative government's willingness to increase the powers of the Welsh Office enhanced the argument for proper public accountability. Second, the growth of quangos heightened the sense of public outrage that a party lacking majority support in Wales should place so many functions and financial resources in the hands of non-elected persons. Finally, the near elimination of Welsh Conservative MPs undermined the argument that public accountability for government in Wales could be adequately and appropriately exercised through the existing parliamentary system.

The Welsh Office

The Welsh Office was established by the Labour government in 1965 in the teeth of opposition from the Conservatives. Initially established with a very limited range of powers, it grew under both Conservative and Labour governments (Jones 1990). In 1975 the Welsh Office acquired significant economic powers arising from Section 7 of the Industry Act which, operating through the WDA, enabled it to develop a coherent programme aimed at attracting inward investment (as detailed above). The new Conservative government in 1979 conspicuously failed to limit the role of the Welsh Office but actually added to its powers. In 1980 the Welsh Office assumed responsibility for negotiating with the Treasury the level of the Rate Support Grant (subsequently the central government support for the council tax) and during the Thatcher and Major administrations it gained administrative responsibility for the health service, agriculture, secondary and further education and finally the university sector in Wales. For most domestic purposes the Welsh Office became the expression and means of government in Wales.

The growth of Welsh Office responsibilities was reflected in the increased numbers of civil servants employed in the Welsh Office. When it was established the Welsh Office had slightly more than 200 civil servants and its total expenditure was somewhat less than £250 million a year. In 1995 that expenditure had reached £7000 million, which represented 70 per cent of public expenditure in Wales. However, while the Welsh Office grew in financial importance and administrative responsibilities, it did not grow in democratic accountability. The Office's political leadership, a Secretary of State and two ministers of state, were all Conservative and thus representative of a minority political opinion in Wales. Four Secretaries of State, Peter Walker, David Hunt, John Redwood and William Hague, were English MPs representing English constituencies. Nor was the Welsh Office's discharge of its duties beyond reproach. In December 1993 the Auditor General published a damning report on the Welsh Office's sloppy accounting which revealed that approximately £100 million of public expenditure was unaccounted for (Comptroller and Auditor General 1993). The opposition parties concluded that a proper degree of public accountability could only be obtained by an elected Welsh assembly.

The growth of quangos

After the creation of the Welsh Office, new quangos came into existence covering most aspects of Welsh life: the arts, sport, health and the countryside; tourism, inward investment, land, housing and economic development; and latterly higher and further education. The development of quangos was so considerable that one political journalist referred to Wales as 'Quangoland' (Osmond 1992). The Welsh quangos taken together were responsible for £1.5 billion expenditure a year by the mid 1990s. Two of the quangos, the WDA (authorising £149 million a year) and Housing for Wales/Tai Cymru (£116 million a year), were amongst the top 40 quangos in the United Kingdom. Even the smaller quangos spent significant amounts: the Welsh Arts Council authorised over £12 million of public expenditure each year. Nor by the mid 1990s was the process of 'quangoisation' complete. The National Health Service hospital trusts brought further quangos in their wake. There were concerns, not confined to party political spokesmen, that the growth of Welsh quangos and the amount of expenditure which they authorised had reached a critical point.

The first concern regarded the power of appointment exercised by the Welsh Secretary of State; whether this form of government patronage was a good or bad thing in itself and whether it was being operated in an appropriate manner. There were some, particularly in local government, who argued that these functions would be better exercised by a democratically elected authority with roots in the community it served. But Conservative governments clearly harboured serious doubts about the legitimacy of local government, which explains why so many powers were stripped away from local authorities and pushed down to 'specialist-function' quangos. Other quangos were given all-Wales responsibilities which could not readily or appropriately be exercised at a local authority level. Furthermore, the prevalence of quangos, both in Britain generally and abroad, suggested that local authorities did not possess elements of expertise and cost-effectiveness which could not easily be duplicated in an alternative institution.

The issue was not one of whether or not there should be quangos but how their membership should be constituted. In January 1993, the Wales Labour Party accused the government of, 'stuffing public bodies in Wales with Tory Placemen' (Labour Party 1993, p.4). In particular, Labour condemned the practice of Conservative politicians, rejected by their electorate, subsequently being appointed by the Welsh Secretary to chair quangos; specifically Beata Brooks, defeated in the 1987 European elections prior to her appointment to the Welsh Consumer Council, and Ian Grist who lost his Cardiff Central seat in the 1992 general election but was appointed within weeks to the South Glamorgan Health Authority. Labour was also concerned about multiple appointments to quangos; for example, people such as Sir Geoffrey Inkin and Dr Gwyn Jones. The clear implication behind these criticisms was that the Welsh Secretary of State should appoint more representative persons to quangos.

The second major concern was that Welsh quangos were not properly accountable to the electorate but were lodged in the semi-secret world of the executive branch of government. During the early 1990s, Rhodri Morgan MP was engaged in guerrilla warfare against the WDA, criticising and highlighting its financial improprieties. In 1993 the WDA was subjected to the ordeal of examination by the respected and feared Public House of Commons Accounts Committee. Various 'skeletons' were discovered and warnings were issued (Public Accounts Committee 1993). But it was also apparent that it was rare for public bodies in Wales to be subject to the attentions of the Public Accounts Committee; there were bigger, more expensive fish to fry in London. The Welsh Affairs Committee could potentially have undertaken regular investigations of Welsh quangos, but the Committee was a flawed instrument; it was not specialist, nor could it be given a wide remit. It was too small to permit an effective sub-committee to operate and it lacked the kind of specialist professional secretariat which would be absolutely necessary if the supervision of Welsh public bodies were to be detailed and rigorous.

Local government reform

The democratic deficit in Wales in terms of the parliamentary system was well illustrated by the case of local government reform. Unlike England, where an independent commission was appointed to make recommendations, the Welsh Office decided in 1991 to run its own consultative process. Welsh local authorities, particularly members of the Assembly of Welsh Counties (AWC) became increasingly disillusioned with the consultation process, feeling that their views were not being taken into account. The counties had always argued that the county system should be largely retained because it was more economic and efficient (Boyne *et al.* 1991). However, in July 1993 the Welsh Secretary announced that the 37 districts and 8 counties were to be replaced by 21 (later 22) new unitary authorities.

The AWC was incensed by the announcement and immediately called for the appointment of an independent commission to produce proposals, an elected assembly to bring quangos within a framework of democratic accountability and, if the government failed to withdraw its proposals, to initiate a policy of non-co-operation. In August 1993 the AWC met with the Convention of Scottish Local Authorities and agreed a joint plan of non-co-operation with the government in both Wales and Scotland. The Welsh Secretary was left with the dilemma of pushing ahead with the reform proposals, despite the opposition of important interests in Welsh local government, or of abandoning them. In July of that year the new Welsh Secretary, John Redwood, appeared to indicate that his mind was not closed when he suggested that, in some parts of Wales, a modified two-tier system might be implemented. But the government's proposals, as presented in the Queen's Speech in November 1993, returned to the original Welsh Office scheme.

Opposition within Wales was considerable and was supplemented by concerns expressed in the English shire counties, where similar proposals were mooted. In what appeared to be an embarrassing climb-down, Redwood announced that the Welsh local government reforms would be delayed by 12 months, a decision which encouraged opponents in the hope that further concessions might be extracted from the Welsh Office. However, the decision to introduce the proposals first to the House of Lords rather than the House of Commons relieved the parliamentary timetable in the Commons and overcame the anticipated 12 month delay. The government then used its majority to push the legislation through parliament. The Local Government (Wales) Act, arguably the most significant Welsh legislation in a generation, became law in June 1994 despite widespread hostility across Wales.

Implications of an asymmetrical party system

The growth of a distinctive Welsh administrative structure in the 1980s and early 1990s highlighted a crucial defect: the lack of popular support in Wales for the Conservative government. A similar argument could have been advanced for various parts of the United Kingdom, but Wales had a distinct political identity and, for the majority of the population, was perceived as a nation in its own right. Consequently, the asymmetrical pattern of electoral support for the two major UK parties raised serious questions in Wales. It was not simply that the Conservatives had never been a majority party in Wales; the extent of the party's weakness created the political dilemma. In the 1992 general election the Conservatives won 6 seats compared with Labour's 27; Plaid Cymru won four constituencies and the Liberal Democrats one. Conservative weakness was even more pronounced at the local government level. In the last election for the old counties and the first election for the new all-purpose district councils, the Conservatives came a poor fourth (Table 3.1).

Table 3.1: Party Representation in Welsh local authorities

Party Representation	*Con.*	*Lab.*	*Lib. Dem.*	*Plaid Cymru*	*Ind.*	*Others*
In old counties (1992)	32	269	28	40	115	10
In new districts (1995)	43	744	74	118	286	14

In 9 of the 22 all-purpose authorities the Conservatives failed to win one seat. Cardiff, which the Conservatives had controlled in the 1980s, returned just one Conservative, a dismal performance repeated exactly in Newport and Swansea. In these circumstances, a Conservative minister in charge of the Welsh Office, making appointments to quangos and participating in the erosion of local authority powers, raised very basic questions about political legitimacy and the government's electoral mandate in Wales.

The depths of the Conservative Party's weakness in Wales also compromised the operation of parliamentary government. The Select Committee on Welsh Affairs had been created in 1979 by the Conservatives as an alternative to Labour's proposal for an elected Welsh assembly, so roundly defeated in the referendum. Nicholas Edwards, then Welsh Secretary, had argued that the problems of public accountability (a major rationale for the assembly) could be resolved within the confines of Westminster parliamentary procedures (Drewry 1985). In 1979 the Conservatives, in their best post-war performance, had won 13 Welsh seats and were able to fill their 6 seats on the 11 member Committee. But successive general elections depleted the number of Welsh Conservative MPs. By 1995, with three of their members serving as junior ministers (two of them in the Welsh Office), the Conservative government was obliged to draft English Conservative MPs to maintain its majority. Of the six Conservatives on the Committee in 1995, for example, only two represented Welsh constituencies, a situation which did little to enhance the Committee's status in Wales.

In December 1995 William Hague, who had become Welsh Secretary following John Redwood's resignation to stand against John Major in the Conservative leadership election, announced another parliamentary initiative: a reform of the Welsh Grand Committee to give a more prominent and visible role to the consideration of matters relating to Wales by the House of Commons (Settle 1995). To this end he declared that the Committee would meet more frequently, up to seven times a year in Wales; that the Prime Minister and members of the cabinet could be called to justify their policies in Wales; and that the Committee's procedures would be reformed to allow oral questions, short debates and substantive discussions. However, the composition of the Committee – all 38 Welsh MPs plus up to 5 others from outside Wales nominated by the Committee of Selection – was unchanged. This strongly suggested that a reformed Grand Committee would be subject to all the political weaknesses of the Welsh Affairs Select Committee.

The question of whether the Welsh interest could be accommodated within the Westminster parliamentary system was also raised during the passage of the reform of the Local Government Bill. Standing Order 86 stated that in the committee stage of any bill relating exclusively to Wales, the Committee should include all MPs representing Welsh constituencies. Because the government realised it would be defeated if the committee were so constituted, it suspended the Standing Order and supplemented its six Conservative MPs from Welsh constituencies with nine Conservative members from English constituencies. This was not the first time that Standing Order 86 had been suspended, but its use in the committee stage of the Welsh Local Government Bill illustrated the ease with which Welsh interests could be overridden (Osmond 1994).

The European connection

The return of devolution to the Welsh political agenda was not the product solely of domestic political events. British membership of the EU added a new dimension to Welsh politics, requiring it to look outwards beyond the UK to the European Community and, in making its case, to define its interests more clearly. In short, the European connection helped to make Wales more self-conscious of its political identity. In establishing its European connection, Wales was obliged to develop two strands: one formal and the other informal.

The formal strand was developed by the Welsh Office through its Economic Regional Policy and European Affairs Divisions. The Divisions dealt with the social aspects of industrial decline, tourism, conservation and regional/structural development programmes. They consulted with and advised local authorities on future EU funding policies. The Economic Affairs Division was active within the Welsh Office, ensuring that all Divisions were aware of EU policies and Commission directives. All of this helped develop an awareness of the EU dimension.

The Welsh Office also adopted a proactive European policy, largely as a result of Peter Walker's initiative when he was Welsh Secretary, setting up links with the four 'Technological Tigers': Baden-Wurttemberg, Catalonia, Lombardy and Rhone-Alpes. The intention was to promote technological collaboration, joint research and development, and cultural and civil service exchanges. Although the degree of collaboration was limited, the initiatives taken were nonetheless significant. The initial agreement was signed by the Welsh Office and the Baden-Wurttemberg government in March 1990 and set in train a series of academic staff/student exchanges between colleges of the University of Wales and the Universities of Mannheim, Heidelburg and Tubingen. Joint projects were established between the respective civil servants of the Welsh Office and Baden-Wurttemberg covering industrial training, traffic congestion and land reclamation. While Wales was not then at the cutting edge of technological innovations, the links established provided an example of dynamic inter-regional co-operation which was not dependent upon London as an intermediary and promised much for the future.

The effectiveness of these inter-regional links may be judged as limited. However, with legislative, financial and administrative functions deriving from Westminster there were powerful inhibitions upon the main Welsh actors and the European Community. Welsh local authorities were inhibited from entering into agreements with European regional/local authority organisations because of their limited legal and financial powers. The Welsh Office was inhibited from pushing the Welsh case because it had to balance a specific Welsh interest against a more general British interest; and the European Commission, although eager to establish contacts with British regions, was under no illusion as to where political power resided and in its negotiations dealt exclusively with the UK government.

It was because of a perceived sense of weakness that attempts were made in Wales during the 1980s to create an informal consultative network. First, there was a deliberate policy by local authorities to emphasise the Welsh regional dimension by associating the Assembly of Welsh Counties with European regional organisations such as the Conference of Maritime Regions, the Assembly of European Regions, the Council of Regional and Local Authorities and the Atlantic Arc. Second, there was the sustained campaign to create a centre in Brussels dedicated to co-ordinating the lobbying activities of a variety of Welsh organisations. Welsh local authorities had been pushing for this development since the early 1980s but the Welsh Office withstood the pressure, arguing that the Welsh interest could best be served by inter-departmental discussions between the Welsh Office and the various 'lead' departments in Whitehall. Despite this the WDA took the initiative in April 1991 and announced it was to set up a centre to add to the voice of the WDA and other Welsh bodies in Europe.

The Wales European Centre was opened in February 1992 to represent Welsh public and private sector interests and to put Wales in the hearts and minds of the decision-makers in Europe. Welsh local authorities had always been enthusiastic for such a centre and had set up a working party to plan for its operation at the AWC conference in Swansea in 1985. But the lead player was undoubtedly the WDA and its ability to cut a crucial deal with the Welsh Secretary of State, David Hunt a staunch enthusiast for the European Union. This led to a decision being made in less than 72 hours with only minimal Welsh Office involvement (Lewis 1995).

The early evidence suggests that on balance the Welsh European Centre could be counted a success: the Welsh MPs positively supported it and the profile of Wales in Brussels was improved. But there were problems: the costs constantly increased and contributions could not be guaranteed, the system of seconding staff from Welsh organisations reduced efficiency by too frequent a turnover, and the Welsh Office was not fully reconciled to the Centre as an alternative representative of the Welsh interest. However, in the absence of alternative regional institutions the Wales European Centre provided an important new focus and platform for Welsh interests in Europe.

The need for further debate about institutional change to improve the representation of Welsh interests in Europe nevertheless continued to be raised, for example by a damning report by the Welsh Affairs Select Committee in late 1995 on the Welsh Office's performance in the EU (Welsh Affairs Committee 1995). The introduction of new regional institutions, including an assembly, remained, therefore, an issue upon which private and public sector opinion and opposition political opinion could still converge.

The revived devolution debate

The series of successive Conservative election victories, the impact of the Thatcherite agenda and the perception of a democratic deficit in the administration of public policy in Wales, progressively transformed the attitudes of both the general public and political activists to devolution. It is against this background that one can explain the Labour Party's cautious moves towards renewing its commitment to an elected Welsh assembly.

The Labour Party began the process of reviewing its policy on devolution in the aftermath of the 1992 general election. A special Commission was set up to consult all sectors of Welsh political life to produce a policy which would gain support both inside and outside the party. The Commission Report in May 1995 roundly condemned the democratic deficit and recommended a directly elected Welsh assembly which would, 'help deliver policies for economic regeneration, the health service, and educational training' (Wales Labour 1995, p.4). A revised Report in 1996 expanded on plans to reform the system of quangos, notably recommending a reformed WDA (Wales Labour 1996). However, aside from the assurance that the assembly could pass secondary legislation (hardly a major function), it was clear that Labour was recommending a model for devolution very like that rejected in the 1979 referendum: an executive body with no financial or legislative powers (see Chapter 1). Furthermore, the role of the Secretary of State was not clearly defined; the incumbent would remain part of central government yet have responsibility to act on behalf of the assembly in negotiating the level of the block grant with the Treasury. The Commission also proposed that the local government committee system rather than the cabinet model would apply and that elections would be by the 'first past the post' method, a mechanism destined to provide continuous one-party rule by Labour.

The response to Labour's proposals fell far short of enthusiastic. One member of Labour's Commission resigned and set up a ginger group because he believed that the policy was not sufficiently radical. Some Labour MPs representing valley constituencies expressed unease with any devolution policy, which they regarded as a concession to nationalism, a conclusion which might have had something to do with the fact that in most valley constituencies the only effective opposition has been provided by Plaid Cymru. The weak and ambiguous proposals suggested that the Wales Labour Party was still a reluctant devolutionist and that the enthusiasm expressed by Labour's Shadow Secretary of State, Ron Davies, was not shared by party activists. For many political commentators it appeared that devolution for Wales was only on the agenda because of the Scottish proposals and that Wales, as it had been in 1979, was again being dragged along on Scotland's coat-tails. At one stage the discontent amongst valley MPs was such that Ron Davies' position in the shadow cabinet appeared to be under threat, with the possibility that his position as Shadow Secretary would be occupied by a less enthusiastic proponent of devolution. However, this danger was averted by Davies' unexpected success in coming third in the shadow cabinet elections in November 1995. In addition, Kim Howells, one of the most reluctant devolutionists amongst the Welsh Labour group of MPs, who had been appointed Labour's spokesman on English regionalism, was effectively marginalised. His position was always seen as a strange appointment given his political attitudes, but it became embarrassing when Howells spoke out against devolution on a visit to Scotland and used the emotive phrase the 'Balkanisation of Britain' which drew obvious parallels with the events in the former Yugoslavia. The Labour leadership was outraged. Tony Blair administered a public dressing down and in July 1996 Howells was moved sideways to Trade and Industry.

These events hardened the Labour Party leadership's commitment to Welsh devolution. But there remained a small hard core of Welsh Labour MPs highly sceptical of devolution and uncompromising in their commitment to 'first past the post' elections to the Welsh assembly despite Labour's plans for proportional representation for the Scottish parliament. This potential for division both before and after a general election was further increased by Tony Blair's decisions in June 1996 to invite the Welsh Labour Party Executive to incorporate a proportional representation element into plans for the election of a Welsh assembly, and to provide for a pre-legislative referendum on devolution. First, the proportional representation decision incensed sceptics. Second, despite his strong commitment to devolution, and his response to some pro-devolutionist critics who doubted that reform could occur without a specific mandate or be successful without the application of proportional representation, Blair also angered a majority of pro-devolutionists because the referendum pledge threatened the very possibility of devolution. Overall, then, one may conclude that the Labour Party developed a commitment to Welsh devolution in the early to mid 1990s which was more strongly based than in 1979, but internal politics remained hugely problematic.

The changes in political attitudes in Wales during the 1980s and in the early part of the 1990s contributed to a far more broadly based groundswell of opinion in favour of devolution. By the mid 1990s a sense of a Welsh political identity, not necessarily linked to nationalism, had become more pronounced. The Welsh counties, all of which had opposed devolution in the 1979 referendum, had by 1990 established a new consensus in support of devolution. In June 1991 the AWC committed itself to a Regional Council for Wales and justified its proposal in European terms, noting how the most successful European countries had regional bodies which played a vital role in promoting the economy, giving the people in the region a voice in how their services were run and organised, and also a sense of self-esteem. The AWC concluded that, 'the absence of such a regional council in Wales is not only an undemocratic omission, but a self-imposed handicap' (Assembly of Welsh Counties 1992). This handicap was highlighted by the AWC's inability to influence the government's proposals for local government reform or even to persuade the government to set up an independent commission to advise on the reformed structure of local government. The experience proved to many county councillors the necessity of institutions which would express more effectively the Welsh interest.

The changed opinions of Welsh local government councillors were reflected by the general public. During the 1980s, public opinion had been largely apathetic about Welsh devolution. By the 1990s the situation had changed. Polls conducted between 1990 and 1996 consistently showed a clear majority for devolution and an elected Welsh assembly. The various polls were not strictly comparable because the sample size was not constant nor were precisely the same questions asked, but some constants can be identified. Prior to the 1992 general election an NoP poll showed a clear lead for devolution, with 47 per cent in favour of an elected assembly for Wales, 31 per cent opposed and 21 per cent in the 'don't know' category. The poll also indicated that Labour, Liberal Democrat and Plaid Cymru supporters strongly favoured devolution. Only Conservative voters were opposed, and even amongst them a sizeable minority (31%) supported devolution. Significantly, when asked for their opinion if Scotland were to have a parliament, support for Welsh devolution rose to 61 per cent.

Polls conducted during 1994 and 1995 revealed certain inconsistencies. Some polling organisations, particularly Beaufort Research, registered a high proportion of 'don't knows', usually slightly more than a third. Other polls, NoP and MORI suggested a declining proportion of 'don't knows'; down from 21 per cent in 1992 to 10 per cent in 1996. All polls, however, indicated at least a 2:1 majority in favour of devolution. In January 1996, a MORI poll registered 67 per cent in favour of Welsh devolution. Commenting on the poll, Robert Worcester concluded that, 'the Welsh do not think they are well governed under the British system. They see it as out of date, unresponsive to the needs of the Welsh people and in need of drastic overhaul' (Worcester 1996).

The evidence from the polls did not suggest a dramatic rise in support for Plaid Cymru; public support for the party remained remarkably stable throughout this period. What it did reveal was a profound unease with the structures of government in Wales and an assertion of 'people power', a conclusion reinforced by the consistently high level of support for a referendum to decide the devolution issue as well as other policy issues.

Conclusion

Welsh politics underwent profound political change during the 1980s and early 1990s. This is not to be understood in terms of the importance of nationalism and responses by the Labour Party out of electoral expedience, but in terms of broader changes in the British and European contexts to the practice of Welsh government. The most significant of these was the change to Welsh political culture effected equally by government privatisation and the growth of a global economy. The virtual disappearance of traditional basic industries, the growth of a manufacturing base including some high technology companies, and the establishment of a financial service sector in Cardiff, all contributed to the change. The success of the WDA in attracting multinational companies to Wales brought more foreign businessmen, more attuned to global economics than parochial politics. Trade unionists and local politicians also became more aware of international forces.

At the same time as the political culture of Wales underwent profound change, Conservative governments conducted changes in the administrative structure of Welsh governance which raised concerns about a democratic deficit. Developments at the Welsh Office, increases in the use of quangos and approaches to consultation in Wales with respect to local government legislation, all highlighted problems of accountability. In addition, the Conservatives' disastrous electoral record raised concerns over the legitimacy of Westminster government, especially when the paucity of Conservative Welsh MPs led to the suspension of Westminster conventions which had allowed for special Welsh representation. Finally, the increased role of the EU over a wide range of policy issues questioned the centrality of the British connection to Welsh interests, and stimulated debate over whether Westminster institutions were to be criticised not only for how democratically they governed Wales at home but also for how they represented Welsh interests in Europe.

Changes in Welsh political culture after the early 1980s established a priority of promoting the Welsh interest in Europe and the wider world, rather than simply in a British context. Following this, serious doubts emerged as to the ability of existing political structures to represent adequately the Welsh interest. In particular, local politicians sought to establish new structures which related Wales directly to the institutions of the EU rather than those which remained reliant on a generally unsympathetic British government. This is not to say that the London connection became unimportant, but it was no longer seen as the only link which Welsh interests needed to influence. It was in this context that the Labour Party in Wales and other organisations revived consideration of a Welsh assembly, and support for such a step appeared to increase at both the elite and popular levels. It remained to be seen however, what effects the internal divisions of the Labour Party and anti-devolutionist campaigners would have on popular opinion, issues that would prove crucial in a referendum.

References

Aitchison, J. and Carter, H. (1993) 'The Welsh language in 1991.' *Planet: The Welsh Internationalist* 97, 3–10.

Alter, P. (1989) *Nationalism.* London: Edward Arnold.

Assembly of Welsh Counties (1991) 'The case for a Welsh regional council.' *News: Newyddion* 4 June 1991.

Balsom, D. and Jones, B. (1984) 'The faces of Wales.' In I. McAllister and R. Rose (eds) *The Nationwide Competition for Votes.* London: Pinter Publishers.

Boyne, G.A., Griffiths, P., Lawton, A. and Law, J. (eds) (1991) *Local Government in Wales.* York: Rowntree Trust.

Comptrollor and Auditor General (1993) National Audit Office, 'Welsh Office: Premises Management.' *HCP 1992–93,* 444.

Constitution Unit (1996) *An Assembly for Wales.* London: Constitution Unit.

Drewry, G. (ed) (1985) *The New Select Committees: A Study of the 1979 Reforms.* Oxford: Clarendon Press.

Foulkes, D., Jones, B. and Wilford, R. (eds) (1983) *The Welsh Veto: The Wales Act 1978 and the Referendum.* Cardiff: University of Wales Press.

Jones, B. (1990) 'The Welsh Office: a political expedient or an administrative innovation?' In *Transactions Hon. Soc. Cymmrodorion.* Denbigh: Gee.

Lewis, B. (1995) 'The Wales European Centre: Its Background and Significance.' Cardiff School of European Studies, unpublished Masters dissertation.

Osmond, J. (1992) *The Democratic Challenge.* Llandysul: Gomer Press.

Osmond, J. (1994) 'Remaking Wales.' In J. Osmond (ed) *A Parliament for Wales.* Llandysul: Gomer Press.

Owen, R.G. (1990) 'Assembly of Welsh counties: inter-regional relations.' In *Régions d'Europe.* Paris: Assemblé des Régions d'Europe.

Public Accounts Committee (1993) *Twenty Fourth Report: Welsh Office Appropriations Accounts 1992–93.* London: House of Commons Session 1993–94.

RSMB for S4C (1993) *Language Committees and Leisure: A Study of the Understanding and Use of Welsh in Wales.* Cardiff: S4C.

S4C (1994) *Report and Accounts.* Cardiff: S4C.

Wales Labour (1993) *Who Runs Wales? A Briefing Paper on Quangos in Wales.* Cardiff: Wales Labour Party.

Wales Labour (1995) *Shaping the Vision: A Report on the Powers and Structure of the Welsh Assembly.* Cardiff: Wales Labour Party.

Wales Labour (1996) *Preparing for a New Wales, a Report on the Structure and Workings of the Welsh Assembly.* Cardiff: Wales Labour Party.

Welsh Affairs Committee (1995) *Fourth Report, Wales in Europe, Volume 1, Report together with the Proceedings of the Committee.* London: House of Commons Session 1994–95, HCP, 393-i.

Settle, M. (1995) 'Major will have to face Welsh MPs says Hague.' *Western Mail,* 1 December 1995, p.1.

Worcester, R. (1996) 'Westminster out of touch say voters.' *Western Mail* 27 January 1996.

CHAPTER 4

Conservative Governments, Scotland and Wales

A Perspective on Territorial Management

Jonathan Bradbury

Introduction

Following the 1987 general election, successive Conservative governments recognised that they faced problems emanating from Scottish and Welsh politics. First, they perceived a need to address the territorial problem of increasing criticism against the existing constitutional settlement by which Scotland and Wales had been governed. Second, they were forced to admit that such territorial dissent was also a party problem in that it was channelled into poor electoral support for the Conservative Party and a questioning of the overall legitimacy of London-based government and politics. As Gamble (1993) noted, this led Conservative governments in the late 1980s and early to mid 1990s to address the question of territorial management in order to sustain the existing constitutional settlement and to ensure broad compliance with Conservative policies. Most analysis of this development tends to be from a periphery perspective, and stresses the remoteness of Conservative government from the realities of everyday concerns in Scotland and Wales and the resulting incoherence and/or injustice of central government policy. The ineffectiveness of territorial management in this era has become a commonplace assumption. This chapter is not intended as an apologia for Conservative policy but does argue that Conservative governments developed territorial management with serious intent, and that whilst the potential for success was questionable, a more equivocal assessment is generally appropriate.

Before proceeding it is important to understand the methodological assumptions of examining the policies of Conservative governments via a territorial management perspective. First, it assumes that decision-making in many areas of government business is strongly influenced by considerations of the nature and preservation of the Union of Scotland and Wales with England. Second, it assumes a principal actor focus on the governing elite as the determinant of decision-making. Bulpitt's (1983) analysis suggests that this comprises the Prime Minister, a centre governing elite, and the secretaries of state for Scotland and Wales and their territorial governing elites. Third, this perspective draws upon an understanding of the historical evolution of a constitutional settlement whereby the government of Scotland and Wales has been informed by characteristics of both a unitary state and union-state tradition (Urwin 1982). Since the eighteenth century, government has been based upon the primacy of government from Westminster – the supremacy of parliament – combined with a readiness to make policy in sympathy with distinctive Scottish and Welsh demands. The latter has ensured the provision of distinctive governing arrangements through administrative devolution and parliamentary innovation, and the granting of net subsidies through higher levels of per capita public expenditure than for England (see Chapter 1). This settlement was developed in the search for territorial consensus, and may be understood as the traditional framework for territorial management.

It should be further noted that this chapter makes reference to three contemporary formulations of territorial management. First, there is assimilationism, an approach which takes full advantage of the unitary state dimensions of the British state, assimilating Scotland and Wales to an English norm, relatively excluding respect for specifically Scottish and Welsh concerns and privileges (Mitchell 1995). Second, there is unionism, an approach which conversely develops the union-state characteristics of the British state. Of course, all engaging in territorial management would call themselves unionist – in favour of the Union – but being unionist here is given the specific meaning of emphasising that the nature of government shows respect for the diversity of interests in constituent territories of the Union, their concerns and privileges. Both assimilationism and unionism are developments of the existing constitutional settlement. Third, there is devolution, an approach which dilutes the primacy of government from Westminster in favour of developing the political autonomy of constituent territories. Some take the view that such an approach is consistent with the development of the union-state characteristics of the British state. More conventionally, it is seen as a measure designed to preserve the Union by means of an entirely new constitutional settlement which is quasi-federal in character (Bogdanor 1979).

The chapter analyses the approaches taken by the Thatcher and Major governments, first to Scotland and then to Wales. It is argued that Conservative governments after 1979 did much to move away from a traditional approach to territorial management, developing an assimilationist approach to territorial management at different times in both Scotland and Wales. The development of a unionist approach nevertheless continued to be influential, and after 1990 an attempt was made to reassert a traditional balance in territorial management in Scotland, and then after 1995 in both Scotland and Wales. Conservative governments did not flirt with devolution as was the case in the late 1960s and early 1970s. Overall, these developments in Conservative territorial management proved to be problematic. The chapter concludes by looking at the options left open for Conservative approaches to territorial management.

Scotland

The Thatcher governments

At the advent of the Thatcher era the issue of territorial management was not high on the political agenda. Following the failure of the devolution referendum in 1979, the Thatcher governments simply assumed the constitutional stability of the Union and asserted an unambiguous hostility to devolution. Nevertheless, the Thatcher governments did affect the nature of government in Scotland. This was unavoidable given their intention to provide a general project for the modernisation of Britain, necessitating policies which needed uniform implementation across the whole of the country. Although Scotland's special arrangements affecting government and public expenditure remained, the implications of what has come to be known as Thatcherism implied a greater reluctance to revise policy in line with particular Scottish sensitivities. Indeed policy reforms to relax government responsibility for levels of unemployment, to privatise nationalised industries and reduce the size of the state, and to deregulate markets and encourage enterprise had a considerable impact in Scotland. In these ways Thatcherism implicitly represented an assimilation of government policy in Scotland to a British norm, thus accentuating the operation of the unitary characteristics of the state (Mitchell 1995).

At the 1987 election, voting indicated renewed sympathies with constitutional change and left the Conservatives with only 24 per cent of the vote and just ten seats in Scotland. The third Thatcher government faced up to the fact of a 'Scottish problem' and the need to develop a strategy of territorial management. In her memoirs Mrs Thatcher conceded that as a result of the Thatcher reforms, Scotland had lost many jobs in traditional industries and in 1987 'jobs in uncompetitive industry continued to be shed and unemployment remained higher than in England' (Thatcher 1993, p.618). She also conceded the long-run factors leading to diminishing support for the Conservative Party in Scotland: notably the erosion of a base of Orange Unionist support, the high level of council housing occupation, and identification of the Conservative Party as an English party insensitive to Scottish issues and problems. These factors contributed to the 1987 result. Nevertheless, she claimed that during the 1980s underlying Scottish economic fortunes improved, with Britain's transformed reputation attracting foreign companies to Scotland and building up Edinburgh as a major financial centre. The oil industry continued to thrive. Moreover, it was unfortunate that unemployment had started to fall in Scotland only four months before the 1987 election. Confidence in the economic revival of the Scottish economy had yet to feed through (Thatcher 1993, pp.618–619). Hence she continued to interpret the imposition of her policy agenda as something that had aroused short-term opposition, but which was nevertheless in the long term good for Scotland. There was no need to take account of these Scottish concerns, and therefore an assimilationist approach ought to be maintained.

Instead Mrs Thatcher concluded that the deeper problem underpinning the dissent against Westminster rule lay in the continued power of a Scottish Conservative elite which was sceptical of Thatcherism and wished to present Scotland as a special case. Under criticism, a Conservative Secretary of State was always inclined to safeguard the Conservative position in Scotland by championing Scottish interests against the Conservative government in London. George Younger, Secretary of State until 1986, had taken just this approach, raising the spectre of separatism and Conservative electoral defeats in Scotland if his requests were not met. For the most part Westminster government accommodated these appeals, but such an approach had been received with increasing irritation by Mrs Thatcher. After the 1987 election, Thatcher concluded that continuation of this type of response would sell short the gains from Thatcherite reforms, with the attendant dangers of maintaining the legitimacy of state dependency in Scotland and breeding continued support for the Labour Party. In the long run it would militate against an appreciation of the actual benefits of Conservative policy and increase Scottish antipathy to both the constitutional settlement and the Conservative Party. Mrs Thatcher, therefore, decided that the Scottish problem existed not because of too much exposure to her policies but rather too little; and that the Thatcher approach should be promoted more positively with an intensification of reform and emphasis on its benefits in order to convert the Scottish electorate to a Thatcherite outlook. Hence Mrs Thatcher decided to intensify the move towards assimilationism, in the belief that attack was the best form of defence (Cooper 1995; Thatcher 1993, pp.619–621).

Consequently, after the 1987 election Mrs Thatcher initiated legislation to privatise electricity and transport, establish Scottish Homes, reform education and health, restructure the Scottish Development Agency as Scottish Enterprise, and introduce the community charge a year earlier than in England and Wales. To promote these reforms Mrs Thatcher visited Scotland on six occasions during 1988. In her speeches she sought to disassociate Scottish political identity from state intervention and to ally it instead with the Thatcherite ethics of enterprise and self-help. She argued that there was a native culture of Scottish enterprise, typified by Adam Smith, which had been dulled by state intervention in the twentieth century, and which should be reactivated. Whilst implementing a policy programme which made no concessions to distinctive Scottish demands, she did not extend assimilationism, however, to the point of dismantling Scotland's special governmental arrangements or ending its comparative advantage in public expenditure. Indeed there were further developments during the Thatcher years of administrative devolution, relating to housing, nature conservancy, training and enterprise, and higher education. Similarly, the operation of the Barnett formula, which determined the territorial allocation of public expenditure, was even more favourable to Scotland during the 1980s than expected. On the other hand, the Thatcher rhetoric did not celebrate the infrastructure of unionism or publicise the new developments within that tradition. Instead the merits of alternative forms of government began to be championed, notably the quangos, whose boards were controlled by government appointees. These were developed to take over central and local government functions and delivery programmes, thus bypassing what were perceived to be the islands of resistance to the Thatcherite agenda in the traditional state bureaucracy. Nor did Mrs Thatcher prevent English Conservative backbenchers from criticising Scottish over-representation in the House of Commons or the higher levels of public expenditure per capita. Moreover, she showed little concern that, as a result of there being only ten Scottish Tory MPs, with three holding ministerial positions, the Scottish Affairs Select Committee did not sit in the 1987 parliament. In these ways Mrs Thatcher prepared the ground for future development of the process of assimilation to the English norm (Cooper 1995; Heald 1994; Mitchell 1995; Thatcher 1993).

Mrs Thatcher promoted her message to the Scottish public over the heads of the Scottish Conservative elite and, as a result, faced political difficulties. Malcolm Rifkind, appointed Secretary of State by Mrs Thatcher in 1986, promoted the enterprise culture in his speeches, but in truth he was a politician of the traditional Scottish Tory elite, consistently defending special Scottish interests and the distinctive arrangements for Scottish government and public expenditure. Moreover, he initially opposed the introduction of the school opt-out legislation in Scotland, and although carrying through several Thatcherite measures, in 1990 he started to dissent publicly from the Thatcher government's general handling of Scottish affairs. This stance was most evident over the issue of the community charge. The Scottish party had actually asked for its early introduction to neutralise the intense criticism that had followed revaluation of the rates, but when its practical implications became clear, Scottish party leaders criticised the government for what they saw as the introduction of an unpopular tax with Scotland acting as the guinea pig. This was followed by Scottish outrage at an announcement in the 1990 budget that a community charge benefit would be paid but would not be backdated for Scotland, despite the fact that the charge had been implemented earlier there. Rifkind, faced with intense criticism, took up the cause and succeeded in persuading Mrs Thatcher to agree to a special payment, something in which he then publicly revelled as a victory against London. Rifkind took a similar line in arguing the Scottish case over the proposed closure of the Ravenscraig steelworks. At the 1990 Scottish Conservative Party Conference, when faced with criticism about the general lack of consideration for Scottish interests in the Thatcher policy agenda, he even went as far as to hint at the possibility of devolution (Cooper 1995; Thatcher 1993, pp.621–623).

Mrs Thatcher's more natural ally in the Scottish Office was the junior minister, Michael Forsyth, who was responsible for health and education reform. In 1989 Mrs Thatcher insisted that he should also become Chairman of the Scottish Conservative Party. Rifkind had a difficult working relationship with Forsyth and he opposed Forsyth's promotion. It was over this issue that the underlying tension between the Thatcher project and the Scottish Tory elite finally erupted. In the summer of 1990 it appears that Rifkind mobilised the Scottish Tory elite, including Willie Whitelaw and George Younger, against Thatcherism through a campaign to oust Forsyth from the Chairmanship. By then Mrs Thatcher had her own troubles. She agreed reluctantly to Forsyth's removal as party Chairman in Scotland, although he was to remain a minister. Mrs Thatcher recorded that, 'it had been a brave attempt to bring the Scottish Tory party into the latter half of the twentieth century' but the appointment of Lord Sanderson instead, 'was taken as a sign that the attempt to extend Thatcherism to Scotland had come to an end' (Thatcher 1993, p.623). She concluded that the configuration of forces that led to this outcome was but a rehearsal for her own downfall as Premier later in the year.

The Thatcher era represented a considerable departure from the Conservative Party's historic approach to Scottish government. Mitchell (1995, p.1377) reminds us that the party had hitherto positioned itself as that which, in defending most staunchly the integrity of the British state, respected diversity, and specifically the union-state tradition in the government of Scotland. In contrast, under Mrs Thatcher the Conservative Party at Westminster repositioned itself politically as much less sympathetic to diversity and the union-state tradition, pursuing instead an assimilationist approach. She sought to neutralise dissent by facing it head on, seeking to make the Scots come to terms with change through a mixture of persuasion and coercion. Mrs Thatcher has claimed that this approach reaped ever greater economic success. The problem was that this was simply not sufficiently appreciated, meaning that the Thatcherite political revolution in Scotland was not achieved (Thatcher 1993, pp.623–4). In hindsight it would appear that the Thatcherite onslaught came too late and was too short-lived to have any chance of dislodging the views of the Scottish Tory establishment or persuading the public to a Thatcherite outlook. Rather, for the short period it lasted it succeeded in angering Scottish feeling further. The Scottish Conservative elite was alienated and it was this period that saw the creation of the Scottish constitutional convention and a serious debate once more about the options for devolution.

The Major governments

When John Major became Prime Minister in 1990 the Thatcher legacy was a highly problematic one. The scale of the third election victory in 1987 had encouraged Mrs Thatcher to take her agenda into spheres of policy where it was both more difficult to achieve workable solutions and derive electoral benefit, and upon which there stood far firmer opposition even within her own party. In so doing she underestimated the difficulties ahead. Taking on the challenge of gaining the support of the Scottish public for her policies over the heads of the Scottish Tory elite was a case in point, and she suffered for it. Major's inheritance was the expectation that, nevertheless, he would try and continue the Conservative revolution in British politics whilst also placating the opposition that ultimately had overwhelmed Thatcher. In the case of Scotland this meant finding a marriage between continued pursuit of the Thatcher policy agenda and a revival of the Tory tradition of respect for Scotland's special rights within the Union of Great Britain. This was a hand which involved appearing to play both with conviction *and* with an eye to consensus, always a difficult one to play.

It was in this context that a new approach was formulated. At first glance there appeared to be little change. Both Major governments, except for the abandonment of the community charge, continued with the Thatcher medicine of privatisation, deregulation and administrative reform. The closure of Ravenscraig was announced, and unpopular policies with respect to water organisation, local government reform, VAT on domestic fuel, and the Rosyth naval base were pursued. The Scottish Office also joined in the process of civil service reform. However, prior to the 1992 general election Major announced that also he would adopt more of a listening approach to Scottish concerns so as to re-establish a consensus style of government. To help him he appointed a new Secretary of State, Ian Lang. Lang was potentially a much better collaborator from the Scottish Tory elite than Rifkind. First, he was prepared to pursue the policy agenda. Second, whilst clearly in favour of respect for the union-state tradition, there were clear limits as to how far he would push the Scottish case. In contrast to his views in the 1970s, he was opposed to devolution as he now believed that the relations between a Scottish parliament and Westminster would always be marked by conflict. Hence whilst continuing radical policy reform, Lang sought to help Major re-establish consensus by other means within the existing constitutional settlement. He shared the view with leading one-nation Tories, such as Edward Heath and John Biffen, that this best involved attention to the special arrangements by which Scotland was governed, a view to which Major was also apparently persuaded (Cooper 1995, pp.1390–92).

This line of thought formed the basis for a new tilt towards unionism: to erode dissent by celebrating and promoting the distinctive union-state characteristics of the government of Scotland, and to think about how they might be extended within the existing constitutional settlement. If the Scots were reminded of the advantages that they enjoyed under existing arrangements then it would be a powerful antidote to calls for constitutional change and might arrest the Conservative decline. Hence whilst some English Conservative backbenchers continued to criticise special arrangements for Scotland, Major chose rather to emphasise their existence and the threat to the benefits they would bring if constitutional change occurred. As a result, in the 1992 general election campaign Major carried a dual message in Scotland: that only a Conservative government could deliver both a successful enterprise economy and preserve the long-held special benefits of the Union. Major sought to re-inspire feelings and memories that he felt had been left untouched for too long by reminding the electorate of the advantages for Scotland of existing arrangements, and to compare them favourably with the uncertain consequences of devolution or independence (Major 1992). To cement the new emphasis on unionism Major promised to take stock of governing arrangements for Scotland after the election to see if they could be improved. In the event Major took much comfort from the 1992 result. The achievement of 24 per cent of the vote and 11 seats could not be presented as a convincing performance, but it was an improvement on 1987 despite three years of attention from Mrs Thatcher and despite the dire predictions of electoral pundits. Major felt vindicated in his stance and the result strengthened his resolve to continue to pay attention to the Union with Scotland during the next parliament.

The 'taking stock' exercise that followed led to the publication of a White Paper, *Scotland in the Union – A Partnership for Good* (Cm 2225 1993) in March 1993. The first half of the paper detailed the existing special benefits of the Union for Scotland, relating to the economy, parliamentary business, the law, and the advantages of the Scottish Office and devolved administration. Measures for promoting Scottish interests in Europe were emphasised, including the creation of Scotland Europa in 1992; the staging of a meeting of the European Council in Edinburgh in December 1992; and plans for a Europartenariat in Glasgow in December 1993. Lang was also adamant that Scottish interests in Europe were best promoted through existing representative arrangements in the EU Committee of the Regions and through the attendance of Scottish Office ministers at meetings of the EU Council of Ministers. The paper confirmed the government's commitment to maintaining these arrangements, and a plea was made for much greater appreciation of the historic legacy of the Union in preserving Scottish interests both in Britain and Europe than had been allowed for in the political debate in Scotland. Overall, this public detailing of the existing arrangements governing the Union was clearly a further attempt to turn round public opinion on constitutional change by jogging the memory over its benefits.

The second half of the White Paper conceived the basis of recent Scottish dissent in terms of the problems of lack of time, accountability, debate and transparency in the handling of Scottish parliamentary business and government. It made a series of proposals which were then debated in parliament (Cm 2225 1993; Hansard 1994). In responding to the prescribed problems it was recognised that, 'constitutionally, the most significant of the proposals relate[d] to the Parliamentary arrangements for the handling of Scottish business' (Cm 2814 1995a, pp.15–16). The government was careful to maintain that increased responsiveness to Scottish considerations could be made without diminishing parliamentary supremacy or, indeed, the opportunity for debating Scottish issues in the full House of Commons. What was proposed were additional opportunities for consideration of Scottish parliamentary business, which were to be provided by widening the powers of the Scottish Grand Committee. These included greater use of a power under 1948 Standing Orders of the House, for the Committee to stage the substantive debates of second readings of bills, which in practice were likely to be law reform bills and private members' bills; a new procedure for debating secondary legislation; more time for deliberative debates; and the introduction of adjournment debates. Scottish Office ministers were also to make more ministerial statements to the Committee; the Secretary of State was to hold additional question times before the Committee; and Scottish Office ministers in the House of Lords were also to be answerable to the Committee. The reform of the Committee was hailed as the creation of a mini House of Commons for Scotland within the orbit of the UK parliament. To facilitate this up-grading, it was envisaged that the Scottish Grand Committee should no longer have its meetings bunched in June and July, but meet according to an advance timetable of meetings for the whole parliamentary year, starting in 1994–95. It was envisaged that it would meet on up to 12 occasions per parliamentary session, with question times every second or third session. It was also hoped that there could be more meetings of the Committee in Scotland. The message was that Scotland's interests would be more clearly heard within parliament.

Tacked on to these proposals were commitments to allow special standing committees on Scottish bills, to sit in Scotland if necessary to hear evidence. There was also promise of more administrative devolution to the Scottish Office with respect to training and further education, industrial support, supervision of the Highlands and Islands airport, the Scottish Arts Council, care in the community and supervision of European Social Fund expenditure. The Scottish Office was itself to be more visible in Scotland, with information points in all major towns and cities. Devolution to communities and individuals was emphasised through the establishment of Scottish Enterprise's network of local enterprise companies and in the application of citizen's charters. Finally, a pledge was made to use the Millennium Fund in part to reforge the Union. Overall, *Scotland in the Union*, in making these new proposals on governing arrangements, sought to amplify further the Government's continuing commitment to a traditional unionism.

The bulk of the proposals in *Scotland in the Union* had been implemented by 1994. It is clear, however, that during 1995 Major continued to be worried by the Scottish problem in view of opinion polling in favour of home rule and the woeful electoral performance of the Conservative Party in the elections for the new local authorities. He did not lose heart in the general strategy for managing dissent in Scotland; rather the opposite as he became increasingly convinced of its broader utility. For, as Arnold Kemp (1995) argued, from a party perspective, his Scottish policy, as well as directly countering opposition plans for constitutional change, drew attention specifically to the tax-raising powers in Labour Party proposals for a Scottish parliament. This was useful in helping to continue to portray the Labour Party as a high tax party. Moreover, his staunch unionism in Scotland was a very good antidote to arguments that Major instinctively was prepared to sell out the interests of the Unionists in Northern Ireland. In continuing with his strategy all that Major decided to do in fact was to improve upon the initiative of 1993–94.

Following his leadership election victory in July 1995, he appointed Michael Forsyth as Secretary of State. After the initial shock of the appointment of the former *bête noire* of the Scottish Tory establishment had died down, the decision became explicable on two grounds. First, it appeared that Forsyth had shifted his political position since the days when he acted as Thatcher's Trojan Horse at the Scottish Office. He remained committed to a Thatcherite policy agenda, but had left behind the assimilationist rhetoric of the Thatcher era (Forsyth 1995a). In terms of arguing for the Union and against constitutional change, Forsyth now actively promoted the special arrangements for Scotland and looked for new ways to build upon them. Second, for all the scepticism about Forsyth in Scottish Tory circles he was the Scottish Tory that the Labour Party and the SNP feared the most (Thatcher 1993, p.622). A more populist and combative politician than Lang and possessing a sharp intellect, he had a much better chance of promoting the Major government's message in Scotland. In short, Forsyth was the politician most likely to make the Major approach towards managing territorial dissent in Scotland work.

Few would deny the gusto Forsyth brought to the position of Secretary of State, a notable incident being his attendance in a kilt at the première of 'Braveheart', the Mel Gibson film. Forsyth continued to bring forward radical policies regarding water organisation and offered new proposals regarding the privatisation of Scottish Office crofting land. But most attention focused on the constitutional dimension of his agenda and the consultative approach which in part accompanied its development. In November 1995, following promises made during Major's October Party Conference address, Forsyth announced further proposals for Scottish government reform within existing constitutional arrangements (Forsyth 1995b).

First, in relation to the Scottish Grand Committee he announced two new proposals, which were implemented through changing House of Commons Standing Orders on 20 December. The Committee was henceforth to be able to hold third reading debates, as well as the second reading debates allowed for under the Lang initiative. More dramatically, he proposed that UK ministers other than the Secretary of State for Scotland would now be able to attend the Scottish Grand Committee, put motions and answer questions, though not vote. Both Major and the Chancellor, Kenneth Clarke, had already agreed to attend meetings in 1996. Forsyth also made much more of the Scottish Grand Committee meeting in Scotland, preferably in various locations to make people aware of its debates. Overall, he claimed that, 'these Grand Committee measures have the dual benefit of bringing government closer to the Scottish people while simultaneously reinforcing Scotland's position in the Union. We can achieve all of this without a Tartan Tax and without the 45.1 million pounds running costs of a Scottish parliament' (Forsyth 1995b, p.15).

Second, following a suggestion made by Campbell Christie, General Secretary of the Scottish Trades Union Congress, Forsyth proposed to expand the consultative role of the Scottish Economic Council to consider Scottish Office resource allocation; Scotland's place and performance in the global market; the industrial base; the skills base; and overall economic performance. The Council's membership would be broadened and non-members would be invited to committees of the council when appropriate, 'so that it becomes truly a Council for Scotland' (Forsyth 1995b, p.17). Finally, Forsyth responded positively to proposals from the Consortium of Scottish Local Authorities (COSLA) to give local government more autonomy. The framework of control was to remain, including central power to cap local council tax and regulation of council performance through publication of performance data. However, Forsyth accepted some of COSLA's proposals, including allowing councils more autonomy in the spending of capital allocation and giving them the right to make their own byelaws. Through these various actions, Forsyth hoped to show that Scottish interests, at both elite and community levels, could be promoted within existing constitutional arrangements.

The Forsyth initiative represented the continuation of a mode of territorial management which after 1990 had emphasised the unionism of the Government. Overall the Government's approach was a hybrid one, which sought to continue the Conservative policy revolution by using all the powers of unitary government, whilst at the same time attempting to combat the unpopularity of such policy by showing convincing respect for Scotland's special place in the British state as a voluntary Union – an approach which tried to draw on the advantages of the traditional approach to territorial management. It remained open to question, however, as to whether this approach would achieve more effective management of dissent than was possible under Mrs Thatcher and whether it underpinned a possible revival of Conservative Party fortunes. Of course, much rested, as Thatcher always recognised, on the state of the economy and the extent to which any improvement was associated by the general public with Conservative economic management. In terms of the lean towards unionism, the master-stroke, if one existed, was thought to be the enlisting of senior cabinet politicians to legitimise the Scottish Grand Committee as a credible alternative to a

Scottish parliament. For the reality of the 1994–95 parliamentary session was that meetings of the Scottish Grand Committee were no more taken notice of than before the Lang initiative. By contrast, the Scottish media was intensely interested in the Committee meetings in Scotland in 1996, particularly when the Prime Minister and other senior Cabinet ministers were present. As a consequence, the opposition parties were forced to take the Committee more seriously and allow the possibility that it might yet emerge as Scotland's debating chamber. As the parties prepared for the 1997 general election it was apparent that the case for more far-reaching plans for home rule could yet lose their thunder, especially if regard for the Forsyth initiative was complemented by successful exposure of the problems of proposals for devolution, notably on issues of finance, representation and inter-assembly relations.

It was also clear, however, that dissatisfaction with the imposition of an ideologically driven Conservative policy agenda on an unwilling electorate and its mixed economic effects was not likely to diminish easily. Similarly, there remained many doubts about the credibility of the Lang and Forsyth initiatives to help in buying off dissent. Both initiatives were supported by the opposition parties for the ways in which they improved upon, in particular, parliamentary scrutiny. But George Robertson, Labour's Shadow Secretary of State, and Jim Wallace, leader of the Scottish Liberal Democrats, stressed that the Scottish Grand Committee following its reform remained little more than a talking shop. The Committee could only debate second and third readings of bills which were deemed uncontroversial by the House of Commons. Even then it could not take a decisive vote on either reading, as that power remained with the full House of Commons. In practice, the work referred to it would rely on the goodwill of English MPs acting in the full House, a significant minority of which deplored special treatment for Scotland. Similarly, in its day-to-day work it would be dependent on the Scottish parties co-operating through the 'usual channels', something which had been conspicuous by its absence for some years. Above all, the opposition parties were able to point to the fact that measures for improving consultation and scrutiny were of little comfort when the most important policy decisions remained imposed by a Conservative government, reliant on a Westminster, not a Scottish, majority (Clouston and Wintour1995; Hansard 1994). In short, Major's mix of assimilationism and unionism had been clearly percieved as asymmetrical, and it was going to take either growing support for the modern Conservative policy agenda or a favourable reception to the theatre of the Lang and Forsyth initiatives for the Major government's approach to territorial management to reap electoral improvement or, should it come to it, public support for a 'no' vote in a devolution referendum.

Wales

The Thatcher governments and the Walker–Hunt era

The approach taken by the first two Thatcher governments in Wales and Scotland was strikingly similar. With respect to Wales, too, there was an assumption of constitutional stability, whilst implicitly the implementation of the Thatcher policy agenda suggested a trend towards assimilationism. In the 1987 general election, the Conservative result in Wales was also poor. However, the Thatcher government's perception of a Welsh political problem was much less marked than in the case of Scotland. While the election result had not been good, Welsh voting behaviour did not demonstrate the same level of territorial dissent as that of Scotland. Support for Plaid Cymru was proportionally far less than was the case for the SNP. Nor did the dominant vote for the Labour Party in Wales imply majority support for devolution. The leader of the Labour Party, Neil Kinnock, had never been a committed supporter of Welsh devolution, the Welsh Labour Party itself was split over the issue, and it remained a peripheral concern with many voters. Nor was the result in Wales of any great significance for the Conservative Party in electoral terms. There were far fewer seats at stake than in Scotland and the party had never done that well in Wales. Hence it is perhaps not surprising that Mrs Thatcher's memoirs rate barely a mention of Wales, as there was not sufficient reason to take the personal interest that she did in Scotland. Instead she left the issue to her new Secretary of State, Peter Walker, an experienced politician who, it was felt, could be trusted to improve the Conservative position and deflect the dissent that did exist. In so doing she granted him much more autonomy over political strategy and day-to-day management than that made available to Malcolm Rifkind, the Scottish Secretary.

The outcome of the approach taken in Wales has been claimed by Peter Walker to have been markedly distinctive in a number of respects. First, whilst Walker shared Thatcher's desire to create an enterprise culture he did not have the same confidence that the fortunes of the Welsh economy could be left solely to market forces. He believed far more in the concept of private and public sector partnership and a role for the state in plugging gaps where capital and initiative were not forthcoming. Similarly, Walker did not share Thatcher's relegation of poverty and deprivation to the realm of personal responsibility. He was concerned at Wales' range of social problems, notably high unemployment and bad housing. As a one-nation Tory he believed firmly in the state taking responsibility for the most poorly off in society. His views as a whole implied a greater emphasis on the need for public expenditure than was the case with the Prime Minister. Such views appeared to complement well the Welsh predilection for the politics of community, co-operation and partnership, and he took the stance with Mrs Thatcher that he would govern Wales according to these beliefs or not at all. According to Walker she quickly assented, suggesting that the arrival of Walker at the Welsh Office was to mark a halt in the assimilationist tendency which had previously prevailed. Thatcher's backing of Walker's approach in Wales would allow a return to the traditional Tory approach to territorial management: old-style unionism, in which government sought to adapt central policies to the distinctive needs of the territory concerned, both in terms of policy content and political style.

Walker's memoirs indicate that considerable efforts were made to pursue this approach and undoubtedly it met with some success (Walker 1991, Chapter 15). With Thatcher's support he achieved small increases in expenditure on a range of programmes to clear land for development, build roads and expand the funding of the Welsh Development Agency (WDA) to generate new development. Indeed the WDA came into its own in the 1980s, sending teams to Japan and the USA to promote Wales as a base for location of new plants to supply the British and EU markets. Walker took a personal role in such promotion and joined in trade visits to Japan, Korea, Germany and the USA. He supported the WDA's strategy of working in partnership with local business agencies and local authorities in order to ensure successful accommodation of new enterprise on the ground. This included encouraging local authorities to speed up the planning process and to provide land for private housing for new company employees. Local authorities, of course, proved willing partners as the WDA developed a successful track record in attracting inward investment. As a corollary to this partnership approach, Walker consulted trade unions about inward investment policies and encouraged single-union deals in return for productivity agreements.

Walker also emphasised the importance of special regional development initiatives. He pushed for the building of the second Severn Bridge to capitalise on the opportunities of the M4 road link between South Wales and England. He ensured the completion of the project started under Walker's predecessor, Nicholas Edwards, to dual the whole of the A55 in North Wales, and subsequently promoted it as 'the road to opportunity'. Walker also established the Cardiff Bay Development Corporation, after a suggestion made by South Glamorgan County Council, to clear the old docks developments and create tourist and leisure industry opportunities. Finally, Walker introduced the Valleys Initiative, by which he sought to reverse the decline of the old mining communities through an integrated programme of land clearance, economic development, road and school building, and social provision. The result overall was a substantial growth in inward investment, accounting for 22 per cent of all British inward investment in 1987–90.

Among the companies which were attracted were Bosch, Toyota and Ford, each in their different ways creating knock-on effects on employment through demand for components and other semi-finished materials and services. During this period unemployment in Wales fell from 13 to 6 per cent, with the level in the valleys falling faster than anywhere else in Wales.

For Walker, success in tackling problems in deprived communities was the cornerstone of his economic and social programme, a priority characteristic of Conservative regional policy in the 1960s and 1970s. He did, however, see other key aspects to his role as Secretary of State. For example, he acknowledged the distinctive cultural dimension in Welsh politics by introducing the Welsh Language Board. Overall, Walker believed that he commanded support in Wales for his whole programme, and perhaps the clearest endorsement of his approach was that when Walker chose to step down, Mrs Thatcher appointed a successor, David Hunt, who was broadly committed to its continuation, a decision accepted by John Major on becoming Prime Minister. Walker had made many key strategic decisions, but Hunt still managed to make some notable developments, including the 1993 Welsh Language Act. Indeed Hunt sought to develop the consensual approach to governing Wales further. In 1993, when the Lang initiative was launched in Scotland, Hunt tried to advance similar proposals in relation to the operation of the Welsh Grand Committee. In the spring, he proposed to a meeting of the Committee that it could meet every other week, and hold question times, set debates and adjournment debates in a manner similar to that of a full meeting of the House of Commons (House of Commons 1993). These proposals, however, were allowed to wither on the vine when Hunt was promoted within the cabinet in 1993. It was at this point that the period of territorial management established by Walker came to an end. Its distinctiveness from the broad thrust of Thatcherism has been endorsed by many commentators. Gamble (1993, p.83), for example, concluded, 'under Walker and Hunt the Welsh Office has practised not the disengagement favoured by Thatcherite ideology but an interventionist industrial policy.'

Such appreciation of the distinctiveness and apparent success of the Walker–Hunt approach to governing Wales, nevertheless, needs qualification. First, Walker and Hunt largely worked through a system of quangos, of which the WDA was the prime example. Power of appointment was with the Secretary of State and the quangos came to be controlled predominantly by members or sympathisers of the Conservative Party. Quangos allowed the Secretary of State on many issues to bypass the views of elected local government, which was predominantly controlled by the Labour Party. Whilst it is perfectly reasonable to suggest that quangos can operate in sympathy with broader civic preferences, revisionist commentators have noted how the Welsh quangos in practice brought a clear Conservative agenda to bear on public policy (Morgan 1994; Morgan and Roberts 1993). For example, Griffiths' (1994) account of Welsh Office policy on the Cardiff Bay Development Corporation shows how a partnership approach with elected local authorities and professed concern with the broader needs of the development area rapidly disintegrated even under Walker into partisan preference for Conservative appointments to the Corporation and a narrow focus on property development. More broadly, Griffiths (1996) argues that the policy agenda pursued in Wales during the Walker–Hunt era was much closer to Thatcherite prescriptions than to those of local concerns. His position is that the structural constraints imposed by the British system of government, with all the attendant consequences arising from Treasury and cabinet controls, were bound to make distinctiveness in Welsh government rather more rhetoric than reality. Hence, while recognising the unionism which did indeed characterise much of the approach of Walker and Hunt to government in Wales, there is a danger in underestimating the policy assimilationism to an English norm which in practice may have penetrated the day-to-day administration.

Second, the effectiveness of the Walker–Hunt era can be exaggerated. Perceptions of economic improvement owed a lot to a relative worsening of the situation in south-east England. Furthermore, Welsh perceptions of economic improvement were in any case muted as inward investment and new jobs were accompanied by the driving down of real wage rates and increases in part-time and contract working that were general features of British labour market development in the early 1990s. There was also growing concern about the Conservative grip on Welsh governance that developed with the concentration of power in quangos. This was highlighted in the hearings of the Public Accounts Committee of the House of Commons in 1993 when irregularities concerning payments, expense claims and recruitment in the WDA were exposed. As a result, 'the carefully packaged image of the Welsh Development Agency (WDA) as a dynamic institution manned by tireless, bright people working selflessly to improve economic conditions in Wales has begun to unravel' (Griffiths 1994, p.1026). Whatever the other effects of the Walker–Hunt era, the increasing importance of quangos as the vehicle for the delivery of public policies undoubtedly contributed to Welsh disenchantment with the government and support for constitutional reform.

In summary, it is clear even during the Walker–Hunt era that Welsh government was increasingly conducted through unelected quangos by which a Conservative interpretation of Wales' needs could be brought to bear, not necessarily with as much benign sympathy as that claimed from the centre. This aroused concerns and undoubtably the consensual tone of the Walker–Hunt mode of territorial management did not fully placate Welsh concerns about the centralising and anti-democratic tendencies of Conservative governments. Nevertheless, despite these reservations, it is reasonable still to conclude that in comparison with the approach taken in Scotland in the late 1980s, between 1987 and 1993 Wales experienced a departure from the clearly assimilationist approach, necessary for the uniform implementation of the Thatcher state reforms. Government was conducted with far more sympathy to the perceived policy needs of Wales, and with a style which was much less obviously politically confrontational. In terms of territorial management, the Walker–Hunt approach was clearly more successful in minimising politicised dissent against Conservative government than could be said of the approach taken in Scotland up to 1990.

The second Major government

The appointment of John Redwood to succeed Hunt as Secretary of State in 1993 changed the political scene in Wales. It was symptomatic of the fact that the Welsh problem was still seen as of a different order of magnitude to that of Scotland. Major, like Thatcher before him, viewed the Welsh position as such that he was prepared to grant a relatively high level of political autonomy to the management of the Welsh Office. There appeared to have been no prior agreed strategy when Redwood was appointed. It was purely coincidental that Redwood's appointment marked a change in approach which bore a close resemblance to that of Mrs Thatcher's agenda of territorial management in Scotland in the late 1980s. It was nevertheless highly significant because the approach in Wales, as in Scotland, helped to crystallise opposition criticisms into a case for constitutional reform.

During his period of office, from 1993 to 1995, Redwood was in many ways constrained by the work of his predecessors. Projects were already in progress which depended on levels of public expenditure to which Redwood would have taken exception. These included Welsh Office support for European initiatives, various regional development schemes and a high level of grant aid to companies directly from the Welsh Office or the WDA. Whilst Redwood after leaving office was critical of the WDA as land 'magpies', when in office he was publicly supportive of its work. Similarly, he had to honour commitments with respect to existing initiatives. Nevertheless, in his rhetoric he placed more emphasis on the development of an enterprise culture in Wales, seeking in particular to focus efforts on helping small and medium sized businesses. He was noted for his hands-off approach in encouraging development against the wishes of environmentalists. Indeed his anger at environmentalists' successes in blocking development led Redwood to brand them as reminiscent of 'European neo-Nazis' and to cut the funding of the Countryside Council for Wales by a sixth. He also emphasised the need to apply New Right ideas to public sector provision. Most famously he spoke out against moral decay and its financial consequences for the public sector, singling out the problem of unmarried mothers. To reform the state in Wales he championed the reform of local government structure to create leaner, fitter local government. Similarly he implemented administrative reforms in the NHS to make savings on management posts and to achieve a higher proportion of funding being spent on clinical work. He actively promoted the Citizen's Charter, a popular schools initiative, and imposed reforms on the Welsh Office which led to the creation of more executive agencies, the application of market testing and staff reductions (Cm 2815 1995b). Not surprisingly, given his commitment to the Thatcherism of Wales, Redwood also displayed little sympathy for Welsh sensitivities and immediately dropped the proposals for reform of the Welsh Grand Committee which Hunt had latterly brought forward to replicate developments in Scotland.

Overall, Redwood adopted the philosophy that government was best approached by giving the electorate a stronger rather than a watered-down version of Thatcherism, and by seeking to persuade and coerce the electorate into the belief that it was actually good for them. In practice, such an actively assimilationist approach proved to be a failure. It was during Redwood's tenure that the abuses of the Welsh quangocracy came to light and this, combined with his 'messianic' approach, raised serious question marks over the legitimacy of Conservative government in Wales. Redwood, an Englishman with no Welsh connections, representing a constituency in the south-east of England, seeking to implement the brand of Conservative policy furthest from Welsh sympathies, appeared like a colonial viceroy rather than a democratically accountable politician. Not surprisingly, the Redwood era saw a significant hardening of the position of the non-Conservative Welsh political class in favour of some form of constitutional change. The appalling Conservative losses in the 1995 Welsh local government elections appeared to signify a wider public contempt for the Conservative Party. In effect John Major, in appointing Redwood, had succeeded in creating the perception of a Thatcherite legacy in Wales that Mrs Thatcher had herself not left. Thus by 1995 Wales, as well as Scotland, was seen by Major as posing serious territorial and party problems, although those in Scotland were considered the more serious.

Of course, the demonstrable failure of his approach in Wales may have been enough to cause Major to consider Redwood's removal, but in 1995 the wider politics of the British Conservative Party forced a new development. Redwood had increasingly promoted his approach in Wales as a right-wing blueprint for the government of Britain as a whole, another 'guinea pig' affront which hardened Welsh opinion against him. It was logical, then, that it should be Redwood who was ultimately to emerge as the challenger to Major in the July 1995 leadership contest. Redwood's resignation to fight the challenge and his subsequent defeat left Major not only with the need to appoint a new Secretary of State in Wales but also, in making the appointment, to impose his own political agenda as against Redwood's previous right-wing crusade. It was in this context that for the first time following the re-emergence of territorial management in Westminster politics after the 1987 general election, a uniform approach was adopted across Scotland and Wales. With the appointment of William Hague as the new Secretary of State, the approach to territorial management adopted in Scotland after 1990, and relaunched with greater momentum under Michael Forsyth from the summer of 1995, was replicated in Wales.

Hague was to echo Forsyth's promotion of Conservative successes in developing an enterprise economy. He did not flinch from supporting a hard financial settlement for Wales in the 1995 budget. His background as a former social security minister under the right-wing Peter Lilley, had left him with the reputation of being keen on rolling back the frontiers of the state. Hague had much in common with Redwood on these matters. However, Hague took much greater care to avoid confrontational rhetoric and specifically to appease environmental interests by restoring the budget of the Countryside Council for Wales. At the same time, like Forsyth in Scotland, he balanced policy assimilationism with a more profoundly pro-Unionist rhetoric and respect for the union-state characteristics of Wales' governing arrangements. The readiness to respond to Welsh criticisms of the unresponsiveness of the British government, and to promote the advantages that Wales derived from existing constitutional arrangements, was highlighted by Hague's announcement in November 1995 of reforms of the Welsh Grand Committee which were similar to those simultaneously announced by Forsyth in Scotland. Of course, there is no separate body of Welsh law. Hence it was not suggested that debates of second or third readings of bills would be heard in the Welsh Grand Committee. However, Hague proposed that the Committee might meet more often, perhaps six or seven times a year, as opposed to the paltry eight meetings between 1992 and 1995. He also suggested that half the meetings could be held in Wales, some possibly outside Cardiff. The Committee could hold short debates in addition to those addressing government business. There would be a facility for Welsh Office ministers' question times at some meetings and other government ministers might attend the Committee to take part in debates, make statements and be questioned on how UK-wide policies affected Wales. With these proposals Hague believed, 'the Welsh Grand Committee has the potential to ensure that Welsh interests are kept high on the agenda in Parliament' (Welsh Office 1995; Settle1995).

At the same time, Hague followed Redwood in vociferously opposing devolution. Indeed both Hague and Forsyth vigorously made the case that devolution would create an unnecessary and costly extra tier of government; that it would reduce the power of the Secretary of State, leading to the abandonment of the position and its influence within the British cabinet; that it would lead to the reduction of MPs at Westminster; and that it might well be the precursor of independence. The prospects of such arguments having an impact on territorial dissent in Wales were probably greater than in Scotland. While the position of the supporters and critics of the government's stance remained much the same as in Scotland, government backers in Wales knew that they would be able to exploit two important differences from the Scottish situation. First, the non-Conservative political elite had remained divided over constitutional change: both within the Labour Party over the need for it and between the opposition parties over what form it should take. Second, the Conservative Party would be able to appeal to an underlying Welsh sentiment which historically had put a high premium upon the defence of Welsh cultural identity but a questionable emphasis upon the assertion of a Welsh political identity. The uncertain consequences of constitutional reform would remain the most effective weapon in Conservative territorial management in Wales. It is significant, nevertheless, that the approach in Wales taken by the Major government had at last been harmonised with that in Scotland. The issue of preserving the Conservative revolution and the territorial union under existing constitutional arrangements were closely interconnected in the Major statecraft: it all survived or fell together.

The Conservative Party and options for territorial management

In Scotland two modes of territorial management were adopted after 1987. Thatcher's assimilationism was followed by Major's tilt towards a compensating unionism. In Wales three modes were followed. Walker implemented a largely traditional method of attempting to achieve territorial consensus. Redwood applied a Thatcher-style assimilationism. Hague then replicated for Wales Major's preference for a compensating unionism. An examination of the Conservative legacy of territorial management gives lie to the argument that Conservative governments did not apply themselves seriously to addressing perceived Scottish and Welsh problems. Nevertheless, their attempts had to confront significant political obstacles. Moreover, it was only from 1995 that territorial management apparently became a more general Conservative project, managed from the centre. The earlier phases of territorial management in Wales can be associated with the stances taken by particular Secretaries of State to a much greater extent than was the case in Scotland. It was only after the appointment of Hague that the approaches towards territorial management in Scotland and Wales appeared to be harmonised. This approach can be characterised as policy assimilationism balanced by a unionist tilt towards respect for territorial interests through governmental reform, which tried to hark back to the traditional Tory approach to governing Britain.

In the run-up to the 1997 election it was clear that the Major approach would not be altered substantially in the short term. In Scotland, this would mean the implementation of existing proposals to strengthen the Grand Committee as a preferable alternative to a Scottish parliament, and the promotion of local government reforms in terms of delivering more genuine devolution of power. In Wales, similar promotion of Conservative policy achievements and the existing machinery of government was to be expected. Prior to the election, looking at developments in Conservative thinking in the longer term, however, three lines of development in Conservative policy seemed possible. Each would primarily focus on solving the 'Scottish problem', as thinking about the 'Welsh problem' remained poorly developed despite an awareness of its existence.

First, there was the possibility of a continuation of the existing approach, with a tendency if territorial dissent remained a problem for the Conservative leadership to feel compelled to move yet further towards unionism. In this context the most advanced option consistent with the strategy of the Major governments were to be found in the recommendations of the Douglas-Home Report which informed the Conservative Party election manifesto of 1970. This proposed the creation of a directly elected assembly for Scotland, called a convention, which dealt with second reading, committee and report stages of bills, leaving third reading and House of Lords stages to Westminster. The supremacy of the UK parliament would be maintained by virtue of its power to determine which bills could be dealt with by the convention in this way – essentially uncontroversial bills – and by its ultimate power of vote on the third reading. If the Scottish Grand Committee were to be given these convention powers, which would entail voting as well as debating powers at all intermediate stages of bills, and always met in Scotland, then the Major approach might be taken to its logical conclusion. As Bogdanor concluded, 'the Douglas-Home proposals in fact offered the maximum degree of devolution possible within the continuing framework of the unitary state' (Bogdanor 1979, p.109). Failure of such proposals would mark the end of the viability of Major's approach.

Alternatively, it appeared that the party could come under the influence of the one-nation strand of Toryism which was still strong in the party, especially the Scottish Conservative Party. This element had long considered devolution for Scotland a realistic option in developing the Union, duly considering the Thatcher approach eccentric and abhorrent, and the Major approach potentially confused and minimalist. In 1968 the Conservative Party under Heath showed that they were prepared to go as far as supporting a devolved assembly in line with the Conservative principle of diversity, and in the 1987 Queen's Speech debate Edward Heath advised considering the devolution option in response to the renewed Scottish problem (Bogdanor 1979, p.108; Cooper 1995, p.1387). Within Scotland even in the 1990s there was party support for devolution lurking beneath the surface. An ICM poll in early 1995, for example, showed that 45 per cent of Scottish Tories favoured devolution, only 6 per cent less than Labour support, and it was quietly admitted that a number of prominent Scottish Tories remained in favour of an Edinburgh parliament (Clouston 1995). Such views were based in part on principle. They were also informed by realism. Many Scottish Conservatives had begun to be reconciled to the inevitability of devolution and were doubtful of their chances if they entered the first elections for a Scottish parliament as the anti-parliament party.

A third line of policy development appeared possible if a candidate more clearly of the Right were to become leader. In these circumstances the party might continue with the Major approach in the short term but in the longer term would be more likely to have a fundamentalist debate as to whether it was predominantly an English party, which was ready to call Scotland's bluff and threaten separation if there were not compliance to assimilationism. Indeed it was apparent that the influence of the 'sod off' school of English Conservatism might become increasingly influential in the Parliamentary Party.

Whatever the case, it was apparent that it was clear that the interest within the Conservative Party in the mid 1990s in finding a solution to the 'Scottish problem' was set to continue. The project for the modernisation of Britain that the Thatcher governments offered was clearly perceived at the centre as having placed considerable pressures upon territorial consensus, pressures which the Major governments' efforts at territorial management had only offered a start in releasing. In due course it was possible that solutions emerging from the Scottish debate might also complement more specific thinking about the 'Welsh problem'. This chapter, therefore, might be seen in hindsight as only offering an analysis of the opening shots in the

Conservative battle to determine the political arrangements by which the Union with Scotland and Wales is held together and developed in the context of substantial stae reform and in the face of pressures for major constitutional change.

References

Bogdanor, V. (1979) *Devolution.* Oxford: Oxford University Press.

Bulpitt, J. (1983) *Territory and Power in the United Kingdom: An Interpretation.* Manchester: Manchester University Press.

Clouston, E. (1995) 'Scottish Tories uncomfortable on home rule.' *The Guardian* 14 January 1995.

Clouson, E. and Winton, P. (1995) 'Tories counter-attack on Scottish Constitution.' *The Guardian* 1 December 1995.

Cm 2225 (1993) *Scotland in the Union – A Partnership for Good.*

Cm 2814 (1995a) *Serving Scotland's Needs, The Government's Expenditure Plans 1995–1996.*

Cm 2815 (1995b) *Departmental Report by the Welsh Office, The Government's Expenditure Plans 1995–96 to 1997–98.* London: HMSO.

Cooper, J. (1995) 'The Scottish problem: English Conservatives and the Union with Scotland in the Thatcher and Major eras.' In J. Lovenduski and J. Stanyer (eds) *Contemporary Political Studies 1995.* Belfast: Political Studies Association.

Forsyth, M. (1995a) *A Charter for the Millennium.* London: Conservative Political Centre.

Forsyth, M. (1995b) 'The Richard Stewart Memorial Lecture.' 30 November 1995, 32pp.

Gamble, A., Holliday, I. and Peels, G. (1993) 'Territorial politics.' In P. Dunleavy *et al.* *Developments in British Politics 4.* London: Macmillan.

Griffiths, D. (1994) 'The Welsh Office and policy exceptionalism in the 1980s: some reflections.' In P. Dunleavy and J. Stanyer (eds) *Contemporary Political Studies 1994.* Belfast: Political Studies Association.

Griffiths, D. (1996) *Thatcherism and Territorial Politics, a Welsh Case Study.* Aldershot: Avebury.

Clouston, E. and Wintour, P. (1995) 'Tories counter-attack on Scottish constitution.' *The Guardian,* 1 November 1995, p.2.

Hansard (1994) 'House of Commons Scottish Business,' 11 July, columns 762–803.

Heald, D. (1994) 'Territorial public expenditure in the United Kingdom.' *Public Administration 72,* 147–175.

House of Commons (1993) 'Minutes of the proceedings of the Welsh Grand Committee 8 March – 14 July 1993', House of Commons papers 92/93 847.

Kemp, A. (1995) 'Time to grasp the thistle.' *The Guardian* 25 February 1995.

Major, J. (1992) *Scotland in the United Kingdom.* London: Conservative Political Centre.

Mitchell, J. (1995) 'Unionism, assimilation and the Conservatives.' In J. Lovenduski and J. Stanyer (eds) *Contemporary Political Studies 1995*. Belfast: Political Studies Association.

Morgan, K. (1994) *The Fallible Servant: Making Sense of the Welsh Development Agency.* Cardiff: University Papers in Planning Research No. 151.

Morgan, K. and Roberts, E. (1993) *The Democratic Deficit: A Guide to Quangoland.* Cardiff: University Papers in Planning Research No.144.

Settle, M. (1995) 'Major will have to face Welsh MPs says Hague.' *Western Mail,* 1 December.

Thatcher, M. (1993) *The Downing Street Years.* London: HarperCollins.

Urwin, D. (1982) 'Territorial structures and political developments in the United Kingdom.' In S. Rokkan and D. Urwin (eds) *The Politics of Territorial Identity Studies in European Regionalism.* London: Sage.

Walker, P. (1991) *Staying Power.* London: Bloomsbury.

Welsh Office (1995) press release, 30 November.

CHAPTER 5

The Restructuring of Local Government in Scotland

Ronan Paddison

Introduction

During the 1980s the Thatcher governments embarked upon a concerted drive in Scotland to impose their policy agenda on a largely sceptical and unreceptive population. A key aspect of their approach was a desire to establish greater central control over local government. In the 1990s, the precise strategy of the Major governments was less certain, but once again policy adopted towards local government offers some insight into underlying thinking. A key element of Conservative policy on local government right across Britain was the reform of structure. Consequently, in seeking to explore the nature of the Major governments' approach towards Scotland, this chapter focuses on the restructuring experience in Scotland, in which a two-tier system of regions and districts was replaced by a single tier of unitary authorities. The discussion is presented in four sections. The first focuses on the rationale for reform, initiated by the last Thatcher administration and echoed by the succeeding Major government, critically examining two of the essential claims made for the shift towards unitary authorities, the clarification of accountability and the removal of the friction inherent in the two-tier system. Section two critically assesses further government claims that restructuring would foster a greater sense of community identity with local government. Section three then develops the argument that restructuring was essentially an exercise in achieving greater central control over local government, without seriously engaging with the concerns of other key players with an interest in the outcome, notably the local communities themselves. This suggests a continuity in the approaches of the Thatcher and Major governments towards local government, and in the policy of assimilating Scotland to English norms that broadly characterised the substance of

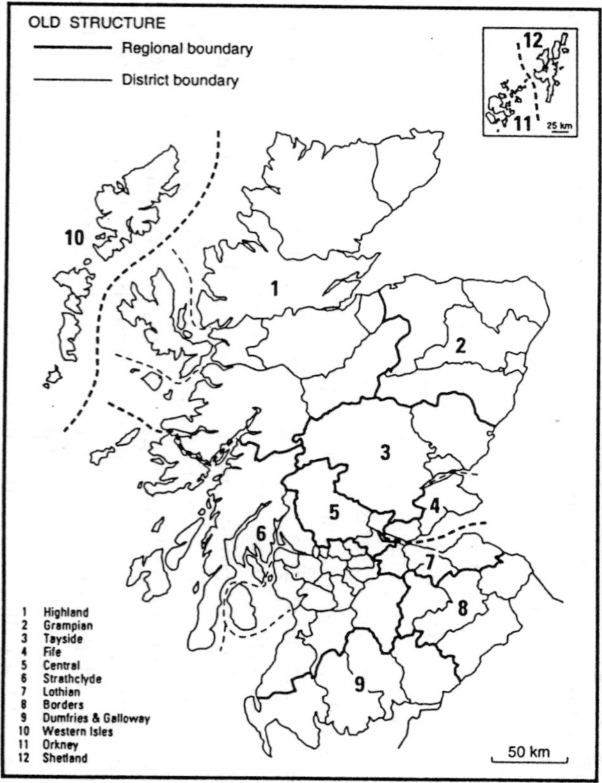

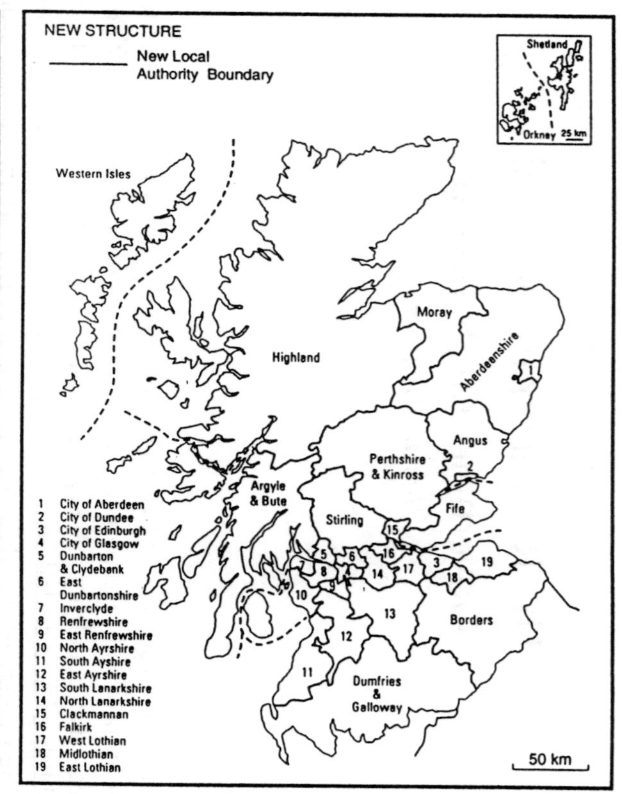

Figure 5.1 Old and new Scottish local government structures

Conservative government after the 1987 election (see Chapter 4). A conclusion, nevertheless, argues that in practice the attempt to improve the capacity for imposing a Conservative policy agenda through local government restructuring created new problems in terms of centre–local conflicts, although public responses remained uncertain.

The Major government's rationale for reform

The Local Government (Scotland) Act passed into the statute books in November 1994. It abolished the existing regional and district councils in favour of 29 unitary councils, which were duly elected in April 1995, taking over their duties a year later (Figure 5.1). These joined three already existing unitary islands councils, to make 32 local authorities in all. The case for this reform was originally spelt out by the government in its consultation paper of 1991 (Scottish Office 1991). As in the English and Welsh exercises, the argument was expressed largely in terms of the shortcomings of the existing two-tier system. First, in duplicating administrative structures, such as personnel, financial and legal services, the system was wasteful. Second, because of the development of an enabling role, rather than one devoted to direct service provision, it was contended that the way in which local authorities discharged their statutory functions had changed materially over the period since the Wheatley Commission (Wheatley Report 1969) had made its recommendations. The Wheatley Report had concluded that a unitary structure, whatever its other benefits, was difficult to reconcile with the need for large-scale strategic co-ordination and local service provision, particularly for education, social work and land-use planning. However, the shifts in the responsibilities of local government, it was now claimed, had made such a dichotomy less salient, paving the way for a unitary system. Third, the existing two-tier system clouded accountability because of the confusion amongst the electorate as to what functions were the responsibility of the regions and the districts. Finally, the two-tier system was also the cause of friction and delays, particularly on projects which required joint action.

Midwinter (1992) has tellingly criticised the first half of this rationale, questioning in particular whether there were likely to be cost savings following the removal of the regional councils as well as the assumption that local government had become an 'enabling mechanism'. A more detailed examination of the second half of the rationale provided in the consultation paper – the problem of accountability and the removal of regional and district conflict – is the focus of the discussion here.

The claim that there were major problems of accountability in the two-tier structure lay at the heart of the proposal to create unitary authorities. The evidence to support the argument is far from convincing. In a survey conducted in the early 1980s and reported by Young (1984), those services which were most frequently used – notably housing and education, but also refuse collection – were correctly attributed to the responsible tier of local government by a majority of respondents (between 55 and 73%). For services likely to be used less frequently, only a minority were able to make a correct identification. These findings were corroborated broadly in a comprehensive survey of public knowledge of local government in Scotland conducted in 1995 (Table 5.1). For most local government services at least half of those questioned were able to identify correctly which tier was the responsible authority.

Table 5.1: Identification of service providers, Scottish Local Government (1995)

	Don't know (%)	*Regional Council* (%)	*District Council* (%)	*Council – could not specify* (%)	*Central Government* (%)	*Quango* (%)	*Hospital Trust* (%)	*Total* (%)
Schools	10	62	14	11	2	1		100
Libraries	12	27	49	11		1		100
Hospitals	18	40	10	6	5	16	5	100
Street Cleaning	5	11	77	6		1		100
Police	18	60	11	7	3	2		100
Cemetaries	23	18	50	8		1		100
Unemployment Benefit	20	25	19	11	23	1		100
Home Helps	15	33	39	10	3	1		100
Roads Maintenance	8	53	31	7				100
Tourism	27	32	23	10	1	7		100
Prisons	28	36	9	8	16	3		100
Gas Supply	21	17	10	7	1	43		100
Parks, etc.	7	20	60	12		1		100

Source: Scottish Office (1995)

Difficulties arise in the interpretation of these survey results, notably the question as to what defines a 'satisfactory' level of knowledge – a point which is usually overlooked, probably because of its ambiguity. Clearly, interpretations of survey results do differ in the emphases they try to make. Commentating on Young's survey, Midwinter (1992) argued that the correct allocation of services was 'basically quite high', though the judgement appeared to have been made in a relative sense, in that there had been considerably lower levels recorded in a similar type of survey in England. On the other hand, in the 1995 Scottish survey – in which admittedly the level of 'correct' answers was lower than the earlier survey, but in a number of cases remained at above 50 per cent – knowledge of service provision was described as 'low' (Scottish Office 1995). Insofar as even a level of 60 per cent leaves a substantial proportion of the electorate confused ultimately as to where accountability properly resides, the threshold of what defines a satisfactory level is likely to be high. But a high threshold may be unrealistic – surveys of voter knowledge of local government (such as being able to name their local councillor) tend to demonstrate low levels of knowledge.

The presumption that in moving to a simpler structure accountability would be increased was questionable for several reasons. As was frequently stated, the necessity within single-tier systems to enter into joint service arrangements would blur accountability (Leach *et al.* 1991). From the outset of the reform process, the government conceded that some services would need to be administered on a joint basis, either regionally, as in the case of the police, fire and valuation services, or sub-regionally, as for land-use planning and, in Strathclyde, public transportation. Other joint service arrangements were likely, particularly given the small size of some of the unitary authorities. For example, authorities in the former Lothians Region fairly promptly negotiated the operation of a number of social services on a joint basis.

In practice, the structure of accountability had become more complex not primarily because of the two-tier local government structure but because of the changing administrative configuration resulting from the growth of quangos and public–private partnership agencies which had local impacts but which were external to the formal system of local government. Its reform had taken place against a complex pattern of both centralisation and decentralisation (Lloyd 1994). Some services, such as tourism and local economic development, had operated on a 'conjoint' basis, provided for by government, public and private sector agencies and quangos. While citizen demands over service provision focused on the mainline services of housing and education, transparent lines of accountability were of no less significance in the case of local economic development given the impact it could have on a locality's future mode of development. What is of significance here is that, as Table 5.1 shows, the correct identification of service provision was considerably lower for those provided by central government and quangos, including those such as health care in which there had been substantial shifts of administrative structure. As much as it was expected that unitary authorities would simplify accountability for the electorate, the development of joint service arrangements, together with the complex network of other agencies, including quangos, which had local impacts, would also tend to blur the lines of accountability.

The claim that a unitary structure would avoid the conflict that characterised the two-tier structure also needs to be scrutinised. Such conflict, it was argued, reduced effectiveness by weakening the co-ordination of service delivery, particularly where related functions, notably housing and social work, were provided by different tiers of local government. In large measure, it had been these difficulties which had led to the establishment of the Stodart Committee review of the two-tier structure in Scotland, and which reported in 1981 (Stodart Report 1981). This was concerned mainly with effectiveness and the proper allocation of functions between regions and districts. It avoided the question of territorial reorganisation and the issue of unitary authorities, even though both were mentioned in submissions made to the Committee.

There is little doubt that as far as the four major cities were concerned there had been considerable, and ongoing, tension with the regional authorities. Having functioned as all-purpose authorities under the earlier system, the cities were consistent in resenting the loss of status. This was particularly so in the case of Glasgow, which a few years after the 1975 reorganisation had commissioned a report presenting the case for its re-instatement as a unitary authority. In its submission to the Stodart Committee it had argued that the division of responsibilities undermined its ability to tackle the problems of multiple deprivation in the peripheral estates. These tensions persisted, affecting working relationships and the effectiveness of local government, as the moves towards (intra-authority) decentralisation adopted separately by Glasgow and Strathclyde illustrated. Consensus between the authorities as to the structure and objectives of decentralisation would have had beneficial impacts on the effectiveness of service provision and local participation, yet not only were the schemes drawn over different geographical territories, but the fundamental differences in the expectations the councils had for their programmes resulted in the city having two weakly co-ordinated systems. Elsewhere in Scotland region/district conflict was more episodic, its salience increasing in the other urban centres such as

Inverness, which itself had argued the case for unitary status to the Stodart Committee.

Clearly, however, replacing the two-tier structure by unitary authorities was not of itself going to be a panacea for achieving a more effective local government system. This was to be also dependent on the improvement of management structures within the councils. Decentralisation measures, which were made mandatory for the unitary authorities under the 1994 Act, provide a case in point. Their effectiveness was to be dependent in part on overcoming departmentalism and on the adoption of roles which co-opted community support. Again within Glasgow, existing practice showed how even for such an elementary decision as the definition of a common set of boundaries, co-ordination between service departments was not easily achieved. Nor were the arrangements for structure planning, sub-regional joint committees, likely to remove the conflicts which had arisen during the previous 20 years.

Closer scrutiny of the claims made by the government, as these two examples illustrate, tend to show that the case for a unitary system was by no means obvious. The Wheatley Report in fact argued that the decision between an all-purpose and a two-tier structure needed to take into account the advantages and disadvantages of each. Ultimately, opponents of the reorganisation argued that the limited timetable of consultation and even more of analysis, together with the failure to heed the demand for Scottish devolution, had prevented anything like a proper evaluation. As the Consortium of Scottish Local Authorities (COSLA) expressed it, 'the [Scottish Constitutional] Convention is seriously concerned that the whole question of the structural re-organisation of local government has been dealt with in such an inadequate, superficial and cavalier way' (COSLA 1993, p.9).

Restructuring, boundaries and identity

A further part of the government's rationale for reform was that the two-tier system, in that it weakened accountability, also blurred political identities. This undermined the ability of the electorate to control the fiscal and policy behaviour of local government. A unitary structure, it was claimed, would help to foster the sense of community identity on which local government should be based. In the English reform the notion of community identity was spelt out in the guidance given to the Local Government Commission, which made the recommendations for structure reform. Along with cost and functional considerations this was to be used as an important factor in assessing alternative territorial configurations (Department of the Environment 1992). In some of the Commission's deliberations, the importance of community identity and of expressed preferences clearly played a key part

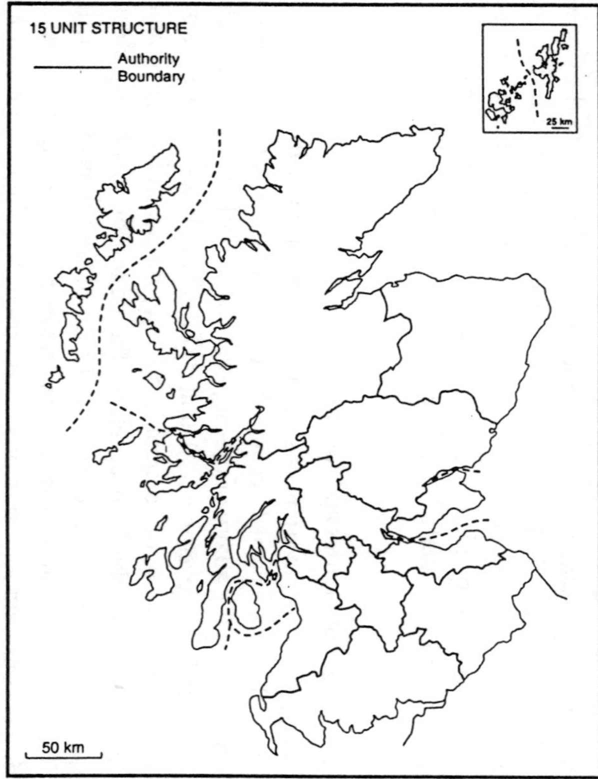

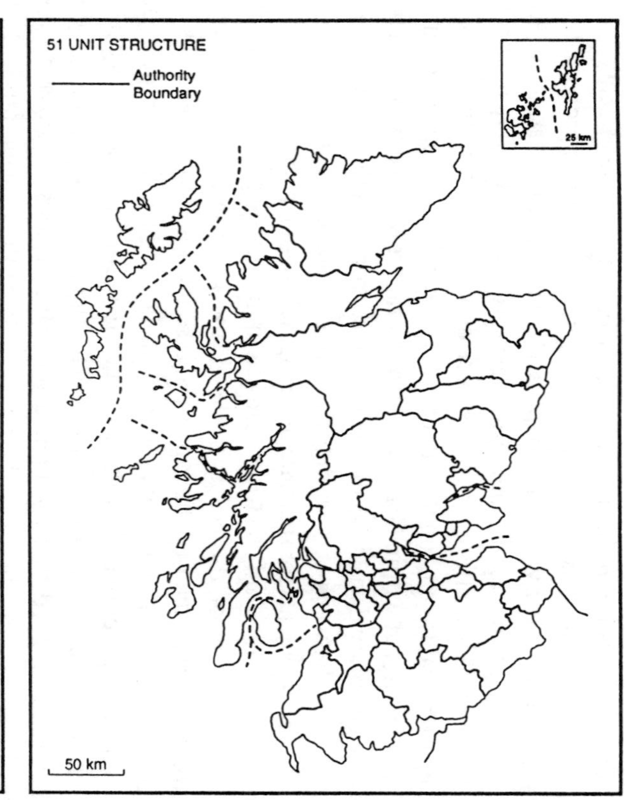

Figure 5.2 Alternative Scottish Local Government proposals (Scottish Office 1992)

in helping to explain the mix of two-tier and unitary arrangements which resulted in England.

However, in the Scottish reform, although community identity was defined as also important to the designation of boundaries, the Scottish Office's approach to reform tended to play down its significance in practice. This followed inevitably from the less 'open' nature of the reform process where the opportunity to gauge public opinion was limited to little more than the invitation to comment on the alternative maps suggested in the consultation paper. (Two of the alternative configurations suggested are shown in Figure 5.2.) Furthermore, in an attempt possibly to defuse the 'boundary problem' it was made plain that the boundaries of the new unitary authorities would generally follow existing regional and/or district council divisions, although, as in England, there was the suggestion that the new councils could adopt a 'back to the future' solution by resorting to the former counties.

Ultimately the use of community identity had only limited influence in the definition of the new councils. In terms of conforming to pre-existing communities it was in the rural areas that its application was the more apparent, with some authorities (including Perth and Kinross, Angus and Mearns, and Argyll and Bute) matching, though not precisely, former counties, and others (such as Dumfries and Galloway and Highland), matching the former regional councils. Conversely, in the more urbanised central belt, and particularly outside the major cities, the delimitation of many of the councils owed more to political and administrative expediency, amalgamating adjacent districts to create new authorities within which any affective sense of community was limited. In other cases districts were severed in more blatant attempts to gain partisan advantage.

The use of community identity as a criterion for delimiting the new structure was itself problematic. As the consultation paper recognised, most citizens feel loyalties towards a range of areas, 'but on balance...may consider that the main area with which they identify is relatively small, and that smaller authorities are better at identifying and fostering the loyalties of those they represent' (Scottish Office 1992, p.17). There was indeed sufficient evidence from the previous round of reform in Scotland (and from elsewhere) to support this argument, and the government implicitly recognised the validity of the need to tailor the working of local government to the community scale in the requirement for the new authorities to present proposals by 1997 as to how they intended to decentralise their operations. Why the logical implications of this were not followed can only be explained by the fact that it was politically unacceptable.

Furthermore, defining the basis of community identity in atavistic terms overlooked the capacity of local government itself to manufacture feelings of community. As a number of the unitary authorities were to demonstrate in their 'shadow' year, fostering a sense of community identity – through logos and other symbols – was an important early task, particularly for those embracing areas in which there was relatively little sense of collective identity. The use of promotional techniques repeated the process initiated following the 1970s' reorganisation when the then new authorities, particularly the regions, embarked upon ongoing programmes of 'community imagineering'. Historic counties, notably Fife which was successful in both reorganisations, retaining its territorial integrity both as a region in the 1970s and as a unitary authority in the 1990s, were able to harness a strong sense of collective identity. Yet authorities which lacked such an historical basis were able also to engineer and foster collective identity. Though measurement of the impact of such campaigns is lacking, there is little doubt that Strathclyde Region had become part of local public consciousness, though whether for most electors this association was construed in net positive or negative terms is a moot point.

Reform as control

The striking contrast between the 1970s reform and that of 1994 is that while in the former there was consensus overall on the need for change, in the latter radical change was implemented in the absence of any such consensus. Indeed there was considerable opposition from local authorities acting through COSLA, which for a time after the Bill had been passed pursued a policy of non-co-operation. It should be noted, however, in line with the outcomes likely from the proposals, that opinions did differ on the need for change. Predictably, a majority of the regional councils, seven of the nine, were opposed – those likely to become unitary authorities differing from the majority opinion. Conversely, less than half of the district councils argued that the case for change was not proven. Some, notably Glasgow, adopted an intermediate stance, arguing that while the case for wholesale reorganisation had not been made, it, along with the three other major cities, should be reconstituted as a unitary authority. As in any exercise of territorial restructuring, competition between existing authorities for status within the new structure deflected opposition which would otherwise have been directed at the centre. These divisions were to resurface once the Act had been passed and preparations were being made to install the new authorities, and were evident in a schism between those Scottish councils for and against a campaign of non co-operation mounted to stall implementation.

Public opinion, too, was hardly generally supportive of change. Survey evidence was consistent for most of the period after the 1970s reorganisation in suggesting that there were high levels of satisfaction with how councils performed as service providers (Tables 5.2 and 5.3). Though this is different from claiming that electors were satisfied with the working of local government *per se* (or its structure), that most were satisfied with its performance as a service provider is an important pointer to likely answers to these wider questions. Opinion polling, then, provided unconvincing evidence of support for the case for single-tier local government. Even though during the consultation process opinion shifted marginally towards favouring the change, overall there was only limited support amongst the electorate. This was matched by the non-local authority responses to the second consultation paper, which had set out the options for restructuring. Of the more than

Table 5.2: Satisfaction with council services overall, Scottish Local Government (1995)

	Very Good (%)	*Good (%)*	*Neither (%)*	*Bad (%)*	*Very Bad (%)*	*Don't Know (%)*	*Total (%)*
Regional Council	10	70	10	6	–	3	100
District Council	13	67	12	5	–	2	100

Note: Less than 0.5% but greater than 0

Source: Scottish Office (1995)

Table 5.3: Satisfaction with individual services, Scottish Local Government (1995)

Services District	*Very Satisfied (%)*	*Satisfied (%)*	*Neither (%)*	*Dissatisfied (%)*	*Very Dissatisfied (%)*	*Total (%)*	*Number (N)*
Council Housing	8	50	15	8	9	100	648
Street Cleaning	18	61	10	9	3	100	987
Parks	20	60	9	8	3	100	972
Refuse Collection	22	69	4	4	1	100	989
Region							
Road and Pavement Maintenance	·3	39	13	32	13	100	994
Schools	12	68	10	8	2	100	651
Social Work	18	56	18	7	2	100	434

Source: Scottish Office (1995)

3000 submissions, mostly from community and other local groups, the single most frequent response was to question the need for reorganisation (COSLA 1992).

In this context one is usefully reminded of Schattschneider's dictum that 'all organisation is bias'. The restructuring of Scottish local government appears to have been no exception. Indeed once the details of the reforms became known there were widespread accusations of gerrymandering, that the restructuring was a 'political fix'. Initiation of the reform and its implementation were perceived as having been inspired more by partisan objectives than they were by those of good governance, while the case for change and how it should be implemented territorially was perceived as lacking any substantive research foundations. As rhetorical as some of the reaction was, such objections had some basis. By comparison with the careful analysis preceding the 1970s reform, and its long period of political gestation, the hurried nature of the no less comprehensive 1994 reform could hardly be more striking. Further, in restricting the debate, a key argument within Schattschneider's dictum, in particular the refusal to consider options other than that of a single-tier system, the structural outcome appeared to have been decided largely from the outset. Certainly the approach to reform in Scotland lacked the flexibility of that adopted in England, where an apparently independent Local Government Commission was given responsibility for recommending structural reform.

If the background to the restructuring is considered more critically, it is clear that the dissolution of the regional authorities in Scotland, the single biggest change of the reorganisation, was always a political likelihood, if not a certainty. Indeed the new councils had hardly been created in 1975 before there were demands for their replacement. They were considered too large and bureaucratic, too remote being the commonly heard accusation, particularly of Strathclyde which, as the largest European local authority, numbered not significantly less than half the population of Scotland. Hindsight was not necessary to appreciate that in favouring the city region approach for the definition of the upper tier authorities, it was inevitable that the modernising of local government in the 1970s would create some disproportionately large local authorities, and that this in turn would generate its own political reaction. As with the claims of gerrymandering, terms such as 'remoteness' and 'too large' are ambiguous, and in the absence of any rigorous research to suggest the contrary, can too easily become hijacked and mythologised for partisan reasons. Large authorities are remote because they are large; the apparent elegance of what is in fact a tautology becomes self-evident, in which its scrutiny is a pointless exercise precisely because it must be true.

However, there were more precise reasons for the apparent inevitability of reform which followed from the 'Thatcher project' for local government in England. In 1972, a two-tier system of local government had also been established in England, both for the metropolitan and shire counties. In 1986 the second Thatcher government abolished the Greater London Council and the metropolitan counties, with the effect, as Leach *et al.* (1991) claim, that the, 'reorganisation structurally destabilised the system of local government in Britain...(so)...that few now expect the existing (1990) system to survive until the end of the century, whichever party subsequently gains (or retains) power nationally' (p.1). More specifically, in abolishing the metropolitan counties and elevating the metropolitan boroughs in England to all-purpose status, the 1986 reorganisation gave fresh impetus to the old complaint expressed by the larger non-metropolitan districts in England that the continued existence of upper tier non-metropolitan county councils reduced the districts' status. The same was true in Scotland, where the four larger cities, in particular Glasgow, had long complained at the loss of powers to regional authorities. If, following the streamlining of the English metropolitan counties, it was to be claimed by the government that the strategic capacity of the upper tier authority, over land use and related activities especially, could be managed by the districts through an indirectly elected joint board or committee, the rationale for retaining the regions in Scotland was considerably weakened. Added to which, in the shift towards the new enabling role of local government, notwithstanding any strategic responsibilities it might have, large authorities and the retention of a two-tier structure appeared dysfunctional.

Nevertheless, in developing local government restructuring it was to be expected that policy would differ between Scotland and England. For, viewed from the periphery, one of the hallmarks of the 1980s was that as much as the Thatcherite reforms sought to ensure that change was applied uniformly throughout the British state, how policies became implemented tended to accentuate differences between member nations (as well as separate localities within them). This was especially true in the field of local government, where in Scotland and England there were different local government systems, and in Scotland there was the Scottish Office, which was able to play a mediating role between the central state and local councils. In several of the major policy reforms affecting local government in the 1980s – the establishment of Urban Development Corporations (UDCs), the introduction of the poll tax and the restructuring of local government, for example – how change was introduced (or not, in the case of the UDCs) accentuated the differences between English and Scottish practice. Such expectations were borne out in the 1990s. Despite the government's intention to introduce a single-tier local government system of unitary authorities, it was only in Scotland and Wales that its stated preference for unitary authorities was actually clearly achieved.

In an immediate sense the difference of outcome between England, on the one hand, and Scotland (and Wales) on the other, was attributable to the different methods used to identify and install the new structures. Where reform in England could to some extent be developed according to some apparently clear criteria, as a result of the work of the Local Government Commission, reform in Scotland need not, as it was determined primarily by the Scottish Office. There were differences even between Scotland and Wales, where in the latter existing authorities were invited to bid for unitary status, an opportunity pointedly denied to the Scottish regions. For example, as suggested earlier, had public opinion actually been employed in Scotland as a measure of community identity and support for alternative territorial configurations, as was the case in England, it is at least plausible that a mix of unitary authorities and a two-tier structure – the outcome in England – would have found favour in Scotland. As the evidence of the English opinion polls demonstrated, of electors in favour of a unitary structure, only in a minority of cases did the proportion exceed 50 per cent, while affective ties were often equally strong to both the existing district and county (MORI 1994). This had a marked influence on the nature of structural reform. In Scotland, public opinion more seriously questioned the need for change and had no impact.

More fundamentally, the *dirigiste* nature of the reform process undertaken by the Scottish Office and the straightforward removal of the regional councils, reflected the underlying tensions raised by the basic constitutional question of the 1980s: who spoke for the interests of Scotland? As the holding of the referendum on the proposal to remove the water service from local control was to demonstrate, the privatisation agenda lacked support in Scotland; even more to the point, that the vote was organised by Strathclyde Region emphasised to the Scottish Office the ability of local government to mobilise opposition, stake its own claim to electoral legitimacy and promote the case for a Scottish parliament (McNulty 1995). The refusal by both the Thatcher and Major administrations to countenance any form of devolution only served to underline the constitutional question and to partialise the issue of local government reform. Ironically, as many submissions to the consultation exercise were to argue, abolishing the regions and implementing a unitary structure would in fact become logical were Scottish devolution to become a reality.

In this context, it appears appropriate to argue that the reform of Scottish local government should be interpreted as an exercise of the Scottish Office and, by extension, of the British state, to engineer a more compliant system of local government. As elsewhere in Britain, central–local relations in Scotland had been strained. Indeed, the early introduction of rate-capping in Scotland reflected the even greater use to which Labour-dominated councils north of the border had put the local power base – as a bulwark against a Conservative- (and English-) dominated British state. For the Scottish Office, then, imposing a unitary structure was primarily an exercise in increasing local government compliance by first, ensuring clearer lines of accountability between electors and local authorities; second, by reducing the number of local authorities to make them more easily controllable; and finally by eliminating the power base of the large Labour-controlled regions. This argument needs some further clarification.

The proposal to reorganise Scottish local authorities should be seen as part of the continuing drive by the Scottish Office to establish the nexus between local spending and electoral accountability. Here the timing of the first consultation paper outlining the government's restructuring proposals in relation to the abandonment of the poll tax is important. Its demise contained within it an admission that the spending–voting nexus had failed; indeed, as earlier in the 1980s, the electorate blamed central government rather than local government for the financial problems of local government. The existence of the two-tier structure became interpreted as part of the problem, obfuscating the lines of accountability by weakening the ties of community with local government. With the then imminent ending of the poll tax, the decision was to opt for a structure which would tighten the control of local government, both by the Scottish Office and locally, where unitary authorities would strengthen the affective ties with local community.

Consequently, as Boyne and Law (1993) have argued for the Welsh reorganisation, a major factor helping to explain the Scottish reform was the objective of increasing control. In part this could be achieved by reducing the number of authorities, even though of itself a reduction would run counter to the logic of public choice theory. Indeed, as a report by the Adam Smith Institute (1989) had argued, given the move towards a unitary structure and the trend towards the enabling local authority, there were clear opportunities in Scotland to define a larger number of smaller local authorities which would increase competition and consumer choice. Yet the Institute's suggestion that councils in a new structure could have populations of between 40,000 and 60,000, which could lead to as many as 100 unitary authorities, however rational ideologically, clearly lacked political acceptability to the Scottish Office. Even the most fragmented of the three options outlined in the consultation paper, listing 51 authorities, would have resulted in a reduction from the number of existing councils. With the number ultimately established at 32, the number of councils more than halved the span of supervision. Tantamount to recognising the greater control that it would be able to exert over the new structure, subsequent Scottish Office proposals offered greater autonomy for the unitary authorities providing they agreed in turn to 'act responsibly', for example by decentralising downwards to local communities (*The Scotsman* 11 October 1995).

It is clear, however, that the abolition of the regional authorities was more important even than the reduction in the number of councils to the overall objective of increasing central control over local government. Dismantling the regions was envisaged as having the effect of diluting opposition. This was particularly the case with respect to the regions of the Labour heartland of central Scotland for it was their abolition that created the 'structural gerrymander' in favour of the centre. Accusations otherwise of gerrymandering, while part of the normal rhetoric of reorganisation, tended to miss the point by focusing on the impacts of local boundary shifts, where the boundaries of the new unitary authorities differed from the existing local government divisions. While there were opportunities to gerrymander boundaries these were limited; in most of central Scotland Labour's dominance was sufficiently strong to ensure that the gains likely to be achieved by gerrymandering would do little to alter the complexion of the unitary authorities. Indeed most of the boundaries of the new authorities followed existing divisions, and in those small number of cases where they were redefined more clearly along partisan lines, their purpose in most cases sought to ensure that pockets of middle-class voters would be incorporated within those (relatively few) councils likely to be non-Labour-controlled. Such was the depth of Labour control in the urban areas that gerrymandering otherwise would have had little effect. Even so, as Table 5.4 demonstrates, the electoral implications of the White Paper's proposal for 28 unitary authorities did maximise the possible gains for the Conservative Party, potentially more than doubling the number of local councils over which they could aspire to control. In the event, such was the swing against the party in the elections to the shadow unitary authorities held in April 1995, that they ended up losing control in even their safest council, East Renfrewshire, where a coalition of Labour and Liberal Democrats assumed power.

Table 5.4: Political control – alternative Scottish Local Government configurations

Ruling Party	*Pre 1994 Structure* (56 councils)*	*Green Paper Proposals† 24 Unit Option*	*35 Unit Option*	*White Paper Proposal ‡ 28 units*	*Unitary Authorities Post-1996 (32)§*
Labour	22 (39%)	10 (42%)	15 (42%)	12 (42%)	20 (63%)
Conservative	5	2	1	6	0
Independent	16	9	11	9	6
SNP	1	1	1	0	3
Liberal Democrats	2	0	1	0	0
No Overall Control	10	3	6	1	3

* Data refer to district councils only
† Calculations based on pre 1994 voting patterns, Scottish Local Government
‡ Calculations based on pre 1994 voting patterns
§ Election results for 'shadow' unitary authorities, April 1995

Source: Scottish Local Government Information

Conclusion

As a normatively expressed exercise, any form of local government reform is inevitably contested terrain, both as to what should be the nature of local democracy and how, in turn, this is to be implemented within a system of local government which simultaneously meets the needs of functional capacity, accountability and accessibility. As elsewhere in the UK, the Major government's reorganisation in Scotland was conducted against the background of a lack of consensus as to the proper role of local government and, indeed, in contrast to the previous round of restructuring in the 1970s, on the necessity of reform. Neither was surprising given the legacy of central–local relations and the repositioning of local government within the local state in the 1980s, conditions which in Scotland were given a further twist by its constitutional position and by the deepening crisis of legitimacy of successive Conservative governments. The governments' stated rationale for local government restructuring does not bear up well under critical analysis, and the analysis presented here suggests that the principal interest of the Major governments in local government restructuring was to extend central control.

Whilst little could be done to prevent restructuring, the gains of central control in practice, however, immediately seemed doubtful. Events during the 'shadow year', 1995/96, suggested the continuation of conflicts and contradictions characterising UK–Scotland and Scottish Office and local government relations during the 1980s and early 1990s. For the Conservatives the failure to gain control in any of the new unitary authorities was made worse by the fact that proportionately the domination of the Left was strengthened. Relations between the Scottish Office and the shadow authorities also became strained as a result of the appointment policies to senior posts of the new councils and payment schemes for councillors. At the same time, the Secretary of State announced the relaxing of controls over a wide range of functions. Though these included the relaxation of some financial controls, significantly rate-capping remained. As much as the objective of the restructuring exercise for the Scottish Office was one of control, partisan factors were to ensure that in practice controlling the behaviour of the unitary authorities would continue to be a source of considerable conflict.

Paradoxically, while public opinion was opposed to reform at the outset of the process, as reform proceeded more opposition was directed to the intention to privatise water (part of the proposed legislation) than it was to the principle of restructuring. To many electors the discourse on local government reform may have lacked transparency; the interpretation of what different modes of local government, single or two tier, regional and/or more local, meant in terms of service delivery and local taxation, problematic enough in its own right, was made more difficult by virtue of the partisan atmosphere in which debate was conducted. Ultimately, in responding to any process of restructuring questions of structure are of less importance to the local citizen than is the performance of local government, and in particular its ability to be responsive to political demands. Following this, recognising that many of them were relatively large and could lack accessibility, unitary councils were given a legal obligation to devise decentralisation proposals which would improve their responsiveness and accountability. As ever, the ultimate test for the success of government policy lay in how well local government complied and whether the result over the long term meets public demands.

References

Adam Smith Institute (1989) *Shedding a Tier: Reforming Scotland's Local Government.* Glasgow: Adam Smith Institute.

Boyne, G. and Law, J. (1993) 'Bidding for unitary status: an evaluation of the contest in Wales.' *Local Government Studies 19*, 4, 537–557.

COSLA (1992) *The Future of Local Government in Scotland. Response to the Consultation Paper.* Edinburgh: COSLA.

COSLA (1993) *Local Government Reform: A Summary of Non-Local Authority Responses.* Edinburgh: COSLA.

Department of the Environment (1992) *Policy Guidance to the Local Government Commission in England.* London: Department of the Environment.

Leach, S., Davis, H., Game, C. and Skelcher, C. (1991) *After Abolition.* Birmingham: INLOGOV, University of Birmingham.

Lloyd, M.G. (1994) 'Learning from experience: regional reports and local government organisation in Scotland.' *Local Government Policy-Making 21*, 2, 34–40.

McNulty, D. (1995) *Referenda and Citizen's Ballots.* Commission for Local Democracy Report No. 15. London: Commission for Local Democracy.

Midwinter, A. (1992) 'The review of local government in Scotland – a critical perspective.' *Local Government Studies 18*, 2, 44–54.

MORI (1994) 'Community identity and the Local Government Review.' *British Public Opinion XVII*, 2, 6–7.

Scottish Office (1991) *The Case for Change.* Edinburgh: Scottish Office.

Scottish Office (1992) *The Structure of Local Government in Scotland: Shaping the New Councils.* Edinburgh: Scottish Office.

Scottish Office (1995) *Baseline Study of Public Knowledge and Perceptions of Local Government in Scotland.* Edinburgh: Scottish Office Central Research Unit.

Stodart Report (1981) *Committee of Enquiry into Local Government in Scotland.* Cm 8115. Edinburgh: HMSO.

Wheatley Report (1969) *Royal Commission on Local Government in Scotland.* Edinburgh: HMSO.

Young, R. (1984) 'Scottish local government: what future?' In D. McCrone (ed) *The Scottish Government Yearbook 1984.* Edinburgh: University of Edinburgh.

Further reading

Commission for Local Democracy (1995) *Taking Charge: The Rebirth of Local Democracy.* London: Commission for Local Democracy and Municipal Journal Books.

McCormick, J. and Paddison, R. (1993) 'Mr. Lang's blueprint for Scotland.' *Local Government Chronicle*, 23 July.

Rallings, C., Temple, M. and Thrasher, M. (1994) *Community Identity and Participation in Local Democracy.* Commission for Local Democracy Report No. 1. London: Commission for Local Democracy.

Scottish Local Government Information Unit (1991) Newsletter No.42.

Scottish Office Environment Department (1993) *Shaping the Future – The New Councils.* Cm 2267. Edinburgh: HMSO.

PART II

British Regionalism and the English Dimension

CHAPTER 6

British Regionalism and the Link with Regional Planning

A Perspective on England

L.J. Sharpe

Introduction

Amidst debates on Scottish and Welsh devolution between the late nineteenth century and the 1970s, regionalism in England was not a subject which merited much serious public attention. Strong regional identities existed, but they seldom found political expression and there was little agreement at a popular level over boundaries or the role of regions in government. There was little that approached the regional ethnic nationalism that could be said to exist in Scotland and Wales. Yet during the post-Second World War period, regional government became a common feature of many West European states. Indeed if we extend the concept as a 'decision space' to include intermediate government in general – the meso, that is, the level between basic communal, or municipal, government and central government *per se* – it became virtually universal among the danger West European states (Sharpe 1993a).

Significantly, the pressures exerted by regional ethnic nationalism, which played such an important part in the continent, were often absent. Instead quite different functional pressures for regional planning played a critical role. From the 1960s Britain shared in the experience of these planning pressures, and in the absence of other stimulants of regionalism, this was particularly important for creating a debate about the need for regional capacity in England. This chapter addresses the origins and implications of that debate. Section one explains the errors of those who predicted that the development of modern West European states would be characterised by centralisation, indicating the origins of contrary tendencies towards decentralisation. Section two then explains the role of planning and its impact on regionalism in Britain, and thus in England, in the 1960s and 1970s. The third section discusses the decline of regional planning in the 1980s and assesses the pressures that emerged, nevertheless, to promote regional reform in England in the early 1990s. Overall, the chapter suggests that whilst regional planning was important for stimulating debate, the pressures for English regionalism remained brittle in the 1960s and 1970s, and appeared even less robust in the early to mid 1990s.

The origins of regionalism: the errors of the centralisation thesis

Decentralisation of the modern unitary state was not one of its predicted characteristics for a whole host of distinguished social scientists in the past from Mill to Marx, rather the reverse: centralisation was the future. Laski, for one among many, was confident in the late 1930s that the unitary state would remain the norm and that its centralisation was an inevitable consequence of modern political development. Indeed, where federalism existed he predicted its demise (Laski 1939). The key assumption of the centralisation thesis, which almost certainly profoundly affected Laski's prediction, was that centralisation of government was essential for equalisation. In this view, equalisation implemented by the centre via public services and progressive income taxes was the key feature of the welfare state since it sought to minimise the impact of both the life cycle and trade cycle on the individual, thus ensuring a general minimum standard of welfare for all. This being so, and given both the inequality of resources between sub-national areas and evidence that prosperity and need were often in an inverse relationship, it was assumed that centralisation would become a key feature of the developing welfare state.

There were, however, three problems with this perspective. First, centralisation in practice was not always the best path to equalisation. In some cases in order to equalise personal life chances the welfare state had to strengthen decentralised institutions in order to make them capable of providing services at least to some national minimum standard (Hansen 1993). Equally, the shift from visible and progressive income tax to indirect and much less progressive taxes – a trend which was common among all Western states – weakened the sheer capacity of the centre to redistribute, thus breaking the link between centralisation and equalisation. In short, in order to redistribute on a just basis, the centre's source of revenue had itself to be raised on a progressive basis.

Second, the centralisation thesis was also faulty in the sense that it was almost wholly economically determinist and thus downgraded the autonomy of the political system in a democracy. This is not to say that the economy, as it unified and specialised, did not centralise; it did. The error lay in the assumption that the political system would, as a mere epiphenomenon of economic forces, centralise as well. In fact, as peripheries declined economically and their cultures were metropolitanised, so they sought political means to counteract this trend by demanding decentralised defensive institutions (Sharpe 1993a).

This expression of the autonomy of the political system leads us to the third source of criticism of the centralisation thesis, and this has to do with what may be called 'democratic maturation'. At its heart, citizenship in a democracy implies two rights for each citizen: the right to develop his talents to the fullest and the right to identity (Rokkan and Urwin 1983, p.191). The first right is, of course, on all fours with the equalisation imperative of the welfare state discussed earlier, but the second implies the right to choose one's nationality or ethnicity. In a multi-cultural society (i.e. most democracies) this right to identity may mean a rejection of the dominant culture of the state in favour of a political system which recognises the right of minorities to have special institutional arrangements which recognise their distinctiveness. Moreover, the right to identity might also imply that if the citizen has the right to select his leaders and affect their policies, he must also have the right to choose the arena (i.e. territorial area) in which such choices are to be made.

What the economic determinist centralisation thesis left out of the account was that this second right intensified as democratic modes and practices took hold in society. In short, all democracies have had a dynamic derived from the length of time that their democracy has been established. The more mature the democracy, the more strongly the two rights are asserted. This process was especially evident in minority culture peripheries, for it was spurred on by the economic peripheralisation generated by the undoubted centralisation of the economy. The onward march of democracy throughout the world led not only to a growing number of sovereign states (the total number has trebled since the creation of the United Nations), but also to an increasing degree of decentralisation in existing states. Here probably lies the origin of the so-called 'unexpected revolution' that so surprised scholars in the early 1960s, when regional ethnic nationalism seemed suddenly to appear in the multi-cultural states of the West.

It is possible to add a further error in the centralisation thesis which also had its origins in the failure to recognise the dynamics of the process of democratic maturation. This was the strong public dissatisfaction with the centralisation inherent in the early model of the post-Second World War welfare state, especially in Scandinavia. This dissatisfaction manifested itself in two broad ways. First, there was a conscious attempt to transfer power to the sub-national level; perhaps the extreme case being Denmark, where this resulted in over 60 per cent of public sector expenditure being conducted at the local government level (Kjellberg 1988). However, it was clearly evident in the rest of Scandinavia as well, where there were such developments as the 'free commune' and 'free county' movements (Rose 1990). The second major change in response to public dissatisfaction with the early welfare state was *privatisation*, which was common throughout the West, especially in the UK, from the early 1980s. In this case there was no transfer within the public sector (from centre to locality), but rather transfer out of the public sector to the market. Perhaps both changes can be seen as a shift from the essentially centralist notion of *need*, that is something defined and tackled by the central government, to the concept of *preferences*; that is to say something desired from the bottom up, by the consumer of public services.

In reality, the modern Western state decentralised in the final quarter of the twentieth century against all predictions to the contrary. Insofar as expenditure patterns of different levels of government were a measure of power distribution, the decentralist trend was confirmed, certainly for the immediate post-Second World War period (1950–73), by the clear rise in the sub-national level of government's share of total public expenditure, which rose in 22 Western states as compared with central (or federal) government (Sharpe 1988). Only in 2 of the 22 (Ireland and Switzerland) did the central share of total government expenditure not consistently decline over this period. The median decline of the centre's share for the period for the whole group was 16.1 percentage points. This decentralist shift slowed down during the later, post-oil shock, period but the trend was maintained nonetheless (Sharpe 1988). To what extent these decentralising trends were in response to the democratic maturation process is impossible to assess. However, it seems likely that they were, given the overt decentralist trends in Scandinavia just discussed and not dissimilar trends in Southern Europe. These latter trends were manifested in the creation of regional governments in Italy and France following the social upheavals of the 'hot autumn' in Italy and '*les evenements*' in France, not to mention the dissolution of Belgium into a federal state.

To return to our starting point, which was to attempt to explain the near universality of meso growth or its refurbishment in Western Europe, it is difficult not to conclude that the origin of the trend was largely political. That is to say, the Western state decentralised as a result of various popular pressures: the onward march of democracy, it seems, led to decentralisation, and that link viewed in historical terms should not surprise us. After all, despite usually being cast as the star of the democratic drama, the individual citizen in reality has had very little purchase on his government. Indeed, in most democracies – even the smallest – his influence has usually been minuscule. It should therefore be expected that as the individual over time became more aware of his marginality he sought to remedy it. Decentralisation offered as good an opportunity as any for such remedial action. This was because decentralised government involved dividing up power so that it was more accessible to the average citizen and also because it offered additional opportunities, besides his vote at national elections, to participate. Indeed, it vastly multiplied the opportunities to become an elected member who actually participated in government, from the 500 or so members, say, of the national legislature to the many thousands manning local councils up and down the national state. In short, decentralisation came to be seen as the future for most democracies, whatever the impact of the 'right to identity' strand of the democratic ideal.

The origins of regionalism: the role of planning

Yet having made a strong case for the *political* origins of regionalism, I wish now to emphasise in the rest of the chapter that political factors were not the whole story. This will not be to refute the impact, for example, of the usually cited regional ethnic nationalism for other Western states. But for the UK there were additional, what may be called functional, factors which in conventional analyses tend to be played down because they do not seem so interesting, or as important, as the pulling and hauling of competing ethnic groups. The additional factor I wish to emphasise as making a key contribution to regionalism is planning, whether it be land use or economic. Taking the UK as an exemplar, I will seek to show that the perceived needs of planning also played a critical role in bringing regionalism to the fore in the UK, especially England, if not, as in some other countries, actually precipitating regional government.

First we must begin with some conceptual clarifications. Broadly speaking, when referring to the concept of the planning region as a determinant of politico-administrative boundaries, it is possible to identify two distinct types of region (Sharpe 1972). The first may be called the *city region* or *nodal region* (Hall 1970). The region in this sense is the 'influence area' of a, usually large, urban centre. That is to say, it is an urban-centred area and its boundary is determined by the extent to which the territory surrounding the urban centre is tributary to it, that is, in terms of journey to work, shopping and services, economic links and so forth (Dickinson 1962). In short, the city regional government seeks to internalise all the externalities that the urban centre at its core generates. It is essentially a concept which, as Bennett has argued, seeks to ascertain the 'true' extent of the modern city in socio-economic terms as opposed to the concept of a city in purely bricks and mortar terms, so that the resulting boundary 'tends to increase administrative size beyond the range of normal activities of the majority of people and emphasises work (or production) over social objectives' (Bennett 1989).

This concept was of considerable importance in the discussion of redesigning, or modernising, local government in the 1960s (Royal Commission 1969), although few modernisation schemes in fact actually applied the concept in all its rigour for the reasons given in the quotation from Bennett. Important as the city region concept was in determining politico-administrative boundaries, it is not a concept of regionalism I wish to apply further in this chapter. The concept of regionalism we will be concerned with is the somewhat different, *economic planning region*. In general, this tends to be more extensive than the typical city region, and its main application was as a component of the new level of state economic planning that emerged in Western Europe in the late 1950s and early 1960s. Unlike the city region, the configuration of the economic planning region is not determined by uniform technical criteria such as the journey to work or labour density, but by a varying mixture of traditional, political and economic criteria (Despicht undated). Very occasionally, a genuine city region may be designated as an economic planning region, quite often because even the economic planning region may require some nodality. In the main, it is fair to say that in the determination of the boundaries of the economic planning region the rule of thumb predominates. Part of the reason for the heterogeneity of the determinants of an economic planning region is that, unlike the city region, there has to be a uniform level of government covering the whole territorial extent of the state, and thus some regions end up being to all intents and purposes 'residuals' that are left over after more coherently economic or political regions have, as it were, chosen their own boundaries. It follows that such residual regions lack a very high degree of homogeneity of any kind.

Surveying the vast literature on regional government and politics around the Western world, it becomes clear that, insofar as that literature has been concerned with the causes of regional ethnic nationalism, as we have noted, it has usually been identified as being the primary cause (see, for example, Esman 1977; Rokkan and Urwin 1983; Sharpe 1993b; Tiriakin and Rogowski 1985). To repeat, the point I wish to emphasise is not to deny the link between regional ethnic nationalism and the emergence of regional government, but rather to claim that if the UK, and especially the English, experience is at all typical, the development of regionalism had a number of other causes as well, including, as we shall see, local government modernisation, conscious political decentralisation and economic modernisation (Viot 1971).

Why was this so? At the risk of over-simplification, there was the profound influence of the French indicative planning model which became popular in Western Europe in the early 1960s, especially in Belgium, Italy, Spain and the UK. It must be emphasised in parentheses that such over-simplification is risky for regional planning in that the indicative model did not have a very coherent rationale. Moreover, discussion of planning in the abstract is peculiarly susceptible to a great deal of largely meaningless verbiage (Faludi 1973). When planning is allied with regionalism this tendency is even stronger. As a European Commission document asserted in 1969, 'regional policy has become fashionable: in spite of (or perhaps because of) this; it is not always quite clear what it is all about' (Viot 1971). Moreover, even in France, the virtual inventor of the system, one cannot help but be struck by the absence of coherence of objectives or precision of purpose in the setting up of the regional machinery if accounts in English are any guide (Viot 1971).

Bearing such cautionary thoughts in mind, we may say that regional planning was evolved by the French in their concerted aim of modernising the French economy as an alternative to the traditional state-based Gosplan planning model, which had been derived from the Soviet Union and had been popular in Western war-time economies, particularly the British. Whereas the Gosplan model disaggregated the national economy by sectors – for example, the steel industry, the vehicle-building industry, the rubber industry – and implicitly assumed uniform contextual conditions for each, the indicative planning model disaggregated the economy *territorially* by region on the grounds that context was vital. For example, if overall economic growth was to be achieved government intervention needed to be fundamentally different in the declining Midi than it did in the vibrant Greater Paris area. The Midi may have needed heavy state investment as a boost to its largely run-down agricultural economy, whereas Greater Paris may have needed governmental intervention in order to *suppress* its economy because of the dangers of wage-push inflation. In order to achieve such flexibility the indicative model required that it was possible for government to pursue *different* policies on each region in the name of a unified overall policy aim of faster economic growth. Moreover, also unlike the Gosplan model, the task was not simply that of mobilising resources in relation to a consensus (forced or unforced) over goals, but of achieving overall economic growth in a modern democracy where consent was paramount and there was no agreement on overall goals. Thus indicative planning involved public consultation and co-operation at all stages of the planning process. The most important of such consultation processes in the context of this chapter was the creation in the 1960s of centrally appointed 'missions' of civil servants at the regional level in co-operation with representative bodies of the region, the collective task of which was to draw up a regional plan within the parameters set by the centre. The role of the regional machinery was largely advisory, as the following official task description of the British case indicates:

> 1 to work out broad objectives for each region and so provide a comprehensive framework within which decisions in particular sectors can be taken;
>
> 2 to advise on the formulation of national policies where these can significantly affect the regions;
>
> 3 to advise on the application in the regions of national policy,
>
> 4 to stimulate interest within each region and build up a common approach within each region to its problems. (Cullingworth 1974)

Regional planning in Britain in the 1960s very quickly became a fashionable activity in government, the popularity of which far outstripped the capacity of either its practitioners or promoters' capacity to define clearly what they were up to. It was developed subsequently not only through the establishment of regional economic planning councils, but also through structure and local planning roles for local authorities and increases in grants of regional aid. One of the reasons for this popularity was what can only be called the 'futurism neurosis', that is to say, the fear that if government failed to ascertain the future and plan for it, costly disaster would ensue. To recognise the importance of planning was to recognise the new dynamism of the post-war economy. In the planning field this fear was engendered by the discovery in the early 1960s that urbanisation had proceeded during the 1950s at a pace that no one had previously even dreamt of and that such growth was creating urban agglomerations which required massive amounts of infrastructural public investment. These agglomerations were on a vast territorial scale and this fact led to the other strand of the futurism neurosis which was the assumption that the sense of locality was dead. The new community form, it was argued, was on a regional and not a local scale since most people, by at least the year 2000 if not sooner, would have personal means of transport and this meant a much more dispersed lifestyle. The normal restraints limiting the growth of urban centres were, in short, being torn asunder. The operative community was, it was argued, inescapably regional.

Another source of regional planning's modishness was that the region came to be seen as the territorial unit best suited to modern production methods. This claim soon got mixed up with the need to decentralise the state itself. Indeed regional government came to be seen by some as a kind of panacea for most of the alleged ills of industrial democracies. Very little real evidence was produced for all of these assumptions and predictions, and none of them took cognisance of territorial subjective attitudes – the sense of regional identity among the population – which might reasonably have been thought to be an essential prerequisite of regional government.

The crucial feature of the application of regional planning in Britain in the mid 1960s for the purposes of this chapter was that it had the effect of settling the crucial problem of *boundaries*, especially in England. Had the new regional machinery started with boundary definition there could have been a lengthy period of wrangling, with possibly permanent, perhaps irreconcilable, animosities of territorial groupings being established. This possibility was all the greater given the highly problematic criteria involved. But the swift establishment of a set of boundaries at a point when no one was quite sure what the whole process was about, or what was at stake, gave the new boundaries a surprising degree of legitimacy and stability. Of course, it was not always plain sailing elsewhere. In France, for example, the regional pattern was deliberately designed so as to cut across ancient provinces so that both the traditional Normandy and Brittany provinces were divided into two. Less politically threatening regions and the ancient Langue d'Oc province were completely ignored. In Britain no such tactic was open to the centre since the boundaries of Wales and Scotland were already far too well established and could not possibly be brushed aside in the French manner. Nonetheless, very much enlarged, and thus rival, counties within the new regions of Wales and Scotland were created, and in the Scottish case were actually called regions. These potential rivals, however, had little impact on the enhancement of Scotland and Wales as unified territorial actors in British politics, a process exemplified by the ease with which the 'Scottish economy' and 'Welsh economy' became established concepts in political discourse very soon after the designation of the two areas as being regions, despite the fact that in reality they embraced a highly fragmented economic structures with little internal economic coherence.

The second contribution that the new economic planning institutions gave to the evolution of regionalism was the implied official recognition that post-war economic growth had not been shared uniformly throughout the state. In short, the new regional planning apparatus brought on to the political agenda the existence of extensive regional inequality. A new regional politics was thereby born which combined the new-style French planning for economic growth with the traditional British planning process which sought to equalise the disparities between the poor peripheral regions of the North and West and the highly prosperous South East. This latter process had its origins in the policies launched in the 1930s to combat the highly uneven impact of the slump. In linking these two planning traditions the popularity of the new planning system was considerably strengthened. This crucial mixture of egalitarian and economic efficiency objectives has dominated regional planning in Britain ever since.

In a rather more abstract sense the new regional machinery provided a very welcome degree of intellectual *terra firma* by appearing to reconcile two quite different planning forms as well. These were *land-use planning* (town and country or physical planning in British parlance), that is the planning of investment in space; and *economic planning* – the planning of investment over time (Viot 1971). Not only were the two types of planning reconciled, but so too were the two levels of government involved: central governmental economic planning and local governmental physical planning. In Britain, where economic planning and physical planning had arisen and were developed in profoundly separate institutional settings, the reconciliation was doubly important. The region could be seen as the buckle which joined the two systems, thus co-ordinating them into an apparently coherent system of government intervention. Another way of putting this is to define regional planning from the centre's perspective as the allocation of investment programmes between regions. From the regions' perspective, regional planning became the distribution of such central largesse (or private sector investment) within the region.

All three of these factors – boundary-making, official recognition of regional inequality and the apparent linking of the two planning systems – gave the regional movement in Britain an added strength that had nothing necessarily to do with the essentially political factors associated with regional ethnic nationalism. There were additional re-enforcing factors in some states. In the southern sector of Western Europe, for example, where reformed local government structures were particularly difficult to effect, the creation of regions took the pressure off the formal local government system to adapt to the pressures of suburbanisation and the problems of externalities. Regional government thus became a relatively painless way of resolving the enormously difficult political problem of locally-based resistance to radical boundary change of local government (Sharpe 1993a).

The decline of planning and the new English regionalism

There was clearly a strong link between the development of regionalism in Britain in the 1960s and the imperatives of planning. This persisted in the 1970s. However, regional planning as a government activity declined after 1979. The reasons for this were threefold. First, there was a marked change in the ideology of central government after Mrs Thatcher's victory at the 1979 general election. Governmental hostility to planning was part and parcel of its stated preferences for the market over government as a determinant of land use and was reflected in all levels of planning. One example of this anti-planning ethos was the abolition of the Regional Economic Planning Councils in 1979. Even more dramatic was the abolition of the Greater London Council and the six Metropolitan Councils in the mid 1980s, largely on the grounds that their primary planning functions were no longer relevant. Similar hostility to planning was also clearly reflected in the Thatcher government's abolition of the Regional Development Grant in 1988, which was a major blow to the whole process of regional economic planning. Overall, the amount of regional industrial aid from the centre declined from £0.8 billion in 1980 to £0.2 billion by 1991. As one group of observers summarised the position on regional planning in 1992:

> Over the past ten years regional development agencies in the UK have experienced a complete transformation of their powers and functions. Employment has been downgraded as an objective of policy. Interventionist powers, particularly of direct investment in the private sector and of factory building have been curtailed. Regional development agencies have become much more market-orientated seeking to support private business and encourage entrepreneurship. They have been required to involve the private sector in most of their own economic development functions and to dispose of land property and investments. (Danson *et al.* 1992)

A similar attack on planning at another level was the downgrading of the local structure plan.

A second reason for the decline in planning was the ending of the post-war Western boom following the quadrupling of the crude oil price in the 1970s. The recession which followed quickly raised the level of unemployment throughout Britain, so that the disparity between the poor peripheral regions and the South could no longer be exemplified by the markedly different unemployment rates, despite the fact that the overall prosperity gap between the poorer and richer regions continued to widen. In short, the arrival of universal unemployment at levels hitherto unknown since the 1930s seriously weakened the underlying employment rationale of regional policy. Apparently unable to do much to alleviate the new unemployment level, government had suddenly, it seemed, become less important.

The final aspect of the collapse of conventional regional economic planning policy was the realisation by the 1980s that regional planning had largely ignored what was emerging as the most urgent planning issue: the decay and degradation of the inner cities. Regional planning in Britain had always been profoundly anti-urban and in consequence indifferent to the large industrial city, as the immense importance allocated to the New Towns in regional planning had up until the 1980s amply testified. Some idea of this strange indifference, perhaps hostility, to the inner city in the old regional planning ideology can be gleaned from a 100-page summary by a group of experts on regional planning policy published in 1970. Nowhere in the whole study was the inner city so much as even mentioned (Labour Party 1970). Yet by the early 1980s such had been the decline of the inner cities, a process exacerbated by the failure of public housing schemes constructed in the 1960s, that government action was felt to be essential. In consequence there occurred a massive switch of resources from the traditional regional aid policies to the inner cities. The combined effects of these three changes had the effect, at least in England, of seriously diminishing formal regional planning as a governmental policy by the mid 1990s.

However, despite the fact that regional planning as an all-embracing approach of central government to include regional economic planning, land-use planning and specifically regionalist administrative structures, was seriously downplayed from the late 1970s, regionalism became a major political issue again in the early 1990s. Both the Labour and Liberal Democrat Parties showed interest in creating regional government in England. Whatever the reason for this renewed popularity for English regionalism, it certainly had very little to do with economic planning. So what were its sources and how seriously should it be treated? Four factors appear to have been important.

One clear causal factor was the continued popularity of devolution (i.e. regional government) in Scotland and Wales. If devolution was to occur then governments for English regions were needed to ensure uniformity for the whole state. The need for such uniformity may have been regarded as being all the more urgent when considerations of representational equity were taken into account. For example, it was recognised that one key argument against the asymmetric granting of regional autonomy only to Scotland and Wales was that in such circumstances it would be unfair to the English electorate, whose MPs would be denied much say on Scottish and Welsh issues (because they were devolved), that Scottish and Welsh MPs would be able to participate in the formulation of all-English legislation in the House of Commons. Another equity question arose because of the extra MPs that both Scotland and Wales enjoyed (in Scotland's case some 23% more than the English average). It was difficult to envisage that asymmetry could persist as well as the extra MPs. Creating regional assemblies in England were then seen as a neat way of resolving both of the equity problems as well as meeting the demands of incipient regional movements in England such as the campaign for a Northern assembly. It was recognised, however, that such a solution would not be perfect if the powers of English regional authorities differed from those of the Scottish and Welsh assemblies. Nor could it resolve all other inequities in the system, such as the consistently higher central financial aid that both Scotland and Wales received. For example, during the period from 1972 to 1987 Scotland and Wales combined accounted for no less than 47.4 per cent of regional cash grants from the centre despite having only 15 per cent of the total UK population (Anderson 1992).

A second reason for the relative popularity of regional government in the first half of the 1990s was the increasing public concern in England at the transfer of public decision-making to non-governmental organisations (quangos) lacking any real public accountability. This process, which was largely derived from a Thatcherite attack on local government, was seen, quite correctly, as an attack on democracy. Since it occurred mostly at the sub-national level, creating regional government was seen as a method for rescuing the transferred services and restoring them to the democratic fold (Jenkins 1995). Allied to this anti-quango case for regionalism was the emergence of a new English regional level of deconcentrated central government, namely the Government Offices of the Regions, created in April 1994. The argument was that the policy integration that these new institutions were intended to achieve between the central Departments of Environment, Transport, and Employment and Education could be devolved to a new elected regional government and would be eminently suitable for it.

Third, we must take account of the impact on opposition party thinking of EU regional policies which became increasingly important after Britain joined in 1973, such that by the mid 1990s these policies absorbed the largest proportion of the EU's budget after the Common Agricultural Policy. The argument in this case was that Britain lost some of these funds because, unlike Belgium, France, Italy and Spain, it lacked a formal regional tier of government. Moreover, British central government, because of the lack of a regional tier, was tempted, despite EU displeasure, into incorporating EU regional funds into its own regional grant arrangements. Again the result was a loss of resources to the regions (Hogwood 1995; Mawson 1996; Tindale 1995).

A final factor enhancing regionalism in Britain as a whole was what may be called the decentralist *Weltanschauung* alluded to at the outset of this chapter. Most unitary Western states, as we noted, had decentralised by the early 1990s and in Western Europe almost all the major unitary states – France, Italy, Spain and Belgium – had created a new regional tier of government; in the case of Belgium to the point of transforming the state into a federation. In short, regionalism was very much an international fashion and as such had a special appeal in Britain, which never lacks vociferous support from that section of public opinion which is for ever anxious to ensure that Britain does not 'fall behind' any international trend in government of which they approve. In particular, creating regions was seen as an essential change that would help to shore up Britain's faltering reputation as a fully committed member of the EU.

Conclusions

To sum up, if the British experience is any guide in the formation of regional, or meso, government in Europe, we must also accord some causal role to indicative planning. It was this phenomenon which first helped to make regionalism so popular in the international market-place of fashionable governmental institutional innovation in the 1960s. In fact the concept of the region took on what can only be described as a glamorous aura in many Western states, and became associated with all that was thought to be good and true among liberal reformers. It was, paradoxically, all the more alluring because of its intrinsic vagueness. No one who lived through the formative period of regionalism in the early 1960s, if only as a peripheral observer of regional planning, can fail to forget that it was a concept which seemed to be on everyone's lips, but which was understood by very few. Being linked to economic growth, to decentralisation and to democratisation gave the regional concept a cachet that was almost irresistible at the time. Although all of these associations declined, and regional planning as an all-embracing approach fell out of favour in Britain from the 1970s, the link with economic regeneration and equality between regions still sustained regional government in those states which developed formal regional systems, such as France, Italy and Spain. It was especially alive in those regions of these three countries that had little in the way of ethnic national movements, and perhaps even lacked much sense of identity.

The sustaining of the regional idea in the 1960s and 1970s, in particular in England, owed much to the development of indicative planning. Consequently, the decline of the regional idea in the 1980s was simultaneous with the abandonment of the regional planning machinery by the Thatcher governments. Yet the regional idea in England re-emerged in the early 1990s without any re-emergent all-embracing planning movement, but instead because of a number of other reasons. In comparison, these did not appear to make a compelling case for English regional government in its own right. For example, a substantial part of the case for English regional government was its necessity as a complement to Scottish and Welsh devolution. There was, nevertheless, some basis to the campaign. In particular, a re-emergent English regionalism owed a great deal to the growing desire for more democracy at the decentralised level to counter the growth of sub-national quangos, which were deemed to lack any local accountability. In this sense regional government was seen as a way of regaining some sub-national democracy after all the losses sustained after Mrs Thatcher's accession to power in 1979. It remained to be seen, however, whether this rather more general pressure for regionalisation in the 1990s than was the case in the 1960s and 1970s would be sufficient to lead to the creation of an entirely new regional level of government; or, indeed, whether different pressures could be identified which would bolster the case for making such an outcome more likely.

References

Anderson, J.J. (1992) *The Territorial Imperative.* Cambridge: Cambridge University Press, Table 4.1.

Bennett, R. (1989) (ed) *Territory and Administration in Europe.* London: Pinter.

Cullingworth, B. (1974) *Town and Country Planning in Britain.* London: Allen and Unwin.

Danson, M.W. (1992) 'Regional development agencies in the UK.' In R. Martin and P. Townroe (eds) *Regional Development in the 1990s.* London: Regional Studies Association.

Despicht, N. (n.d.) 'Background to Europe's regional problem.' In A. Niel (ed) *Priorities in Regional Development.* Peterlee Development Corporation.

Dickinson, R.E. (1962) *The City Region in Western Europe.* London: Routledge.

Esman, M.J. (ed) (1977) *Ethnic Conflict in the Western World.* Ithaca: Cornell University Press.

Faludi, A. (1973) *Planning Theory.* Oxford: Pergamon Press.

Hall, P. (1970) *The Theory and Practice of Regional Planning.* London: Pemberton.

Hansen, T. (1993) 'Intermediate-level reforms and the development of the Norwegian welfare state.' In L.J. Sharpe (ed) *The Rise of Meso Government in Europe.* London: Sage.

Hogwood, B.W. (1995) *The Integrated Regional Offices and the Single Regeneration Budget.* London: Commission for Local Democracy Research Report No. 13.

Jenkins, S. (1995) *Accountable to None.* London: Hamish Hamilton.

Kjellberg, F. (1988) 'Local government and the welfare state: reorganisation in Scandinavia.' In B. Dente and F. Kjellberg (eds) *The Dynamics of Institutional Change.* London: Sage.

Labour Party (1970) *Regional Planning Policy.* London: Labour Party.

Laski, H.J. (1939) 'The obsolescence of federalism.' *The New Republic 98,* 367.

Mawson, J. (1995) 'The re-emergence of the regional agenda in the English regions: new patterns of urban and regional governance?' *Local Economy 10,* 4.

Rokkan, S. and Urwin, D. (eds) (1983) *Economy, Territory and Identity.* London: Sage.

Rose, L.E. (1990) 'Nordic free-commune experiments: increased local autonomy or continued central control?' In D. King and J. Pierre (eds) *Challenges to Local Government.* London: Sage.

Royal Commission on Local Government in England (1969) 'Vol II. Memorandum of Dissent by D. Senior, one of the most systematic and forceful treatises advocating the city regional concept for local government modernisation.' Cmnd 4040. London: HMSO.

Sharpe, L.J. (1972) 'British politics and the two regionalisms.' In W. Wright and D. Stewart (eds) *The Exploding City.* Edinburgh: Edinburgh University Press.

Sharpe, L.J. (1988) 'The growth and decentralisation of the modern democratic state.' *European Journal of Political Research 16,* 3.

Sharpe, L.J. (ed) (1993) *The Rise of Meso Government in Europe.* London: Sage.

Sharpe, L.J. (1993). 'The European meso: an appraisal.' In L.J. Sharpe (ed) *The Rise of Meso Government.* London: Sage.

Tindale, S. (1995) *The Government of the English Regions – Options for Reform.* London: Institute for Public Policy Research.

Tiriakin, E. and Rogowski, R. (eds) (1985) *The New Nationalism of the Developed West.* Boston: Allen and Unwin.

Viot, P. (1971) 'Through regional planning towards regional administration.' In E. Kalk (ed) *Regional Planning and Regional Government in Europe.* The Hague: IULA.

CHAPTER 7

The Shifting Institutional Framework of the English Regions

The Role of Conservative Policy

Murray Stewart

Introduction

The historic fragility of English regionalism is widely recognised. No democratic governmental form developed at the regional level and until the 1990s there was negligible political debate. Indeed, there was little agreement about the existence or nature of regional identities, a fact reflected by overlapping and confusing definitions of regions which led to a multiplicity of mutually inconsistent boundary overlays. The region was seldom seen as a focus for the exercise of administrative discretion or professional expertise; in terms of civil service careers it was at best a stepping stone, at worst a graveyard.

For some, indeed, there existed only what Brian Robson has termed a, 'more punctiform economic geography in which regional advantage counts for less but attributes of localities matter more' (Robson 1993, p.1). Sharpe has consistently demonstrated the frailty of regional forces and the difficulties in building regionalism in an essentially unitary state dominated by a sovereign parliament (see Chapter 6). Theoretical interpretations of the weakness of the region are paralleled by a view held by many of the minimal practical importance of regional administration and the insignificance of what might be regarded as the main manifestation of regional planning – regional planning guidance.

The Thatcher years exemplified the weakness of the regional idea. A philosophical attachment to the unitary state and parliamentary sovereignty, an absence of any real sense of place or of spatial differences within Britain, a pathological dislike of Europe (with its obvious attempts to build a Europe of the Regions), and the dismantling of all machinery concerned with strategic or long-term planning (including most obviously the Greater London Council and the Metropolitan County Councils), all militated against any development of regionalism. Small wonder then that commentators in the 1980s frequently referred to a 'regional vacuum' in England.

In the first half of the 1990s, however, there was a revival of regionalism fuelled as ever by the Scottish and Welsh devolution debate but also by recognition of the pressures to sustain visibility and presence within the European political debate. Indeed, there was rather more to this development than some commentators appreciated, a development whose character may be hypothesised in terms of a struggle to fill the regional vacuum. This was not a struggle which stemmed from the sudden rediscovery of the inherent importance and identity of English regions. It was rather a struggle between four actors, each seeking for different reasons to occupy territory perceived to be empty, or at least to limit the ability of others to extend their sphere of influence and power. Figure 7.1 illustrates this territory in the most simple form.

Figure 7.1 The regional actors in Britain

The struggle was over the resources and the political and administrative power which could be deployed at the regional level. The prize at stake was influence and control over what may be discovered as an important arena of British territorial politics. The actors were four: the European Union, Westminster (the political parties at national level), Whitehall (the civil service) and 'Localities' (local authorities, Training and Enterprise Councils, Chambers of Commerce and other organisations operating, at the sub-regional level, the system increasingly known as 'local governance'). The focus of this chapter is the particular institutional arrangements which were designed for the mediation of these competing interests in the early to mid 1990s.

In focusing upon institutional arrangements the chapter echoes those theoretical perspectives which emphasise the relationship between the particular form and function of organisational arrangements and the wider structures of power within which they are established. Benson, for example, links the concept of the policy sector with a hierarchy of levels of analysis – the rules of structure formation, the structures of interest representation and finally the organisational arrangements within the sector (Benson 1983). Only exceptionally applied to the territorial distribution of power (Mawson and Skelcher 1980), as opposed to its employment in relation to specific policy sectors such as education, Benson's framework emphasises the importance of institutional arrangements in both shaping the policy sector and reflecting the dominant interests within that sector.

A different strand of relevant theorising is that which derives from analysis of the implications of post-industrial and/or post-Fordist globalisation for institutional structures, and which links regulation theory to new systems of urban and/or local governance (Jessop 1994; Mayer 1994; Painter 1991). Although regulation theory was developed primarily with reference to national levels of politics and administration, Lipietz' definition of a mode of regulation (1992, p.2) is in principle applicable to sub-national levels: 'An ensemble of norms, institutions, organisational forms, social networks and patterns of conduct which will sustain and guide post-Fordist accumulation regimes'.

That such '*ensembles*' (reflected as regimes, coalitions, networks or partnerships) are the stuff of contemporary local governance is widely accepted. Less widely considered is the extent to which institutional innovation fosters new modes of regulation and dilutes the traditional strength and autonomy of local political forces (Stoker 1994).

This chapter explores the emergence of such a regional mode of regulation, with particular reference to England in the period under discussion. The first section provides a brief assessment of the interests and motivations of the four actors argued to be seeking to colonise the regional space. This establishes in particular the importance of examining the institutional changes which were initiated from, and determined by, Westminster and Whitehall during the period of the second Major government. The second section discusses two such changes through which Conservative policy-makers sought to transform the institutional base for regional governance: first, the creation of the Government Offices of the Regions (GORs) and the Single Regeneration Budget (SRB) (also discussed in Chapter 8), and second, the 1992–96 review of the structure of local government in the shires. A concluding section discusses the ways in which the English regional space during this period was occupied by the centre, ultimately arguing that the shifting institutional framework in the English regions was, therefore, more characterised by centralisation than by a nascent countervailing English regionalism.

Actors at the regional level

The European Union

By the early 1990s the aspirations of the European Commission to bypass the nation state and to establish a Europe of Regions (and perhaps a Europe of Cities) had been widely asserted. Additionally simply to manage relations with the periphery the EU had sought to operate in conjunction with some form of regional system, whether formal or informal. The long-standing commitment to regional policies, to redistribution between growing and declining, richer and poorer regions and to investment in programmes and funding which supported structural change, made this necessary. The EU thus without doubt was interested in reinforcing, and probably co-opting, regional interests.

EU influence at the regional level was enhanced more specifically by the way in which the long-standing argument between Brussels and the UK government over additionality was resolved during the early 1990s, largely it appears in the favour of Brussels. By the terms of the agreement, Structural Fund grants could continue to be technically treated as public expenditure by the government but they had to be acknowledged as additional to planned national expenditure. In this approach the government was obliged to identify forecast Structural Fund receipts separately from existing programmes. Thus the public expenditure planning totals for regeneration programmes within the responsibility of the Department of the Environment (DoE), for example, had to make allowance for £563 million of European Regional Development Fund grants (including £399 million local authority credit approvals) in the three years from 1995–96, over and above the more specific expenditure programmes within particular programme budgets (DoE 1995). Consequently public expenditure planning totals were in principle larger than they would otherwise have been, although it is impossible to judge whether, in order to accommodate Structural Fund grants within the overall planning total, it was decided that cuts would have to be made elsewhere. Nevertheless, following the agreement the government sought a higher take-up of available Structural Fund grants, and the Single Regeneration Budget in England and other domestic funds were utilised as matching or leverage funding to claw resources 'back' from Brussels. In order for this to happen, all structural fund bids had to be set within a regional framework. The instrumental impetus from Brussels to the production of regional frameworks thus cannot be underestimated regardless of the political arguments.

Local authorities had themselves long been more aware than Whitehall about the opportunities in Europe, and the establishment of a Brussels office, or at least presence, was relatively common amongst local authorities or groups of authorities in the late 1980s (see Chapter 11). The European Commission did nothing to discourage such direct links, and indeed welcomed any opportunity to bypass national networks and establish an alliance with municipalities. This reflected the common feature of all three-tier systems: that top and bottom combine to squeeze the middle.

In general the establishment of the Committee of the Regions, the doubling of the Structural Funds for the 1994–99 period, the redefinition of Objective 1 and 2 areas, and the use of the Structural Funds to support a new set of Community Initiatives reinforced the European Commission's influence on UK regionalism. Although the proportion of total Structural Funds allocated to the UK fell, the absolute amount rose significantly, accounting for £67 billion in the period 1993–97 (House of Commons 1995). The £900 million funding for the United Kingdom through ten Community Initiatives also had both sectoral and spatial implications.

The creation of the Committee of the Regions by the Maastricht Treaty on European Union, was symbolic of the increasing institutionalisation of regionalism in Europe. The Committee of 189 members (24 from the UK) was given an advisory function at Community level as a mouthpiece for all the regions and local authorities of the EU. It had to be consulted on issues of social policy and education, culture, public health, trans-European networks and transport, telecommunications and energy, and economic and social cohesion. There was some ambivalence about the influence and impact of the Committee within the structures of the EU in its initial phase of operation, meaning that it became an issue as to whether the inter-governmental conference to review the Maastricht Treaty would strengthen its role. Nevertheless if the struggle for its first Presidency and the energy which a Franco/German/Spanish alliance invested in exercising control are any guide, some nations at least saw it as an important focus for resource lobbying. Goetz (1993) reminds us that the German *Länder* were the catalysts for the creation of the Committee of the Regions and look to increase its potential to exercise influence, albeit still within a framework of inter-governmental co-operation.

Westminster

For differing reasons, during the first half of the 1990s a widespread commitment to some form of regional administration, if not regional government, also emerged amongst all the parties at Westminster. For the Labour Party regional government was seen as part of a package of citizenship reforms aiming to reverse the trends of centralisation during the Conservative governments after 1979. Regional government would also offer an appropriate level of government for addressing a number of the strategic economic issues of industrial recovery and for establishing Regional Development Agencies. Finally, for the Labour Party the regional level potentially offered an administrative tier capable of containing and making more accountable regional 'quangoland'. The Labour Party proposals for regional government, ratified in 1996, envisaged a first stage of appointed regional chambers based on existing regions, with members drawn from local government councils and other interests represented on policy sub-committees. Subsequently (and optionally), directly elected governments might be created for regions, not necessarily conforming to existing regions but probably based on areas where unitary authorities were the predominant form of local government.

For the Liberal Democrats the significance of Europe was even more pronounced and the region was seen as representing a tier of government and administration from which the strongest possible European alliances could be built. Looking downwards the Liberal Democrats placed most stress upon community responsiveness and their proposals were expected to reinforce the role of neighbourhood councils, parishes and decentralised area committees within a structure of unitary local authorities.

More intriguing was the development of Conservative interest in administrative regionalism, expressed most publicly in the 1992 manifesto but not widely or formally recognised elsewhere. The genesis of this shift lay less in any conversion to the notion of regions and more in the recognition of a threat from others. Thus there was a concern to head off any real move towards a Europe of the Regions or a Europe of the Cities. The Major government was keen to contain the Brussels influence on regions to a minimal administrative level rather than allow any political thrust to develop. The need to suppress oppositional political voices as well as pre-empt a Euro/Regional alliance was also part of the agenda, just as was the abolition of the Greater London Council and the Metropolitan County Councils in England in the 1980s, and subsequently the abolition of the arch Europhile authority in Scotland, Strathclyde Regional Council.

Second, there was a recognition of the need to counter the perceived threat from other parties, and the consequent need to pre-empt the regional thrust of Labour and Liberal Democrats and to ensure that the Conservatives could not be accused of ignoring the regional dimension to economic management. The naming of 20 ministers as 'Ministers for Cities' in 1990 was indicative at the least of a feeling that territorial politics did matter and that a presence on the periphery was important, whether symbolically or substantively.

Third, there was a Tory precautionary move to occupy the territory thought likely to be left vacant following the demise of the county councils. The latter, until the 1990s traditionally Tory, fulfilled the function of intermediate government between Whitehall and the smaller towns of the shires. The outcome of the Local Government Review (see below) was the retention of the bulk of county councils together with a shift to a greater Conservative voice in those hybrid counties where the Labour vote was hived off into urban unitary authorities. Nevertheless, the emergence of a significant number of unitary, possibly recalcitrant, Labour authorities (as well as a single local authority association) led the Conservative Party to accept the need to continue to control the sub-national ground.

Finally, there was a managerialist justification to the Conservative conversion to some form of regionalism. The contract culture of purchaser, provider and quasi-market had inspired the development of inspection, enforcement and regulation, and raised concerns that some greater governmental presence in the field was necessary. Bulpitt's dual polity thesis might suggest that these functions could have been sensibly left to local interests under central policy supervision (Bulpitt 1983), but the evidence of the 1980s and 1990s is that Conservative governments regarded a presence beyond Whitehall as indispensable to the implementation of their policies, even if Conservative opinion ran counter to increasing the autonomy – or the bureaucracy – attached to regional administration.

Whitehall

Complementary to the thrust of Conservative thinking, and inevitably reflecting the direction of prevailing government strategy, there was also a Whitehall interest. Threatened by rationalisation, by a significant reduction in civil service functions and jobs, and by the advent of Next Steps agencies, the mandarins discovered that there was more to administrative life than the Whitehall village (Heclo and Wildavsky 1974). Theoretically the shake-out from Whitehall allowed only for the retention of a core executive, the central departments of state which co-ordinate policy and establish strategy. Much else was privatised or put out to agencies. This was a major threat to both the administrative and executive traditions of the civil service, and a natural counter move was to colonise at least some additional areas.

It should be remembered that the emphasis in the organisation of Whitehall upon functional division at the expense of territorial integration and co-ordination is a long-standing one deriving from Haldane (Cmnd 9230 1918). The traditional response to problems of lack of co-ordination was to identify the potential lying in the Prime Ministerial role, in cabinet and cabinet committees, in the creation of very large departments, in the establishment of specific innovations (such as the Central Policy Review Staff in the 1970s), and in the expenditure management functions of the Treasury. Indeed, historically discussion of the 'core executive' (Dunleavy and Rhodes 1990) revolved around the question of co-ordination, but territorial co-ordination was generally discussed in terms of the particular circumstances and administrative arrangements in Scotland, Wales and Northern Ireland. Dunleavy's analysis of the architecture of the central state (Dunleavy 1989) recognised the issue of territorial organisation and budgets, but did not address questions of area-based, multi-departmental programmes (such as urban regeneration) or the conceptual nature of inter-departmental and/or interdependent bureau budgets.

However, the introduction in 1994 of the GORs and SRB, and the consequent interest of the Treasury in the management and control of public expenditure at both national and regional levels, enhanced the status of the region in Whitehall eyes. Public expenditure within the DoE's urban budget line had been volatile, unpredictable and uncontrollable, in part as a consequence of the interdependence between public and private expenditure in the property and development cycle (Stewart 1994a). By contrast, the SRB provided the basis for tighter control as well as making it easier for the Treasury to reduce current spending levels and/or resist bids for additional expenditure.

A further focus for Treasury interest (already mentioned in relation to Europe) was the prospect of using the SRB as the lever to draw in (or back) expenditure from European funds. After years of stubborn resistance to European programmes and adherence to a strict principle of non-additionality, the Treasury came to recognise that money received from Europe should be seen as additional, albeit within firm public expenditure planning totals. The Treasury took the view that if enhanced regionalism and regional frameworks were to be a prerequisite for the generation of successful European funding bids, it followed logically that the Treasury itself would be happy to acknowledge the regional case provided such frameworks allowed no scope for the additional generation of local government spending.

These shifts, orchestrated through the GORs, were manifestations of the regionalisation of state functions. Hogwood (1995) noted that in the context of the continuing enhancement of this regional, meso-level of administration, two key questions were raised: first, if the central state was being 'hollowed out' did the region represent a new source of administrative and bureaucratic security; and second, what might be the implications for career trajectories as a consequence of the restructuring of Whitehall? In addition, it was clear that regionalisation enhanced the public visibility of civil servants: the DoE Annual Reports (DoE 1994a; DoE 1995) started to identify by name the Deputy Secretary Commands in the DoE, including the ten Senior Regional Directors (three of the original appointments being women). It also led to increases in the number of staff in the regions. In December 1994, for example, as much as 14.1 per cent of DoE staff worked in the GORs, whilst a further 47.1 per cent were employed in agencies or other executive organisations, many located outside Whitehall and in the regions. Only 21.7 per cent of DoE staff were deployed on policy work, with a further 16.5 per cent on central services. Lastly, it is widely acknowledged that by the mid 1990s the more active involvement of regional staff in hands-on programmes (e.g. Estate Action Task Forces and Urban Development Corporations) had heightened the capacities – and interests – of civil servants in regional work.

Localities

Following the move towards a Single European Market and the abandonment by the Thatcher governments of mechanisms of regional co-ordination, there was also a trend towards the need for a shared 'place marketing' between localities (throughout Europe not just the UK), of the need for voice, visibility and promotion, and for the organisation of local interest at a scale above that of any conceivable level of local government. Robson (1995) argues that locality visibility superseded regional visibility in importance, but it may also be argued that even if positive local attributes were deemed as necessary, they were nevertheless seen as insufficient conditions for competitiveness in a global market. There were, for example, important scale economies in regional or sub-regional groupings. The inevitability of such groupings was merely reinforced by the fact that international organisations such as the EU made it clear that they would simply not negotiate with a multiplicity of small areas (see above).

From the late 1980s, therefore, there was some coalescence of local interests. This was based on the standing conferences of local authorities such as the London South East Regional Planning Conference (SERPLAN), The West Midlands Regional Forum and the Northern Regional Councils'

Association, which had existed in all the regions since the planning era of the 1960s and 1970s. These groupings became engaged in the preparation of strategic frameworks of varying kinds and developed their work considerably. Amongst other activities the standing conferences became involved in the preparation of draft regional guidance, which in turn provided the basis for the formal regional guidance given by the Secretary of State as background to structure planning. It has to be said, however, that neither the process nor the substance of work on regional guidance generated much status or respect for regional issues. In part this may have been because English regional boundaries remained in many ways incoherent and unsatisfactory for regional planning purposes. At least two of the regions, in which regional guidance moved ahead fastest (the South East and the South West), had little semblance of being a coherent aggregation of localities. The South East represented a giant doughnut better considered in halves if not in quarters, possibly justifying a planning framework which includes either quadrants of London or perhaps an overall integrated London and South East strategic statement as the basis for two, three or four sub-regional plans. The 'South West' was not one region but two-and-a-half sub-regions: the 'far South West', the West of England and part of the southern South East.

Regional coherence was further strained, however, by the emergence of sub-regional groupings. South Coast Metropole, for example, brought together a Portsmouth-, Southampton, Bournemouth, Rouen, Le Havre and Caen-based network of port-related, cross-Channel interests which straddled two English regions. In the South West, Action South West pressed its Atlantic Arc status and lobbied hard for the 'far South West' (Action South West 1995), as did the Western Development Partnership for the West of England sub-region (Western Development Partnership 1995). The development of regional guidance was dominated by the interests of the far South West, largely because the Northern counties did not become sufficiently actively involved. District councils were marginalised in the debate on regional guidance, with the consequence that there was little allegiance or commitment to the guidance documents. In other regions – the East Midlands, the Northern region or Yorkshire and Humberside – similar sub-regional differences diluted guidance as a collective product owned and recognised by all organisations in the 'region'.

Westminster, Whitehall and institutional change at the sub-national level

It was within this context of competition between four main competitors for regional territorial weight that emergent institutional arrangements became significant. Such arrangements gave practical meaning to any redistribution of influence, and provided a structure within which new sources of authority and power were to be exercised. In the first half of the 1990s, two key changes in institutional form in the English regions evolved as a result of Conservative government policy: the GORs and a reorganised system of local government. Each in principle offered scope for the emergence of dominant interests. The GORs, and the SRB, were hailed (albeit by ministers) as a new localism, the return to responsive and devolved sub-national structures. The Local Government Review in theory represented the opportunity to shape a new structure of sub-national government capable of at least articulating the regional interest, if not producing regional democracy. However, both the creation of the GORs and the Local Government Review may be interpreted as the further encroachment of an ambitious centre into territorial politics and administration. The remainder of this chapter examines each briefly in turn before coming to some concluding observations.

The GORs and SRB

Much institutional innovation and experimentation throughout the 1980s took the form of the establishment of ad hoc, often single-purpose and largely centrally controlled, agencies. The practice of much policy intervention was thus centralised, fragmented and competitive, and in effect diluted the impact of locality-based structures of power and influence, most notably the power of elected local government. Whilst the espoused values were those of co-ordination and integration, in practice the context was one if not of disintegration at least of complexity and fluidity (Audit Commission 1989; National Audit Office 1990). In the early to mid 1990s moves in regeneration policy on the surface appeared to address the problems of fragmentation, as well as to fulfil the Conservative Party's 1992 manifesto commitment to shift the balance of power away from Whitehall and towards the regions. Central to these moves was the SRB. The SRB reflected a departure from an urban, predominantly inner city, policy insofar as it entailed the abolition of the list of 57 designated urban areas and brought all cities and towns – and rural areas – within the potential remit of regeneration policy, increasing the geographical scope as well as the competitive nature of governmental action. Identified need, as reflected in a new index of local conditions (DoE 1994b) was to take second place to capacity to deliver.

In practice the SRB brought together a range of programmes but did not offer increased resources. Indeed the SRB envelope was planned to decrease over the first three years of its existence from £1447 million to £1314 million in 1996–97 (Hansard 1994). This represented a cut of £133 million (over 10%) from 1994–95 levels, and between 1993–94 (the year in which SRB equivalent programmes peaked) and 1997–98 there was a planned reduction in SRB of almost £300 million. In constant 1994–95 prices this amounted to a cut of 22 per cent (Hansard 1994, para.4.21).

Although presented as a single budget, the SRB was also pre-allocated to specific programmes, and top slicing for Urban Development Corporations, English Partnerships and Housing Action Trusts accounted for 40 per cent of the planned 1995–97 SRB total (DoE 1995). Additional commitments – to City Challenge and to continuing Estate Action schemes – made further inroads into the budget and only some £100 million was available for 'new' bids in 1995–96. The issue of pre-commitment became more significant as the programme was reduced, because although in principle the falling away of commitments released resources, in practice cutbacks in the overall budget meant that fewer new projects could be funded. Nevertheless a third and fourth round of SRB in 1996 and 1997 were confirmed in the 1995 autumn budget announcements.

The reductions in funding were, however, to be experienced unevenly. Urban Development Corporation spending was expected to fall by some £87 million between 1994–95 and 1997–98, but Housing Action Trust expenditure was to remain level and English Partnership expenditure was to increase by £29 million. The reduction in resources was therefore to be largely carried by the remainder of the programme – the programmes of other government departments and the programmes involving schemes initiated by local government. Of the reduction of £133 million identified above, £120 million was to be carried by these latter programmes.

Hence the SRB operated in a manner that was far less flexible than was initially suggested. It represented less a renewed localism than a realigned centralism, reflecting a resource shift towards centrally controlled institutional forms of regeneration and tighter expenditure management systems (Hogwood 1995).

The SRB represented a significant shift in administrative function to the regions. The changes effected, however, were of a very specific kind, involving the decentralisation of administration as opposed to the devolution of power and influence. What was involved was the deconcentration of central government functions to a regional base, providing a welcome territorial decentralisation of governmental presence and activity but offering no increase in autonomous local decision-making to locality interests. The new localism, therefore, had three main characteristics. It involved a managerial localism echoing many of the long-standing criticisms of the way in which functional programmes had failed to come together at the local level and thus promised co-ordination and integration. It involved a competitive localism demanding that localities respond to the challenge of change by engaging in active marketing and presentation of their areas to government. Finally it involved a corporatist localism seeking to involve a variety of local interests in the development of local vision, priorities and bids for resources, and to remove further regeneration policy, from the arena of overt and formal local politics (Stewart 1994b).

The GORs and the SRB, therefore, marked the emergence of an important new presence for central government in the regions. It was not, however, a presence which in the medium term offered more resources or local autonomy. Instead the GORs and SRB offered a reinforced centralism in the locality in which the competition for resources, for growth and for economic development were intensified and managed through new Whitehall outposts in the regions. In the metaphor of the struggle for political and administrative territoriality, the conclusion must be that the GORs represented a powerful and coherent central occupation force in the regions.

The local government review

In 1992 the Local Government Commission (LGC) was established by the government to review the structure of English local government, with the primary aim of introducing a system of unitary authorities to replace the existing two-tier system. In an interim report the LGC further stated that as part of its work it had a significant interest in the issue of regional capacity in relation to Europe and strategic economic development (LGC 1993). Apparently it was intended that, 'the review should aim to strengthen the institution of English local government and provide a structure which can wield sufficient resources to be able to maintain a strong voice not only in Britain but in a new Europe of regions' (para. 12 (iii)).

In addition the LGC identified a range of issues relating to scale: 'The commission believes that...the size of the [new unitary] authorities will best be determined by reference to the need to...facilitate strategic approaches to regional economic development and infrastructure, transportation coordination and environmental issues' (para. 37).

This implied that the LGC was well aware of the need to build a system of local government which incorporated a capacity to operate at a strategic sub-regional or regional level and which countered the forces of centralism emanating from the EU, and from Westminster and Whitehall. In its specific reports on individual review areas, there was again explicit reference to the need for strategic planning, together with recommendations as to how to carry forward the structure planning process (the function for which the LGC was formally allowed to make recommendations for joint arrangements). In terms of its proposals as to how a strategic regional capacity might in practice emerge, however, the LGC contributed very little. The key issue that the LGC needed to confront was that structure plans had to be prepared within a framework which was inevitably territorially larger than any authority that the LGC proposed. The LGC discussed this issue in mid review, but in the face of mixed reaction from Commissioners concluded only, 'that it would recognise the regional dimension in its structural recommendations with particular reference to joint arrangements' (LGC 1994, para.48).

The role and function of regional guidance thus came on to, and went off, the reorganisation agenda.

The key influence proved to be the LGC assumption that regional guidance was essentially centralist in character (being ultimately the responsibility of the Secretary of State). From a localist standpoint, therefore, the LGC presumed that regional guidance should be demoted in importance in the interests of building a locally accountable strategic framework:

> The Commission is invited by the Policy Guidance to consider whether there would be advantage in unitary authorities preparing plans within the framework of sub-regional planning guidance either prepared by groups of authorities themselves or issued by the Secretary of State. However the Commission believes that this option is unlikely to provide the clear lead required... The Commission has yet to be persuaded that Government regional guidance can or should provide a sufficient mechanism for resolving local inter-territorial conflicts. (LGC 1993, para. 59)

> The Commission believes that in general locally agreed joint arrangements offer the best starting point, and are preferable to reliance on strategic guidance in keeping the decisions at a local level...strategic decisions have to be implemented...and locally agreed joint arrangements may deliver a better local policy package than a separate authority, especially through a structure imposed by the Secretary of State. (LGC 1993, para. 62)

In the LGC's mind, therefore, the strategic framework had to derive from a bottom-up process which was more likely to build consensus and commitment and hence produce an implementable plan. A firmly localist philosophy was embodied in the LGC's thinking, with local democracy being sustained as a core value. Yet the LGC, 'harbours no illusions about the inherent problems in establishing workable arrangements capable of taking hard decisions that transcend the immediate interests of the constituent authorities in the interests of the area as a whole' (LGC 1995a, para. 219).

All the evidence was that such joint arrangements were inherently difficult and probably doomed to failure. Whilst being philosophically attached to joint local arrangements the LGC, 'also recognises that they are unlikely to be as effective and efficient as a statutory joint authority established especially for the purpose, which would more readily be able to overcome local self interest' (LGC 1995a, para. 220).

Despite these fears the LGC placed the onus firmly upon local government to develop practical joint arrangements for structure planning. But having rejected the possibility of new unitary authorities and/or hybrid county authorities jointly preparing regional guidance, the LGC avoided any further discussion of whether or how a regional or sub-regional framework might be put together. It thus failed to address the invitation of the initial 1992 Policy Guidance to consider the sub-regional issue, and in so doing missed the opportunity to introduce a locally bottom-up element into strategic planning above the level of the structure plan.

Instead the LGC returned to the question of how to ensure that joint arrangements for structure planning could be put in place. Here the LGC clearly believed that the threat of the big stick would be sufficient to bring the new local authorities to heel:

> The Commission nonetheless sees the key element in securing effective joint arrangements as being the special powers conferred on the Secretary of State by the Local Government Act 1992. Section 21 empowers him to establish a joint authority to take over any functions conferred on a local authority as a consequence of structural change and which will be carried out in accordance with joint arrangements, and it appears to him that satisfactory joint arrangements have not been made, or will not be in force when the structural change comes into operation, or have ceased or will cease to be in operation. The Act confers on the Secretary of State a continuing responsibility for securing that satisfactory joint arrangements are maintained, and the power to intervene where they are not. In the Commission's view, if this were widely understood to be a real sanction, and the circumstances under which the Secretary of State would envisage intervening were well understood, that would do much to bind the new authorities together in locally agreed joint structure planning arrangements. (LGC 1995a, para. 221)

Thus although Local Government Review offered the opportunity to develop a debate about the way in which local authority activities could be aggregated into a regional or sub-regional dimension, the outcome of the Review was to demote the regional issue (Leach 1994; Stewart, Gaster and Smart 1997).

The pattern of local government following the 1992–96 Review was complex (*Local Government Chronicle* 1996; LGC 1995a, 1995b). It resulted in plans for 46 unitary authorities in the shire areas. Nineteen of these were to be in five all-unitary former county areas; the remaining 27 unitary authorities were to lie within 19 county areas which, as a result would become hybrid (being a mixture of unitary and two-tier arrangements); 15 county areas were to retain the status quo. Despite the formation of a single local authority association, the outcome was not one which necessarily inspired confidence in the ability of local government to engage in collaborative sub-regional strategic activity given the prevailing structures. Indeed the emergence of the hybrid solution in 19 county areas (together with the fact that under Section 21 of the 1992 Local Government Act joint arrangements could not be enforced in status quo areas) suggested that there would be a more traditional battleground. The structural solutions reinforced affective rather than effective communities, and exaggerated old town and country tensions. It was expected that inevitable arguments over Standard Spending Assessments would exacerbate the problem. Local political energies and administrative expertise would, therefore, have to be diverted to the management of inter-authority issues at the county scale as opposed to building supra-authority capacity at the regional level.

A restructured system could provide, with authorities working collaboratively, continuity in the networks which had begun to exercise influence at the European level. Nevertheless, institutionalised conflict between authorities might make this problematic. Clearly, the key issue at the end of the Review remained that, 'new authorities, fewer in number and potentially with a single peer group local authority association will have to choose between the perpetuation of a poor record in co-operative relations or a new record of co-operation designed to create coherent regional voices, heard equally in London and Brussels' (Bradbury 1993, p.16).

A shifting institutional framework and the new regionalism

To assess the balance of influence and power at the English regional level we can revisit the struggle described earlier. Figure 7.2 illustrates the potential parity between the four actors, but a more accurate picture, Figure 7.3, suggests the growing marginalisation of the locality in practice.

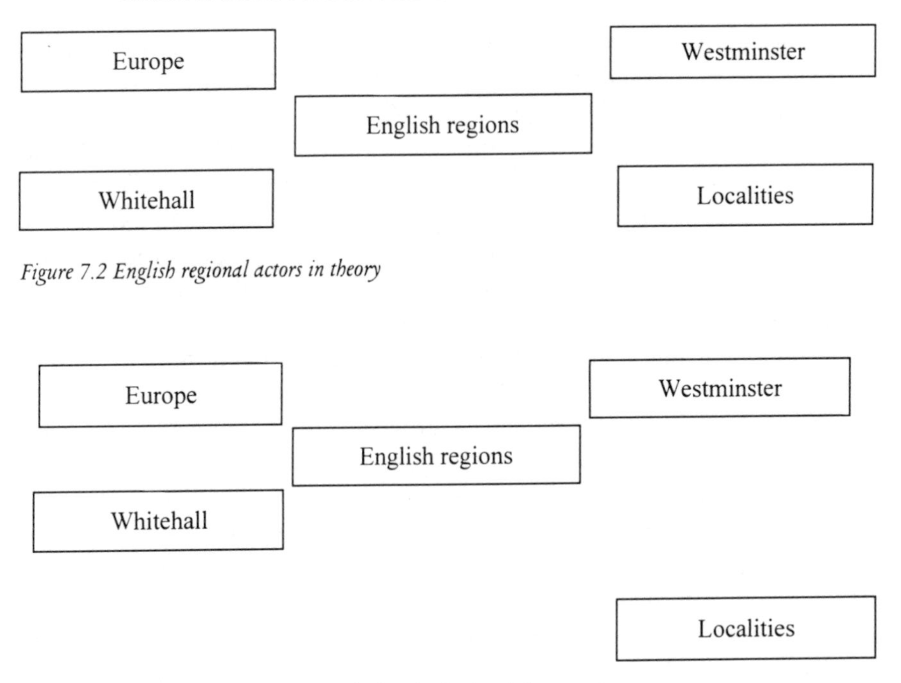

Figure 7.2 English regional actors in theory

Figure 7.3 English regional actors in a shifting institutional framework

During the first half of the 1990s three of the main actors became dominant. The EU clearly was active at the regional level. At Westminster the political parties all appeared to have something to gain from a regional presence. Through the GORs the civil service also developed a strong interest at the regional level. Overall the GORs represented the successful implementation of a Conservative strategy to fill the regional space with a central administrative capacity rather than allowing it to be filled purely by elected representatives from localities.

The representatives of the localities could have participated as a powerful fourth actor if there had been the will and the capacity to build a critical mass of aggregated local influence and power at the regional or sub-regional level. The likelihood, however, of this happening, or being allowed to happen, remained an open question. In regard to land-use planning the work of the Local Government Commission failed to stimulate collaborative working above the structure plan level. Indeed the Commission, whilst clearly well aware of the regional issue, felt itself to be limited by the legislation framed by the Major government. It therefore proved either uninterested or unwilling to address the broader issues of strategic planning (as opposed to more localised issues of community and service arrangements) and to deliver a local government system with a regional dimension to it.

In the future, government policy might well seek to manage the English regional space in a similar manner to that which was developed in this period. Most likely this would be supported by Whitehall, as its interests would be well served by an expanded regional role. Indeed a number of benefits to civil service aims became clear during the initial phase of the GORs. First, the procedures for arriving at agreed programmes for the use of Objective 1, 2 and 5(b) funds involved the development of Single Programming Documents defining the amounts and purposes of the grants and the conditions attached. Second, monitoring committees (serviced from the GORs) were given the management of Structural Fund support. Third, Regional Challenge, top slicing £160 million from the Structural Funds for competitive bidding, represented a further top-down Whitehall intrusion into the relationship between the European Commission and localities. EU actors would also probably acquiesce in any continuation of this approach. During the early 1990s there was certainly tension between the Commission and Whitehall over both the membership of monitoring committees (House of Commons 1995) and the extent to which the institutional arrangements for drawing up Single Programming Documents and for monitoring the implementation of these programmes should reflect national or local interests. The top-down climate was, however, pervasive. Not least through the establishment of machinery for the management of European programmes, there was overall a surprising convergence of Brussels, Whitehall and Westminster interests, a powerful coalition of interests, all standing to gain from the new regional arrangements.

By the mid 1990s, the most plausible scenario in the absence of a change to a government committed to devolution, was that locality interests would be increasingly marginalised as the centre colonised the regions. Localities, although in principle standing to gain from a system in which the region could operate as the vehicle for a bottom-up aggregation of collective local interest, were also concerned with the possible threat of regionalism to their own autonomy and with the difficulties of joint working. Local authorities were heavily engaged in managing with reduced resources, in responding to the challenge of compulsory competitive tendering in, and in in-fighting following reorganisation. There remained tensions between cities and surrounding areas, and the local private sector was stretched between planning for recovery from recession on the one hand and contributing to the management of government initiatives (e.g. Training and Enterprise Councils, health and authorities and trusts and so on) on the other.

In some areas there were powerful coalitions of local interest which had accessed national and European funding, and sub-regional and regional groupings such as SERPLAN and the West Midlands Regional Forum of

Local Authorities had become both more numerous and more visible. Nevertheless, whilst such groupings appeared impressive compared with earlier English experience, they paled into insignificance when compared with the capacity, organisation and political sophistication of their European counterparts. Moreover, it was questionable whether the regional ground would be captured by the interests of locality looking upwards as opposed to the interests of the centre spreading outwards, particularly in the context of a Conservative government. The terminology of local government in this respect tended to be more that of defence, retrenchment and consolidation than of expansion and advance. The situation, however, remained highly fluid. There was evidence, as Chapter 9 shows, that local government by the mid 1990s was beginning to recognise a need to come together more formally at the regional level and to work with other regional players in relating to the GORs.

The overall implications of all these developments were ambiguous. For regionalism itself the prospects were positive. During the early to mid 1990s a regional infrastructure was created, albeit dominated by the centre, which had within it the potential to facilitate a more explicit territorial redistribution of power in England. In the immediate political climate of the mid 1990s, however, the prospects for region building from a democratic, bottom-up base remained uncertain. Even against the background of a change of administration, it was an open question as to how much real power from Whitehall and the GORs a newly elected government would cede to indirectly or directly elected structures within the English regions.

References

Action South West (1995) *Regional Policy. Memorandum of Evidence to the Trade and Industry Committee.* House of Commons, Fourth Report, Session 1994–95, HC 356–II. London: HMSO.

Audit Commission for Local Authorities in England and Wales (1989) *Urban Regeneration and Economic Development: The Local Government Dimension.* London: HMSO.

Benson, J.K. (1983) 'Interorganisation network and policy sectors.' In D. Rogers and D. Whetton (eds) *Interorganisation Coordination.* Chicago: University of Chicago Press.

Bradbury, J. (1993) 'The politics of local government reorganisation and English regionalism.' Paper at the ESRC Research Seminar 'British Regionalism and Devolution in a Single Europe'. University of Strathclyde, 15 September.

Bulpitt, J.G. (1983) *Territory and Power.* Manchester: Manchester University Press.

Cmnd 9230 (1918) *Report of the Machinery of Government Committee (The Haldane Report).* London: HMSO.

DoE (1994a) *Annual Report 1994. The Government's Expenditure Plans 1994–95 to 1996–97.* Cm 2507. London: HMSO.

DoE (1995) *Annual Report 1995. The Government's Expenditure Plans 1995–96 to 1997–98.* Cm 2807. London: HMSO.

Dunleavy, P. (1989) 'The architecture of the British central state: parts I and II.' *Public Administration 67,* pp.249–275; pp.391–417.

Dunleavy, P. and Rhodes, R. (1990) 'Core executive studies in Britain.' *Public Administration 68.*

Goetz, K. (1993) 'German federalism and European integration: compatibility and adjustment.' Paper to the ESRC Research Seminar on Regionalism and Devolution.

Hansard (1994) *House of Commons Proceedings,* Session 1993–1994, vols.240–242, 31 March and 25 April.

Heclo, H. and Wildavsky, A. (1974) *The Private Government of Public Money.* London: Macmillan Press.

Hogwood, B.W. (1995) 'The Integrated Regional Offices and the Single Regeneration Budget.' Research Paper 13, Commission for Local Democracy.

House of Commons (1995) *Regional Policy. Fourth Report of the Trade and Industry Committee, Session 1994–95.* HC 356–I. London: HMSO.

Jessop, R. (1994) 'Post-Fordism and the state.' In A. Amin (ed) *Post Fordism: A Reader.* Oxford: Blackwell.

Leach, R. (1994) 'The missing regional dimension to the local government review.' *Regional Studies 28,* 8.

Lipietz, A. (1992) *Towards a New Economic Order: Post-Fordism, Ecology and Democracy.* Oxford University Press.

Local Government Commission (1993) *Renewing Local Government in the English Shires: A Progress Report.* London: HMSO.

Local Government Commission (1994) 'Minutes of Meeting – 24 February' (unpublished).

Local Government Commission (1995a) *Renewing Local Government in the English Shires: A Report on the 1992–95 Structural Review.* London: HMSO.

Local Government Commission (1995b) *The 1995 Review of 21 Districts in England: Overview Report.* London: HMSO.

Local Government Chronicle (1996) The new shape of Britain's local government. July.

Mawson, J. and Skelcher, C. (1980) 'Updating the West Midlands regional strategy: a review of inter-authority relation.' *Town Planning Review 51,* 2.

Mayer, M. (1994) 'Post Fordist city politics.' In A. Amin (ed) *Post Fordism: A Reader.* Oxford: Blackwell.

National Audit Office (1990) *Regenerating the Inner Cities.* HC 169. London: HMSO.

Painter, J. (1991) 'Regulation theory and local government.' *Local Government Studies 17,* 6.

Robson, B. (1993) 'Regions, cities and networks.' Paper presented to the EDRC Research Seminar 'British Regionalism and Devolution in a Single Europe' University of Strathclyde, 24 March.

Robson, B. (1995) *Regional Policy.*

Stewart, M. (1994a) 'Value for money in urban public expenditure.' *Public Money and Management 14,* 4.

Stewart, M. (1994b) 'Between Whitehall and town hall: the realignment of urban regeneration policy in England.' *Policy and Politics 22,* 2.

Stewart, M., Gaster, L. and Smart, G. (1997) *The Work of the Local Government Commission: Oversized Cloak or Emperor's Clothes?* York: Joseph Rowntree Foundation.

Stoker, G. (1994) 'Regulation theory and local government.' *Local Government Studies 17,* 6.

Western Development Partnership (1995) *Regional Policy. Memorandum of Evidence to the Trade and Industry Committee.* House of Commons, Fourth Report, Session 1994–95, HC 356–II. London: HMSO.

CHAPTER 8

The Origins and Operation of the Government Offices for the English Regions

John Mawson and Ken Spencer

Introduction

This chapter examines in more detail the Government Offices for the English Regions (GORs) established in April 1994 (see Chapter 7). It assesses both the factors which led the Major government to introduce this novel form of regional government, as well as how the GORs operated in terms of the policy making process and in implementation of government policies within the regions. The first part of the chapter sets out some of the underlying pressures which led to the re-emergence of the regional dimension as an issue in public policy. It then goes on to explore the government's response to the mounting pressures on its urban and regional programmes and their administration, leading to the 1992 Conservative Party manifesto commitments (Conservative Party 1992, p.39) and the November 1993 announcement (Department of the Environment 1993a) to establish a new strengthened regional machinery. An analysis is then presented of the internal structure of the offices, their relationships with Whitehall and other government agencies and departments, and with their regions during their first two years of operation. Finally, consideration is given to how far the offices can be said to have met the objectives set for them during this period and how their role was viewed by others.

Clearly, the fruits of such an analysis of the operation of the GORs are limited. It will take some time before the full impact of the organisational changes introduced work their way through into discernible service delivery and policy impacts. Nevertheless it is possible to make some critical observations. The research upon which this chapter draws was funded under the

Economic and Social Research Council Whitehall Programme and is based upon the findings of the first stage of a research project which involved a series of semi-structured interviews in the GORs and in Whitehall undertaken in the autumn of 1995 and the early months of 1996. The authors would like to emphasise that their interpretations and conclusions do not necessarily represent the views of the civil servants interviewed.

Developments underlying the revival of interest in the regional administrative tier

Interest in the issue of the decentralisation of decision-making through strengthened territorial management and the creation of elected regional structures is a matter of policy discourse which has fluctuated over time (Garside and Hebbert 1989). Certainly the tenure of office of the Conservative governments after 1979 is recognised as a period in which the regional dimension of government became unfashionable. Nevertheless, it is during this period that the seeds of a revival of interest can be identified. A number of (not necessarily related) trends and events brought the issue to a head at the end of the 1980s and ultimately resulted in the launching of the GORs in 1994. Regional administration, however, has an earlier pedigree, particularly in regard to land-use planning.

In the early post-war period, against the background of the establishment of a comprehensive urban and regional planning system, the Ministry of Housing and Local Government set up a network of regional offices to manage population overspill from the congested conurbations and oversee transport and other regional planning activities. These were abolished by the Conservative government in 1958. The regional agenda was subsequently resurrected by the Wilson government of 1964, which sought to link national and regional economic planning with physical planning under the Department of Economic Affairs. This system was managed at the regional level through the establishment of nominated bodies known as Regional Economic Planning Councils (EPCs) which were supported by civil servants in so-called Economic Planning Boards whose purpose included the preparation of regional plans (Wannop and Cherry 1994). The abandonment of the Labour government's national plan experiment and the subsequent resistance of the Treasury and other departments to integrated regional development strategies saw a downgrading of the regional agenda in Whitehall. However, the Economic Planning Boards continued to provide a limited mechanism for co-ordination of the activities of those government departments present in the regions. Moreover, regional planning strategies continued to be prepared by the Department of the Environment in partnership with the EPCs and local authority regional forums until the late 1970s (Mawson and Skelcher 1980). Attempts by some of the regional planning teams to introduce disaggregated regional budgets linked to the annual public expenditure round and longer-term financial planning process, together with the desire to integrate public policies and programmes across a much wider spectrum beyond land-use planning considerations, met with stiff resistance from Whitehall departments (Northern Regional Strategy Team 1977). In 1981 the EPCs were abolished and under a more ideological and 'anti-planning' agenda the Conservative government effectively abandoned regional physical planning, only for it to be revived again in the late 1980s under the guise of Regional Planning Guidance as development pressures continued to present problems in more prosperous regions (Thornley 1993).

A second underlying factor which inspired a regional agenda in England arose from political developments emanating from Scotland and Wales. While an elected regional structure for the English regions was strongly opposed by the Conservative government, nevertheless the nationalist vote remained in the background as an issue which could not be ignored by any British political party. The rise of Scottish and Welsh nationalism in the 1970s prompted the Wilson and Callaghan governments to engage in active consideration of devolution. As a result both major opposition political parties considered a commitment to a move to some form of elected regional institutions for the English regions, either in the form of a federal structure as per the Liberal Democrats or regional assemblies in the case of the Labour Party. The continuing significance of the nationalist vote in Scotland and the use of the concept of the 'Europe of the Regions' to justify the case of an independent Scotland, certainly maintained pressure on the Labour Party to support a Scottish assembly, and in turn elected assemblies in the English regions (Coulson 1990). Further, some commentators take the view that the Conservative government sought to enhance its presence at the regional level in England by administrative decentralisation in order to forestall pressures for an elected regional tier.

Aside from these underlying political pressures, developments within the European Community, now the European Union, were seen as a significant contributory factor behind the government's decision to establish strengthened regional offices. During the course of the 1980s, the mechanisms for allocating European Regional Development Fund and subsequently Structural Fund money through a strategic plan or 'programme approach' resulted in tensions surrounding the degree of EC participation in what was regarded as essentially a domestic policy matter (Martins and Mawson 1982). The European Commission's continuing insistence on the production of detailed regional strategic documents and financial programmes, prepared on a social 'partner' basis with local institutions and representative bodies, reinforced the message of the importance of a strong co-ordinated central government administrative presence at the regional level, not least in Treasury circles (Stewart 1994a).

In the realm of business and trade, the launching of the Single European Market, the European Economic Area and enlargement of the Union further heightened awareness of the opportunities and competitive threats of a trading bloc of over 380 million people. Business leaders became increasingly concerned about the weakness of the business support infrastructure in the English regions compared with that of some European competitor regions (Coopers and Lybrand 1992). Related concerns were expressed about the organisation of inward investment, the lobbying for, and management of, European funds, and the future of regional strategic planning against a background of uncertainties arising from local government reorganisation. The management of these functions and the division of responsibilities between various agencies in this regard resulted in further complications at the sub-regional level as Chambers of Commerce, Training and Enterprise Councils (TECs), and local authorities and their regional associations/forums have vied for leading roles (Bennett, Wicks and McCoshan 1994). To this complex institutional map at the regional and sub-regional levels must be added the role of statutory bodies such as the New Towns Commission, the Rural Development Commission, English Partnerships and the development agencies established by the former nationalised industries. Given the increasingly complex and multifaceted nature of the regeneration task and the need to co-ordinate the overlapping programmes and roles of a myriad of agencies, many of which were funded by central government, it was recognised that organisational capacity at the regional level needed to be strengthened in areas such as partnership and network development (House of Commons, Trade and Industry Committee 1995; Lewis 1992).

Such arguments surrounding the question of co-ordination could equally have been applied in other realms. Water, waste, electricity, gas, telecommunications, and radio, television and cable experienced a decade of liberalisation and privatisation leading to a patchwork of private utility companies, often with a strong regional organisational framework (Marvin and Cornford 1993). Given the significance of these services for economic development, physical planning and social policy, some critics have argued for a regional as well as a national regulatory framework, perhaps along the lines of the US State Utility Commissions. Elsewhere in the public service the move to establish 'arms length' Next Step agencies – such as the Benefits Agency, the Highways Agency and the Employment Service – raised similar questions about the strategic dimensions of public service delivery in cities and regions, against the backcloth of an increasingly fragmented public domain.

This problem was most stark, perhaps, in the field of urban regeneration, and it was therefore not surprising that it is from this direction that some of the greatest pressure emerged for change. By the end of the 1980s, it was becoming evident that the 'patchwork quilt' of government programmes, alongside a panoply of agencies engaged in economic and urban regeneration, often with no formal relationship with either government offices or local authorities, was causing confusion and leading to duplication and wasted effort (Audit Commission 1989). Criticisms along these lines by the Audit Commission and the National Audit Office were further strengthened by the personal experience of business leaders asked to head various government initiatives and by ministers who were given responsibility for the co-ordination of government policies in specific cities (House of Commons, Public Accounts Committee 1990; National Audit Office 1990).

It was against the background of these pressures that the 1992 Conservative Party manifesto made a commitment to the introduction of Integrated Regional Offices (IROs) in the English regions and the creation of a Single Regeneration Budget (SRB) alongside other mechanisms to improve co-ordination such as One Stop Shops/Business Links and the Urban Regeneration Agency, subsequently retitled English Partnerships (Conservative Party 1992, p.39). Such proposed changes, however, must also be considered alongside reforms in the internal management of the civil service. These included the launch of the Efficiency Unit and the Financial Management initiative in the early 1980s followed by the Citizen's Charter (1987), the Next Steps initiative (1988), market testing (1991) and finally the establishment of the Office of Public Service and Science headed by a cabinet minister after the 1992 general election (Her Majesty's Government 1994).

The underlying philosophy behind such developments was the delegated provision of public services in which control and responsibility would be pushed down and out of the central government machinery, wherever possible through the use of market or quasi-market mechanisms. However, in policy terms this fragmentation of the public domain led inevitably to tensions. Freedom to manage resulted in demands that the centre yield power. However, the increasingly federated character of the civil service, and the absence of an integrating and coherent strategy for public service provision at central government level, also raised the question of what compensating co-ordination mechanisms would be required. It is in this context that the potential scope of the territorial dimension of public administration was recognised as one useful mechanism for facilitating greater cohesion in certain overlapping policy fields.

The Secretary of State for the Environment, for example, in launching the IROs in November 1993, commented that they would, 'provide their customers with a more comprehensive and accessible service...meet the widespread demand for a single point of contact...bring services closer to the people they serve, simplify the government machine and improve value for money' (Department of the Environment 1993a, p.2). However, in this regard the historical experience of centralised and compartmentalised character to decision-making in the civil service suggested considerable difficulties for the co-ordination of central government policies at the regional level (Morran 1993). With no single civil servant clearly responsible for government policies, not all government departments present in the regions and only limited inter-departmental co-ordination machinery through the Planning Boards, it was to be expected that problems should surface in various policy areas such as European funding and urban regeneration (Stewart 1994b).

The sixth Report of the Treasury and Civil Service Select Committee 1988–89 highlighted some of the difficulties when it pointed out that there was no disaggregation on a consistent basis of public expenditure information for the English regions nor were there adequate attempts to examine or plan the inter-relationships between programmes and their impacts. This situation was contrasted with the position in Scotland, Wales and Northern Ireland which had the benefit of co-ordinated political management, devolved territorial departments, block budgets and expenditure switching discretion between programmes within these blocks. The Committee noted that this discretion was valued by the Secretaries of State concerned since, 'it assists policy co-ordination and financial management...moreover it permits substantive policy differences and adjustment of UK policy measures in the light of different traditions and circumstances' (House of Commons, Treasury and Civil Service Select Committee 1989, p.2).

The role and structure of the GORs

In April 1994 the government launched its new network of ten integrated regional offices in the English regions (GORs). Civil servants in the Training Enterprise and Employment Division of the Department of Employment and the Departments of Environment, Transport and Industry were made accountable to one Senior Regional Director (SRD) (Department of the Environment 1993a, 1993b). Subsequently in 1995 the Department of Education was merged with the Department of Employment adding a further significant dimension to the work of the GORs. Reporting to the four Secretaries of State, each SRD was made responsible for all staff and expenditure routed through their office and for ensuring that the necessary co-ordination and links were established between main programmes and other public monies. In addition GORs were to seek to maintain close links with those departments without a regional presence. In parallel with the launch of the GORs, the SRB was established, drawing together 20 separate programmes totalling some £1.4 billion in 1994/95 from five departments: the Department of the Environment, Department of Trade and Industry, Department of Employment, Home Office and Department of Education and Science. Its purpose was to provide flexible support for regeneration and economic development and was made available throughout each region. A proportion of the SRB was to be allocated on the basis of annual bids, submitted to the GORs (in the short term the sum available was relatively small). Drawing on the City Challenge experience, the bids were led by local authorities and/or TECs or other appropriate bodies such as those from the private or voluntary sectors. The SRB was made the responsibility of the Secretary of State of the Environment and in making decisions about funding he was to be guided by a Cabinet Committee for Regeneration (EDR). This considered regeneration policies and their co-ordination, set the guidelines for the SRB and selected the bids. To facilitate the process a network of 17 sponsor ministers was established to advise EDR ministerial colleagues on regeneration issues related to their own particular city or area.

In order to implement the GORs policy initiative centrally, a Deputy Secretaries' Management Board was established, responsible to the four Permanent Secretaries. This was to deal with administrative matters and overall policy direction of the GORs and to meet the SRDs on a monthly basis. It was serviced by an inter-departmental group, the Government Office Co-ordination Unit (GOCU) headed by an Under-Secretary in the Department of the Environment. A set of overall objectives was established for the GORs, and within this framework each SRD was given a degree of local autonomy to develop structures and processes appropriate to the local situation. The overall objectives may be summarised as: (1) to achieve operational requirements of departments and ministers; (2) to contribute local views and experience to the formation of government policy; (3) to promote a coherent approach to competitiveness, sustainable economic development and regeneration, using public and private resources and through the exercise of its statutory responsibilities; (4) to develop the skills and methods of working of staff to achieve these objectives; (5) to develop local partnerships with, and between, all the local interests to promote and secure these objectives; and (6) to provide a single point of access and deliver high quality services on Citizen's Charter principles (Department of the Environment 1993b).

While the GORs were all established with a broadly similar range of functions, management structures and relationships with Whitehall, there were, nevertheless, some important differences worthy of note. Undoubtedly the most significant related to the Government Office for London (GOL), which was to service a cabinet sub-committee and consequently established direct access to ministers from all the key government departments which impacted on the capital. Both GOL and the Government Office for Merseyside (GOM), as urban focused regions, took over large-scale regeneration programmes including responsibility for the two highest spending Urban Development Corporations (UDCs). GOM also inherited oversight of the Objective 1 European Programme for Merseyside. In contrast, the South East and Eastern Offices took on comparatively few economic development or regeneration programmes of any significance, nor were they to have access to sponsor ministers. Reflecting the size of the regions, they inherited a number of physically separate office buildings in different locations established by the former departmental government offices. The South West region was the only GOR which had a full sub-office, covering the counties of Devon and Cornwall. In 1996 it became the first area outside London to be allocated a minister responsible for the whole of the GOR region.

It is important to note that the GORs, when established, did not encompass a number of government departments which may have had significant policy and operational relationships with the four parent departments at the regional level, for example the Department of National Heritage, the Ministry of Agriculture, the Home Office and the Department of Education (although in the latter two cases special co-ordination arrangements were set in place and in 1996 the Departments of Employment and Education merged). It is evident that a focus of the work of the GORs, arising from the programmes of their parent departments, was that of environment, infrastructure, regeneration and economic development. Another interesting feature of the GOR structure is that there was to be no direct line management relationship between the SRDs and the Next Step agencies of the four parent departments or other departments, even where such agencies had a significant regional presence and impact in policy terms, for example the Highways Agency, the Employment Service and the Benefits Agency. Likewise, the GORs were not given a line management relationship with the various non-departmental public bodies such as the Rural Development Commission, the Housing Corporation and the National Rivers Authority which, moreover, have their own regional structures and boundaries. English Partnerships, which was established during the same time frame as the GORs, also has a different regional framework, despite having an operational relationship with the GORs in the field of economic development and regeneration.

The SRDs

Reflecting the significance of the initiative and the need to oversee senior civil servants from the former government offices, the new SRDs were appointed at the Under-Secretary grade 3 level, while in the case of the SRD for London the position was filled at Deputy Secretary grade 2. The latter appointment was made against the background of the unique position of London as the capital city and the requirement to service the cabinet Sub-Committee for London. The Regional Directors were appointed under open competition and were widely seen as being recruited from the ranks of the most experienced and able civil servants, 'highfliers' tipped to reach the highest positions in the civil service (Department of the Environment 1993c).

The Directors were given three year contracts, which led some to question whether this was a sufficient period to master such a complex and innovative brief and whether a longer time span should have been given before they moved on to their next position. In some parts of the civil service eyebrows were raised as to the wisdom of 'highfliers' taking such risky appointments in career terms. Undoubtedly the SRDs ran the risk of offending parent departments, senior civil servants and ministers if they articulated too strongly a regional perspective.

Their role was prescribed by the six objectives set for the GORs by ministers. It can be summarised in various ways, but undoubtedly included acting as a spokesperson for government policies in the region, contributing to policy development by providing the regional perspective, managing departmental programmes, and carrying out a networking and facilitating function to promote regional development with other key actors. The tensions in fulfilling these tasks in practice were considerable. Establishing, for example, a new integrated range of functions at the regional level challenged the traditional lines of management responsibility and political accountability at the centre. The SRDs were also under detailed public scrutiny within the regions as the voice of government. Internally there were staffing problems arising from integration, as well as policy choices and compromises which had to be made between departments. The practice of the GORs and the reality of these tensions in their first two years of operation are discussed further in the following sections.

The management of the GORs

Undoubtedly one of the key internal management issues with which the SRDs had to grapple (in the implementation and management of policies and programmes), was their accountability to four separate Departments of State. Their scope for management discretion was prescribed by service level agreements or memoranda which set out what was expected of the GORs in relation to a department's policies across the board or in relation to individual significant programme areas. In constructing these agreements there was a tension present between the priorities of 'head office' departments in ensuring that their main line policies and programmes were given priority by the GORs and the desire of the regional offices to focus rather more on issues of co-ordination, integration and giving policies a regional flavour. There is a view that some departments took a rather defensive position in constructing these memoranda in a far too prescriptive form in order to ensure that their departmental objectives were given priority.

In the initial phase of operation the GORs bid on an annual basis for resources to carry out their departmental and regional office functions through a system known as GO-MINIS, linked to the public expenditure cycle. The GORs prepared a set of proposed activities and set of objectives for the forthcoming year which were then negotiated at the centre with the parent departments and GOCU. Once approved, the GO-MINIS documents were translated into annual operational plans and specific plans for the individual divisions or directorates within the GOR. The GORs also translated their operational plans into annual reports for ministers and for wider public consumption.

Aside from those policy areas with an explicit territorial focus, no regional office dimension was introduced into negotiations between the Treasury and individual departments. In financial management terms, lines of accountability for programmes ran to the relevant nominated budget holder at the centre. Departments operated different financial management systems which meant that programme co-ordination and integration at the regional level were sometimes difficult.

In terms of the internal management of the GORs the SRDs were given a degree of freedom to structure their offices to reflect local circumstances. They brought together their senior management teams, comprising heads of directorates, on a regular weekly or monthly basis. There were a wide range of responses to the opportunities presented by the merger of the functions of four separate departments. A number of common themes were nevertheless discernible. In most offices the opportunity was taken to bring together the management of the common offices services and the personnel function. Strategic management, research, the SRDs' secretariat and ministerial visits were also areas where progress was made. In terms of programme areas the opportunities for integration presented by the GORs resulted in the transfer of functions or greater co-ordination, mostly notably in relation to European programmes and the SRB. Another area receiving attention in a number of offices was the question of the co-ordination of TEC business service contracts between the Department of Trade and Industry and the merged Department for Education and Employment.

To facilitate the co-ordination theme in relation to locally established policy priorities and the national themes established by ministers, viz. competitiveness, regeneration and sustainability, the GORs established various cross-office working groups. Another organisational response to the co-ordination agenda was made through the management of certain activities in geographical sub-divisions. In some cases this was limited to the management of a single function as, for example, in the sub-division of London by GOL in order to oversee the SRB. Other GORs established area teams in order to exchange information and co-ordinate policies and initiatives, for example Yorkshire and Humberside and the West Midlands. In the case of the South West, a sub-office was established to cover Devon and Cornwall, while in the case of the South East functions were managed by area teams supported by functional specialist back-up groups in a form of matrix management. This latter approach was by far the most radical example of office restructuring.

In establishing these new methods of integrated working the SRDs experienced a number of management difficulties. Undoubtedly one of the key issues concerned the merging of staff from five departments with very different histories, professional backgrounds and organisational cultures. Different departmental policy priorities and associated professional values meant that on occasions there were differences in the perception of, and attitudes towards, particular policy issues or problems. Flexibility in personnel management was inhibited to some degree by the fact that staff remained employees of their parent departments. In practice this meant that there were variations in terms and conditions of service amongst staff working alongside each other and carrying out similar functions. It also meant that it proved difficult to transfer staff to a higher grading in a different department. Another related management problem concerned the inheritance of government buildings from the former regional offices which naturally presented a physical barrier to the successful integration of functions. A policy of co-location was adopted in the case of a number of the GORs, but was limited across the board by problems of finance and the opportunities presented by the termination of leases.

Relationships with the centre

Turning to the question of relationships with Whitehall, the overall management and co-ordination of the GOR initiative was provided by the management board of four Deputy Secretaries from the parent departments who met on a monthly basis. The Chairmanship of the management board rotated on a six monthly cycle and was serviced by GOCU, which was located in the Department of the Environment. Senior civil servants from the parent departments were charged with the task of liaising with the GORs directly and attending the management board and GOCU meetings. The board determined the agenda for the monthly meeting of the SRDs, which addressed personnel, administrative and policy matters, and received briefings and engaged in discussions with Departments and/or on occasions ministers.

There was no single minister with a brief to oversee the overall development of the GORs, and it was suggested that this was possibly a weakness in the structure which meant that it would prove difficult to maintain the momentum of the initiative within the Whitehall machine. In practice most day-to-day policy issues were dealt with directly with the ministry concerned, through the relevant directorate of the GOR. There were mechanisms in place for regular meetings between the senior staff of the GORs and civil servants at the centre responsible for specific programmes/policy areas. In addition the SRDs established a system of 'twinning' whereby directors divided up amongst themselves responsibility for taking the lead in monitoring policy areas and taking initiatives on particular issues.

Overall, it is difficult to gauge the consequences for the policy process of the establishment of the GORs. There is evidence that ministers in the initial phase of operations were impressed with the improved quality of information made available to them (House of Commons, Trade and Industry Committee 1995, p.xiv). However, it would be a mistake to assume that the GORs themselves were able to exert any great influence in Whitehall on regional issues. There were examples of action taken by SRDs which influenced policy, for example in relation to the access of regional airports to the internal domestic US markets, and in pressing against specific regional cuts in the road programme. It would appear, however, that there were no significant changes in the policy machinery at the centre to accommodate a regional input, either through the management board or the establishment of other policy co-ordination mechanisms.

Indeed there were complaints that when policy was developed in Whitehall the involvement of the regional level was either not considered at all or the regional perspective was introduced at too late a stage for the GORs to have any significant influence. A further criticism was that while the GORs had to secure a common position on sensitive policy issues between the various departments at the regional level, when the decisions were then referred upwards to parent departments there seemed to be a lack of awareness or understanding that a prime role of the GORs was to secure policy co-ordination and that this had necessitated on occasions compromise in relation to central departmental priorities. Of course, it needs to be recognised that some parent departments had a greater tradition of dialogue with their regional offices, and the degree of influence which could be exerted was partly dependent on the departmental origins and political skills of the SRD. Overall, it was clear that the exercise of influence and quiet diplomacy would take time to yield results and by its very nature the success of this type of approach would not always be very visible.

The issue of measuring the impact of the GORs was something which was exercising the attention of those charged with their development in Whitehall as well as the GORs themselves. Basic input/output measures for various programmes were already built into the GOR operational plans arising from the GO-MINIS. However, it was when the wider aims of the GORs were considered that difficulties arose in relation to aspects such as co-ordination, integration, influence and partnership development and so on. As one measure of performance review, some GORs commissioned customer/client surveys. Internal staff attitude studies were also undertaken. No definitive performance evaluation framework was established, but existing operational plans and annual reports contained a mix of both the six national objectives set for the GORs and their translation into more specific local objectives.

Clearly it was a key part of the GORs' remit to establish a regional flavour to national policies and achieve greater cohesion in their administration. Ministers consistently took the position that they did not wish to see a return to what they regarded as the ineffectual all-encompassing and rigid blueprint plans of the former Economic Planning Councils. Yet equally the SRDs clearly needed a set of regional priorities, performance measures and guidelines to manage their office effectively.

The development of regional priorities or strategy

In a number of policy areas and in the management of several major programmes, the SRDs had the opportunity to exercise a considerable degree of regional discretion/influence in the decision-making process. These included competitive bidding for SRB and European funds, housing investment programmes, negotiation of contracts with TECs and UDCs, content of regional planning guidance and so on. Against this background there was a quite widely held view in the regions amongst local authorities, representatives of the business community, the Regional Trades Union Congress and the voluntary sector that there should be a published regional framework which indicated the way in which the decisions of the GORs were determined, and that locally representative bodies should participate in the process of formulating such priorities. Clearly such expectations were fuelled by the publicity hype surrounding the launch of the GORs. The Department of the Environment press release accompanying Mr Gummer's announcement in November 1993, for example, stated that the initiative involved, 'sweeping measures to shift power from Whitehall to *local* communities and make the government more responsive to local priorities' (Department of the Environment 1993a, author's emphasis).

The GORs were caught in the crossfire between differing perceptions of the nature of regional reform and the role of the GORs. This debate surfaced in the press and in criticisms from members of the Public Accounts Committee and the Chairman of the Trade and Industry Committee that the SRDs had far too much discretion, influence and choice in a number of policy areas and that there was insufficient public scrutiny of their activities, either regionally or nationally (Foster 1995). In this context the SRDs were faced with a difficult balancing act. They had on the one hand to pursue the objectives set for them in promoting a coherent approach to competitiveness, sustainable economic development and regeneration, developing local partnerships to secure these objectives and contributing local views and experience to the formation of government policy. At the same time they had to resist pressures for a too open and dirigiste form of regional administration and strategic planning since they were the servants of ministers and the Whitehall machine for whom such an approach was an anathema. Inevitably, for operational purposes regional priorities were required in a number of policy and programme areas, whether or not they were the subject of wider consultation and were ultimately made public in a strategy document. The tensions present in this situation were illustrated in the debate surrounding the operation of the SRB.

An explanatory note issued by the Department of the Environment in November 1993 setting out how the new SRB system would operate indicated that the GORs would submit their recommendations for successful SRB bids within the context of a regional regeneration statement which would be submitted to the Secretary of State and the Ministerial Committee for regeneration (Department of the Environment 1993d). In the event, the final bidding guidance document made no reference to this document. Subsequently the Department indicated that such formal annual statements or strategies setting out priorities for regeneration would not be prepared, since, 'to do so could limit the flexibility and local partnership-building capacity which the GORs are seeking to encourage in order that local needs can be better addressed on a more responsive basis' (House of Commons, Trade and Industry Committee 1995, p.171). The subsequent level of overbidding in SRB round 1, however, led the local authority associations to argue in evidence to the House of Commons Environment Committee (July 1995) that if such strategies had been prepared a great deal of time and effort could have been saved and that, 'regeneration statements would have formed a useful background against which to judge bids and place them in context' (House of Commons Environment Committee 1995, p.54). Moreover, the House of Commons Trade and Industry Committee concluded in its report on regional policy in March 1995 that, 'there was no inherent reason why a regional strategy could not be robust and flexible in format' (House of Commons Trade and Industry Committee 1995, p.1v).

Many SRB practitioners took the view that, in any case, the GORs were forced by necessity to operate a set of 'bottom drawer' regional priorities in order to manage the system (albeit covertly). Moreover, it is argued that the GORs were already engaged in the preparation and/or approval of a range of economic, regeneration, environmental and European strategic documents, so that regional priorities were already established in most of the key policy areas. These included Regional Planning Guidance, Community Support Framework documents for EU Structural Funds, TEC and UDC corporate plans, local authority land use and economic development annual plans, Transport Plans and Programmes (TPPs), Housing Investment Programmes (HIPs), and so on. The documents were checked for consistency in the GORs, and some offices engaged in internal exercises drawing out the key regional priorities. What was needed, so ran the argument, was a single clear public statement which would greatly assist the longer-term investment and planning decisions of both public and private organisations in the regions (Fell 1995).

Policy dialogue, partnerships and co-ordination

Beyond the preparation of formal statutory documents, a number of the GORs in their initial phase of operation also began to engage their regional and local partners in a dialogue about the future of their regions. In view of the sensitivity of preparing a regional strategy most GORs proceeded cautiously, the West Midlands being the only region which produced an explicit list of ten regional priorities. Others, such as Yorkshire and Humberside, used opportunities such as the Competitiveness White Paper or the commissioning of research on their regional economy to highlight regional issues and engage in debate on priorities, sometimes in working parties with representatives of various interest groups such as the business community or the local universities (Government Office for Yorkshire and Humberside 1995a, b). Significantly, however, the GORs did not operate within the framework of a policy forum such as the old EPCs, where the key regional institutions came together to hammer out an agreed regional view with government. Indeed this left the GORs vulnerable to the accusation that on occasions they engaged in a process of picking and choosing the bodies or individuals which they consulted with on a particular issue or policy in order to get the right message for ministers.

There can be no doubt, however, that the SRDs made considerable efforts to participate regularly in formal regional meetings such as those organised by standing conferences of local authorities, TEC regional groups and the regional bodies of the Confederation of British Industry, as well as meeting informally key regional decision-makers in the public and private sectors. Where appropriate they sought to address perceived gaps in the regional consultation and decision-making structures.

In terms of partnership development within the regions, the GOR role was greatly facilitated by the opportunities presented by the establishment of the Business Link network and the operation of the SRB, which provided the resources and rationale for intervention. A number of GORs undertook audits of partnerships in their region and where necessary provided active support in development or restructuring. SRDs and other senior staff regularly attended and/or monitored partnerships in a number of GOR regions. It was recognised that more needed to be done in terms of the training of staff in networking skills, particularly for those regions where there had been little previous experience of this type of role.

The formal co-ordination of agencies and organisations, particularly in the fields of economic development and urban regeneration, was, however, more problematic. The House of Commons Trade and Industry Committee (1995), for example, commented on the 'bewildering profusion' of economic development bodies in the regions. It noted that in Lancashire, for example, there were some 40 organisations active in the field receiving public money and another 24 receiving funds indirectly. The Department of Trade and Industry's statement that the GORs, 'help co-ordinate the efforts of other agencies where this is necessary' was dismissed as 'complacent' in the face of what the committee interpreted as clear evidence of wasteful expenditure (House of Commons, Trade and Industry Committee 1995, p.1ii). It was argued that there was a need for a more proactive response, fostering organisational capacity through the preparation of agreed regional and local plans to co-ordinate the activities of different agencies and allocate tasks:

> Any small business which turned up at a bank seeking funding without a business plan would be sent away to prepare one: indeed, government funded organisations would advise it on how to do so. In contrast the government is willing to allow large sums of money to be spent on economic development without any form of plan to co-ordinate that spending for maximum effectiveness. (House of Commons, Trade and Industry Committee 1995, p.1iv, para. 111)

It could be argued, however, that the Committee's references to the co-ordination role of the GORs was perhaps too harsh in the light of their functions and responsibilities *vis-à-vis* Whitehall.

It has to be recognised that the GORs' first two years of operation provide a very limited basis for assessment. Moreover, given the disposition of management responsibilities, one has to recognise that the challenge of developing a cohesive approach at the regional level amongst a diverse set of agencies and public sector funding regimes required a sustained effort of networking, bargaining and negotiation by the SRDs across departmental and agency boundaries. Indeed, during this period the solution to many of the key problems of co-ordination faced at the regional level lay beyond the immediate sphere of influence of the GORs within the wider organisation of the civil service and associated agencies, and particularly in the Whitehall decision-making machinery. The fact that the SRDs had to report to four Secretaries of State and operate within four separate departmental policy-making and financial management systems inevitably presented difficulties in terms of policy integration. Moreover, the GOR initiative was not accompanied by any fundamental changes in the policy-making machinery at the centre to accommodate a regional dimension arising from the new GOR structure. Nor was there any significant devolution of policy discretion to the regional level.

Conclusion

The decision to establish the GORs can be seen as a radical departure from the centralised and compartmentalised traditions of the civil service, and for this reason was greeted with some surprise by practitioners, policy-makers and academics alike. It should be noted that without the enthusiastic support of a small number of influential senior ministers it is unlikely that the manifesto proposals would have survived the Whitehall policy-making machinery. Outside Whitehall there was quite widespread support in principle for the idea of the integrated government offices (House of Commons, Trade and Industry Committee 1995, p.xiv), with the greatest controversy surrounding issues of accountability and the degree of participation of local democratic institutions in their work. However, much of the debate was misinformed as to the role and full extent of the responsibilities and powers of the GORs. Partly such misunderstandings stemmed from the government's own launch press statement which implied that the GORs would involve a 'transfer of power from Whitehall to local communities' (Department of the Environment 1993a). In practice, their key function was to strengthen the presence and improve the quality of central government decision-making in the regions, particularly in relation to the activities of the four parent departments. Initially at least, certain local and regional bodies held a number of unrealistic expectations as to the role of the GORs which created tensions and problems for the SRDs in the execution of their task. One assumption was that they would act in an advocacy manner for their regions in the resource allocation process. Another was that they would be able to represent in a comprehensive overarching manner all government policies, including those in the social policy area.

While it might be argued by some that the GORs immediately enjoyed too much power and that there was insufficient scrutiny of the decisions taken by the SRDs, it could equally be argued by those wishing to see more co-ordinated and geographically sensitive government policies and programmes at the regional level, that the SRDs were not given sufficient direct influence over a wide range of government institutions and hence expenditure in the regions. The GORs, for example, did not encompass all government departments present in the regions. Nor did they incorporate major aspects of government activity delivered through Next Step agencies or non-departmental bodies. In seeking to address this issue any steps taken to strengthen the powers and responsibilities of the GORs would, of course, require an appropriate strengthening of democratic accountability at the regional level.

Clearly, it was always going to take some time before the full impact of the organisational changes introduced in the GOR initiative worked its way through into discernible service delivery and policy impacts (Ritchie 1996). Indeed, prior to the 1997 general election, more restructuring was set to take place, co-location was planned for a number of offices and there were plans for an expanding range of initiatives in partnership developments, networking and so on. Nevertheless, it is possible to come to some preliminary observations on the progress of the GORs and the views held by others about their performance. In the first two years of operation, surveys undertaken by various national local authority and business representative bodies indicated that the concept of the GOR had been well received but that there was disappointment that they had not opened up to a more active involvement of local institutions in their work (Association of District Councils 1995;

Fell 1995). In terms of the management and delivery of government programmes there was no clear discernible pattern, with some organisations reporting improvements while others noted no differences either at the regional level or in relation to central government. This response was perhaps to be expected.

Personnel and management issues arising from the merger of the four separate departments certainly absorbed a great deal of senior management time, both in the regions and in Whitehall, and deflected attention from broader policy considerations surrounding the role and development of the GORs. The development of the GORs took place at a time of significant restructuring of civil service departments which led to a reduction in middle and senior posts. This did not help the climate of integration.

Nevertheless, despite these difficulties the GORs operated in a far more integrated fashion than regional offices of central government had ever done before (Ritchie 1996). Civil servants were given the explicit role of speaking on behalf of their GOR when they visited their clients, rather than on behalf of individual departments as was the case in the past. Organisational innovations also occurred to facilitate enhanced inter-departmental working through thematic working groups and area teams.

The then Minister for Trade and Industry, Tim Eggar MP, commented to the Trade and Industry Committee: 'the IROs are intended to provide a more efficient delivery and more responsive delivery within a framework which is set down centrally; their civil servants, previously part of the culture of a particular department, are increasingly being welded together as teams, as people who are working for the more efficient delivery of programmes for that region'. He cited the example of a meeting held in the North East with the other sponsor ministers to consider the competitiveness of the North East as a region '...we are able to address the key issues in a more structured way than was previously possible' (House of Commons, Trade and Industry Committee 1995, p.xiv).

The establishment of the GORs certainly eased the introduction of the SRB and, indeed, the SRB itself was a mechanism which assisted the offices in developing more corporate working. Despite the various procedural problems arising from the operation of the SRB process, the introduction of this radical new form of regeneration policy was a significant achievement. There was notable progress in other areas such as the establishment of Business Links and in the management of European programmes. The provision of support for, and development of, various local and regional partnerships was another feature of the new-style government offices, as was the engagement of key local decision-makers and institutions in informal and more formal discussions surrounding key regional issues. There were, nevertheless, shortcomings in the development of the skills of civil servants in networking partnership development and other forms of organisational capacity-building at the regional/sub-regional levels.

In relation to the major programmes of the parent departments, there were clear benefits in bringing together under a single management umbrella the environmental, land use, infrastructure, economic development and regeneration policy instruments. However, in terms of a wider integration of public policies at the regional level to include the social policy arena, much less was possible (let alone contemplated) given the lines of organisational accountability. Even within the environmental, economic development and regeneration policy fields there were structural problems arising from the line management relationships of the Next Step agencies and non-departmental public bodies. Finally there is the question of the relationship with the centre. The GORs offered a significant opportunity to transform urban and regional governance, and specifically the workings of the civil service both in Whitehall and the regions, an opportunity which was largely missed. The full potential can only be realised, if the principles of subsidiarity are applied, with the devolution of powers and responsibilities downwards to the regions and wherever appropriate from the GORs to elected local government and other representative bodies. Equally the centre must adapt its structures to accommodate a regional input into decision-making in Whitehall. As the House of Commons Trade and Industry Committee pointed out, while the GORs were accountable to particular ministers for each programme there, 'appears to be no ministerial responsibility for their co-ordinating role, which is the crucial aspect of their work' (House of Commons, Trade and Industry Committee 1995, p.xivii, para. 90).

In conclusion, there can be no doubt that the GORs represented a significant development in the machinery of government at the regional level, and despite the various criticisms which have been made of their role they seem likely to remain in one form or another. Under one political scenario they could become the building blocks of a devolved democratically elected regional structure or a more regionally accountable form of governance. Alternatively they could remain as a powerful instrument of administrative decentralisation maintaining the power of Whitehall in the regions.

Note

This chapter draws upon research undertaken by the authors for a research project entitled: 'Whitehall and the reorganisation of Regional Offices in England'. The research was funded under the ESRC Whitehall Programme.

References

Association of District Councils (1995) *Integrated Regional Offices.* London: Economic Development Committee, 5 May.

Audit Commission (1989) *Urban Regeneration and Economic Development: The Local Government Dimension.* London: HMSO.

Bennett, R., Wicks, P. and McCoshan, A. (1994) *Local Empowerment and Business Services. Britain's Experiment with Training and Enterprise Councils.* London: UCL Press.

Conservative Party (1992) *Manifesto 1992: The Best Future for Britain.* London: Conservative Council Central Office.

Coopers and Lybrand (1992) *Growing Business in the UK. Lessons from Continental Europe: Promoting Partnership for Local Economic Development and Business Support in the UK.* London: Business in the Community.

Coulson, A. (1990) *Devolving Power: The Case for Regional Government.* London: Fabian Society.

Department of the Environment (1993a) 'John Gummer announces measures to bring new localism to improved government services.' News Release, 4 November. London: Department of the Environment.

Department of the Environment (1993b) 'New Regional Offices', 'Single Regeneration Budget', 'Cabinet Committee', 'Sponsor Ministers' and 'City Pride.' Factsheets Nos 1–5. London: Department of the Environment.

Department of the Environment (1993c) 'John Gummer announces appointment of senior regional directors.' News Release, 14 December. London: Department of the Environment.

Department of the Environment (1993d) *Single Regeneration Budget. Note on Principles.* London: Department of the Environment.

Fell, M. (1995) 'The CBI's views on the government offices in the regions.' Paper given at the Association of Metropolitan Authorities Annual Conference, Sheffield, 12 October.

Foster, J. (1995) 'MPs attack powers of regional viceroys.' *Independent on Sunday,* 5 February.

Garside, P.L. and Hebbert, M. (1989) *British Regionalism 1900–2000.* London: Mansell.

Government Office for Yorkshire and Humberside (1995a) *Competitiveness in Yorkshire and Humberside. A Regional Perspective.* Leeds: GOYM.

Government Office for Yorkshire and Humberside (1995b) *Change and Renewal. The Yorkshire and Humberside Economy.* Prepared for GOYM by M. Campbell, M. Foys and J. Froud. Leeds: Leeds Metropolitan University.

Her Majesty's Government (1994) *The Civil Service. Continuity and Change.* Cm 2627. London: HMSO.

House of Commons, Environmental Committee (1995) *First Report. Single Regeneration Budget. Minutes of Evidence and Appendices. Session 1995–1996 Volume II.* London: HMSO.

House of Commons, Public Accounts Committee (1990) *Thirty-third Report. Regenerating the Inner Cities.* Session 1989–90, Vol.216. London: HMSO.

House of Commons, Trade and Industry Committee (1995) *Fourth Report, Session 1994–95.* London: HMSO.

House of Commons, Treasury and Civil Service Select Committee (1989) *Sixth Report, Session 1988–89.* London: HMSO.

Lewis, N. (1992) *Inner City Regeneration. The Demise of Regional and Local Government.* Studies in Law and Politics. Milton Keynes: Open University Press.

Martins, M. and Mawson, J. (1982) 'The programming of regional development in the European Economic Community: supra-national or international decision making?' *Journal of Common Market Studies XX,* 3, 229–244.

Marvin, S. and Cornford, J. (1993) 'Regional policy implications of utility regionalisation.' *Regional Studies 27,* 2, 159–165.

Mawson, J. and Skelcher, C. (1980) 'Updating the West Midlands Regional Strategy.' *Town Planning Review 51,* 2, 152–170.

Morran, G. (1993) 'Time for a dialogue on the regions.' *Local Government Chronicle* 19 February, 18–19.

National Audit Office (1990) *Regenerating the Inner Cities.* London: HMSO.

Northern Region Strategy Team (1977) *Strategic Plan for the Northern Region.* Newcastle: Northern Regional Strategy Team.

Ritchie, D. (1996) 'The role of the Government Offices of the Regions in regional identity and development – achievements of the first two years.' Paper delivered at Queen Mary, Westfield College, Public Policy Seminar, What Future for British Regions?, London, 15 April.

Stewart, M. (1994a) 'Regionalism, devolution and economic dynamism – the shifting institutional framework?' Paper given at ESRC Regionalism and Devolution Research Seminar, 9 May, London School of Economics, London.

Stewart, M. (1994b) 'Between Whitehall and town hall: the realignment of urban regeneration policy in England.' *Policy and Politics 22,* 2, 133–146.

Thornley, A. (1993) *Urban Planning under Thatcherism. The Challenge of the Market.* 2nd edition. London: Routledge.

Wannop, W. and Cherry, G. (1994) 'The development of regional planning in the UK.' *Planning Perspectives 9,* 1, 29–60.

CHAPTER 9

The English Regional Debate

Towards Regional Governance or Government?

John Mawson

Introduction

In contrast to the great seriousness with which periodic demands for Scottish and Welsh devolution have generally been treated, English regionalism was once famously described as the 'dog that never barked' (Harvie 1991). However, evidence of developments in the politics and administration of the English regions during the first half of the 1990s suggested that this relative evaluation was no longer entirely appropriate. In this period certain underlying economic, political and administrative developments led to new forms of regional governance. This development was often linked closely to the particular policies of the Major governments (see Chapters 7 and 8), but it was also related increasingly to approaches in sub-national government, involving central and local government and other key institutional players working together through various forms of partnership and network. Furthermore, it can be argued that a great deal of common ground across the political divide was established in respect of the practice of English regionalism. As a result, it was evident that such trends towards regional governance were likely to persist irrespective of the prevailing political philosophy at the centre.

At the same time, the Labour Party in opposition developed proposals designed to make the new regional capacity subject to greater accountability. It provided, in the first instance, for indirectly appointed regional assemblies or chambers, comprising local politicians and representatives of other regional institutions, and then for a staged move from such nominated regional bodies to directly elected regional assemblies, which would inevitably be subject to political and constitutional pressures. This sparked considerable debate in the mid 1990s over the possibility of moving to a fully fledged system of English regional government.

This chapter seeks to examine these developments by placing them initially in an historical context. Having charted the emergence of regionalism in the first half of the century, the chapter focuses in detail on the events surrounding the Labour government's devolution proposals of the 1970s. It highlights the failure to resolve satisfactorily the English regional question and the way in which this played a significant part in the ultimate failure of the devolution project for Scotland and Wales as well. The chapter goes on to explore why the regional issue took on increasing significance in the latter part of the 1980s and how the Conservative government and the opposition parties responded with new policy agendas. The challenges of a new form of regional governance are examined, focusing on the increasing role played by local government and the business community. Having explored the features of the Centre-Left agenda for the regions, the chapter explores the longer-term prospects for English regionalism.

The origins of the English regional debate

It is instructive to reflect that many aspects of the contemporary debate concerning regionalism in England were present in the latter decades of the nineteenth century and in the years up to the First World War. During this period there were bitter political disputes surrounding the form and structure of the British state. They related in particular to the issue of Irish home rule and the reform of the House of Lords, but the decentralisation of government administration was an issue of more general importance underlying the establishment of elected county councils in 1888. The English dimension was taken a stage further when the Labour Party Conference of 1918 declared the aim of, 'separate statutory legislative assemblies for Scotland, Wales and even England with autonomous administration in matters of local concern' (Labour Party 1918, p.70). However, when a Speaker's Conference on devolution (1919–20) addressed parliamentary concerns about 'Home Rule All Round', England was treated as a single unit for devolved government rather than proposing regions within England.

It was during this period that the emerging academic disciplines of sociology and geography began to study the region as a physical, social, cultural and political entity. Moreover, some of the founding fathers of the town planning profession, such as Sir Patrick Abercrombie and Raymond Unwin, saw the value of regions as one key focus of planning practice and were to go on to influence heavily the Royal Commission on the Distribution of the Industrial Population and Industry (Royal Commission 1940), which established the legislative framework for the post-war system of land-use planning and regional policy (Hall, Thomas, Gracey and Drewett 1973).

An important influential figure in the early academic and professional discourse surrounding regionalism was the Scottish intellectual and polymath, Sir Patrick Geddes, who advocated the adoption of regional surveys. One of the driving forces behind his regional interest was a hostility to the overwhelming influence of the capital city in every aspect of British society. In commenting on contemporary politics Geddes was to observe: 'The movement of politics is no longer a question between Empire and nationalist Home Rule, between Ulster and Irish Free State; it is really between centralised government – and civic regionalism' (quoted in Defries 1927, p.238). Geddes commissioned the geographer C.B. Fawcett to write the influential book, *The Provinces of England: A Study in Some Geographical Aspects of Devolution*, which was an elaboration of arguments contained in an earlier academic paper, 'the natural divisions of England' (Fawcett 1917). In this study Fawcett made the key connection between the achievement of successful devolution to Scotland and Wales and the need to resolve the issue of regionalism in England. Fawcett did not see the English regions as the building blocks for a federal system, but rather as playing an administrative role in receipt of functions devolved by parliament. After the end of the First World War, however, debates surrounding territorial politics died down and the next half century was marked by a broad constitutional consensus extending across the political spectrum. Regionalism was kept alive by a small band of political advocates, academics and professionals, particularly those engaged in the emergent town planning profession.

Ultimately, however, regionalism was to resurface as the political and institutional certainties of the post-war welfare state began to break down in the 1960s and 1970s. As part of the Wilson government's experiment with French-style national indicative planning, Regional Economic Planning Councils (EPCs) were established in 1964 to prepare regional strategies linking economic and physical planning. Later in the 1960s the centralisation of power became a more explicitly political issue following the growth of nationalism, and led again to a perceived need for decentralisation of powers to elected regional bodies. This issue was debated by the Kilbrandon Commission, which reported its proposals for devolution in 1973 (see Chapter 1). The report noted that there was a general demand from people in England, 'to win back power from London' (Royal Commission on the Constitution 1973, paras 1–7), and consequently advocated as part of its scheme the creation of English Regional Councils. The majority report suggested that these should be advisory; a minority report advocated parity with the suggested assemblies for Scotland and Wales.

Labour's election manifesto in late 1971 committed the party in general terms to the establishment of elected regional authorities in England as a complement to its devolution proposals for Scotland and Wales. But once in office, while pressing ahead with its home rule proposals for Scotland and Wales in the form of a draft bill, it chose to issue a consultation Green Paper for England, *Devolution: the English Dimension*, since, 'consultation undertaken in the summer of 1974 showed not only much greater desire for change in Scotland and Wales than England but also a clearer view as to what form it should take' (Her Majesty's Government 1976, para. 3). The Green Paper emphasised a key problem which had been regularly raised by the Labour MP for West Lothian, Tam Dalyell, in parliamentary debates, namely the question as to whether Scottish MPs should have the right to vote on English legislation in subject areas which were devolved to Scotland, especially if Scotland were to continue to have the same number of MPs at Westminster. The Consultation Paper concluded with various ways in which the double representation problem could be addressed. It rejected the notion of an English assembly or assemblies with legislative powers, since this would amount to a form of federalism and an unbalanced one in which one partner would have 85 per cent of the regulation and resources. Instead it plumped for a series of regional assemblies with legislative powers overseeing a range of strategic functions.

The Labour government, however, subsequently abandoned this proposal on the grounds that it lacked support. On this basis English regionalism was buried once again. This decision also had disastrous results for the broader devolutionary scheme. In particular, the failure to provide an economic and political counterweight to the perceived advantageous position of Scotland (at a minimum a development agency for the North) was to lead to problems in the passage of the devolution legislation. English MPs, particularly from northern constituencies, showed their dissatisfaction by supporting legislative amendments to the Scotland and Wales Acts which they felt would reduce the prospects for devolution.

These included the Cunningham amendment, which required a referendum on devolution with a vote of 40 per cent of the registered electorate as a threshold for the affirmative vote to succeed. The failure of the 'yes' vote to attain the requisite level in the referenda of 1979 led to the collapse of parliamentary support for the government (most particularly the support of the Scottish National Party) which by then was in a minority position. Clearly, failure to address the English regional question satisfactorily had been one significant element in creating both of these outcomes.

Labour Party regionalism and its critics, 1979–96

Following the unsuccessful outcome of the devolution referenda, the Labour Party's commitments were watered down in the 1979 election manifesto. Indeed support for a Welsh assembly was withdrawn and there was no mention of regional devolution in England. The election of the Conservative government in 1979 effectively killed off devolution as an immediate political issue. The lack of interest shown by the general public and the absence of any great enthusiasm for English regionalism amongst key constituents within the Labour Party, such as local government, the trade unions and regional representatives, added to the devolution *débâcle* and put the issue on the back burner for a decade. Despite the campaigning efforts of John Prescott, then the Shadow Regional Affairs Spokesperson, who issued in 1982 a detailed economic and political case for elected regional authorities and development agencies in the *Alternative Regional Strategy* (Miller and Mawson 1986; Parliamentary Spokesman's Working Group 1982), the case for English regionalism did not figure in the 1983 manifesto and only led to a commitment to consultation on regional structures in the 1987 manifesto. Even the federalist Liberal Party, which had strongly advocated elected English regional government in the 1970s, recognised political realities and retreated in the 1983 and 1987 elections to taking action in England, 'as the need and demand is established' (Liberal Party 1987). In the case of the Conservative Party, the 1970s flirtation with devolution and regionalism under Edward Heath was firmly squashed by the strongly centralist Mrs Thatcher.

However, the outcome of the 1987 general election and the response of the Labour Party in Scotland brought the devolution issue back to the fore. Labour Party activists felt more frustrated than ever that overwhelming electoral support in Scotland had no impact in Westminster and many who had been hostile or lukewarm to devolution now became active supporters. The implications for England of a strongly renewed Labour Party commitment for constitutional change in Scotland were signalled in a speech by Brian Gould, Shadow Environment Spokesman, in May 1990. He claimed that, 'this new commitment by Labour to regional devolution is an important moment in British politics' (Gould 1990). Subsequently, in 1991 the Labour Party published a Consultation Paper, *Devolution and Democracy* (Labour Party 1991) which highlighted the issues in more detail, particularly the democratic deficit at the regional level in England, and the need for a more effective and accountable regional structure to access European funding and to facilitate economic development. Based on earlier party documents, it suggested a phased approach to elected regional government in England in which the move from unelected regional structures would be based on the widest consensus possible. The 1992 manifesto drew on the Prescott report in emphasising the key role of regional development agencies. It also resurrected proposals for elected assemblies for the English regions but without making a firm commitment to their introduction in the first term of a Labour government.

The other two major parties also responded to the revival of the regional agenda in their manifestos. Of particular importance was the Conservative attack on the destabilising effect of the devolution proposals on the Union. The party nevertheless recognised the validity of a number of the emerging arguments concerning the weakness of the regional administrative structure in the English regions, and so the Conservative manifesto also stated that it would strengthen the machinery for co-ordination in the regions. New, integrated regional offices of the appropriate Whitehall departments would be established so that business and local government would have 'only one port of call' (Conservative Party 1992, p.39). Thus the Conservative solution was to be one of administrative decentralisation as expressed in the introduction in 1994 of the ten Integrated Regional Offices, subsequently known as Government Offices for the Regions (GORs).

Meanwhile the Labour opposition, in formulating new proposals for England to accompany Scottish and Welsh devolution, embarked upon a wide-ranging consultation exercise in the run-up to the production of the party's local government policy document, *Rebuilding Democracy, Rebuilding Communities* (Labour Party 1995a). Initially the proposals for English regional reform were to be prepared alongside the party's local government policies. However, the tensions present in resolving the relationship between the two tiers was such, particularly against the background of the complex and varied outcome of local government reorganisation, that the brief was split when Jack Straw became Shadow Home Secretary in the spring of 1994. The apparent uncertainties in Labour policy were sharply criticised by John Major as part of a general attack on the incoherence of Labour's proposals and their damaging consequences for the stability of the Union (Major 1995). The ferocity of the attack drew media attention, and for the first time in many years the English regional dimension began to be considered as a significant political issue.

Labour responded swiftly to the Conservative attack. A Labour spokesman commented to the press that John Major's pitch for the English nationalist vote had helped the opposition by highlighting the issue at an early stage, thus giving time to formulate policy (Castle 1995). The skeletal framework of a new strategy which Straw and his team had been working on was then presented to a meeting of the Parliamentary Party early in February 1995, and was revealed in an interview on BBC 1's *On the Record* programme. Labour's sensitivity to the accusation that regional government would create more bureaucracy was highlighted in Straw's statement: 'One thing we are clear about in England – you cannot establish regional assemblies as well as having shire counties and districts underneath them' (Straw 1995a). This position was reiterated in a speech by Tony Blair, by then Labour Party leader, in St Helens when he argued that the fact that the Major government's restructuring of local government in England (see Chapter 7) had reduced only 8 of the 39 shire county areas to anything like a tier of unitary district authorities, meant that the creation of elected assemblies would take, 'longer than had been anticipated' (Blair 1995). In a clearly orchestrated campaign, 'party sources' were quoted as saying that the need to subject local government to a further reorganisation and to consult widely made the establishment of elected regional bodies ahead of a second election highly unlikely. Meanwhile, Labour remained determined to press ahead with addressing what it regarded as a democratic deficit in the regions, expressed in the form of quangos and powerful government offices, by proposing the establishment of indirectly appointed regional bodies comprising councillors who would work in parallel with these bodies on regional policy matters and oversee and scrutinise their activities. Such bodies would represent the first stage in the move to elected assemblies. The approach was to be sketched out in greater detail in a consultation document in June 1995, the outcome of which was to be presented to the party's Policy Forum and Conference in the autumn of 1996. This outcome raised concerns amongst two opposing groups in the debate: on the one hand there were those in local government who saw the development as a potential threat to the strategic role of local authorities; and on the other the advocates of elected regional authorities within the party, particularly from the North of England, supported by outside pressure groups such as the Campaign for a North of England Assembly, who were concerned about possible delays (Tommaney and Turnbull 1992).

At the same time, Labour's more detailed plans provoked further comment from their political opponents. The essence of the Conservative case against Labour's regional government proposals was succinctly summarised by Whitehead (1996) as follows: that regional government would add additional tiers of bureaucracy to sub-national government; that it would be expensive to set up and administer; that it would be constitutionally improper; and that it would have no legitimacy or popular mandate. In a speech to the Association of Metropolitan Authorities (AMA) Local Government and Regionalism Conference in March 1995, the Minister for Housing and Local Government, David Curry, elaborated the Conservative case (Curry 1995). Taking an historical perspective he argued that English nationality had a much earlier, and more coherent, centre than in many European countries and that regional identities folded at a much earlier stage in England.

Curry went on to consider the claim made by the advocates of regional government that the EU was constituted in such a way as to make necessary such reforms in order to successfully access its Structural Funds. His view, however, was that the funding arrangements between the EU and the English regions were well worked out and did not necessitate formal governmental structures. He argued that local partnerships, whether they emerged as part of domestic policies or as part of European programmes, were likely to be more effective than the institutional partnerships that regional government would enforce. Nor did he consider that strategic planning and other service functions required regional government since regional mechanisms had been developed where necessary, such as in the case of Regional Planning Guidance: 'It's brought together groups of local authorities and I think it will get better as time goes on and what is interesting is that one is seeing the development of different regional forums which have helped to give this more substance. The West Midlands Forum, for example' (Curry 1995).

Turning to 'one or two practicalities' surrounding Labour's ideas, David Curry highlighted the difficulties of defining regions and implementing regional government only in situations, 'where there were unitary authorities and where people wanted it'. He pointed out that a very heterogeneous system of local government had emerged from the Local Government Review and he did not detect any great appetite to go down this course again:

> I go around the country and I talk to many leaders of different sorts of councils. The number of them that will tell me over coffee that the concept of regional government is the biggest elephant's graveyard is legion… And where's the demand? I have to tell you that in my surgeries in Skipton, no-one has come to talk to me about regional government.

In relation to the so-called democratic deficit at the regional level, he questioned, 'if you're going to pour every quango into this new tier how do you expect to get rapid, responsive, effective handling of the various different issues that come up?'. As to the GORs: 'They are accountable to their ministers and they are accountable to Parliament… So I would prefer to try and make our system work through the Regional Offices, through the partnerships, through that sort of consultation and see whether we can't deal with them more effectively that way' (Curry 1995).

At the same conference the Liberal Democrat Home Affairs Spokesman, Robert MacLennan, presented a perspective which in many ways involved a far more radical restructuring of political and institutional forms than that proposed by Labour. He pointed out that his party had long favoured decentralisation of government, a commitment set out in the party constitution and elaborated upon in the 1993 policy document *Here We Stand* (Liberal Democrat Party 1993). In justifying the approach he stated that many of the arguments which were apposite in Scotland for regionalisation applied with equal force in England, though not all. The debate was not over whether to decentralise but how it should be done. The Liberal Democrat aim was not to create a new sub-national tier of government, but rather to replace existing appointed bodies such as quangos and other government agencies in the regions with institutions which were democratically accountable. The Liberal Democrats proposed between 9 and 12 elected regional assemblies assuming various responsibilities from central government and quangos, but with a major focus on regional development.

MacLennan pointed out that while their proposals for the Scottish parliament, Welsh senedd and English assemblies meant they would have different powers, they would nevertheless all have a common foundation based on a set of guiding principles, including election by a system of single transferable votes; the structure of government would be determined by the subsidiarity principle; power would be brought down from Westminster rather than up from local government; there would be some limited taxation powers; and disputes between government bodies would be decided by a Supreme Court. He reminded the audience that earlier statements made by the Liberal Democrats had envisaged the establishment of English regions taking up to six years preceded by a Parliamentary Commission which, following consultation, would produce boundary proposals. MacLennan indicated that he favoured such a process, which would allow for the emergence of a variable structure based on consultation.

The new regionalism: the view from business and local government

As the views of the political parties on the need for a new regional agenda became increasingly focused, so other key actors with an interest in the regional issue began to recognise the force of the arguments for change. The underlying tensions between central and local government surrounding relations with Brussels all fuelled the debate. These related particularly to the accessing of European funding, the recognition of the need to improve the co-ordination of government programmes at the regional level, question marks over the transparency and accountability of government agencies and institutions within the regions, and a recognition of the need to strengthen the organisational and administrative framework of economic development within the English regions. During the course of 1994 and 1995, a number of these issues were aired during the House of Commons Trade and Industry

Committee review of regional policy under the Chairmanship of the Labour regional spokesman, Dick Caborne. The Association of British Chambers of Commerce argued in evidence to the Select Committee that a stronger regional voice was needed if Britain's views on regions were to be properly represented in Europe, and that this could best be accomplished by a regional forum which also provided an advisory and co-ordinating remit in economic development (House of Commons Trade and Industry Select Committee Report 1995, para. 138). Concerns about regional co-ordination and the transparency and accountability of government were also raised by the Confederation of British Industry (CBI). In January 1995 Howard Davies, the then Director General of the CBI, said that:

> Regional businesses have definitely welcomed having a single port of call for government in their region. But curiously, rather than appease enthusiasm for regional autonomy and make them think that government really does care about the world beyond the M25, the Integrated Regional Offices seem to have had the opposite effect. It has woken them up to what they have been missing. (Davies 1995)

Following this, Davies launched a regional business agenda initiative to reflect what he saw as, 'a growing consensus that a regional focus for decision-making across the public sector needed to be created which allowed input from the business community'. He pointed out that a survey of CBI members in England and Wales had revealed, 'a general dissatisfaction with the balance of power between the Centre and the regions' (Fell 1995, p.4). This message was relayed to all the political parties, but the effectiveness of the CBI lobby became most immediately evident some months later when the government announced that business representatives would be appointed to the management board of the GORs in Whitehall.

It was not just the business community, however, which recognised and responded to the increasing significance of the regional agenda. Regional issues had always been a matter of concern for local government in relation to issues such as transport, planning, environmental issues, regeneration, economic development and European funding. Over the years the need to engage in policy development, advocacy and the implementation of various strategic initiatives at this geographical scale had necessitated the creation of regional joint machinery, although much of this type of work had been undertaken through the county councils. Perhaps the best known examples of local authority joint working were the so-called 'standing conferences', or regional local authority associations, which had their origins in the early post-war attempts to disperse population and industry from the congested cities and required the preparation, monitoring and review of regional plans. Such activity became progressively less relevant with the emergence of the inner city problem and the 'ideological' antagonism towards planning during the Thatcher era. Nevertheless, the activity survived in some regions viz. the South East, West Midlands and North East. This continuity of experience was matched elsewhere by a revival of joint working during the latter part of the 1980s in response to the need to provide Regional Planning Guidance for central government. Work was extended into other activities such as economic development and the preparation of European strategies. Indeed a particular spur to the development of regional strategies came from officials of the EU's Regional Policy Directorate who, much to the annoyance of central government departments, actively encouraged local authorities to prepare such strategy documents with other regional 'social' partners as a backcloth to the allocation of funding under the new round of EU Structural Funds. In the case of some regions, such as the North West, it was the need to work together on these documents which proved the catalyst in renewing regional collaborative working and helped forge a new regional consensus amongst previously competing local authorities and sub-regions (North West Regional Association and North West Business Leadership Team 1993).

With the restoration of a comprehensive geographical coverage of regional working by the early 1990s, and an increasing recognition of the need to articulate local authority interests at the regional level, a decision was taken to establish an English Regional Association (ERA) in 1993. A subsequent survey conducted by the ERA then showed that the composition of the nine regional local authority associations, now styled Regional Associations (RAs) encompassed all the local authorities in England (bar three councils) including counties, districts, metropolitan districts and London boroughs (ERA 1995a). The majority of the RAs focused their activities on regional planning, and environmental, transportation, waste, economic development and European issues. However, there were variations in emphasis, with the South East and South West Regional Planning Conferences, for example, focusing largely on land-use planning matters, while at the other end of the spectrum the North of England Assembly and West Midlands Forum had more wide-ranging policy agendas.

The survey further showed that the main decision-making bodies of these organisations, which generally met three or four times a year, comprised nominated representatives with differing formulae for appointment on a geographical and/or local authority category basis. None of the associations had non-local authority members, but most had observer consultee positions and/or formal/informal links with central government, business organisations, trade unions, voluntary sector and other elected representatives – such as Committee of the Region members, MPs and MEPs. The great majority of secretariat offices were permanent, serviced by officers from the various authorities, and four of the nine maintained a Brussels office. The ERA itself developed regular officer and member meetings to discuss matters of mutual interest, exchange information and engage where appropriate in lobbying on policy issues.

At their meeting in Falmouth in March 1995, against the background of the regional debate and Labour's emerging proposals, the RAs resolved that there should be a devolution of various central government regional functions and powers to local authority organised regional working (ERA 1995b). They also took the view that, given the decentralised and fragmented nature of central government activities at the regional level, the relevant government agencies should be required to consult and seek the views of regional and local interests through agreed regional mechanisms provided by the RAs (ERA 1995b). The ERA and individual forums went on to launch a European Action Programme in the run-up to the Inter-governmental Conference, and to organise a series of seminars and conferences in different regions on the issue of devolution to the English regions and their future role in this respect (Mawson *et al.* 1996).

Given the traditional role of the three national local authority associations in presenting a local government perspective to Whitehall, it was perhaps inevitable that there should be some 'behind the scenes' debate and tensions as to the precise role of the RAs in expressing a local authority view on regional and European issues. With the proposal to merge the national associations on the agenda during this period (subsequently agreed in 1996), some took the view that it would be better to leave the construction of a regional interface with the new Single Local Government Association (Association of County Councils, Association of District Councils, Association of Metropolitan Authorities 1995). During the course of 1994 and 1995 the AMA and the Association of District Councils (ADC) both launched reviews of their positions on the regional question, while at the same time lending support to a study on regionalism commissioned by the Local Government Management Board (Stoker, Hogwood and Bullman 1995).

In earlier periods of debate, regionalism in England was regarded with scepticism, if not outright hostility, by a significant number of senior and more influential local government politicians, reflecting the perceived threat to local government's strategic role. This was particularly the case with civic leaders of some of the larger cities and the county councils. In addition, this opposition was always a potent force within the Labour Party policy-making machinery whenever the party flirted with the idea of regionalism. During the course of the 1980s and early 1990s, influential local government experts and academics, such as Professor John Stewart of the Institute of Local Government Studies and Professor George Jones of the London School of

Economics, led a fierce intellectual assault on the idea of regional government whenever the idea re-emerged in the political arena (Jones 1988). The nub of their argument was that a regional tier would exercise over local authorities many powers operated by central government, and that it would be responsible for the provision of strategic services which would otherwise be the responsibility of local authorities. Because the regional assemblies would be elected, Jones and Stewart took the view that they would feel that they had the legitimacy and authority to press their priorities on local authorities. Thus they argued from a local government perspective that the introduction of elected regional assemblies would be a proposal for centralisation (Jones and Stewart 1985).

Given the above arguments, it was a measure of the changing context by the mid1990s that the local authority associations were prepared to entertain seriously the possibility of some form of elected regional tier. In February 1995 the ADC held a policy workshop to consider the various options, ranging from constitutional reform (Cornford 1995) to more limited measures, which might be introduced prior to legislation in the first term of a government moving towards elected assemblies. In the latter case proposals were presented on the role which could be played by the RAs working in parallel with the GORs and what changes would be required at the interface between Whitehall and the regions (Mawson 1995). In attendance at the workshop was the Labour Party's Local Government and Home Affairs team, charged with the responsibility for preparing Labour's proposals for the English regions. Some months later the ideas were reiterated in a paper produced by the Institute of Public Policy Research (Tindale 1995) and in May, reflecting the growing significance of the regional agenda, the AMA published the findings of its working party on *Regionalism: The Local Government Dimension* (AMA 1995a).

The paper highlighted the fact that, 'England already had an extensive system of regional administration', which it termed 'creeping executive regionalism', reflected in the establishment of the GORs and the wide range of government agencies which, 'are not accountable locally and are only indirectly accountable to Parliament' (AMA 1995a, p.1). The AMA argued that it was necessary to ensure that the English regions had the capacity and political and institutional infrastructure to respond to the pressures facing them. Priority needed to be given to remedying the democratic deficit, and local government's regional structures could provide a basis for achieving this, at least in the short to medium term, prior to elected assemblies. However, it was argued that the idea that simply to require the GORs to be accountable to elected members appointed by authorities in a region would solve the problem was a gross simplification.

To begin with, the GORs were only in control of limited aspects of central government policies and programmes. It would be necessary to consider what responsibilities currently undertaken by central government agencies could be undertaken at the regional level; which functions should remain within the remit of the GORs; which could be transferred to regionally accountable decision-making bodies; and which could be devolved downwards to local authorities in joint working machinery. The whole question of coterminosity of regional boundaries would need to be addressed, with the simplest and speediest starting point being a move to the boundaries of the GORs.

Labour's consultation proposals: a choice for England

The AMA's discussion document was clearly designed to influence the developing thinking within the Labour Party. When the Labour Party consultation document was released in July 1995 it reflected the debates which preceded it, adopting a cautious and staged approach designed to address the problems and criticisms which had been raised (Labour Party 1995b). The paper rehearsed the argument that there was a strong case for a democratically accountable regional tier in England irrespective of what was seen as the entirely unrelated debate concerning Scotland and Wales. It highlighted the need for improved co-ordination at the regional level and the weakness of the institutional capacity of the English regions in regard to matters such as economic development and accessing funding from Brussels. The need to make the government offices, quangos and other agencies more open and accountable to the regions and their local authorities was also emphasised. The emergence of regional local authority working, as represented by the RAs, was seen as the building blocks for a new democratic regional structure. However, the approach needed to be a phased one.

In September 1995, Jack Straw set out the thinking which underlay the proposals in a speech to the Regional Studies Association (Straw 1995b). He argued that Labour could not be accused of creating a further tier of bureaucracy since it was the Conservative government which had done that, rather the task was to make regional government accountable to the people it served. In drafting the proposals Straw suggested two apparently conflicting trends had to be taken into account: first that there was a need all over England to make the existing system of regional government more responsive and accountable to people in each region, and second, that support for directly elected assemblies varied across the country, 'so the question was how to secure change which allowed those regions with strong support for elected assemblies to move ahead at their pace and not at the pace of the slowest'.

The solution was to be a two-stage process with the creation of indirectly elected regional chambers made up of a relatively small number of nominated councillors (40 was suggested). *A Choice for England* proposed that nominations would come from an electoral college based on a formula reflecting a geographical and political balance. The chambers would co-opt other regional partners from business (the CBI, Chambers of Commerce, Trades Union Congress (TUC), voluntary organisations) to key policy committees and regional development organisations. They would be serviced by the current secretariats of the RAs, and hence it was suggested that their running costs would be funded by the local authorities. There would be no tax-raising or legislative powers, and they would be set up quickly and initially without the need for legislation. Their responsibilities would cover European funding, economic development, transport and land-use planning, and they would have formal rights of consultation with the GORs and powers of scrutiny over regionally based quangos, Next Step agencies and privatised utilities. They would also have the responsibility for managing the establishment of the directly elected assemblies.

A Choice for England stated that consideration would be given to transferring certain functions held by the GORs and quangos to the regional assemblies, or at least sharing responsibility with the GORs. The regional boundaries of the chambers would conform in the case of most regions to those of the GORs, since the exercise involved formalising, extending and making more accountable some of the existing structures of regional government. However, when it came to elected assemblies it was likely that there would be more controversy and hence the need for consultation, as, for example, in the case of the South East region. In relation to the costs of such bodies, the claim was made that these would be negligible since there was inherent inefficiency in the present system of regional policy with duplication, overlap and waste which had been identified by the House of Commons Trade and Industry Select Committee (House of Commons 1995). Independent auditors and the Audit Commission would ensure that no additional expenditure was involved in the establishment of directly elected assemblies.

As to the timescale, Straw stated that it would vary from region to region and would be dependent on three safeguards, which were suggested not as insurmountable hurdles but as practical steps to ensure that the policy was implemented by consent. In the case of the first condition:

> it seems to us that the plan for the Chamber should be drawn up by democratic representatives in the region rather than by some unelected commission or Whitehall. The second condition – of Parliamentary approval – would be straightforward. Our intention is that this would be by Parliamentary Order, after a short debate under powers provided

> by the principal act establishing the concept of regional assemblies... The third condition is that of popular consent possibly by a region wide referendum... Without a clear test of public opinion, the establishment of these bodies could get bogged down in impossible to resolve arguments about whether the public really wanted them...the assemblies might then have an air of impermanence about them and in turn fail to attract the best of elected members and officers.

The phased approach, according to Straw, was necessary not only to address the need for popular consent but also because shire counties could not generally co-exist with a system of elected regional assemblies, since it was argued that in the fields of land-use planning, transport, economic development and European aid (all of which would be key functions of the regions), there would be considerable overlap with the activities of the county councils. Nevertheless, the requirement for a two-tier system was not set in stone. He accepted that in some very sparsely populated counties there may be exceptions to the general rule of unitary local government.

Straw suggested that Labour's previous plans for elected assemblies had been stillborn in part because of the statist blueprint approach which would have imposed from above a standard model everywhere all at once. Rather, an organic approach had to be adopted:

> I've no wish to start a competition between the North, the North West and the South West but there's little doubt in my mind that they are the regions with the strongest developed regional identity, not least because they are also the regions furthest distant from London. All have developed regional institutions. The North, for example, has shown the way with the Northern Development Company and the North of England Assembly. Real partnerships have got going in that region. I know that there is a good deal of evidence for example which points to strong popular support for an elected assembly in the north. The beauty it seems to me of the scheme proposed is that given these regional strengths, the north does not have to ask anyone else about where it is in the queue. It can push itself to the front of the queue. Once that happens it will create a dynamic which other regions can then follow.

As far as London was concerned, the Labour Party was already committed to the establishment of an elected strategic authority, but the final details would also be subject to a confirmatory test of public consent such as a referendum. How such an authority would relate to regional chamber(s) or assemblies elsewhere in the South East remained to be spelt out.

The Regional Policy Commission

In June 1996 the Labour Party launched the second key component of its proposals for the English regions in the form of *The Report of the Regional Policy Commission* (Regional Policy Commission 1996). The Commission had been established some 12 months earlier under the Chairmanship of the former EU Regional Policy Commissioner, Bruce Millan, at the instigation of Labour's Deputy Leader, John Prescott. Working under the framework of the proposals contained in the *Choice for England*, the report was designed to develop regional economic policies which would complement the emerging proposals for regional political structures.

Central to the Commission's thinking was the establishment of a regional development agency (RDA) for each region under the remit of the relevant chamber or assembly. This mirrored earlier Labour Party thinking in the *Alternative Regional Strategy* and Labour's 1994 policy statement, *Winning for Britain* (Labour Party 1994), which acknowledged the valuable practical experience of local authority, controlled enterprise boards or companies as one model for the proposed RDAs. Under the Commission's proposals these bodies would take control at the regional level of the management of regional economic policy, the European Structural Funds and other regeneration programmes such as the Single Regeneration Budget. The RDAs would also subsume the work of the Rural Development Commission, English Partnerships and the inward investment agencies. They would adopt constitutions which would enable the participation of other regional partners such as the CBI, regional TUC and the voluntary sector in the preparation of a regional strategy, and where appropriate they would participate in, or foster, sub-regional or local partnerships engaged in various aspects of economic development including the raising of private sector finance. At a national level it was suggested that there should be a minister of cabinet rank with special responsibility for the regions to enhance inter-departmental co-ordination and take responsibility for the GORs. Alongside these national roles it was also envisaged that there should be an assessment of the regional impact of public expenditure.

The proposals contained in the Commission document were not formally ratified by the Labour Party decision-making machinery. However, it was clear that in carrying the support of senior Labour Party figures they were likely to be taken seriously in providing the framework for future policy development. Indeed, the wider significance of these developments was highlighted in a press leak in May 1996 which suggested that the Labour leader was seeking to avoid a rebellion of English MPs against the Scottish devolution proposals by supporting the immediate implementation of the proposals for the RDAs (Condon 1996). Labour Party sources were quoted as saying that the promise of the speedy introduction of RDAs would be sufficient to persuade the 40-strong Northern group of MPs, second only to the Scottish MPs within the Parliamentary Party, to drop its plan to disrupt the devolution legislation in protest at the lack of the immediate establishment of elected assemblies in England. A North East MP, John McWilliams, was quoted as saying: 'We can now support our Scottish colleagues wholeheartedly over devolution knowing that we can expect their support in return. All we ever wanted was fair treatment if devolution was on for Scotland'.

The strengthening of the RAs

The developments surrounding English regionalism in the two year period between 1994 and 1996 were to lead to the commissioning of a number of studies by various research foundations and institutions into the regional question, and there was a heightened awareness and interest in the issue amongst politicians, policy-makers and practitioners to a degree which had not been experienced since the mid 1970s. There was, moreover, a growing momentum behind the work of the RAs, with seminars and conferences organised for officers and members to explore the potential role which the RAs might play (West Midlands Regional Forum 1996). The prospect of an election within a comparatively short time frame, which suggested the possibility of a change in government, and in turn the emergence of a new regional structure based on the building blocks of local authority regional organisation, was undoubtedly a major factor behind a spate of reviews of RA roles and constitutions. Further pressures leading in the same direction were the strengthened presence of central government in the regions as represented in the work of the GORs, and the establishment of a single local government association by April 1997 with an electoral college organised on a regional basis. Irrespective of the outcome of the general election, it was recognised that for all the reasons listed above (and others), local government would need to speak with a more powerful single voice at the regional level.

Remarkably, even associations such as the East Midlands Regional Planning Forum, covering an area without a strong regional identity, were actively considering bringing all their members together within a strengthened constitution and wider remit. Similarly, the South West Regional Planning Conference had set in train discussions with its regional CBI and TUC to establish a regional chamber on a voluntary basis by October 1997 (South West Regional Planning Conference 1996). Recognising that the North East would be regarded as the front runner in the implementation of the Straw proposals, a detailed Consultation Paper on a three-stage move to the establishment of an elected regional assembly and development agency, was approved by the North of England Assembly of Local Authorities at the beginning of 1996 (North of England Assembly 1996). Meanwhile, in Yorkshire and Humberside, another region with a history of both municipal and sub-regional rivalries, a single Yorkshire and Humberside Regional Assembly (YHRA) was launched in the summer of 1996, merging the two former regional local authority bodies. Significantly, while explicitly tailored to fit the framework of a regional chamber, the establishment of the new assembly was welcomed by the Minister of Housing and Local Government, David Curry.

The YHRA decision-making body comprised the 22 leaders of the member authorities supported by a Chief Executives' Advisory Group and four specialist member/officer groups covering key policy themes: sub-regional issues in the four county areas, lobbying, networking and partnership development. The rationale for the approach was spelt out by the Chief Executive of Bradford Metropolitan District Council, Richard Penn, in a seminar paper in April 1996 when he argued that no single agency could have the capacity solely to regenerate its own area, so that the two key concepts underpinning the YHRA strategy were partnership and subsidiarity (Penn 1996). Modern regional policy, he suggested, involved a combination of traditional inward investment and indigenous development policies, but to this needed to be added the promotion of innovation, development of institutional capacity and fostering of networks of public and private sector bodies to develop best practice and participate in joint initiatives. The success of such an approach was dependent on the capacity of the partners to exploit and integrate the resources they shared in order to maximise the use of the region's social and physical capital. The issue of effective institutional capacity, he argued, helped to explain why different regions achieved different levels of success.

Richard Penn suggested that the best examples of success in this approach were at sub-national or regional level because of the combination of geographical closeness, personal knowledge and shared cultural values. The regional level was important, he argued, because much innovative activity took place in the form of industrial clusters and because regional analysts were beginning to recognise that the regional level was the most appropriate level for the design and delivery of support programmes for such clusters, particularly in the case of small and medium sized enterprises. The major obstacle to the achievement of this in England was, in his view, the institutional deficit. Penn suggested that the Conservative government's establishment of the GORs was partly an acceptance of this problem but, 'the longer term possibility of a "bottom up" approach represented by the Regional Assembly creates better possibilities for the development of networking capacity' (Penn 1996, p.9).

The response to New Labour's regional agenda

While the reorganisation of the regional associations reflected a growing recognition that the regional level was likely to be a long-term basis for significant development, the response to the Labour Party consultation exercise was also indicative of how seriously regional reform was now being taken at a national level within local government circles.

The AMA's submission on *A Choice for England*, for example, was broadly supportive of the Straw approach, but saw the first indirect stage as a necessary transitionary interlude to the establishment of directly elected assemblies which, it argued, would make possible more genuine devolution of power from the centre (AMA 1996). It was for this reason that the AMA wished to see a five year timetable for staged change. It also questioned the need for a mandatory referendum in each region, taking the view that it would only be possible to draw definitive conclusions with a large turnout and majority (in favour or against). It was contended that the chambers could not take on the role envisaged for them with the level of staff resources available to the existing regional associations, and thus there would need to be a transfer of resources from central government. As to the role of any new regional body, it would be necessary to be clear about lines of responsibility since the attempt to make a regional office accountable both to ministers and a regional chamber would lead to fragmentation and confusion. As well as the obvious regional strategic roles for the regional body, the AMA supported the position that regionally based quangos, Next Step agencies and privatised utilities would be subject to scrutiny as to their regional impact. Further, the AMA argued in some cases that it might be appropriate to transfer their regional functions to the chambers. As to the mechanisms which could be deployed by a chamber in carrying out its monitoring role, these might include requirements to consult the chamber; appointment by the chamber of board members to the relevant organisation; or the use of House of Commons Select Committee-type scrutiny commissions. Once directly elected regional assemblies were established, relevant organisations could be required to submit their strategic plans for approval; a client–contract relationship might be developed where funding was provided; the assembly might appoint all members of an agency's board; or the regional functions of an activity might be transferred to the control of the assembly.

The Association of County Councils (ACC) was unable to set out an agreed cross-party position on regional assemblies, but its Labour Group submission to *A Choice for England* did not oppose the principle of elected assemblies whilst agreeing with the requirement for evidence of popular support based on the experience of regional chambers (ACC Labour Group 1995). Perhaps not surprisingly, given the tensions between the county and district tiers of local government over strategic responsibilities, the ADC presented a generally supportive statement on the Straw proposals (ADC 1995). In a lengthy 40-page submission most of the detailed attention focused on the role of the chambers since it was felt that this was the most immediate challenge and the model which might persist for some time, if not indefinitely, in some regions. Nevertheless, the ADC response acknowledged the potential weaknesses of an indirectly elected stage and questioned the logic or need for Labour's 'triple safeguards' in moving to elected assemblies. As with the AMA response, it was argued that greater funding would be needed to resource the chambers and more attention needed to be given to what functions would be transferred from central government. In relation to the composition of the chambers it was argued that all local authorities should have a place, with weighted voting to reflect the different sizes/types of local authority. Other relevant bodies would be given the opportunity to be represented but it would not be appropriate for representatives of such organisations to have a role in the decision-making process on a par with local authority representatives. As far as regional boundaries were concerned, the ADC, in common with the AMA report, argued that the debate about boundaries ought not to be allowed to sidetrack and delay the introduction of regional chambers. To this end it was suggested that the regional chamber/GOR boundaries should be coterminous.

A third significant commentary on the chamber/assembly model came from the work of the Constitution Unit based at University College, London which was established in April 1995 to enquire into the implementation of various constitutional reform measures. Funded by a number of charitable research foundations, it carried out a research programme on the introduction of devolved assemblies in Scotland, Wales and the English regions. While not formally responding to Labour's consultation exercise, nevertheless its report on *Regional Government in England*, published in July 1996, clearly focused on the Straw proposals. It critically reviewed the emerging Centre-Left model for the English regions and explored various practical issues surrounding the process of implementation.

In terms of planning a parliamentary legislative programme, it emphasised the distinction between a process of relatively rapid transition from chamber to assembly, as distinct from a slower process envisaged by the ADC in which the chambers might play a more significant longer-term role. In the case of the former scenario, legislation would be needed to provide for regional assemblies from the outset, in which case the transitionary role of chambers would be less significant. With the slower transition, chambers would need the active co-operation of Whitehall departments, the Next Step agencies and other statutory bodies to fulfil their role. This could best be accomplished through a White Paper, which would identify chamber roles and functions; set out formal relationships with other government departments and agencies; give directions to quangos; set out mechanisms of voluntary collaboration such as jointly produced 'charters'; establish the framework of a regional strategic plan and how it would relate to Whitehall policy-making; set out the constitutional parameters and geographical boundaries of the chambers; and lay out what steps would need to be taken to move to the establishment of elected assemblies. Thus chambers could make a start without legislation. However, the Constitution Unit argued that there would be limitations on what could be achieved without a statutory basis. They might lack the necessary authority, funding would be dependent on voluntary agreement, the extent of their activities would derive from their constituent local authority powers, which could be contested, and there would be heavy dependence on the willing co-operation of Whitehall and its agencies.

The advantage of moving to directly elected assemblies, it was argued, would be that clear lines of political accountability would be established, thus making possible the devolution of central functions. Such transfers, however, would have implications for the management of central government and, clearly, the wider the range of functions the greater the prospects of political difficulties and dispute. The Constitution Unit set out a range of possibilities for assemblies, from a minimalist model incorporating only limited chamber functions to one with an enhanced range of activities but short of those of a Scottish parliament involving legislative powers (see Figure 9.1).

Other critical issues needing to be resolved according to the Unit included relationships with local government, and specifically whether the assemblies would allocate resources to local authorities and other public bodies within the region. The funding of assemblies would also be a controversial matter, with various options including block grant, a regional income or sales tax, a precept or a levy on local government. It would be necessary to determine whether the same boundaries needed to be maintained for chamber and assembly stages, and if there were to be changes, how they would be chosen. Finally, the composition of assemblies and the electoral mechanisms would require resolution. Given the geographical distribution of party support and the strong possibility of one-party domination in a number of regions, it was

Minimalist

1. The strategic responsibilities of chambers
   - strategic land-use planning
   - transport
   - economic development
   - co-ordination of European funding bids
2. The voice of the region
3. A statutory right of consultation on strategic or business plans for the Regional Development Agencies
4. Similar responsibilities for other key bodies (which would need to be given clear regional structures and budgets). For example:
   - regional arts associations
   - sports councils
   - health authorities
   - regional arms of Highways and other key Next Step agencies
   - English Partnerships
5. Consumer consultative arrangements for public utilities
6. Statutory right of consultation by government on defined issues

Advanced

As for minimalist model plus:

1. Assuming the functions of GORs in some or all of the following fields:
   - education and training
   - industry
   - urban regeneration (including allocating Single Regeneration Budget
   - environment and transport
2. Assuming responsibility for powers over agencies, or regional arms of agencies, working in the above fields, covering:
   - approval of strategic land
   - assembly being 'client' for the agency
   - appointment of all board members in the regions
   - formal transfer of some or all functions in the regions
3. Determining the allocation within the region of an allocated block of Lottery funding
4. A block of expenditure allocated by government to cover the above, with virement permitted

Source: Constitution Unit (1996)

Figure 9.1: Constitution Unit options for English regional reform

suggested there was a strong argument for a system of proportional representation.

Conclusion

It is evident in reviewing the debate surrounding the English regional question in the mid 1990s that the concept of regionalism was interpreted in several different ways by commentators. Some looked at the issue purely in a formal political and administrative sense, exploring the prospects of alternative models of government such as administrative decentralisation, devolution and federalism (Tindale 1995), while others considered the question much more from the perspective of spatial planning (Wannop 1995). Some researchers widened the debate and asked questions about the nature of the regional problem and how this was being translated into new forms of governance (Harding, Evans and Parkinson 1995). Undoubtedly, as the focus of regional concerns shifted over the course of the post-war period, so in turn did the debate about appropriate institutional and governmental structures.

The 1960s, for example, was a period in which the regional dimension was explicitly linked to wider economic concerns about the competitiveness of the national economy and the need to secure balanced growth across the country as part of anti-inflationary policies. For a brief period a technocratic managerialist perspective prevailed in which the application of the French model of indicative planning sought to link national economic priorities with comprehensive regional land-use and socio-economic strategies prepared on corporatist lines by indirectly appointed regional EPCs. While national economic planning quickly disappeared following the demise of George Brown's Department of Economic Affairs, the EPCs persisted in their work of preparing tripartite regional strategies throughout the 1970s, reaching a pinnacle with the *Strategic Plan for the Northern Region* (Northern Region Strategy Team 1977). However, the attempt to produce comprehensive regional strategies ran against the grain of Whitehall departmentalism and Treasury concerns about the regional disaggregation of public expenditure.

By the mid 1970s the focus of debate amongst the political parties had shifted to the possibility of regional government in England as a complement to the need for devolution of Scotland and Wales. While Labour remained committed to regional economic policy and planning, the underlying momentum was undoubtedly based upon the political pressures arising from nationalism. In this respect the failure of Labour to achieve a satisfactory political and economic formula capable of resolving the various concerns of

English MPs about devolution led to a parliamentary backlash and the ultimate collapse of the legislation.

At this juncture it is evident that there was little political or policy rationale within England to support the case for some form of regional government that would have been sufficiently strong to override the objections of prominent national Labour Party figures, opponents of regionalism in local government or the apathy of the general public.

During the course of the 1980s Conservative governments dismantled the remaining elements of Labour's regional machinery and adopted a strong 'pro Union' status quo position in regard to the constitution. It was nevertheless in this period that new pressures emerged which were to lead to the re-emergence of the regional agenda in England (Mawson 1996). The fragmentation of the public realm arising from privatisation, the establishment of arms-length agencies and the marketisation of public services, when taken together with a limited and poorly co-ordinated presence of government departments, highlighted the need to improve management at the regional level. The business support structure and institutional capacity for handling regional development and inward investment was widely seen as inadequate in comparison with that of other EU countries and Scotland, Wales and Northern Ireland. Moreover, the need for civil servants to manage the implementation of European Structural Fund programmes at the regional level and prepare regional strategies to access European funding resulted in pressures from the Treasury. Added to these administrative and policy considerations there were those outside government circles who expressed political concerns about the accountability and openness of government agencies and quangos at the regional level.

There were also more fundamental changes in the policy context within which regional activities were taking place. The dismantling of traditional regional economic policy reflected the evening-out of inter-regional unemployment disparities (albeit at a higher absolute level than prevailing in the previous three decades) and the increasingly diverse, complex and unpredictable nature of spatial economic change, often with greater variations within than between regions. Given the powerful forces of economic restructuring unleashed by the Single European Market and the increasingly interdependent nature of the international economy, commentators argued that there was a need for policy interaction at several scales from international down to local (Albrechts *et al.* 1989; Amin and Thrift 1994). Within this new context the region was seen by many influential policy-makers as playing a critical pivotal co-ordinating role, as expressed in the many debates surrounding the 'Europe of the Regions'. To facilitate this new role the view was that there was a need to devolve powers downwards from national governments in order that policies could be shaped to local circumstances. The task of the region was to provide direction and co-ordination to the wide range of institutions and agencies established to facilitate economic, social and physical development. The marshalling of resources, human, financial and institutional, was to be accomplished by facilitating networks and partnerships within and between public and private sectors. In this process the aim was to devolve responsibility downwards in applying the principles of subsidiarity and negotiating an efficient division of labour in terms of the roles and responsibilities of different organisations. Regions which succeeded in developing their institutional capacity were seen as the ones best capable of responding to the opportunities and threats of the modern economy.

It was against the background of these new approaches to regionalism and the political pressures on the government described above, that the GORs were established in 1994 by the Conservative government. In examining their remit it is clear that one of their key purposes was to strengthen regional institutional capacity (whether this was achieved in the most effective manner remains an open question – see Chapter 8). Early successes included the introduction of the Single Regeneration Budget, which placed a premium on the development of local partnerships as part of the bidding process. The GORs also managed the Regional Challenge, established the network of Business Links, developed a regional dimension to the competitiveness White Paper, and more generally facilitated local and regional partnerships. One of the weaknesses of their role, however, was a reluctance by ministers to allow the GORs to engage in any form of open formal debate with the key regional players in the development of various regional strategic priorities. As a consequence, the Senior Regional Directors periodically were subject to criticisms that they were powerful, unaccountable bureaucrats who were in a position to pick and choose regional opinions and play off one group of regional actors against another. However, it was significant that businessmen within the regions were offered positions on the management boards of the GORs and that the Minister of Housing and Local Government supported the initiative by local authorities to establish a voluntary chamber in Yorkshire and Humberside. In his speech on regionalism in 1995, David Curry argued that government encouragement of regional joint working on issues such as Europe and Regional Planning Guidance had fostered the development of the RAs. This form of regional governance worked well, and therefore he saw no need to establish formal political structures to replace it. Interestingly, similar thinking was present in a study by Harding *et al.* (1995), which sought to test the widely argued case that the experience of regional government elsewhere in Europe had played a significant role in fostering regional development. They concluded that when evidence was cited of growth arising from a well-developed institutional capacity, it was as often based on informal and non-statutory relationships as on the existence of formal democratic structures:

> Depending on the powers and responsibilities vested in them and their capacity to mobilise other regional interests, regional authorities might encourage improvements in regional economic performance in the longer term. But to assume that a transformation in economic circumstances will follow automatically upon any form of regional democracy is a leap of faith. (Harding *et al.* 1995, p.2)

It is clear that as a consequence of these developments in regionalism there was support for a move to a strengthened presence for the key players, for example the GORs and local authority regional associations, in order further to develop networks and partnerships with other regional and sub-regional partners such as the CBI, the Chambers and the Training and Enterprise Councils (TECs). It was envisaged that such a move would be based around a desire to enhance institutional capacity through formal and informal voluntary links, both within and between public and private sectors. It would also build upon agreements negotiated between the local authority associations, TECs, the voluntary sector and others on the development of joint working at regional level (AMA 1996; West Midlands Forum 1995, p.2).

In this respect, therefore, there was much common ground around the building blocks of the GORs and RAs. However, it was clear that a Labour agenda would go further in economic development, with a more proactive approach. This would entail, for example, the establishment of RDAs, the removal of constraints on the role of local authority companies in economic development, a more strategic approach to the role of TECs, and the mobilisation of private finance through vehicles such as investment bonds. There would also be a strengthening of relations, directly or indirectly, with the other government institutions which had a major impact on the region and which hitherto had not had a formal management link with the GORs; institutions such as the Next Step agencies, English Partnerships and the Rural Development Commission. The establishment of scrutiny, accountability and control mechanisms would not only be an element in extending the economic policy remit of the regional bodies, it would also be seen as addressing the problem of the democratic deficit.

Turning to the longer-term agenda of regional government, in the event of a change in administration, it was felt that there was sufficient parlimentary support to legislate for the staged model. To some observers the package offering the establishment of chambers throughout England and the prospect of moving to elected assemblies in a second term was a pragmatic response to the political reality of varying enthusiasm for regionalism and the need to avoid further costly local government reorganisation. Further, it had the advantage of 'going with the grain' of developments in regional governance and was a comparatively low cost solution, even with some additional central government financial support to the chambers.

The promise of early legislation to establish the RDAs was thought necessary to help secure the passage of devolution legislation by encouraging the support of the powerful North East block of Labour MPs, as well as others from the North of England. Moreover, it was argued that those regions which took early steps to establish elected assemblies would set in train a 'domino effect', with other regions following quickly behind not wishing to lose comparative advantage. It was thought, therefore, that the Straw staged approach could be interpreted as a robust strategy fitting in with the short-term 'low cost' priorities of New Labour and addressing immediate political pressures arising from devolution, whilst at the same time providing the scope for a more ambitious form of elected regional government in England in the longer term. There were some, however, who took the view that the complexities of achieving elected regional authorities were such that the interim phase of nominated chambers and/or strengthened regional partnerships might, *de facto*, become a permanent feature if the transitionary process became bogged down in political and constitutional problems. This scenario was attractive to those in local government who, whilst welcoming the opportunity to exercise greater influence over government offices and achieve more openness and accountability at the regional level through regional chambers or formal partnerships, were nevertheless concerned about the threat which elected regional authorities posed to the role and responsibilities of local government. However, as the Constitution Unit argued, such indirectly nominated chambers in anything other than a short time frame might well find difficulties in exercising influence within Whitehall and could quickly lose authority within their regions if it was seen that the chambers commanded few real powers, resources and political clout. The Unit saw the chambers as serving a useful purpose as a transitionary vehicle, but probably having much less utility as a permanent feature. Others took the view that a strengthening of regional governance was a sufficient and adequate response to the prevailing circumstances. Formalising and building upon existing regional networks and partnerships reflected existing trends in building regional organisational capacity.

For those wishing to see more fundamental constitutional change, the Straw approach could be interpreted as a cynical ploy. The so-called 'triple safeguards' on this interpretation could have been suggested simply to ensure that major reform remained a distant and unlikely prospect. In the event it was noticeable that the outcome of the Labour Party's consultation exercise in the summer of 1996 resulted in the 'watering down' of some of the perceived hurdles, notably the insistence on a mainly unitary local government as a precursor to elected regional authorities and the broadening of the acceptable tests of popular support to reflect more closely the multi-stage, multi-track approach seemingly acceptable in Spain. In conclusion, in the mid 1990s the outlook for English regionalism remained unclear but, nevertheless, one which was likely to see further development of regional governance if not government.

Note

This chapter draws upon research undertaken by the author for a research project entitled 'Whitehall and the Reorganisation of Regional Offices in England' undertaken with Professor Ken Spencer. The research was funded under the ESRC Whitehall Programme.

References

Association of County Councils, Association of District Councils and Association of Metropolitan Authorities (1995) *One Voice for Local Government.* London: AMA.

ACC Labour Group (1995) *ACC Labour Group Response to A Choice for England Consultation Paper.* London: ACC.

ADC (1995) *ADC Response to the Labour Party Consultation Paper, A Choice for England.* London: ADC.

Albrechts, L., Moulaert, F. Roberts, P. and Swyngedouw, E. (eds) (1989) *Regional Policy at the Crossroads. European Perspectives.* London: Jessica Kingsley Publishers.

AMA (1995a) *Regionalism: The Local Government Dimension.* London: AMA.

AMA (1995b) *A Choice for England – AMA Response.* London: AMA.

AMA (1996) 'Promotion of economic partnerships at local and regional level'. *AMA Development Committee. Agenda Item 18.* London: AMA, 26 January.

Amin, A. and Thrift, N. (eds) (1994) *Globalization, Institutions, and Regional Development in Europe.* Oxford: Oxford University Press.

Blair, A. (1995) quoted in *The Independent* 14 February.

Castle, S. (1995) 'Labour treads softly on devolution'. *Independent on Sunday* 12 February.

Condon, T. (1996) 'Blair buys off home rule rebels'. *Scotland on Sunday* 12 May.

Conservative Party (1992) *Manifesto 1992: The Best Future for Britain.* London: Conservative Council Central Office.

Constitution Unit (1996) *Regional Government in England.* London: Constitution Unit, University College, London.

Cornford, J. (1995) 'English regional government.' Paper given at ADC Policy Workshop on Regional Government in England. London: ADC, 15 February.

Curry, D. (1995) 'Regionalism – the government's perspective.' Paper delivered at the Association of Metropolitan Authorities/Birmingham University, School of Public Policy Conference, Westminster Hall, Regionalism: the Local Government Dimension. London, 20 March.

Davies, H. (1995) 'Regional government.' Paper delivered at regional newspaper editor's annual lunch. Newcastle, 6 January.

Defries, A. (1927) *The Interpreter Geddes: The Man and his Gospel.* London: Routledge.

English Regional Associations (1995a) *A Survey of the English Regional Associations.* London: ERA.

ERA (1995b) 'English Regional Associations Move Ahead.' ERA press release. London: ERA, 30 March.

Fawcett, C.B. (1917) 'Natural divisions of England'. *The Geographical Journal* February, 124–125.

Fell, M. (1995) 'The CBI's views on the government offices in the regions.' Paper delivered at Association of Metropolitan Authorities Annual Conference. Sheffield, 12 October.

Gould, B. (1990) 'Power to the regions will be the last legacy of the next Labour Government.' Centre for Local Economic Strategies, Spring Lecture. John Rylands Library, Manchester, 24 May.

Hall, P., Thomas, P., Gracey, H. and Drewett, R. (1973) *The Containment of Urban England,* 2 vols. London: PEP/Allen & Unwin.

Harding, A., Evans, R. and Parkinson, M. (1995) *Regional Government in Britain – An Economic Solution?* Research Findings, 47. Joseph Rowntree Trust. York: Joseph Rowntree Trust.

Harvie, C. (1991) 'English regionalism: the dog that never barked'. In B. Crick (ed) *National Identities. The Constitution of the United Kingdom.* The Political Quarterly. London: Blackwell.

Her Majesty's Government (1976) *Devolution: The English Dimension – A Consultative Document.* London: HMSO.

House of Commons, Trade and Industry Committee (1995) *Fourth Report, Session 1994–95.* London: HMSO.

Jones, G.W. (1988) 'Against regional government'. *Local Government Studies* September/October, 1–10.

Jones, G.W. and Stewart, J.D. (1985) *The Case for Local Government.* London: Allen and Unwin.

Labour Party (1918) *Report of Labour Party Conference.* London: Labour Party.

Labour Party (1991) *Devolution and Democracy.* London: Labour Party.

Labour Party (1994) *Winning for Britain.* London: Labour Party.

Labour Party (1995a) *Rebuilding Democracy, Rebuilding Communities.* London: Labour Party.

Labour Party (1995b) *A Choice for England: A Consultation Paper on Labour's Plans for English Regional Government.* London: Labour Party.

Liberal Party (1987) *Election Manifesto*, quote in F.W.S. Craig, British General Election Manifestos 1959–1987. Dartmouth, 1990.

Liberal Democrat Party (1993) *Here We Stand.* London: Liberal Democrats.

MacLennan, R. (1995) 'Regionalism – a Liberal Democrat perspective.' Paper delivered at AMA/Birmingham University Conference. London, 20 March.

Major, J. (1995) quoted in *The Times*, 6 January.

Mawson, J. (1995) 'The interim phase. Is it possible to achieve a greater degree of regional accountability prior to legislation?' Paper given at ADC Policy Workshop on Regional Government in England. London: ADC, 15 February.

Mawson, J. (1996) 'The re-emergence of the regional agenda in the English regions: new patterns of urban and regional governance'. *Local Economy 10*, 4, 300–325.

Mawson, J., Hall, S., Gibney, J. and Bentley, S. (eds) (1996) *The English Regional Associations of Local Authorities. The 1995/96 European Work Programme.* Birmingham: School of Public Policy, University of Birmingham.

Miller, B. and Mawson, J. (1986) 'The Alternative Regional Strategy: a new regional policy for Labour. Chapter 5.3 in P. Nolan and S. Paine (eds) *Rethinking Socialist Economics.* Oxford: Blackwell.

North of England Assembly of Local Authorities (1996) *Regional Government. Consultation Paper.* Newcastle: NEA, August.

Northern Region Strategy Team (1977) *Strategic Plan for the Northern Region.* Newcastle: NRST.

North West Regional Association and North West Business Leadership Team (1993) *Regional Economic Strategy for the North West.* Wigan: NWRA Secretariat.

Parliamentary Spokesman's Working Group (1982) *Alternative Regional Strategy: A Framework for Discussion.* London: Labour Party.

Penn, R. (1996) 'The need to develop a strong regional democratic voice.' Paper given at Queen Mary/Westfield College Public Policy Seminar, What Future for British Regions? London: QMW, University of London, 15 April.

Regional Policy Commission (1996) *Renewing the Regions. Strategies for Regional Economic Development.* Sheffield: Sheffield Hallam University.

Royal Commission (1940) *Royal Commission on the Distribution of the Industrial Population.* London: HMSO.

Royal Commission (1973) *Report of the Royal Commission on the Constitution.* London: HMSO.

South West Regional Planning Conference (1996) *Regional Identity for the South West.* Taunton: SWRPC.

Stoker, G., Hogwood, B. and Bullman, W. (1995) *Regionalism.* Local Government Management Board: Luton: LGMB.

Straw, J. (1995a) quoted in the *Daily Telegraph*, 13 February.

Straw, J. (1995b) 'Labour and the regions of England.' The Regional Studies Association Guest Lecture. Labour Party Press Release. London: Labour Party, 28 September.

Tindale, S. (1995) *Devolution on Demand. Options for the English Regions and London.* Institute for Public Policy Research: London: IPPR.

Tommaney, J. and Turnbull, N. (1992) 'Taking the north into the 21st century: the case.' A Paper for the Campaign for a North of England Assembly, Newcastle.

Wannop, U.A. (1995) *The Regional Imperative. Regional Planning and Governance in Britain, Europe and the United States.* London: Jessica Kingsley Publishers.

West Midlands Regional Forum (1996) *Regionalism and the West Midlands Region. Proceedings of a Conference.* Stafford: WMRF.

West Midlands Regional Forum of Local Authorities (1994) 'Regional Collaboration for Economic Development.' Draft Local Authority/TEC/Voluntary Sector Joint Working. WMRF Regional Chief Executives' Group. Stafford: WMRF, 23 November.

Whitehead, A (1996) 'English regions: the emerging political agenda of implementation.' Paper delivered at Political Studies Association Conference, English Regions – Will They Happen? Southampton, 14 February.

Further reading

Her Majesty's Government (1986) *Competitiveness. Creating the Enterprise Centre of Europe.* White Paper. London: HMSO.

North West Regional Association/North West Business Leadership Team (1992) *Regional Economic Strategy for North West England.* Wigan: NWRA.

Parliamentary Spokesman's Working Party (1992) *The Alternative Regional Strategy.* London: Labour Party.

PART III

Local Government, European Union and British Regionalism

CHAPTER 10

British Local Government in the European Union

Michael Goldsmith

Introduction

Following the passage of the Single European Act in 1986, the day-to-day work of the European Commission increasingly involved contact with the sub-national levels of government of the member states. Such levels of government exhibited a considerable diversity in their structure, finances and functions (Batley and Stoker 1991; Goldsmith 1992; Norton 1994), but forms of regional government were present widely throughout the Union and were by far the most common intermediary in EU politics between the supra-national and local levels. Nowhere was the impact of the new dynamics of European integration felt more than in Britain, but in terms of sub-national representation, Britain was the odd one out. Elected local government had to take on the intermediary role in the absence of an elected regional level. Consequently, in considering the developments in British sub-national politics arising from the changing European relationship in the late 1980s and early to mid 1990s, this chapter will chart the growth of British local government activity upon the EU stage, highlighting some of the particular developments which this growth revealed through four case studies. This account of local authority activity in an EU context provides insights into local and regional dimensions of politics and policy-making, which offers a qualified view of the development of new regional capacity. The chapter concludes by considering some likely further trends.

The EU and British local government

At the outset it is important to remember why the EU, and particularly the Commission, developed an interest in working with local government. Subsequently, the Union's involvement with sub-national government was based upon the Maastricht Treaty of 1992, which confirmed the subsidiarity principle as one of its main provisions. This principle, which required European activity to be undertaken at the lowest capable level of government, was of course differently interpreted by member states, but in many of them it confirmed and enhanced the involvement of regional and local governments in European affairs. Such involvement became increasingly important from the mid-1980s, especially as the process of enlargement and further moves to European integration necessitated parallel strategies to foster economic and social cohesion.

From the point of view of the Commission, Goldsmith (1993) has suggested that there were three main reasons why it sought to work with regional and local authorities in this era. First, given that economic, political and social integration were the key objectives of the EU, the Commission sought to adopt strategies which would further those objectives. In practice, the Commission was less administratively coherent than one might have expected; this factor and its small size meant that it became dependent on others with regard to policy-making (Edwards and Spence 1994). Authors such as Rhodes (1992) noted that, as a result of this, Commission officials developed large numbers of policy communities, each more or less self-standing. Commission officials had a particular interest in developing these corporate-style policy communities, since such groupings allowed them to manage an increasingly complex and burdensome consultation process. This approach, and the programmes to which it gave rise, helped to create a clientelistic relationship with consultees, of whom regional and local authorities were but one set. While it may not have been an overt and conscious strategy of building support, it is true to say that the Commission enjoyed many dependents, for whom it could produce benefits. It is possible that in return for such benefits, the Commission may on occasion have received bureaucratic or political support for its own European-wide objectives (Mazey and Richardson 1992). Furthermore, it was clear that as the Commission sought to bind regional and local government to it in some way, such links were seen as a way of breaking down what the Commission perceived to be some of the more parochial and nationalistic pressures from the member states. As such, the Commission effectively had an incentive to adopt a strategy of incorporation of interests, one not totally dissimilar to that adopted by some national governments.

Second, and more mundanely, the Commission needed information on which to base its policy proposals. Brussels, as writers such as Greenwood, Grote and Ronit (1992), Andersen and Eliassen (1993) and Mazey and Richardson (1993) suggested, was by the early 1990s a lobbyist's paradise. For their part, lobbyists were willing and able to provide information to the Commission's directorates. Indeed there were some suggestions that the Commission itself had encouraged the development of such groups in order to increase its access to information and opinion, viewing regional and local government as an important counter to the dominance of member states and the Council of Ministers. Given the largely clientelistic nature and style of many of the Commission's relationships with differing interest groups, the development of a close and mutually dependent relationship with the world of local government was hardly surprising.

Third, when it came to the implementation of policy, the Commission lacked the resources to oversee the working of its directives and regulations. The monitoring and implementation of its programmes therefore frequently fell to sub-national government. As the scope of EU legislation was extended, so national governments became concerned to ensure that the increasing use of sub-national government did not undermine the primacy of their position. This inevitably led to various tensions (John 1994).

Against this background, then, it is interesting to consider how British local authorities adapted to the increasing pressure upon them to relate in some fashion to Brussels. The first point to be made in this context is that the situation was a rapidly developing one. At the turn of the decade, both Audit Commission (1991) and Eurolog (1992)[1] surveys revealed that most British local authorities were ill-prepared for the onset of the Single Market, and that those who were really active in Europe represented a small minority. However, the early 1990s witnessed considerable change, leading to a situation in which there were far fewer authorities who had not adopted a conscious approach towards their management of the European issue. In reality, it was the period after the 1986 Single European Act which saw the most significant progress, a period during which there was considerable movement towards an enlarged European market and the development of the European Structural Funds.

In the first instance, the lead tended to be provided by a number of larger Scottish and Welsh authorities, which were soon followed by cities such as

---

1. The Eurolog survey (1992) was undertaken in seven European countries, covering the state of local government involvement with the then EC. The British study was undertaken by Mike Goldsmith (Salford University) and Liz Sperling (Liverpool John Moores), and is reported in Goldsmith and Klaussen (1997).

Birmingham, Sheffield and Manchester. At the forefront was Strathclyde, under the political leadership of Charles Gray, which played an active role in the development of the Regions of Traditional Industry (RETI), a group of European local authorities from declining industrial regions. Created in 1984, RETI could claim to be one of the longest serving networks of regional and local authorities, covering more than two dozen European-designated Objective 1 and 2 regions, including within Britain several types of authorities and regions: Strathclyde, Fyfe, South Wales, Greater Manchester, Merseyside, South Yorkshire and West Yorkshire/Humberside. The city of Birmingham was also quick off the mark, using its membership of Eurocities, a network of over 30 European 'second cities', as a means to pursue its particular urban problems through exchange of best practice and lobbying. In addition, authorities such as Doncaster, Barnsley and Sheffield were active in launching a European-wide Coal Communities Campaign which resulted in the European Commission proposing a special EU coalfield regeneration programme, RECHAR, funded by the Structural Funds. It was not surprising, given that a significant proportion of the UK's overall receipts from the EU came under the general heading of the Structural Funds, that authorities in those regions classified under EU regulations after 1988 as Objective 1 or 2 were the most active on the European front. Within the UK, Northern Ireland and Merseyside were the two areas which were classified as Objective 1 regions with less than two-thirds of EU GDP per capita, and thus it is they who reaped the greatest benefit from EU munificence. Rather more parts of the country were classified as Objective 2 (effectively declining industrial regions), including Greater Manchester, Strathclyde, Birmingham, West and South Yorkshire, and parts of the North East. Other parts, particularly the more rural areas suffering significant economic and social deprivation, were eligible for funding as part of the Objective 5b classification. This ensured aid for counties such as Devon and Cornwall.

Following on from early experience, local authorities gave increasing attention not merely to the direct accessing of European funding but also to adopting a longer-term, more proactive strategy to exert influence over the manner in which EU policies were shaped to ensure access to future programmes attuned to their particular needs. Increasingly authorities worked together at sub-regional and regional levels in orchestrating lobbying activity and jointly funding a Brussels presence. Such developments were paralleled by an increasingly sophisticated corporate approach within local authorities. For a long time, most of the officials dealing with European matters were likely to be found in either a chief executive's department or else in the department with responsibility for economic development. In an increasing number of cases, however, a separate European Unit or group was established, and many of these were given more proactive roles to play in promoting awareness of European issues across all departments of the authority, as well as other local players such as the voluntary sector and business community.

Finally, in addressing the rapid development of the scope of local authority activity on an EU stage, it is worth noting the steep learning curve displayed by many local authorities in their activities. Authorities quickly came to understand how to exploit the various programmes and initiatives which came on stream in the mid and late 1980s. In particular, Birmingham and Merseyside were able to reap considerable benefit from their involvement in pioneering integrated operations programmes as well as their ability effectively to negotiate with Brussels' officials directly on these and other matters (Redmond and Barrett 1988). Quickly other parts of the country, for example Devon and Cornwall, the North East, and South and West Yorkshire, followed suit. By the turn of the decade, and at the time of the review of EU activities by the Audit Commission in 1991, those authorities who were active were operating in a highly proactive fashion, and sometimes to the discomfort of central government. In the early to mid 1990s this momentum was being maintained as a wider range of local authorities learnt, first, the importance of networking with other authorities within the UK and across Europe generally, and second, the value of early information about future European initiatives from which they might benefit.

The second point to notice about this period, however, was the relatively narrow base of British involvement. It should be recognised that British sub-national government was involved increasingly in the implementation of EU directives and regulations, especially in the trading standards and environmental fields. This development resulted from the largely non-executive nature of British central government, which inevitably meant that much of the real work in policing these regulations had to be undertaken either by local authorities or else by agencies such as the Health and Safety Executive. EU public procurement requirements provided a further example of the way in which European initiatives involved local authorities. However, all this said, British involvement was largely driven by a concern for economic development and regeneration. This reflected the focus of EU policy concern on regional disparities and on the problems of areas with declining traditional industries.

In this respect, a key issue providing an impetus to the development of European competence in local government was undoubtedly the question of eligibility for funding. Authorities falling outside the main funding categories and areas of eligibility under the Structural Funds had less of an incentive to develop a European competence. Nevertheless, particular note should be made of authorities such as Kent County Council which revealed how an imaginative approach to seeking funding beyond the most obvious programmes can yield dividends. In their case, they were able to persuade the Commission that Kent was a border region with northern France and hence ought to be eligible for cross-border collaborative support in regard to economic development, transport and tourism initiatives through the so-called INTERREG programme. The European Commission had developed a number of programmes such as this which were not linked to specific geographic areas of eligibility, and which local authorities increasingly sought to target as potential sources of funding for anti-poverty programmes, technology transfer initiatives and networks to facilitate the transfer of best practice, and to engage in lobbying. Through such networks local authorities began to build up partnerships or working relationships with their counterparts elsewhere in the EU and beyond. Furthermore, British local authorities, especially through their associations, became increasingly active in other European-wide bodies speaking for local government, such as the Council of European Municipalities and Regions. The politicians and officials who worked with such bodies were very active at both national and European levels in promoting the potential role of local government in implementing EU policies.

The reform of European regional policy in the late 1980s, as well as offering new funding opportunities, also provided an important lesson for regional and local authorities: namely that there was scope for local government to exert influence over the evolution of European policies if it adopted a politically sophisticated approach. After this reform, there was a considerable growth in British local government activity on the European stage, to the point that it reached a level of maturity the equal of or superior to many of its European counterparts. British local authorities, often operating on a regional basis and in partnership with other regional players, opened Brussels offices. They also established and engaged in European-wide networks, as well as worked alongside Commission officials in the development and subsequent implementation of policy. Furthermore, British local authorities increasingly worked in networks with other agencies, notably in the private and voluntary sectors, as well as with higher education. These relationships often reflected similar local partnerships in other EU countries and went some way to respond to Commission (and central government) pressure to develop some form of local or even quasi-regional network.

Finally, it is worth emphasising that a key trend that arose from many of these local government operations was their quasi-regional dimension. As one of the case studies makes clear, Lancashire Enterprises Limited did not only represent Lancashire County Council but worked with many of the district authorities, as well as with metropolitan districts and other bodies in Greater Manchester and Merseyside. In the West Country, Cornwall operated alongside Devon, Somerset and Dorset at the Brussels level. Similar collaborative exercises could be found in the case of the North West Partnership (Burch and Holliday 1993) and North of England Consortium, as well as in Yorkshire and Humberside and the East Midlands. Both Scotland and Wales had long-established Brussels-based European operations. Though there may not have been a formal regional tier in England, the development of such co-operative activities at least sowed the seeds for further activity on a regional scale.

These trends all suggested considerable development in local government operations in relation to the EU in the late 1980s and the first half of the 1990s. However, it is also important to remember a number of points which constrained British local government's ability to play a large role on the European stage. First, as Roberts (Chapter 12) suggests, the absence of any *regional* tier of government placed some limit on the ability of British local governments to operate as equal partners alongside some of their European partners. This was compounded by the restructuring of local government, where in Scotland, for example, the regional authorities which were very prominent in speaking for Scotland on a European stage, were abolished. Local government restructuring in England may have had similar consequences in some areas where the strategic role of the county councils was lost. For example, as a result of Blackpool and Blackburn leaving Lancashire and becoming unitary authorities, it was questionable as to what was left of Lancashire that could speak on some regional basis. Similarly, it was difficult to see how the North West of England could speak with one voice as long as Merseyside took a separate and separatist path. Some of the difficulties associated with this problem are illustrated in the various case studies, although it may be the case that the emergence of the regional associations went some way towards filling the vacuum.

A second constraint on the development of a more proactive role relates to organisational inertia and the conservatism of local government, since many authorities remained largely reactive in terms of their relationship to European initiatives. Those officers responsible for European affairs, particularly in smaller authorities, worked largely on a part-time basis and generally acted as a post office through which details of European initiatives or regulations passed on their route to the department or section supposedly most interested. The manner in which authorities responded to an initiative often depended on how individuals within the department concerned saw the initiative in terms of their overall responsibilities. It was a matter of organisational priorities in terms of day-to-day local authority activity. EU regulations and directives were often seen as yet another set of unnecessary bureaucratic regulations imposed upon an overstretched and underfunded public sector, particularly in activities such as trading standards or environmental areas. Indeed, even finance and purchasing departments had to become involved with EU regulations following the introduction of the public procurement requirements, which required orders above a certain size to be put out to European tender.

A third constraint was the fragmentation and privatisation of much of British local government which meant that the voice of particular areas was much more difficult to articulate. Partnerships had to be established and sustained, and agreements reached between competing interests. Each of the case studies below illustrates the way in which local authorities increasingly set up partnerships and networks with public and quasi-public agencies, as well as with the private and voluntary sectors, as part of their European activities. The case studies also suggest the problems of such activities which arose from the fact that these sectors tended to be less well orientated towards Europe than were many local authorities.

Finally, as John (1994) states, central government was in this period the dominant voice in Britain's relationship with Europe. It was also likely that central government would become increasingly engaged following the UK's stance on subsidiarity and Treasury concerns about accessing European funding. The establishment of the Government Offices of the Regions (GORs), as Chapter 8 suggests, was in part an attempt by central government to ensure the effective co-ordination and management of European programmes and the maximum take-up of European funding, whilst at the same time maintaining oversight over the activities of local authorities in the EU sphere. Though established with a strong overtone of partnership, the GOR initiative was seen by many as an attempt to control sub-national EU relations. This was not welcomed by local government, which, as we have noted, sought through its involvement in the management and implementation of European programmes to develop a closer direct relationship with Brussels. In turn this was a relationship which was not always appreciated by Central Government. In practice, the way in which relationships developed between the GORs, local authorities, the private sector, higher education institutions and the voluntary sector varied. In some cases, such as the North West, the existence of two GORs – one for Merseyside and one for the rest of the North West – meant that there was no coherent voice speaking for the North West region as a whole. Overall, there is some evidence that in terms of the strengthened central government management of EU programmes through the GORs the arrangements worked more effectively in the North, Yorkshire and Humberside, and the East Midlands. However, there clearly remained difficulties in some regions, notably over a willingness to allow local elected members to participate in the forums overseeing European programmes. The West country was mentioned to the author as a 'particularly difficult area' by civil servants involved. Partnerships on this scale were inevitably going to take time to develop and it remained unclear as to whether the new system of regional offices and partnerships would develop to a sufficiently effective level in terms of the management of European affairs.

British local government in the EU: four case studies

The trends identified in the general discussion and the shifting nature of the relationship between Brussels, central government and local authorities in Britain can be illustrated further through case study discussions of developments in the early 1990s. Of course, none of the cases can claim to be truly representative, but they are indicative not only of the way in which local authorities responded to Commission initiatives but also of the distance some travelled in adapting their behaviour. In each case, local authorities are kept anonymous for legal reasons.

A Northern county

The first example, drawn from the North of England, is of a county council which, though better than many at the time, could still be seen as largely reactive rather than proactive in terms of its relationship with Europe. It had established a European team in 1991–92, headed by two non-British officials, both of whom had some experience of working with Europe. The team was part of the county's Economic Development Unit, working mainly, it was felt, on *coping* with EU changes rather than *shaping* them. The authority believed it had developed a better mix of skills in the 1990s in this area, but the team itself took the view that it still lacked sufficient resources to do the kind of job which it believed was desirable in developing a more sophisticated European approach. The team developed a number of European Advice Centres for local industry and the voluntary sector, and within the authority it took the lead in co-ordinating bids for Structural Funds. But the team's main function was to link with other departments and to pass information on to them. Internally its main links were with the Trading Standards Department, though there was an ad hoc group which met on European matters across the authority as a whole from time to time. In practice the authority largely adopted a reactive approach to opportunities from Europe. Furthermore, the adaptation was undertaken at the departmental level and not by the authority as a whole. As such the unit did not lead on European matters generally, but rather responded to requests for assistance from departments. The unit also gave support to the voluntary sector and to private business in its area, and worked with both local Training and Enterprise Councils and other Northern economic development agencies.

The county was a member of the North of England Assembly, an example of the emerging regional coalitions mentioned earlier. This regional association opened an office in Brussels late in 1992 as a means of facilitating existing lobbying and networking activities. Despite this opportunity, however, the county was still an example of a largely reactive local authority in European terms, being relatively poorly linked to Europe by comparison with the leading examples of British local government. It had begun to develop its expertise and to be recognised on the European stage, particularly in developing links with Groningen in Holland and with various European agencies. But overall, at the time of research, this authority was still running its European activities on a largely uncoordinated, decentralised and somewhat ad hoc basis, even if it was more appreciative of European issues than many other local authorities.

A Northern district

The Northern county can usefully be contrasted with another local authority in the study from the North of England, a metropolitan district. In 1990, the authority established a four-man team, the leader of which was well connected to national bodies working in Europe. The *raison d'être* of the team was to deal with EU initiatives for the area as a whole, not just the local authority, and in this regard it saw access to, and dissemination of, European information as critical. It was responsible for the preparation of most of the local authorities' bids and associated lobbying activities. It had been successfully engaged in bids with the local further education college, a museum and local authority organisations. It worked closely with British Coal Enterprises and other industrial partners in accessing European funds through RECHAR, and with the Coalfield Communities Campaign to assist in the regeneration of former mining communities. It had also managed to become involved in an INTERREG scheme.

The view expressed by the team leader was that the, 'local authority cannot afford to ignore the EU honeypot at the end of the rainbow'. As a result the authority became active in a range of networks such as RETI and the Association of European Regions, 'not because they are trendy but because they are purposeful'. As in the previous case study, the authority had joined with a dozen other authorities in its area to form a 'regional' grouping, with a two-man Brussels office. The team felt that the relatively weak voice of local government at the regional level had forced the authority into co-operating with local authorities and other local organisations. It was felt that the partnerships which had resulted, especially with the private sector, had led to better understanding all round and a more effective mechanism for securing European funds. Partnership had become even closer with regional government offices, involving recognition of the crucial gatekeeping role which national government plays in accessing European funds. The EU had provided the stimulus or leverage towards the development of these linkages, even though the resultant funding did not make up for that which the authority had lost from central government. In making cross-national partnerships the authority had also learned the importance of networking and of being proactive, so that joint bids could be made to tap into the full range of EU funding sources and not just the main structural funds, important though the latter were.

This case provides an example of a proactive authority, increasingly aware of the importance of networking and partnership, and of maintaining a good working relationship with central government and its agencies. Its membership of an Objective 2 region undoubtedly helped in fostering a positive approach. However, inevitably there had been some occasions when eligibility for funds was a problem and it had been able to find ways round the problems through its contacts in the Commission and elsewhere in Brussels. Given this experience, at the time of the study the authority was actively seeking to promote one of its elected members as one of the UK members of the Committee of the Regions, through its national local authority association.

The role of Lancashire Enterprises Limited

Further light is cast on the role of British local government in the EU by examination of an extremely active player on the European stage, the former enterprise arm of Lancashire County Council, Lancashire Enterprises Ltd (LEL). Originally established in 1982 as the county's economic development agency, its main objective throughout its history was the economic development of Lancashire. By the early 1990s the organisation had four major concerns: training and employment; property development and asset management; financing the provision of risk or venture capital for start-up companies; and other opportunities for economic development, particularly consultancy. It ran five investment funds, investing anything from £500,000 to £5 million, and its biggest success was the 'saving' of the Leyland end of the Leyland DAF truck company in 1992–93. Initially funded by the County Council, it was privatised in 1989 in order to avoid problems arising from the 1989 Local Government and Housing Act, which placed severe operative constraints on local authority-controlled companies. The County Council retained a 20 per cent equity stake in the company which was floated on the stock market. Given also that its shareholders included Louise Ellman, Labour leader of the County Council, and its Chairman was Jim Mason, former Chief Executive of the Co-operative Wholesale Society, it is doubtful whether LEL was totally free from political control in the years that followed privatisation.

After privatisation, the company not only broadened its financial base by bringing in further investors and borrowing substantial sums from the banks, but it also developed a major international consultancy arm which gained contracts from the Commission, other European bodies, and UK central and local government. This pattern of work was one of the keys to the success of LEL, since it was able to transfer skills and knowledge gained in one area of its work to others.

Broadly speaking, at the time of the research, LEL engaged in three lines of activity. First, it managed European Social Fund (ESF) and European Regional Development Fund bids for its clients, including Lancashire County Council. Second, it ran a number of European projects, for example COMMETT, BRITE, EURAM and STRIDE, for other public and private sector clients, and third, through its consultancy division, it developed programme applications in other EU areas of activity. Its work for the Commission, as well as for some of the other European networks, gave it an insight into the workings of the Commission and the needs of a wide range of interested parties, so it considered itself able both to advise potential clients and to develop bids, especially at an early stage in a new EU programme. To facilitate its European work, it maintained two offices, in Brussels and Luxembourg, the latter being referred to as the Lancashire embassy! In Brussels it maintained a six-person team, let out space to other authorities seeking a Brussels base, and on a scale of operation was at least on a par with most of the Brussels-based offices of regional and local authorities from other EU countries, such as the German *Länder*. So pervasive was the LEL operation that at least one Commission official was quoted as suggesting that LEL 'owned' Brussels. Whether this was a reference to the company's property dealings in the Belgian capital or its close links to many EU directorates was not made clear. What LEL would say is that its Brussels and Luxembourg offices were critical to the process of information-gathering, as well as providing on the spot representation when new initiatives were developing or when some response was required. LEL had also learnt that such close relations with the Commission meant that it could use informal channels to lobby. One respondent remarked that, 'lunchtime drinks tell you more than all the official literature'. Euromarketing was also seen as allowing proper networking in order to ensure that the, 'Commission and European system worked in your favour'. In this way the company was able to work with the Commission rather than against it, knowing that the Commission would generally listen. One example was the way in which it played a leading role in the establishment of a European-wide network to lobby the Commission to establish a programme for those areas experiencing defence industry restructuring and in subsequently securing funding for Lancashire from that programme. This example is not dissimilar to local authority networks such as the Coal Communities Campaign, which led to the RECHAR programme, and a similar one for the shipbuilding industry leading to the RENAVAL programme.

In the early 1990s LEL represented one of the most successful organisations working for a local government in the European field – extremely proactive, one of the leaders in Euro lobbying for regional and local government and extremely skilful in putting successful bids together, yet also clearly aware of the benefits which could come from shaping EU programmes as well as winning funds from them. Well connected, capable of strategic thinking and well placed to work with and for local authorities, LEL was clearly able to continue building on its successes.[2]

The West Country county

A final case study from the survey is provided by a West country county council, whose interest in Europe at the time of the survey was stimulated as much by its classification as an Objective 5 area as by broader policy considerations. It shared this categorisation with large parts of Scotland and Wales, which were its British competitors for Objective 5 funding, but with which it worked when lobbying Whitehall and Brussels. Its interests in Europe meant that it also participated in the growing 'regionalisation' of

---

2. An example of another local government-owned consultancy firm also operating in the same field with some success was the Manchester-based Centre for Local Economic Strategies (CLES). At the time of the research, CLES operated in three main European areas: partly on cultural industries, on transport and infrastructure, and on the provision of training for local authorities about the EU. It also worked for Directorate General XVI on regional policy and for Directorate General V on social policy, mainly on matters relating to Eastern Europe and the Mediterranean area. Its transport work underpinned the Green Links network, designed to improve freight transport from Ireland, across Northern England and Northern Europe out to Germany and Eastern Europe, as well as the Baltic Gateway project, which links the North East authorities with the Baltic states. The scale of CLES was much smaller than LEL: for example its 1992/3 turnover was something like £450,000 compared with LEL's £6 million plus.

English local government in the EU context, since it worked closely with neighbouring authorities which were similarly classified, and which it persuaded to jointly participate with it in its Brussels operation rather than incur the costs of yet another office.

By the early 1990s the authority had a significant European Unit, which had developed its expertise in-house over a number of years in accessing Objective 5 funds. Though not on the same scale as those available for Objective 1 and 2 regions, in a rural context the funds had been nevertheless significant. At the time of the research, the County Council had won support for developments such as an art gallery and a training centre, as well as both Lingua and ESF project funding. All involved significant funding. For example, the art gallery project had brought in almost £1 million.

In operational terms, the unit worked across the authority and with local business and voluntary sector organisations. Its objective or 'bottom line' was defined as economic development and, 'getting the authority further up the scale in Europe'. As an authority it had always had an international outlook, linked strongly to other Celtic areas, and particularly with Finistere in Brittany. The basic function of the European Unit was to share information on EU developments with its internal and external partners and to help in the development of funding bids, especially from the authority. There was a European Co-ordination Support Group, led by the unit, with membership at chief or principal officer level from each department in the Council, each acting as the departmental contact point. The group was set up following a review of the internal management of European activities, which identified the need for greater co-ordination. It met quarterly, information was provided to each departmental contact, and seminars were run on particular issues such as public procurement, revisions to strategic funds and so on. A number of more specific working groups was also established. The group was responsible for developing the authority's overall European strategy, within which each department had its own European strategy setting out how the department expected to be engaged with European issues other than simply funding. This process and structure meant that Europe was linked into the mainstream of the Council's activities. Given the strong economic development focus of much of the county's work, it meant that the European Unit was effectively involved in 'dealing with everything that was important' in the authority.

The main tasks of the Unit were to provide information, to identify and co-ordinate bidding opportunities, and to maintain links with Brussels. The Unit was seen as the key to raising funds because of its expertise, and it had a budget which allowed it not only to respond to Brussels initiatives, but also to develop its own activities in partnership with other authorities, local business and other agencies, as well as with European partners.

The authority's European office was headed by an individual with Commission experience. As a consequence, the authority had a strong group of formal and informal networks in Brussels, including a good working relationship with the Commission, which allowed it to play a part in the development of new Commission initiatives, such as the LEADER programmes developed by Directorate General XVI. The interpretive skills of the Brussels officer were seen as crucial to the county's success in European affairs. Interestingly, the Brussels office was rented from LEL, and the authority maintained working links with that company, sharing information and working together on areas of mutual interest. It was this sharing of information, its interpretation and the ability to network which lay at the heart of much of the authority's European activity. For example, the authority was an active player in the Atlantic Arc group of regions, as well as being a member of the Association of European Regions and the Committee of European Municipalities and Regions. In addition, it was involved with an informal local authority network associated with agriculture, tourism and fishing, in Western France and the Iberian and Greek Peninsulas. The Brussels office had helped in the development of these networks, not only because of its expertise in this respect, but also because local authorities from these areas regularly visited the office to discuss co-operation. The authority believed that the building of such links and networks helped the exchange of expertise between authorities with similar problems, as well as allowing for the establishment of partnerships along the lines sought by the Commission which could be brought to bear when developing new projects and funding proposals.

Despite the authority's active approach, however, the scope for really significant financial gains was seen as being relatively limited. In part this stemmed from the scale of funds available for Objective 5 regions, in part from the fact that areas such as Wales and Scotland had greater resources with which to play the European game and had been at it for longer, as well as difficulties being experienced with central government and, specifically, its attitude towards the funding of local authorities. For example, one local partnership had won significant funds under a Commission initiative, but had not been able to spend all of the money secured because central government had been unwilling to release the matching funds required under the system of annual capital controls. As a consequence, the authority feared that it was in danger of losing subsequent allocations of funds from the Commission and was lobbying hard in Brussels to protect the regional allocation.

This case study is interesting for a number of reasons. First, it illustrates how an authority could make significant progress in the European arena if it took the necessary steps. This implied recognising the importance of obtaining and correctly interpreting information and intelligence, as well as building effective networks at regional and European levels. Second, it also illustrates how far behind local government other parts of the local public, private and voluntary sectors often were when operating within this new sphere of public policy, something hinted at by our other case study authorities. Third, it illustrates some of the difficulties which English local authorities faced in dealing with the EU, and in particular with the Commission, in the absence of a formal regional structure. The authority had spent considerable time and effort in persuading its neighbours, effectively part of the same Objective 5 area, to join with it in its European activities. Progress was made and continued with a widening of the basis upon which the authorities in the region came to approach Europe. Nevertheless, given the limited funds available under Objective 5, and the time, effort and resources necessary to develop such regional and sub-regional partnerships, it was to remain an open question as to whether such efforts could really pay off in terms of EU funding. Last, but by no means least, the case study illustrates some of the difficulties faced by authorities in terms of dealings with central government. Despite excellent relationships with the Commission in Brussels, notable for its willingness to give prior warning of developments well before the Department of the Environment learnt of them and its encouragement to the authority to adopt innovative approaches through support for various new initiatives, such successes could be undermined by a negative centralist mentality in Westminster and an unwillingness to ensure matching funds were available.

Conclusions: local government and Europe in the future

The case studies illustrate a number of common developments in local government work in the EU state in the first half of the 1990s. First there is evidence of the speed at which local authorities moved up the European learning curve once they became involved on the European stage. Even those authorities which could be described as largely reactive still developed reasonably sophisticated modes of working on European matters, whereas the most proactive authorities gained a very significant understanding of all the nuances of the Brussels game at least the equal of the cleverest lobbying organisations.

Second, though in different degrees, the case studies illustrate the importance of information in the European context, as well as its constructive interpretation. For the more proactive authorities early information was a key to later success, all the more so if it was properly understood.

Third, as even the case study of the reactive authority noted, the importance of networking, not only at a local level but also at the European level, was an increasingly important factor in the success of local government involvement in Europe. Since a requirement for partners across Europe was an essential ingredient of most Commission programmes, membership of a network was a key to finding partners. Not only did such networks improve the chances of an individual authority obtaining funds, they were also important channels through which experience was exchanged and new ideas tested. But such partnerships increasingly involved not only local authorities across the EU but also other participants from industry, the voluntary sector and higher education. Proactive local authorities recognised this need and began to develop local networks alongside their European ones – though again the case studies hint at the fact that other sectors were often even less well prepared for Europe than local government.

Fourth, whilst a Brussels base may not have been essential, access to such an office was clearly desirable, especially when staffed by people with a good understanding of the Commission and a 'black book' full of useful contacts. It allowed an authority to begin informally to shape new initiatives, learn early of new opportunities for funding, and engage relevant Commission staff in a meaningful dialogue. Such offices came to be recognised as no longer the latest in 'Eurochic', as suggested by the Audit Commission (Audit Commission 1991), as they became a useful addition for a local authority really anxious to secure extensive European support for its activities.

Finally, the case studies reveal much about the development of the difficult relationship between British local authorities and central government. Whilst undoubtedly some of the early initiatives by local authorities on the European stage came about because of what they saw as a chance to bypass central government and to raise some much needed extra funding, most recognised the need to work closely with relevant central government departments at regional and national level. In most cases relationships at regional level would appear to have been reasonable, with the arrival of the GORs providing an opportunity for better co-ordination all round and for a better dialogue between central and local authorities. Arguments about subsidiarity and additionality, however, continued to cloud the relationship. In the Eurolog survey, for example, central government at national level was seen as the biggest barrier to successful activity by local government on the European stage in Britain. The same was not so true elsewhere in Europe, where central government was sometimes seen as a powerful supporter of local initiatives. As was noted earlier, whilst the creation of the GORs went some way to challenge the need for independence of action by local authorities *vis-à-vis* Brussels, it remained unclear as to whether this could really substitute for the absence of a formal regional tier.

Another factor in the British situation was a reflection of the sophisticated way in which local authorities obtained and interpreted information from their European counterparts, their Brussels offices and the Commission. It would appear that some authorities were simply at least as well, if not better, informed on Commission developments as their central government counterparts. Indeed, local officials were as likely to talk with Commission officials on very similar terms as central government bureaucrats. They may even have done so both more directly and frequently than did GOR officials. In European matters, many local authorities were at least the equal of their regional offices, making it difficult for the latter to impose decisions upon the former. Central government, at the GOR level, therefore, still had to find a working relationship, if not true partnership, with local authorities, and the latter accepted the necessity for such an arrangement, even if they did not always like it.

In this context the emergence of regional coalitions of local authorities sometimes working in tandem with private and other public sector bodies, was a not insignificant development. Such regional coalitions, certainly the stronger and more effective ones, went some way to meet the desire of Commission officials to work with a regional tier of 'social partners', and also gave British local government greater credibility and a stronger voice in such bodies as the Committee of the Regions, the Association of European Regions and the Committee of European Municipalities and Regions. But it also brought into question the interpretation placed upon the subsidiarity principle adopted by central government and Whitehall – namely that it should stop there and should not go down to local government which was seen as lacking capacity in these matters. Herein lay a continuing problem in the central–local relationship, one which the restructuring of British local government was unlikely to help. Scotland was to be an interesting test case, for many of its regions were active players upon the European stage. It was open to question how far the same co-ordinated approach to Europe could be made by the range of unitary authorities that came into existence in Scotland, or how far similar developments in England could help the emergence of proto-regional bodies.

It was always possible, of course, that British central government would encourage regional government offices to work more positively with their regional partners in promoting bids to Brussels and in actively engaging the involvement of the local partners in the allocation and management of the programmes. This was the original intention, though there was a lack of evidence of such intentions being fulfilled; similarly the history of British central–local government relationships suggests that such offices would not easily be allowed to 'go native' and that they would continue to be expected to seek to exercise maximum influence and 'control' over the European activities of their regional partners, especially the local authorities. Even in the context of a government apparently committed to a greater measure of regional devolution, as promised by the Labour Party, it is open to question whether civil servants would in practice be expected to operate differently.

Note

The research on much of what follows was undertaken in 1992–93. Lis Sperling of Liverpool John Moores University assisted with the case studies, assistance for which I remain most grateful. That project was part of the wider EUROLOG project undertaken by a European group, the outcome of which is reported in Goldsmith and Klaussen (1997). Financial support for the project was provided by the Local Government Management Board and by the European Commission, to which I am deeply grateful.

References

Andersen, S.S. and Eliassen, K.A. (1993) *European Policy Making.* London: Sage.

Audit Commission (1991) *A Rough Guide to Europe: Local Authorities and the EC.* London: HMSO.

Batley, J. and Stoker, G. (eds) (1991) *Local Government in Europe: Trends and Developments.* Basingstoke: MacMillan.

Burch, M. and Holliday, I. (1993) 'Institutional emergence: the case of the North West of England.' *Regional Politics and Policy 3,* 29–50.

Edwards, G. and Spence, D. (1994) *The European Commission.* London: Longman.

Goldsmith, M. (1992) 'Local government.' *Urban Studies 29,* 3/4, 393–410.

Goldsmith, M. (1993) 'The Europeanisation of local government.' *Urban Studies 30,* 4/5, 683–699.

Goldsmith, M. and Klaussen, K.K. (1997) *European Integration and Local Government.* London: Edward Elgar.

Greenwood, J., Grote, J.R. and Ronit, K. (1992) *Organised Interests and the European Community.* London: Sage.

John, P. (1994) 'UK sub-national offices in Brussels: regionalisation or diversification.' *Regional Studies 28,* 7, 739–796.

Mazey, S. and Richardson, J. (1992) 'Interest groups and European integration.' Paper presented to PSA Annual Conference, Belfast, April.

Mazey, S. and Richardson, J. (1993) *Lobbying in the European Community.* Oxford: OUP.

Norton, A. (1994) *International Handbook of Local and Regional Government.* London: Edward Elgar.

Redmond, J. and Barrett, G. (1988) 'The European Regional Development Fund and local government.' *Local Government Studies 14*, 5, 19–34.

Rhodes, R.A.W. (1992) 'The Europeanisation of sub-national government: the case of the UK.' University of York, mimeo.

CHAPTER 11

Sub-National Partnerships and European Integration

The Difficult Case of London and the South East[1]

Peter John

Introduction

It can be argued that EU inspired sub-national partnerships are a motor of regionalisation, stimulated by the opportunities of the late 1980s and early 1990s. The argument is straightforward and is made up of the following elements. First, the process of European integration brought sub-national bodies and European bodies closer together through the former's desire for funds and the latter's quest for legitimacy. Second, the allocation of the EU's structural funds on a regional basis served to unite regional actors in formal partnerships and create a coalition of regional interests. Third, incipient regionalism found its expression specifically in local authority-based partnerships which took on a European dimension through working together on the preparation of regional lobbying strategies and setting up regional offices in Brussels. Fourth, given the small size of the Commission bureaucracy, it was administratively convenient to deal with territorial aggregations of representative bodies where there was demonstrable political and geographical cohesion. Fifth, the experience of the bodies working together on European lobbying fed into greater regional political cohesion. Finally, political leaders felt better able to work together on European matters than

1. The details about the partnership in the Lee Valley were obtained by telephone calls to several of the partners. The details about other partnerships were gathered from my earlier work on lobbying and Europeanisation (John 1994a, 1994b, 1996). I am also grateful to Janice Morphet, then of SERPLAN, for an interview where she supplied information on her organisation and other partnership arrangements in the South East and Figure 11.1. This map sets out the pre-1997 local government system as described in the chapter.

on many other potentially geographically competitive issues. Overall, it may be suggested that the coming together of these various forces led to the emergence of a European-based regionalism and that laggard regions tended to follow those with more proactive strategies and structures.

Yet this sequence was rarely smooth. In particular, the success and cohesion of regional partnerships was affected by their administrative and cultural contexts. In some parts of Britain there were good bases for European regional working; other areas, particularly in England, were much less suitable. London and the South East presented the most difficult case for a regional identity as it was a highly complex and differentiated economic and political area which made regional partnerships difficult to form. Indeed, if the thesis of a general tendency towards greater regionalisation of political and administrative structures and policies in this period is to be upheld, it needs to be appraised with its most difficult case in mind, as it is at the weakest link that English regionalism and regionalisation can be said to have either succeeded or failed. Signs of regionalisation in the largest area of England must be observed as well as in the better defined regions, such as the North or the West Midlands. If the South East was the Achilles heel of an emerging bottom-up regionalism – owing to its fragmentation, the problem of how to govern the capital, the relationship of London to the rest of the region, its large size and its unfocused identity – then the microscope needs to be directed to factors which initiated greater joint working, such as European policy and funding.

Before attending to the issues raised specifically by London and the South East, this chapter will begin by clarifying understanding of the meaning of sub-national partnerships in an EU context, and the factors which affected their operations. The second section will explain further the relationship between partnership development and regionalisation, isolating the factors which determined that regionalisation should accompany Europeanisation as well as the qualifications to this general thesis. Section three then focuses on the case study of London and the South East, discussing both voluntary and formal relationships. The chapter as a whole argues for a positive attitude to the potential of partnerships as a new form of sub-national governance, and whilst realistic about the problems in London and the South East, suggests some of the potential even here for the new English regionalism.

European partnerships: definitions

By the mid 1990s the term 'partnership' referred to two related phenomena in the context of European Union: the voluntary relationships between public bodies, and between public and private bodies, formed to co-operate on EU matters following the growth in EU regional funding in the late 1980s; and the formal partnerships required specifically by the rules of the Structural Funds, as reformed following the Maastricht Treaty. To take voluntary relationships first, these emerged from the willingness of public bodies to co-operate with other organisations in an area to bid for funds, to network and to influence policy. Generally, an already existing economic development partnership took on an EU dimension. Often these partnerships were within a local authority's boundaries; less often, but increasingly so, they occurred between authorities as part of a regional association, and encompassed the non-elected public sector and private agencies. There was also a growth in the relationships between the political leaders of local authorities who were interested in European matters; and in the networks of European officers which extended between the elected and unelected sectors.

Second, there was the formal partnership committees. The EU introduced this idea in the 1988 reform of the Structural Funds. Before 1988 the Commission directly administered these funds, with some decentralisation of administration to nation states in the form of 'integrated development operations', a system for managing funds concentrated in a particular area. Because of the expansion of the funds and the bureaucratic difficulty of central administration, the EU handed the management arrangements to nation states in 1988. However, the Commission ensured that the running of the programmes was carried out according to the principle of partnership of the public authorities involved. When the funds were reformed again in 1993 the Commission and Parliament sought to broaden the scope of the partnerships to incorporate a wider range of bodies than just those in the public sectors including the social and economic partners.

While the reformed EU regulation on the management of the Structural Funds seemed to point to the need to institute wide and effective partnerships – as revealed by phrases such as 'close consultations' and 'in pursuit of a common goal' – there were important qualifying phrases which allowed for considerable variation in practice, as was suggested, in particular, by the phrase: 'within the framework of each Member States's national rules and current practices' when referring to the social and economic partners. The phrase was inserted at the request of the British government and sought to ensure that partnership took place within a context fully determined by the member state. At first glance the wording seemed to reaffirm the national gatekeeping model of how European policy was to be implemented in states whilst at the same time extending partnerships, thus validating further Anderson's argument (1990) that the regional funds increased the centralisation of the UK state because they created a close dependence of local government on central government: partnerships were 'top-down'. On the other hand, it was still possible to interpret the regulation in a way which did not allow nation states to dictate exactly the way in which the regulation was put into practice (Economic and Social Committee 1994). Thus the reference to member state practices did not mean that the state could ignore this regulation. The phrase 'close consultations' was stronger than just providing information, it meant the involvement of the partners in all aspects of the decision-making process – preparation, financing, monitoring and ex ante and ex post evaluation – although the final decision about the process and programmes would rest with the competent authority, the member state. The regulation provided potential within partnerships for genuine joint working.

The administrative structure for implementing European funding, of course, differed according to the type of programme, and was handled by different government departments. The main difference in this era was between the European Social Fund (ESF) and the European Regional Development Fund (ERDF). The former was administered nationally, requiring no direct regional input. In practice, it was only the ERDF which had regionally administered partnerships. After the 1988 reform of the funds, the partners were selected by the 'competent authorities', the Department of Trade and Industry or Department of the Environment (in the Government Offices of the Regions (GORs) from April 1994). In each region a programme monitoring committee was established to draw up the Single Programming Document (a summary of the programme area's priorities) to be submitted to the Commission for approval. Subsequently, these committees oversaw decisions about grants and programme delivery and calls for annual reports on the programmes. Until 1993 operational programme committees were also associated with sub-regional programmes. Membership of these committees was dominated by local authorities, national government and the Commission, with some representatives from the private, higher education and voluntary sectors. All committees tended to meet infrequently, once every six months, which would indicate that partnerships were largely superficial. A key factor was the size of some committees. Some, such as the Welsh monitoring committee, had a membership of over 100. However, it would be wrong to judge partnerships purely on the formal proceedings occurring at committee meetings. These meetings became the basis upon which the partners worked together in other contexts. In particular, they led to informal patterns of contact which shaped the agenda of the committees and all the other decisions which occurred in relation to the practical operation of partnerships. Partnerships at the project level also necessitated a further set of relationships. Conversely, much hinged on the relationships between the public authorities which were already in place. The reality of partnership was dependent on prior relationships, particularly between central and local bodies. As Martin and Pearce (1994) and McCarthy and Burch (1994) noted, there was a great variation in such relationships between the regions, particularly in the orientation of the central government civil servants based in the regional offices. Partnership relationships were good in the North, poor in the North West and Yorkshire and Humberside, centralised in Wales and fair in the West Midlands.

The central government context to partnership arrangements was particularly important given the trend towards centralisation in the administration of the Structural Funds. Reform of the funds coincided in England with the integration of the regional offices of the Department of Trade and Industry, Department of Employment (forming part of the Department for Education and Employment), Department of Transport and the Department of the Environment into the GORs and the institution of regional directors presiding over them. Some observers claim the reform could be interpreted as a centralisation of policy (Stewart 1994) which was directly associated with the threat of greater European control over decision-making and the need to occupy a regional space to thwart new developments. While, as Stewart admits, the causal links are difficult to prove, there is circumstantial evidence. The development of the GORs occurred at the same time as the government streamlined the administration of monitoring committees to reduce the layers of bureaucracy. Specifically, the sub-regional programme committees which monitored projects in specific areas were removed. Local authorities argued that this reduced the opportunities for developing sub-regional strategies, lessened partnerships and tightened central control.

Another factor affecting the development of partnerships was the lack of clarity in defining the concept of partnership itself. It was not clear from the meaning of the word what level of contact there ought to be between the bodies: whether it meant participation in decisions, or was more of a symbolic alliance of those affected or benefiting from a programme with one public body taking the lead. The confusion in the term was translated into a wide variety of experiences in practice, particularly as the idea became the 'buzz word' in both central- and local government-inspired economic development initiatives (Hutchinson 1994). Like 'community', 'partnership' was capable of being marketed as a politically neutral term. It is easy to be cynical about its adoption in the European context as it was used to describe any kind of relationship which existed in putting a funding programme together. However minimally a member state implemented the partnership requirements, it was always possible to argue that the state had complied with the regulation.

However, the view of this chapter is that it is possible to take the cynicism too far. While there were examples of superficial and minimalistic relationships, the assumption of the partnership was that innovative, responsive and high quality policies depend on an environment of co-operation, participation and sharing of ideas. Underlying the idea of partnership was a critique of the way in which European funding had been applied to programmes in the past. Not only central actors, but local authorities in the programme areas, had regarded the programmes as legitimate ways of funding existing proposals, such as the off-the-shelf road schemes already developed by highways departments. In Britain, local authorities, with their transport and planning functions, were the lead partners in economic development which entitled them to a fixed sum of money allocated to the Department of Trade and Industry regional offices. In 1995 and 1996, however, there was more competition in the submission of funds and the involvement of other public and voluntary sector partners as well as economic development actors.

The revised concept of partnership involving a wide range of bodies offered an inclusive philosophy to produce better schemes built on best practice. The incorporation of the social and economic partners allowed for a role for the wide range of bodies operating at the local level. It legitimised the partnership of business with public institutions and gave other actors, for example from the voluntary sector, the opportunity to participate. With numerous bodies engaging at different territorial levels, partnerships, both formal and voluntary, could fill the regional space (see Chapter 7). The process coheres with the widespread restructuring of European sub-national government during the 1980s (Batley and Stoker 1990) towards a more competitive and flexible pattern of governance, involving networking and partnerships with all sub-national bodies.

The regional dimension to the EU

Until the late 1980s the main impact of the EU on local government had been on single local authorities. The Europeanised councils were characterised by a large European department or unit, an office in Brussels, a European-style political leader, a proactive funding emphasis and a strong participation in European networks. The main examples were Kent County, Birmingham City and Strathclyde Region. During the mid to late 1980s, the single city or strategic authority model became less feasible. Indeed it became more rational for local bodies to organise their European operations as a partnership between several local authorities and the other local institutions with an interest in European matters.

Four factors were driving this shift in focus. The first and most important change was in European funding. The regulations which allowed some areas to benefit from the Commission's discretion about the allocation of the Structural Funds were changed in 1988. Henceforth, central government made the decisions in the regional offices. At the same time the areas defined as objective 2 became more widely dispersed across the UK, and included new areas such as Stoke-on-Trent and parts of London, making the single authorities less dominant. Another factor reducing the monopoly status of the single local authorities was the expansion of funding into community initiatives. These did not require the Commission to draw a map approved by central government, meaning that local authorities in areas outside the objective 1 and 2 maps were able to receive EU funds. Thus the potential rewards of one authority investing heavily in European operations were diminished. At the same time more local authorities became aware of European dimension as a result of the expansion of the number of competences of the EU in the lead up to the Single Market of 1993, such as in the environment policy area, and perceived that many decisions affecting sub-national government were being taken at the EU level (Baine, Benington and Russell 1992; Bongers 1992). The newly Europeanised local authorities, often as groups, lobbied to change European policy, so as to have the objective 1 and 2 maps redrawn and to create community initiatives on, for example, the rundown of the defence sector. As the rewards for competition could often be a wasted effort and could send a confused message to central government and Commission policy-makers, then it made sense to co-operate as a way to parcel up the funds and to present a united front.

In addition, there was an important change in Commission views about how regional development was to occur. As already noted, the public culture of funding, both at central government and EU level, became more partnership-based with a greater involvement of the non-elected sector, again leading to project proposals less dominated by local authorities. The Commission had shifted its view away from the notion that regional inequality was a result of imbalances and resource depletion, towards the idea that economic success was built on the effective interaction of regional bodies and institutions. The Commission envisaged a synergy driving development, which required more attention to local networks and innovation coming up from below (Bennett and Kreps 1994). In the UK's case, this included Training and Enterprise Councils (TECs), universities, Business Links, the private sector and other public bodies. Hence it made sense for bodies whose areas did not necessarily respect local authority boundaries to see European involvement as a long-term partnership.

The second factor pushing local authorities away from independent action in Europe was the re-evaluation by local authorities of their European involvement. This led to greater moves towards networking and seeking to influence policy (John 1994b). It was an approach which made the return on European involvement less clear, but partnerships with other sub-national European actors, including local authorities, were clearly more cost-effective and also more visible and legitimate in European actors' eyes. This cost saving was most notable in the development of sub-national offices in Brussels (John 1994a). The expansion of these offices reflected the way in which sub-regional or regional groups of local authorities had combined to fund them, such as Yorkshire and Humberside and the Assembly of the North (see Table 11.1).

Table 11.1: British sub-national Brussels offices

Office	*Date Opened*
City of Birmingham	1984
Strathclyde Region	October 1984
Cornwall and Devon counties†	March 1993 (Cornwall since May 1988)
Highlands and Islands*	February 1989
Grampian Region	February 1989
Rural Scotland Liaison Office†	April 1989
Kent European Office†	June 1990
Lancashire Enterprises plc	February 1990
North of England Office†	December 1992
Yorkshire and Humberside European Office†	December 1992
Wales European Centre†	April 1992
East Midlands Counties European Office†	October 1992
East of Scotland European Consortium†	1992
Essex County	January 1991
Local Government International Bureau	December 1992
Surrey County	April 1993
Consortium of Scottish Local Authorities	June 1993
Nottingham Brussels Office†	October 1993
London Brussels Office†	September 1994
Manchester City	October 1994
Hampshire and Dorset Counties†	1995

* – can be considered as one office
† – partnerships
Source: John (1995)

The third factor encouraging regionalisation of local authority activity was the Commission's preference for dealing with more coherent sub-national entities. This was famously announced to partners in the North West by Graham Meadows, of the Commission's Directorate General XVI, who expressed the frustration of Commission officials in having to deal with so many UK local authorities (McCarthy and Burch 1994). In response, local public bodies deemed it sensible to act as a region because the boundaries for the Objective 1 and 2 areas crossed local authority and other public authority boundaries. At the same time the creation of the GORs in 1994 made the way in which decisions about European funding were devolved to the regional level much clearer. Many of the GORs reorganised their European functions to liaise within regions. Thus it made sense for the partners to have a regional voice to try to influence those decisions.

Finally, the move towards more regional working was driven by a general awareness of the opportunities that the EU context offered. Europe presented partners with an incentive to co-operate across local authority boundaries because all the local authorities stood to gain. Hence European involvement provided a different frame of reference from the usual inter-authority disputes, creating an experience of co-operation on transnational goals which had the potential to lessen local political tensions. Indeed the success of co-operating on regional projects led to other types of joint working. An interesting example of this is provided by the Merseyside 'sub-region', where there was a long history of disputes between Liverpool and the outlying districts. Interestingly, despite the conflicts, the former county's five districts decided to fund a joint European office. The same local authorities also carried out joint lobbying to affect the decisions made about the reform of the Structural Funds in 1993 (McCarthy and Burch 1994). Significantly, it was the regional partnerships which took the lead.

However, there were problems in the British experience which provide significant qualifications to the developmental view of the relationship between regionalisation and Europeanisation. The first was the uneven definition of a region in European terms. The Objective 1 and 2 maps were drawn with reference to levels of unemployment (which were in turn were affected by the way central government classified assisted areas). Thus regions, such as the West Midlands, had some parts of their areas covered by Objective 2; others not. In addition, the Commission criteria for examining regions, the NUTS areas, did not focus on regional administrative boundaries but on amalgams of local authority areas. Also the idea that the Commission had a uniform stereotype 'region' which it sought to impose on more differentiated regions was itself a misconception. The variety of types, sizes and levels of tiers of sub-national government was very great across Europe, making Commission specifications of an 'ideal region' difficult. In particular, cities such as Frankfurt and Marseilles sought direct relationships with the Commission and the European parliament. More generally, the lobby group Eurocities, developed on a Europe-wide basis. The diversity was reflected in the composition of the Committee of the Regions, which in its initial phase of operation had members from territories as large as the German *Länder* and as small as English districts.

The second qualification to growing European joint working was the sometimes intense geographical and municipal rivalries which existed within regions irrespective of the common pressures to work together on Brussels offices and regional strategies. Even in regions with a good history of co-operation there were conflicts, usually between the principal city and the other local authorities, such as was occasionally the case between the City of Birmingham and the other West Midlands authorities. In some situations such tensions led to operational splits: for example in the case of Yorkshire and Humberside. Leeds City Council, although part of the regional development association, refused to subscribe to the Yorkshire and Humberside Brussels office. Similarly, in the East Midlands there was a partnership based on the counties and a separate partnership based on Nottingham City, which resulted in two Brussels offices representing the same area. In some UK regions there was a split between a larger region and a smaller or sub-region within it. The most pronounced example of this was the North West, where there was a rivalry between Merseyside and the alliance based on Manchester. The problem was reinforced by the fact that there was also a separate GOR for Merseyside. In the mid 1990s it remained to be seen whether the wider pressures bearing down on the regions, such as the establishment of the GORs and the emergence of a single local authority association, would be sufficient to override these tensions and enable configurations of regional partnerships to develop harmoniously on a more uniform basis.

Finally, the differing geographical and socio-economic make-up of the ten regions affected the cohesion and identity of EU-based regional partnerships. The regions were based on administrative boundaries which did not necessarily correspond to the natural communities of local bodies. The variable cultures and senses of regional identity made it always likely that there would be varying experience of partnerships. In some regions there had been a long history of joint working and co-operation which was based on a shared identity. In these regions a European partnership was naturally grafted on to existing relationships. An example here was the North, which had a long tradition of co-operation, particularly on regional economic development issues. Another example was the West Midlands, where local authorities had been bound together in one administrative region with coterminous boundaries for some time. Other regions were less unified or coherent. Local government restructuring also disrupted relationships, particularly between the larger cities and the counties which tended to adopt a European outlook. The East Midlands was a case of a region with an unclear identity, where there was conflict between Nottingham and the four counties which made up the East Midlands regional forum, and to which further tensions were added by the debate over the future local government structure. Thus the opportunities for greater regional working in relation to Europe were varied. These patterns are exemplified by a more detailed assessment of regional partnerships in the difficult case of London and the South East during the early 1990s.

European partnerships in London and the South East

Throughout the post-war planning era the South East of England was always an imprecise region to identify. In geographical terms it covered an area from Oxford to Dover; and from Colchester to Southampton. For planning and administrative matters it consisted of Greater London and an area covering the counties of Kent, East and West Sussex, Surrey, Hampshire, the Isle of Wight, Berkshire, Oxfordshire, Buckinghamshire, Bedfordshire, Hertfordshire and Essex (Figure 11.1). At the 1991 census this area composed a total population of 17.7 million, which was 36.5 per cent of the English total. By the 1990s it was a region of diversity between the metropolis of London, the high technology-based economies of north Hampshire and Berkshire, the ports of Southampton and Portsmouth, the comparative wealth of Essex, and the rural and poor areas in Kent and Oxfordshire. Its size and diversity made for fragmentation and created difficulty in joint working when contrasted with the more integrated regions in England. The place of London within it caused problems too. Was London part of the South East, to be co-ordinated with it, or were there two regions of London and the rest?

Both underlining and compounding the problem of fragmentation during the early 1990s was the fact that there were few strategic bodies in the region. In London the strategic body, the Greater London Council, was abolished in 1986, leaving many co-ordination matters to the London-wide committees of the locally elected bodies, the 32 boroughs (plus the city of London). One of the most active of these was the London Planning Advisory Committee. In the rest of the South East, co-ordination fell to the formal local government system and the many other governmental- and partnership-based bodies. For the whole of the South East, there was only the London South East Regional Planning Conference (SERPLAN), an association of elected representatives from 12 counties and 98 districts, and the 33

1 City of London
2 Enfield
3 Barnet
4 Harrow
5 Haringey
6 Waltham Forest
7 Redbridge
8 Hillingdon
9 Brent
10 Camden
11 Islington
12 Hackney
13 Newham
14 Barking & Dagenham
15 Havering
16 Ealing
17 City of Westminster
18 Tower Hamlets
19 Hammersmith & Fulham
20 Kensington & Chelsea
21 Hounslow
22 Richmond upon Thames
23 Wandsworth
24 Lambeth
25 Southwark
26 Lewisham
27 Greenwich
28 Bexley
29 Kingston upon Thames
30 Merton
31 Sutton
32 Croydon
33 Bromley
34 Broxbourne
35 Three Rivers
36 Watford
37 Spelthorne
38 Elmbridge
39 Runnymede
40 Epsom & Ewell
41 Rochester-upon-Medway

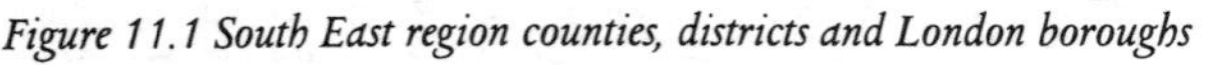

Figure 11.1 South East region counties, districts and London boroughs

Source: The London and South East Regional Planning Conference 1995

London authorities – the full representation of local government. It mainly had a planning remit, though this had widened. It formulated strategies on regional planning, agriculture, demography, the economy, the environment, housing, minerals, transport and waste. In addition, there was the Association of London Government (ALG) which was established in 1995 as a result of the merger of the two previous associations of London local authorities. From a central government point of view, the South East was mainly divided into two regions: the Government Office for London (GOL), which covered the greater London area; and the Government Office for the South East (GOSE), which covered a doughnut-shaped region around London. It should be noted, however, that GOSE and SERPLAN did not cover the same area, the latter taking in part of the area covered by the GOR in the Eastern Region. Thus the South East had started from a weak base for regional co-operation and co-ordination. Unlike other areas, such as the West Midlands, there were few structures and traditions for the emergence of European partnerships.

For European Structural Fund purposes the partnership of bodies in the South East was not extensive because, until 1993, the main UK areas which qualified for Objective 2 funding were in the North, Wales and Scotland. Up until the late 1980s the South East had low unemployment. The exception was that London received some funding under article 10 of the old European Development Regulations in 1989. These projects sought to regenerate economic activity in London's poorest housing estates and were monitored by a partnership between local authorities and central government. The other exception was the ESF (Objectives 3 and 4) to which many South East authorities had successfully applied. Local authorities and representatives from the voluntary sector, higher education and government schemes, sat on the national monitoring committee. One officer representing the ALG sat on the committee.

After 1993 some parts of London became eligible for Objective 2 funding. Partnerships included a wider group of representatives. The East London and Lee Valley partnership did not have to start from scratch as it derived from the earlier Objective 2 funding lobby led by Waltham Forest London Borough. Hence the main monitoring committee was composed of the bodies which allied to lobby for it. However, the committee still represented a highly diverse set of interests, reflecting the fact that it was linked to the complex governance structures of London. The membership comprised representatives from the ALG, the three TECs, the Lea[2] Valley

---

2. Confusingly, there are two spellings, Lee Valley and Lea Valley. Lee is used in the partnership documentation.

Regional Park Authority, English Partnerships, East London Partnership, Stratford Development Partnership, the Dalston and Bethnal Green City Challenges, the North London Business Leadership Team, officers from the councils, and representatives from the Further and Higher Education Funding Council and from the London Voluntary Sector Training Committee.

In general, at the committee level, the experience of partnership was poor. This did not result from an unwillingness to participate, but from the complexity of the situation, the novelty of full partnership and conflicts over goals. In the early period the partnership met infrequently and the Single Programming Document was only completed after a series of revisions. At the higher level there was serious conflict between the partners over where the resources should go, which meant that the committee meeting schedule slipped. It is difficult to ascertain whether because of the conflict there was a good partnership or not. Its existence at least shows that there was a forum for debate. There were also extraneous reasons why the partnership did not jell together. The first was the fact that European policy either changed very rapidly, or decisions about the rules for submission of projects were very late in coming, which slowed matters down and made it hard to assemble a package of projects. One example was when the Lee Valley Partnership was unable to submit its bids because the Commission changed the priorities of the ERDF, downgrading environmental and transport projects. The second was the complexity of the area, as it crossed many local authority boundaries. This made co-ordination difficult. There were also political problems, with certain council members benefiting from ERDF decisions who were not of the party which controlled the authority. Highly factional politics ran deep in the area, with a recent history of bitter conflict between the Liberal Democrat and Labour Parties. The third factor was that the start up of the partnership coincided with May elections in the London boroughs, which changed the political control of Tower Hamlets and meant that it took time to reorientate policy. It appears that in order to push the partnership along, a committee of civil servants within the government office for London co-ordinated affairs, so the centralisation affecting policy in other regions was also in train in London.

One of the interesting features of the partnership, however, was that there were arrangements at lower levels. For example, in Hackney there was a European partnership group which met every two to three months to discuss projects. It was less concerned to discuss strategy than to produce good submissions. Again, unlike the old system of local authority projects, these project submissions were all partnership-based. One example was an arts project in partnership with the British Film Institute to develop a centre in Hoxton. The local council was involved because of its access to matching funding and expertise, and its ability to provide leadership and co-ordination. Another was a multi-media project led by London Guildhall University and the colleges. The government office played a different role depending on the project. Most of the projects filtered up, and were led by local authorities, whilst for the others there was a need for the GOR to take a role. For example, on the Bishopsgate goods yard, which borders two authorities, English Partnership took a role, but with the government office taking the lead.

Further important examples of locally formed partnerships in the South East included the Isle of Thanet area in the South East region, which had as partners local authorities, East Kent Initiative (private sector), higher education, the Tourist Board, the voluntary sector, a water company, English Nature and the Kent training body. The partners had a role in drawing up drafts of the documents, but the final programming document was approved by the government department. The committees met at six-monthly intervals. In addition, there was the Kent and Nord-Pas-de-Calais cross-border project (INTERREG II). The national partnership was mainly based on local authorities with central government and Commission representatives. There was also a joint committee composed of partners from Nord-Pas-de-Calais and separate working parties.

Overall, the conclusion to draw from the experience in London and the South East is that at the regional or programme level partnerships were difficult and as a result often were centrally led. On the other hand, because of the complexity of getting projects together, more successful partnerships emerged at the local level where they were concerned with practical issues. This would seem to echo Bennett and Kreps' concluding points from their survey that, 'where "partnership" relations occur they are more often pragmatic around projects than consensual around goals' (1994, p.138).

The success of formal partnerships in London and the South East in the early 1990s appears to have been limited for a number of reasons. Unlike areas which had long histories of collaborative working, partners in London and the South East found it hard to work with each other because of the complex economic and political geography of the region, and political conflict in London. The changes in the rules of the funds brought in far more actors than previously, which made co-ordination complex. As not much of the area was eligible for funds, partnerships tended to be local, and anyway worked better on the projects. Thus, in contrast to other regions or sub-regions in England, there was little relationship between the formal partnerships on the monitoring committees and wider sub-regional or regional-based partnerships. Finally, there was the general problem of European partnerships, that there were limits to the extent partners could shape decisions. Central government civil servants, responsible to ministers, chaired the committees and set the agendas.

Whilst a key focus in this period was on formal partnership development, it should be noted that voluntary partnerships continued to develop. Indeed these covered a wider area and therefore had the ability to give a wider regional focus. The most prominent was the European activities of the ALG. Before the merger of the associations, the Association of London Authorities led a partnership of inner London authorities, such as Islington and Waltham Forest, which wished to develop a European focus, particularly on social policy. The successful application for Article 10 funding was as a result of this partnership approach. Indeed the Labour-controlled association and some inner city London authorities developed an interest in EU matters which appeared to them to be more progressive and forward-looking than was UK central government policy. The European focus was heightened when London launched a lobby during the Maastricht Treaty negotiations to propose an urban competence for the Structural Funds (John 1996). The attempt to change the drafting of the treaty was perhaps rather ambitious for a group of local authorities, so it was not surprising that the lobby failed. The association then launched a more successful lobby to have an urban definition in the Structural Funds when they were reformed in 1993 – a more realistic objective – which led to the Objective 2 designations discussed above. London authorities lobbied for, and benefited from, the URBAN community initiative. Joint working also resulted in the opening of an office in Brussels in September 1994 which included the TECs and other London public bodies. Thus London resembled the pattern developing elsewhere in the country: the trend towards greater regional or sub-regional partnership, networking and lobbying on Europe. Perhaps because of its London focus the ALG resisted a wider South East identity, although its members were part of SERPLAN.

SERPLAN was the only South East body seeking a regional European remit. Although it was created mainly as an advisory strategic planning association which was to produce reports and guidance for local authorities and central government, in this period it was seeking a European remit as the basis for a broader, regional role. For example, its officers had regular meetings with the Committee of the Regions' members and Commission officials. During 1994 and 1995 there were meetings with all the English regional associations to exchange ideas and discuss strategies which had European themes, such as the European Work Programme, the EU's Transport Strategy, the future of funding, the Delors White Paper and the Inter-governmental Conference in 1996. In fact SERPLAN played an advocacy role in trying to strengthen the presence of English regional associations. It argued that a region of its size, a European mega region, would become more important in Commission policy, as indicated in the European Commission report *Europe 2000+* (CEC 1994). To capitalise on this more proactive role, SERPLAN was seeking to become more like a regional association. In order to reflect the nature of the region it suggested that it could be federated with five constituent parts: London; Hertfordshire, Essex and Bedfordshire; Buckinghamshire, Oxford and Berkshire (BOB); Kent and East Sussex; and Hampshire. It was argued that this federation would also be able to link together the Association of District Councils, regional structure.

Other voluntary partnerships in the South East seeking a European role during the early 1990s were sub-region-based. On the fringes of the South East was the South Coast Metropole, which was a European partnership including Portsmouth, Southampton, Bournemouth and Poole. The last two towns were outside the South East region. The partnership aimed to gain European recognition and funding, and to build relationships across the Channel. Other cross-country partnerships were also seeking a European focus. For example, there was the Thames Valley Consortium, a partnership based on BOB. However, most European operations remained contained within the counties. The main example was Kent, which was one of the pioneer European authorities. It continued to concentrate on the cross-border initiatives (INTERREG I and II) with Nord-Pas-de-Calais. A new European player which emerged in the era was East Sussex, which was successful in obtaining an INTERREG II project with Normandie region. Some wider partnerships were involved in lobbying for the initiative. East Sussex mobilised counties along the South coast to agree a lobbying strategy. Another example of a cross-border initiative was Essex County, which ran a joint office with Picadie region. Thus, unlike other regions where European partnerships were converging on the regional boundaries, those in the South East were either inward-looking in large counties or outward-looking linking with local authorities outside the region or in France. On this evidence, while reflecting the diverse and changing nature of British regional networking in the early 1990s, voluntary partnerships were not, in the South East at least, strengthening regionalism.

Conclusion

British regionalism from the late 1980s had a growing European focus. The advantages of local authorities working together on European issues on lobbying, networking and joint projects surpassed, or at least complemented, the single authority strategy. Regional strategies defined local authority approaches to Europe in the first half of the 1990s in the same way as the pioneer single local authorities did in the 1980s. With the break-up of Strathclyde, the downgrading of European operations in Birmingham, and the way the local government review had weakened strategic local authorities in England, Wales and Scotland, the field was more open for regional partnerships. The trend for more forms of unelected local governance to become involved and for networks to grow made regional joint working more likely.

These trends were incipient in the South East, with growing partnerships based around the ALG, the Thames Valley and the South Coast Metropole. A focus for the whole of the South East was being articulated through the European aspirations of SERPLAN. But the experience of European operations in the South East reflected the fragmentation of the region as well as tendencies to joint working. First, the unified and well-organised European function co-ordinated by the ALG precluded a wider partnership based on the South East, as the association resisted participating in a wider South East identity. For the South East to have worked better, London needed to play an active part. This separation was compounded by the organisation of the GORs, of which three were established covering the South East. Second, the formal partnerships were too small and too marred by conflict to be a basis of a more effective regional strategy. Third, the strong Europeanists in the region were still the single counties, such as Kent, Essex, East Sussex and Hampshire, which had the size and incentive to go it alone in their European strategies, and work in cross-Channel initiatives rather than engage in regional networks. These entities were not greatly affected by local government restructuring. Finally, the size and unclear identity of the region militated against a regional European vision. These factors suggest that, when considering the European push to regionalism and regionalisation from the late 1980s, the South East did indeed present a difficult case, as it did in other aspects of the regional debate.

In the mid 1990s there were still nevertheless some trends which pointed to a growing European role. The Commission's discussion of mega regions, in that it suggested potential implications for policy or funding, offered some incentive for a European South East strategy. It implied also that other English regions would have to merge or work together for these planning purposes, such as a Midlands region or a North, Yorkshire and Humberside region. It was also clear that the enhancement or transformation of SERPLAN could be an incentive for more European strategies. The insistence of the English Regional Association that English counties move away from being individual members to regional groupings offered some further impetus. Local government restructuring, although not making a huge impact in the South East, provided some potential for making a regional partnership more feasible, as it was possible that Southampton and Portsmouth would wish to join partnerships at a wider level than their former counties as they had done already within the South Coast Metropole. These trends suggested, as with other aspects of the apparently amorphous South East, that there was more of a possibility for a coherent regional identity than was generally supposed, though the difficulties remained immense. This conclusion should be seen both in the context of the more general factors pushing towards new forms of English regional capacity, as well the cultural, political and institutional constraints pushing against.

References

Anderson, J.J. (1990) 'Sceptical reflections on a Europe of regions.' *Journal of Public Policy 10*, 417–447.

Baine, S., Benington, J. and Russell, J. (1992) Changing Europe. London: Bedford Square Press.

Batley, R. and Stoker, G. (eds) (1990) *Local Government and Europe.* London: Macmillan.

Bennett, R. and Kreps, G. (1994) 'Local economic development partnerships: an analysis of policy networks in EC-LEDA local employment development strategies.' *Regional Studies 28*, 2, 119–140.

Bongers, P. (1992) *Local Government and 1992.* Essex: Longman.

Commission of the European Communities (1994) *Europa 2000+. Cooperation for European Territorial Development.* Luxembourg: OOPEC.

Economic and Social Committee (1994) 'The Role of the Public Authorities in the Partnership. Opinion of the Section for Regional Development and Country Planning.'

Hutchinson, J. (1994) 'The practice of partnership in economic development.' *Local Government Studies 20*, 3, 335–344.

John, P. (1994a) 'UK sub-national offices in Brussels: regionalisation or diversification.' *Regional Studies 28*, 7, 739–746.

John, P. (1994b) *The Europeanisation of British Local Government: New Management Strategies.* Luton: Local Government Management Board.

John, P. (1995) *A Base in Brussels: A Good Investment for Local Authorities?* Special Report No. 2. London: Local Government International Bureau.

John, P. (1996) 'Centralisation, decentralisation and the European Union: the dynamics of triadic relationships.' *Public Administration 74, 2,* 293–312.

Martin, S. and Pearce, G. (1994) 'The impact of Europe on local government: regional partnerships in local economic development.' In P. Dunleavy and J. Stanyer (eds) *Contemporary Political Studies 1994.* Belfast: Political Studies Association.

McCarthy, A. and Burch, M. (1994) 'European regional development strategies: the response of two northern regions.' *Local Government Policy Making 20*, 5, 31–38.

Stewart, M. (1994) 'Between Whitehall and town hall: the realignment of urban regeneration policy in England.' *Policy and Politics 22*, 133–145.

CHAPTER 12

Whitehall et la Désert Anglais

Managing and Representing the UK Regions in Europe[1]

Peter Roberts

Introduction

In the Single European Act and the Maastricht Treaty the EU placed increasing emphasis upon the region as a common building block for policy and action. In the same period the collapse of the Soviet bloc led to the emergence of a 'New Europe' of former Central and Eastern Europe characterised by a reawakening of regional autonomy and identity beyond the boundaries of the EU. This chapter considers the implications of these developments for the UK regions in the early to mid 1990s and their responses in light of the various forms of regional administrative structure which left local government as the key elected sub-national institution. Overall, the chapter argues that central government's stance towards the issue of regional institutional capacity and the role of local government in this period was such as to have damaging consequences on the ability of the UK regions to respond to the new challenges posed by developments in Europe. Section one provides evidence of the operational deficiencies in terms of seeking to exercise influence over the EU policy-making challenge. Section two suggests that there was also a representative deficiency in terms of responding to institutional change in Europe. This was clearly reflected in the case of UK representation on the EU Committee of the Regions, as well as in respect of the Assembly of European Regions (AER) which had a broader geographical coverage than the EU. A number of the problems experienced by regions in the UK, and especially in England, are illustrated

1 The author wishes to acknowledge the assistance provided by Damien Welfare, Trevor Hart, Jos Gallacher and Franz-Josef Stummann in the preparation of this chapter.

from the author's experience of participating in the preparation of the *Yorkshire and Humberside Regional Strategy* – the region's background strategy for its bid to the European Commission to gain access to the Structural Funds (Yorkshire and Humberside Partnership 1993).

Finally, the chapter considers the implications for the UK regions of the persistence of a democratic deficit, arising from the absence of a formal tier of elected government. This critique is made from a perspective which could be described as European rather than British, and regionalist rather than nationalist, in focus. It is argued that the absence of a measure of devolution of power to the regions, and especially to those of England, limited their search for a clearer identity and role in the EU. Whitehall and Westminster saw the regions largely in an imperialist light: a view which assumed that all power rightfully resided at the centre and that the requirements of the regional 'colonies' were subservient to the needs of the central unitary state. The dominance exerted by Whitehall over the regions of the UK, and especially those of England, reflected the relatively powerless state of localities and regions in a political desert created by excessive central control. In contrast, it was clear that a new balance of power and opportunity between the regions and the centre would have presented new challenges, which included those of providing an effective system of regional planning, and promoting regional development and management in an increasingly competitive Europe.

Localities and regions post-Maastricht: the operational problem

The Maastricht Treaty raised a number of issues of considerable significance for local and regional authorities:

- the implications for local and regional authorities of the aim of economic convergence
- the likely effects of moves to enhance economic and social cohesion
- the consequences of further progress towards the achievement of political union
- the future size and composition of the EU
- the pace of change in the future evolution of the internal structures and policies of the EU.

These matters raised major challenges for regions and localities, and there was a consequent need to develop the capacity of sub-national institutions to tackle such matters in a way which met local and regional needs. In meeting these challenges the further question was raised of where subsidiarity began and ended in the UK context in responding to EU change. Was the concept solely about the redistribution of power between member states and the institutions of the Union, as the British government suggested, or was it also about the decentralisation of power from London to the regions and localities (Roberts, Hart and Thomas 1993)?

In commenting on these issues there were clear differences of view between Brussels and London. At the time of the Treaty, Leonardi and Garmise (1992, p.270) commented on the probability of EU initiatives promoting a regional agenda: 'If before 1992 the Community provided for itself the legal right and the ability to intervene in regional policy, from 1992 onwards it will have the political will to do so'. Such political will was reflected particularly in the establishment of the Committee of the Regions. However, it is questionable whether this new political will was also to be found in the UK. The EU may have wished to enhance the role and function of regions, but in a highly centralised state, such as the UK, the operational capacity to perform this role, and to discharge essential functions, was always likely to be limited. Experience after 1992 bore out this fear. If one considers matters concerned with the day-to-day management of regions, it is clear that the UK regions, and especially the English regions, found it very difficult to play an ideal operational role in the post-Maastricht policy process. In particular there was a lack of organisational and technical competence at the regional level to plan and implement programmes for future development. This was a matter of concern given the lacklustre performance of central government in providing either an integrated and comprehensive strategic vision or a sound democratic basis for the governance of the UK's regions.

In this respect the situation of the UK regions was out of step with developments elsewhere in the Union and in the wider Europe (Barrington 1991). This was symptomatic of the general inability of British central government to pay sufficient attention to the spatial dimension of many aspects of public policy. Criticisms of the lack of adequate regional strategic guidance or policy came from many quarters; but it diminished the capacity to develop either national or regional economies (Roberts 1990). Whilst the recent renewal of interest in regional planning as a result of the new European impetus went some way to answering such criticisms, in the mid 1990s it remained unclear whether regional planning 'risen from the bier' (Wannop 1995, p.187) would develop to full maturity.

This absence of an operational capacity for the governance of regions has been discussed in the literature and was demonstrated on the ground. Even in those regions which had a distinctive level of what Kellas (1991) refers to as 'territorial management', the arrangements were considered flawed in both design and operation. More importantly, in the late 1980s and early

1990s, a period of resource shortages and general tension between the centre and the periphery, the notional control which was exercised by regional administration in Wales, Scotland and Northern Ireland did not appear to be capable of moving outside the parameters set by Whitehall-dominated government. Goldsmith (1986, p.167) observed that despite the fact that different administrative processes existed in the peripheral regions, 'in practice by and large these processes do not appear to give rise to significant variations in policy implementation if the Imperial core is not prepared to countenance such variations'.

In such a situation, and the position obtaining in the English regions was significantly worse than that in the Celtic fringe, there was little chance of developing appropriate regional or local arrangements which offered the chance for a long-term strategic vision to emerge and, more importantly, for it to be translated into action. This was a major problem because a considerable number of operational tasks for sub-national government were associated with the evolution of the specific areas of policy action most likely to be affected by the Single Market Programme and the Treaty on European Union. Whilst it is not the intention of this chapter to deal with all of these tasks in detail, Table 12.1 provides a brief summary of some of the main areas of interaction between the key elements of the Single European Market Programme and those aspects of operational and technical competence which were within the remit of local and regional government. As can be ascertained from Table 12.1, some aspects of local and regional operational competence were more affected by the Europeanisation of policy than others, whilst other elements of the Single European Market affected all aspects of competence. Irrespective of the scale and significance of the impact, the most important feature of the relationship was the considerable span and the growing significance of many of the interactions.

At a regional level there were a number of other tasks which had to be discharged, and it was here that the lack of formal regional government really began to bite. By comparison with regions in many other European member states, the regions of the UK suffered a double disadvantage: they lacked any permanent and formal capacity for the generation and implementation of comprehensive and integrated regional plans; and they lacked a mechanism to ensure the conformity of key actors with any plan which may have emerge and been approved. This disadvantage hindered regions in responding 'adequately to the new requirements arising from deeper European integration' (Wiehler and Stumm 1995, p.249).

In the introduction to this chapter, it was stated that examples from Yorkshire and Humberside would be used to illustrate some of the key issues and features that were present in the UK regions. Whilst it is to the credit of

Table 12.1 The British local authority response to the Single European Market: which functions will be affected?

Elements of the Single Market	*Local Authority Functions* 1	2	3	4	5	6	7	8	9	10	11	12	13	14	15
Standards, testing certification				•				•	•	•	•			•	
Food laws	•								•	•					
Pharmaceuticals									•	•					
Public contracts	•	•	•	•	•	•	•	•		•	•	•		•	•
Telecomms	•		•											•	•
Information tech, broadcasting			•				•							•	•
Financial services	•	•													
Insurance	•	•													
Capital movements		•													
Freedom of movement of employees	•	•	•	•	•	•	•	•	•	•	•	•	•	•	•
Training (including languages)			•										•		
Company law	•										•				
Physical barriers														•	
Animal, plant and fish health, meat hygiene	•								•	•					
Competition policy	•				•										
State aids	•				•		•								
Consumer protection	•				•				•	•					
Environmental policy	•				•					•					
Research and development					•										
Civil protection	•													•	•
Freedom to vote in local elections	•														
Social dimension	•		•		•	•									

1 = Administration/legal
2 = Treasurers
3 = Education
4 = Architects/housing
5 = Planning/economic development
6 = Social services
7 = Leisure/amenities
8 = Technical services
9 = Consumer/trading standards
10 = Environmental health
11 = Direct services
12 = Sewerage/waste
13 = Personnel
14 = Police
15 = Fire

Source: Roberts, P., Hart, T. and Thomas, T. (1993)

all the parties who participated in the Yorkshire and Humberside Regional Partnership that they were able to work together in the production of a European regional development strategy (Yorkshire and Humberside Partnership 1993), there was no guarantee that any of the partners – central and local government, the Training and Enterprise Councils (TECs) and the regional bodies of the Confederation of British Industry (CBI), the TUC and the Chambers of Commerce – would be able to deliver the planned outputs. Even with the subsequent establishment of a single local authority body, the Regional Assembly for Yorkshire and Humberside, to facilitate regional joint working and encourage mutual support, the old evils of Treasury-dominated central expenditure planning together with the absence of any form of regional budget, worked against the achievement of the objectives agreed by the partners and reflected in the strategy.

Although the situation improved substantially during the early 1990s with the introduction of Regional Planning Guidance (RPG) for the English regions, these long-term land-use strategies were not integrated with the earlier European regional development strategies (Roberts 1996). In the case of Yorkshire and Humberside, whilst Draft Regional Planning Guidance acknowledged the parameters within which it was prepared, including a substantial number of national policies and statements, it made no mention of the pre-existing European regional development strategy or the resulting Single Programming Documents (SPD) prepared for the various EU programmes that operated in the region (Government Office for Yorkshire and Humberside 1995). A powerful argument existed, and still exists, in support of the merger of these two regional strategic documents, together with the systems responsible for their production. In future the strategic elements of RPG and SPD should be regarded as two parts of a single integrated regional strategy.

Comparing the situation in the UK in this era with that which obtained in many other member states of the EU offers little comfort. Economic policy in those member states with an established regional tier of government was seen to be as much a matter for regional government as it was for the centre; and this arrangement was normally enshrined in a written constitution. The Belgian regions, for example, enjoyed a considerable degree of autonomy on matters of economic policy and public expenditure. Other aspects of regional policy had long been, in some states, entirely within the competence of regional government. For example, the German *Länder* exercised total competence in the field of cultural policy and they nominated a minister from amongst their members to represent the Federal Republic at meetings of the Council of Ministers.

A further factor which acted to disadvantage UK regions was that in some other member states (this was especially the case in Germany), because the relationship between central government and regional authorities was based upon a lengthy and complex process of negotiation, central government itself was expected to reflect regional requirements within its own policies and programmes (Prodi 1993). This process brought with it the associated benefit of ensuring that central government gave far more attention to the co-ordination and spatial implications of its own policies than was the case in the UK. In such situations, the actions of central and regional government tended to be mutually reinforcing, thereby allowing the emergence and implementation of policies which were both spatially appropriate and to the national benefit.

One parallel in the UK to the broader organisational model which existed in other member states of the EU, could be found in the case of overseas inward investment. In the UK, as elsewhere, development agencies pursued policies designed to attract mobile investment; these efforts were supported by central government promotion and funding. However, even in this case, there was only a partial degree of co-ordination or coincidence between inward investment policy and policies for indigenous development. Inward investment was commonly regarded by both central government and regional agencies as an activity that could be superimposed upon a regional economy, rather than as a progressive addition to the existing economic base of a region. Whilst not wishing to criticise success in attracting new enterprises and jobs to lagging regions, it is worth considering what may have been achieved if resources had been devoted to ensuring the greater co-ordination of inward investment with the restructuring and expansion of indigenous industries.

In concluding on these matters it is important to stress that the issue of the operational competence of regions, whilst linked to matters of accountability and democratic representation, was also a matter of direct practical significance. The merger of the regional offices in England of the Departments of Transport, Trade and Industry, Employment, and the Environment into Government Offices of the Regions (GORs) was intended to provide, 'a single point of contact for local authorities, businesses and local communities' (Department of the Environment 1993, p.1). However, this merger did not, on its own, guarantee any improvement upon the previous situation. Indeed, the integrated decentralisation of Whitehall functions needed to be matched by a far greater degree of autonomy in terms of regional planning and expenditure control than was apparent from the GORs' early operation, if the basis was to be established for effective regional planning, management and development.

An optimistic scenario for the evolution of this operational competence in the UK regions would be based on the French experience. Here the regional prefect was initially advised by a representative commission drawn from local authorities and other organisations in the region (Hansen 1968), and regional capacity developed from the initial integration of departmental activities at a regional level, followed by further instalments of functional decentralisation. In the French case the regionalisation of central government functions led eventually, in 1982, to the establishment of directly elected regional authorities as a 'territorial collective'. A more pessimistic scenario is one which views the establishment of prefects for the English regions as a step towards a form of economic direct rule and further expenditure control. However, whatever the outcome, at least a first step was taken with the GORs towards the re-establishment of an operational capacity for the co-ordination of central government functions at a regional level.

Finally, irrespective of the merits and failings of the arrangements for the territorial management of the UK regions, there was the question of the ability of the regions to influence the future evolution and content of European regional, environmental and spatial policy. In the absence of a truly representative regional collective voice, the only real mechanisms for exerting influence which were available to regions and localities were: indirectly through the European Parliament and the Committee of the Regions; by working directly with individual sections of the European Commission; or through networking with other localities and regions on topics of mutual significance. For reasons partly to do with culture and physical isolation, but also associated with the lack of regional (as against local) political leadership and vision, the UK regions were less influential in such arenas than many of their better resourced and more politically influential French, German, Italian and Spanish counterparts. There were exceptions to this general observation (such as the role played by the Coalfield Communities Campaign in leading the development of EUR-ACOM and the establishment of RECHAR), but such initiatives were few in number. The democratic deficit not only disadvantaged the UK regions over the short term, it also affected their ability to influence the form and content of the future European policy agenda. This created a situation in which the evolution of EU policy could fail to reflect fully the needs of UK regions and thereby place them at a further disadvantage in the future. As Europe broadens and deepens, local authorities and regional interests must respond in a similar manner, but for the UK regions such a response was difficult to organise at anything but a local level.

UK regions and regional organisations in Europe: the representation problem

Concerns about UK regional capability in the early to mid 1990s extended to further doubts about the likely development of appropriate political structures within regions and the arrangements for the representation of regions in the central institutions of the EU. One of the most telling illustrations of the relative political powerlessness and lack of operational capability evident in the UK regions was provided by the case of how a procedure was established in the early 1990s to determine how the UK should be represented on the Committee of the Regions. The Maastricht Treaty (Article 198) established this Committee, consisting of, 'representatives of regional and local bodies', as a formal means of representing the regions. The Committee was to be consulted on matters not just affecting regional policy, but also on other 'specific regional interests' including education, vocational training, public health, trans-European networks and culture, and on broader matters of policy and budget as they affected the regions of the Union.

Whilst it proved to be a relatively easy matter for some member states to nominate members to the new Committee, the process of selecting UK members was far from easy. In the absence of an elected (or nominated) regional tier of government, the interpretation of what constituted a representative of a regional or local body generated a major controversy between local and central government.

The initial response from the UK Government was to consider nominating persons other than local government representatives to the Committee. It was, for example, suggested at one stage that the Secretary of State and two other nominees might represent Wales. However, the various local authority associations took a different view and adopted a common stance, that is, that they were the appropriate bodies to advise the government on the selection of nominees (Local Government International Bureau 1993). One of the difficulties – said to have occurred in the process of translation – originated in the wording of Article 198 of the Maastricht Treaty: the original French 'regional and local authorities' emerged as 'regional and local bodies' in the English version. Despite these difficulties in interpretation, the situation was resolved in May 1993 when an amendment to the Bill to ratify the Maastricht Treaty was introduced and agreed. This amendment restricted membership of the Committee to a person who was, 'an elected member of a local authority' (Williams 1996, p.4).

Having established this important principle, the next stage in the process of nomination was to decide on the spatial distribution of seats. Here a further difficulty existed, because the UK government during the passage of the Bill to ratify the Maastricht Treaty had agreed to an (over) allocation of seats to Wales, Scotland and Northern Ireland: 10 of the 24 UK places on the Committee as against the 6 places originally suggested by local government. This left only 14 seats available for members to represent the English shires and metropolitan areas. On the basis of an initial agreement between the English local authority associations, 8 of the original places would have been allocated to the metropolitan areas. The intention of this allocation was to ensure that each metropolitan county had one representative and that two seats should be available for representatives from Greater London. The government's allocation of seats to Wales, Scotland and Northern Ireland created an imbalance in the overall pattern of representation. Table 12.2 illustrates these difficulties.

Table 12.2: Initial and eventual British representation on the Committee of the Regions

	Local Authority View	*Final Nominations*
English Shires	10	8
English Metropolitan	8	6
Wales	2	3
Scotland	3	5
Northern Ireland	1	2
Total	**24**	**24**

A further complication occurred because the government expressed its intention to ensure that the composition of the English delegation reflected the balance between the political parties represented in local government. The party composition of the English nominations is illustrated in Table 12.3.

Table 12.3: Party balance of the English delegation on the Committee of the Regions

	Conservative	*Labour*	*Liberal Democrat*	*Independent*	*TOTAL*
Shires	3	3	1	1	8
Metropolitan	2	3	1	0	6
Total	**5**	**6**	**2**	**1**	**14**

Furthermore, the government, as well as creating a list of members to represent the UK, drew up a list of alternate members who could replace members of the main list if, for whatever reason, they could not attend the Committee. Each member, therefore, had a specifically named alternate member. The choice of alternate members, however, was based upon party not regional representation. Hence the resulting arrangements meant that the:

- Liberal Democrat member from Sutton had a Liberal Democrat alternate from Cornwall
- Conservative member from Trafford had a Conservative alternate from Bath
- Labour member from Birmingham had a Labour alternate from Barnsley
- Independent member from Richmondshire had an Independent alternate from Bridgenorth.

This mechanism for regional representation was out of step with the spirit of the Maastricht Treaty and left three metropolitan counties without a member, and two metropolitan counties without either a member or an alternate member (Merseyside and West Yorkshire).

By way of contrast, some other member states allocated the national quota of seats to the regional or local level on the basis of the advice received from regional government or local authority organisations. In some cases the entire quota was allocated to the regions (Belgium), in others the quota was allocated mainly to regions (Germany and Spain), whilst in some member states the quota was split between regional and the sub-regional levels (France and Italy). Although there were various interpretations as to what constituted a local, intermediate or regional tier of government, the broad pattern of representation evident in the membership of the Committee of the Regions reflected the cultural and political differences which existed between the various member states (Table 12.4).

Difficulty in distributing the national quota of seats on the Committee of the Regions was not unique to the UK. Greece and Ireland also experienced some problems in the process of allocation due to the absence of a formal regional tier of government. However, amongst the larger member states, the UK was alone in lacking an established representative level of government between central government and local authorities which could be used to assist in the process of allocation. Furthermore, the desire of central government to ensure that the delegation reflected the balance between the political parties resulted in a major imbalance in terms of spatial representation. This did nothing to rectify the weaknesses in UK regional representation.

Table 12.4: State representation on the Committee of the Regions

	Local	*Intermediate**	*Regional*	*Total*
Austria	3	–	9	12
Belgium	–	–	12	12
Denmark	5	4	–	9
Finland	7	1	1	9
France	6	6	12	24
Germany	2	1	21	24
Greece	12	–	–	12
Ireland	2	7	–	9
Italy	7	5	12	24
Luxembourg	6	–	–	6
Netherlands	6	6	–	12
Portugal	10	–	2	12
Spain	4	–	17	21
Sweden	8	4	–	12
UK	16	8	–	24
Total	**94**	**42**	**86**	**222**

Note: * for example, Dutch Provinces

Sources: Assembly of European Regions (1994), Christiansen (1995), Gallacher (1995)

The Committee of the Regions could, in the absence of a formal tier of regional government in the UK, have been considered as a mechanism for assisting in the creation of a sense of political purpose and identity at regional level. An English delegation which, for example, had included three representatives from Yorkshire and Humberside (one each for the two metropolitan counties and one for the two shires) would have helped to enable the sense of strategic purpose and joint working, which had been established through the Yorkshire and Humberside Regional Partnership, to be translated into political representation and practical action. Such an arrangement would have given the region an effective voice and presence at the European level of government.

It is important at this juncture to note the presence of an element of disagreement between observers of the Committee of the Regions regarding its mandate and purpose. A positive and regionalist view was advocated by Morphet (1994), who saw the Committee working in tandem with local authorities to represent and advance regional interests. She saw the Committee as having a vetting role in relation to projects and programmes advanced under the Structural Funds, with the possibility that the integrated regional offices would not have their, 'proposals recognised if they are not fully developed from the bottom-up' (Morphet 1994, p.58). This view was supported by the English Regional Association, which argued for new members of the Committee to be, 'chosen and supported by the regions' (English Regional Associations 1995, p.1). An alternative view was put by Gallacher (1995, p.3), who claimed that a 'common misunderstanding' existed that, 'the [Committee of the Regions] exists to represent particular geographical territories of the Community whether or not these regions have a democratic tier of government'. This divergence of view did not, however, undermine the fundamental strength of the Committee as a moderating force capable of acting upon the views of national governments.

In reality, from a non-UK perspective, the situation on the Committee of the Regions from the start was somewhat more complex, with the major conflict 'between local and regional interests' further divided by the, 'difference between federal or regionalised countries and unitary member states', and cross-cut by a rift between the, 'North and the South of Europe, pitting contributors to the EU budget against beneficiaries' (Hooghe and Marks 1995). These differences reflected variations in interpretation regarding the function of the Committee as well as differences in the style of operation sought by members, which in turn reflected the different traditions present in such a wide range of political cultures.

Despite these differences of interpretation and approach, the Committee of the Regions offered a significant opportunity to the localities and regions of the EU to balance national representation through the Council of Ministers with the needs and opportunities which existed at the grass roots. But in the UK this opportunity was missed. This was deeply regrettable because there were a number of positive signs of the roles which a regional representation was capable of performing.

Amongst the early achievements of the Committee of the Regions was a significant input towards progress in the debate on European regional and spatial policy. As Williams (1995) notes, five of the commissions (or sub-committees) established by the Committee included a spatial planning function within their remit. Commission 1 was concerned, amongst other matters, with regional development, Commission 2 with spatial planning, Commission 3 with transport, Commission 4 with urban policies, and Commission 5 with land-use planning and energy. In short, the Committee established specialist groups that covered most aspects of regional and spatial planning, development and management.

In addition, specific actions undertaken by the Committee included the preparation of opinions on the role of regional and local authorities in the partnership principle of the Structural Funds (Committee of the Regions

1995a) and on urban policy (Committee of the Regions 1995b). The former opinion emphasised the importance of bottom-up approaches to the construction of regional programmes, rather than the central government approaches which had dominated in the past. On urban policy, the Committee was of the opinion that it was vital to construct a coherent and integrated approach to urban problems and it emphasised, within the principle of subsidiarity, the need for local and regional authorities to have a sufficient resource base in order to address such problems effectively.

A final example of the influence of early work by the Committee was its report on institutional reform (Committee of the Regions 1995c), a matter which was at the very heart of the Inter-governmental Conference to review the Maastricht Treaty on European Union. In the opinion of the Committee, the role of sub-national representation which it performed needed to be strengthened, especially in relation to a wider range of policy concerns and through a closer association between the Commission and itself in the development of new areas of policy and legislation. This strengthening of the role and powers of the Committee was supported by the UK members in the form of a submission to the Commission on Institutional Affairs by Charles Gray (1995). The UK submission endorsed many of the arguments advanced by the Committee and, in addition, sought the creation of a legal base for sub-national government.

Although the Committee of the Regions was the formal body created to allow for regional representation within the EU, a number of other important organisations also facilitated regional representation at the European level in the late 1980s and first half of the 1990s. The very existence of such bodies further emphasised the implications of the democratic deficit at the regional level in the UK. One such body was the AER which, in its statute of June 1985 as modified in July 1992, sought to: 'strengthen the representation of the region within the European institutions and facilitate their participation in the building of Europe' (AER 1992, p.2). The organisation provided an important platform for regional interests and it attracted support from the regions, both through their membership of the main body and its committees, and through the high level of political support provided for its activities as a result of the direct participation of a group of senior national and regional politicians. There was a significant UK presence in the AER and a number of UK members played an active role in developing the work of the main assembly and the committees. However, following the abolition of the metropolitan counties and the progressive weakening of the shires in England and the abolition of the Scottish regional authorities, the ability of British members to speak and act with an authoritative voice at the regional level was somewhat diminished.

An important characteristic of the AER was that it was built by the regions based on the, 'understanding that Europe should not be forged alone in Brussels' (Teufel 1995, p.76). This bottom-up approach meant that the AER was both owned and empowered by its members, which were drawn from both formal regional authorities and from regional associations of local authorities. A further distinguishing characteristic of the AER was that its membership stretched beyond the EU to encompass over 280 regions in 23 countries. This extensive membership included a number of autonomous and semi-autonomous regions in the countries of Central and Eastern Europe, as well as member regions from EU nations and from elsewhere in Western Europe. An important function performed by the AER was to act as a neutral meeting ground for international, national and regional politicians outwith the formal structures of the EU, but in a more formal setting than that which was provided by meetings of European political groups and professional organisations that had an interest in regional affairs.

The AER operated through a number of permanent committees which dealt with a variety of operational matters as well as questions of a more academic and ideological nature. An important committee was the Scientific Committee advising the assembly itself; available to all of the permanent committees to offer an opinion on technical, professional and academic matters; and prepared also to provide advice for other European organisations.

By its very existence the AER demonstrated, and continues to demonstrate, the strength of common identity and purpose which was expressed at the regional level of government. The promotion by the AER of regionalism and federalism led to a series of agreements with the EU regarding the operational and political role of regions. It is important to note that the predecessor to the Committee of the Regions was the Consultative Council of Regional and Local Authorities, which was established in 1988 by the European Commission in response to a request from, and lobbying by, the AER. The Committee of the Regions emerged from the Consultative Council following general agreement on the value of the regional perspective provided by the Consultative Council. A further initiative of the AER led to its acceptance as an 'observer' by the Council of Europe in 1987 and this development later resulted, in 1993, in the creation of the Chamber of the Regions within the Council of Europe's Congress of Local and Regional Authorities. Subsequently the Chamber of the Regions provided a neutral forum where the regions of Central and Eastern Europe could meet with their Western European counterparts in a formal setting which was endorsed by national governments.

Despite the healthy level of participation of UK regions in the work of the AER, in the mid 1990s there remained many doubts as to the future. Local government reorganisation was threatening to sweep away many members of the UK contingent – a substantial number of the UK members represented shire counties or Scottish regions – and this suggested a lessening of the influence of the UK, as a whole, on regional affairs in the wider Europe. Indeed some countries had been removed from membership of the AER for failing to comply with the basic criteria for membership. Slovenia, a founding member, was removed in 1992 after gaining recognition as a nation state and delaying the creation of regional government. But the overall trend was for membership to increase and for the commitment of members to the regional cause to strengthen. Reorganisation of local government in the English and Welsh shires and the abolition of the regional councils in Scotland was likely to put back the regional representation of sub-national government in the UK by some 20 years; this threatened to leave a yawning chasm due to the absence of an accountable body that could initiate and regulate strategic thinking and action. The case of the abolition of regional councils in Scotland prompted a visiting Norwegian planner to observe that, 'elsewhere in Europe we are moving towards stronger strategic planning at the regional level, but in Scotland the regions are to be abolished' (Hague 1994, p.13).

Conclusions

A number of conclusions can be drawn from this review of the organisation and representation of the regions of the UK in the EU and the wider Europe during the late 1980s and early 1990s. First, there was a democratic deficit in the UK with the absence of any representative or elected structure of regions that was able to superintend the operation of central government functions discharged at regional level. This was clearly out of step with the situation in many other parts of Europe and created a number of difficulties in ensuring parity of representation both within the UK and at a European level.

Second, irrespective of the political arguments for or against the existence of a regional tier of government in the UK, there was a pressing reason for wishing to maintain a positive degree of influence over the questions of European regional and spatial policy. This had to do with the arrangements for monitoring and review of the Structural Funds and for ensuring that any future revisions of fund regulations would match the circumstances and requirements of the UK regions (Robert and Hart, 1996).

Third, a serious imbalance could be perceived in the form and structure of the UK representation on the Committee of the Regions. Indeed our fellow member states could be excused for considering the British approach to be working against the tide of thinking elsewhere in the Union. This limited the ability of the UK to influence the content and direction of European regional and spatial policy and had the potential to work against the national well-being as well as regional interests.

A fourth cause for concern by the mid 1990s related to the threat to the level of UK representation in the AER. The majority of UK members of the AER had represented shire counties or Scottish regions and it was clear that unless the successor unitary authorities could follow the lead which had been given by the unitary authorities in the English metropolitan areas – which had agreed on a policy of joint membership representing the entire county area as a single 'region' – then the influence of the UK in this important forum would diminish.

Finally, on the basis of their experience from the late 1980s, all involved at the regional level were aware that there was also a case for maintaining a strong presence in European regional organisations in order to influence the form and content of regional planning and development as the EU developed to take in new member states. It was recognised, however, that those existing member states which possessed a strong and effective system of regional government, planning and management were the ones most likely to influence the pattern of development in new member states and at the overall European level. As Bachtler (1992) observed, it was the positive models of regional government and planning which were likely to prove to be the most influential in the widening EU.

For the UK, these initial conclusions imply that there was by the mid 1990s an urgent need to associate the arrangements for the regional administration of central government functions through the Scottish and Welsh Offices and the GORs in England with some form of representative regional body, and to develop workable and lasting procedures and methods for regional planning, development and management. In England, the models of joint working which were offered, for example, by the Yorkshire and Humberside Partnership and the West Midlands Regional Forum provided a starting point in the search for a workable solution. As noted earlier in this chapter, it was possible to forsee success in linking these emergent forms of regional assembly to the devolution of central government functions evolving over time into a more accountable and representative form of regional government. But even this first step was seen by many as too radical in a political climate dominated by traditional concerns in Westminster and

Whitehall to maintain central control, a conclusion that was cause for substantial concern.

References

Assembly of European Regions (1992) *Statute of the Assembly of European Regions.* Strasbourg: Assembly of European Regions.

Assembly of European Regions (1994) 'Lists of the members of the Committee of the Regions.' *Regions of Europe 8,* 90–93.

Bachtler, J. (1992) *Socio-economic Situation and Development of the Regions in the Neighbouring Countries of the Community in Central and Eastern Europe.* Luxembourg: Office for Official Publications of the European Communities.

Barrington, T.J. (1991) 'Local government reform: problems to resolve.' Paper presented at the Regional Studies Association Irish Branch Conference, Dun Laoghaire, 1st March 1991.

Christiansen, T. (1995) 'Second thoughts – the committee of the regions after its first year.' In R. Dehousse and T. Christiansen (eds) *What Model for the Committee of the Regions?* Florence: European University Institute.

Committee of the Regions (1995a) *Opinion on the Role of Regional and Local Authorities in the Partnership Principle of the Structural Funds.* Brussels: Committee of the Regions.

Committee of the Regions (1995b) *Draft Report on Urban Policy.* Brussels: Committee of the Regions.

Committee of the Regions (1995c) *Institutional Reform.* Brussels: Committee of the Regions.

Department of the Environment (1993) 'Environment News Release 731.' London: Department of the Environment.

English Regional Associations (1995) *Draft Report on Membership of the Committee of the Regions.* Barnsley: Yorkshire and Humberside Regional Association.

Gallacher, J. (1995) *Committee of the Regions: An Opportunity for Influence.* London: Local Government International Bureau.

Goldsmith, M. (1986) 'Managing the periphery in a period of fiscal stress.' In M. Goldsmith (ed) *New Research in Central – Local Relations.* Aldershot, Hants: Gower.

Government Office for Yorkshire and Humberside (1995) *Draft Regional Planning Guidance for Yorkshire and Humberside.* Leeds: Government Office for Yorkshire and Humberside.

Gray, C. (1995) *Submission to the Special Commission on Institutional Affairs: 1996 – The View from the UK.* Brussels: Committee of Regions.

Hague, C. (1994) 'If it's not broke, don't fix it.' *Town and Country Planning 63,* 1.

Hansen, N.M. (1968) *French Regional Planning.* Edinburgh: Edinburgh University Press.

Hooghe, L. and Marks, G. (1995) 'Channels of subnational representation in the European Union.' In R. Dehousse and T. Christiansen (eds) *What Model for the Committee of the Regions?* Florence: European University Institute.

Kellas, J.G. (1991) 'The Scottish and Welsh Offices as territorial managers.' *Regional Politics and Policy 1*, 1.

Leonardi, R. and Garmise, S. (1992) 'Sub-national elites and the European Community.' *Regional Politics and Policy 2*, 1–2.

Local Government International Bureau (1993) *Committee of the Regions: Representation of UK Local Government.* London: Local Government International Bureau.

Morphet, J. (1994) 'The Committee of the Regions'. *Local Government Policy Making 20*, 5.

Prodi, R. (1993) 'The Single European Market: institutions and economic policies.' *European Planning Studies 1*, 1.

Roberts, P. (1990) *Strategic Vision and Management of the UK Land Resource.* London: Strategic Planning Society.

Roberts, P. (1996) 'Regional Planning Guidance in England and Wales: back to the future?' *Town Planning Review 67*, 1.

Roberts, P. and Hart,T. (1996) *Regional Strategy and Partnership in European Programmes.* York: Joseph Rowntree Foundation.

Roberts, P., Hart, T. and Thomas, K. (1993) *Europe: A Handbook for Local Authorities.* Manchester: Centre for Local Economic Strategies.

Teufel, E. (1995) 'Political perspectives of the AER.' *Regions of Europe 10*, 76–77.

Wannop, U.A. (1995) *The Regional Imperative.* London: Jessica Kingsley Publishers.

Wiehler, F. and Stumm, T. (1995) 'The powers of regional and local authorities and their role in the European Union.' *European Planning Studies 3*, 2.

Williams, R.H. (1996) *The European Union Committee of the Regions, its UK Membership and Spatial Planning.* Newcastle-upon-Tyne: Department of Town and Country Planning, University of Newcastle-upon-Tyne, Working Paper 52.

Yorkshire and Humberside Partnership (1993) *Yorkshire and Humberside Regional Strategy.* Barnsley: Yorkshire and Humberside Regional Partnership.

CHAPTER 13

Conclusion

The Changing Politics and Governance of British Regionalism

Jonathan Bradbury and John Mawson

The essays in this volume have addressed the linked questions of the manner in which regional developments and policy debates in the early to mid 1990s showed an advance on those witnessed in the 1960s and 1970s, when the regional agenda was last prominent. The essays overall suggest that there were a number of notable changes strongly linked to the changing contexts of state reform and European integration. The purpose of this chapter is to draw them out, explaining their origins and discussing their implications within a broader framework of analysis. We offer three perspectives which arise from observations of how structural change impacted upon political and policy debates, and of how elites, both in the regions and in the parties at Westminster, responded to this change. Section one identifies four novel political and policy-related pressures at the regional level, and discusses their effects in terms of the advent of new forms of regional governance and a broader basis of elite support for devolution and regional reform. Section two considers how the Conservative approach to the government of Scotland, Wales and the English regions changed during the 1970s to one which excited territorial opposition and was inherently more problematic. The final section assesses the development in opposition of Labour Party policy on devolution and regional reform, concluding that the advent of New Labour made some important differences to the validity of the project in comparison to that of the 1970s.

All of the essays in the book, are cautious about suggesting that there was a major transformative effect. Indeed, to a considerable extent they provide echoes of the sceptical reflections of the 1970s discussed in Chapter 1, namely: that pressures for change were generally much weaker than their proponents argued; that Conservative administrations gave more serious thought to the complexities of government beyond the centre and of territorial management than was often appreciated; and that the Labour Party found it rather easier to make critiques of Conservative policy than to develop coherent plans for alternative schemes for devolution. In advancing each of the perspectives on change, the chapter takes due note of the need for equivocation.

The regionalist implications of structural change

It has been suggested that Conservative state reforms and developments in European integration had a considerable impact upon pressures for change in the government of Scotland, Wales and the English regions, and the resulting movements for constitutional reform and patterns of sub-national governance during the early to mid 1990s. This section discusses these pressures, the substantive policy implications, and the problematic nature of this putative new form of British regionalism.

It is generally recognised that the pressures for constitutional reform in the 1970s were primarily separatist and centrifugal in nature: that in Scotland and Wales high levels of support for independence and/or home rule represented increased threats of fundamentalist dissent against the Union. In this context, reformist prescriptions for devolution were to be seen primarily as a sop to nationalism; a Labour Party ploy to stop votes going to the nationalist parties, which had to be imposed on the party in Wales and Scotland against a background of resentment and division. English regional reform was seen then as a constitutionally necessary complement to devolution. A number of recent analyses suggest that pressures for reform in the 1990s essentially arose from the re-emergence and intensification of these nationalist pressures; pressures which apparently resulted from the overbearing Britishness of Thatcherism and the encouragement by European integration of politicised concepts of national identity in Scotland and Wales. Whilst often expressed in terms of great caution as to whether constitutional change would actually happen, the messages concerning the intensification of pressures for such an outcome were unmistakeable (see Harvie 1989; McCrone 1993; Osmond 1994, 1995).

Contributors to this book have no doubt that this kind of analysis is at least partially true. Brand and Mitchell, for example, agree that the major spurs to Labour Party proposals for devolution in Scotland in the 1990s were the perceived re-emergence of the nationalist threat to the Labour vote, and an awareness that an increased element of the Labour vote was pro-independence. Their conclusions do show, however, that we need to be wary of suggesting the re-emergence of separatist nationalism as the only significant motor leading to the resurrection of devolution proposals. Most revealing is the fact that whilst the SNP's political support did not suggest that it should have been seen as a greater threat than in the 1970s, nevertheless the Scottish Labour Party became more united in its support for devolution and proposed stronger proposals than in the 1970s. On Wales, Jones refutes the significance of separatist nationalism altogether and argues that, in contrast to the 1970s, the threat of Plaid Cymru was not the principal factor in reinvigorating the Labour Party campaign for devolution. If separatist nationalism and popular pressure cannot explain either alone, or at all, the pressure for constitutional reform in the 1990s, then what else can? It is argued here that four pressures for change emerged arising from state reform and European integration of which two were political and two were of a functional-policy nature.

First, state reform had a significant impact on the outlook of the Labour Party in Scotland, Wales and certain parts of England, notably the North, in terms of considering which power base best promoted the party's interests. In the 1970s, when the choice was posed as being between independence and the centralised British state, many in the Labour Party in both Scotland and Wales remained committed to the centralised British state as the appropriate agency for handling all domestic affairs. This was seen as the best vehicle through which to seek the aims of equality. Devolution was primarily a policy pushed by the Labour Party machine for electoral reasons as we have seen above, and was not uniformly popular in the Labour Party in Scotland and Wales. By the 1990s there remained significant party support for a strong unitary state; the factors which Birch (1989) and Bulpitt (1983) discussed at great length still had their bearing (see Chapter 1). However, the chapters by Brand and Mitchell, Jones and Mawson all indicate that fewer Labour activists were committed to a continued primary concentration of political power at Westminster than was previously the case.

Several party political reasons for this shift may be offered. The 1980s and early 1990s reaffirmed Labour's historic experience, namely that the party enjoyed power at the centre comparatively rarely, and that Conservative governments used central power in ways abhorrent to them. After years in opposition, support grew for the proposition that when in office a Labour government should carry out reforms to decentralise power so that even when voted out of office at Westminster, Labour could still enjoy rather more use of power than hitherto via its office holding in sub-national government. Labour also became less committed to central power because as a result of Conservative state reforms it was apparent that even if the party attained office there would be less central power to use in the pursuit of party objectives than there used to be. Assuming the influence of the New Labour project over a Labour government, there were few expectations that what power there was left at the centre would be used to carry out interventionist state objectives anyway. Hence demands for devolution emerged from territorial groupings within the Labour Party to secure greater governmental autonomy at the regional level in order to allow at least a partial pursuit of democratic socialist objectives. In addition, it should be noted that the broad context of European integration bolstered the Labour Party in Scotland and Wales and parts of England in their campaign for decentralisation. The development of regional level government in a number of states on the continent in the 1980s provided precedents for British devolution which were simply not present in 1979. The Spanish experience of rolling devolution provided some reassurance for the argument of the constitutional viability of variable levels of devolution for different territories within the state; and the French example of evolving regional government from indirectly elected authorities to full regional government provided a model for developing English regional reform.

The second novel pressure for change related to a development in the expression of the politics of identity in Scotland and Wales. This arose from the experience of the 1980s and early 1990s, when there was a questionable mandate for Conservative policies in territories which so heavily voted against the Conservative Party. Resentments at Conservative rule were further intensified by the imposition of the Thatcher policy agenda without recourse to considering the distinctive needs of Scotland and Wales. For example, anger about the appointment procedures and political composition of quangos, at control of the Welsh Office by Secretaries of State with an English background, and at the overriding of special conventions of territorial representation in parliament are all forcefully described with respect to Wales by Jones. This resulted in perceptions of a democratic deficit and sparked concerns about the need to find alternative means of speaking for the nation in Scotland and Wales, leading to a much higher and broader level of commitment among peripheral elites to devolution than was the case in the 1970s. The change was striking. With respect to Scotland, Brand and Mitchell show that the Labour Party was again at the heart of the campaign in the early to mid 1990s but, whilst there were some dissenters, the party became overwhelmingly in favour of change. Moreover, there was evidence to suggest that this shift occurred not merely to counter the SNP. A growing number of members, based in Scottish Labour Action, became enthusiasts for home rule on the basis of a politicised Scottish identity. Elite commitment to the campaign for a Scottish parliament, based on the constitutional convention, also included a majority of Scotland's political and civic leaders, including representatives of the Liberal Democrats, and religious, trade union and local government leaders. This suggests that there was a much broader consensus within Scottish elites in favour of devolution in Scotland than a focus merely on the Labour Party would suggest. Moreover, from the late 1980s they came together in a constitutional convention, showed how a parliament might work in practice, and agreed specific proposals for a future Scottish parliament.

Similarly, in Wales, Jones shows that a more concerted movement grew over the need for devolution. He accepts that the key focus of the movement for change was again the Wales Labour Party and that there were again internal party divisions over the issue. Indeed opposition from a hard core of Welsh Labour MPs placed severe limits on how far the contents of the proposals could go. However, Jones illustrates how the number of public dissenters in the early to mid 1990s was fewer than in the 1970s, and that the national Labour Party commitment to devolution in Wales hardened rather than weakened after 1992. More of the non-Conservative elite also became pro-devolution. Liberal Democrat representatives and trade union, local government and religious leaders, as well as part of the business community, also signalled their support. Of particular interest was the fact that the Association of Welsh Counties, which was hostile in the 1970s, was one of the principal supporters of devolution in the early 1990s as a vital component of any scheme to improve Welsh government. This only serves to highlight the fact that the case for reform of territorial representation in Scotland and Wales became more broadly accepted in elite circles and on a rather different basis from that of the 1970s.

In contrast to the narrowly party political origins of the push for devolution in the 1970s, as a means for the Labour Party to combat the electoral threat of the separatist parties, the case for devolution in the early to mid 1990s was put more positively as a good thing in its own right: to provide for a more democratic representation of Scotland and Wales in the British political system and better government. To place a broad understanding on this subtly different expression of the politics of national identity, this phenomenon may be seen as an example of what Gladstone, in debates over Irish home rule in the nineteenth century, referred to as 'local patriotism' (Bogdanor 1979, p.13). This patriotism expresses itself as a desire to take more control of one's domestic affairs as a nation whilst retaining loyalty to the overarching framework of the British state and looking to the British government to determine external affairs. Taken at face value this kind of politicised national identity would seem less threatening to the overall stability of the British state.

These political pressures were important in their own right but need to be viewed in relation to the two kinds of policy demand which were also present at the regional level in this period. First, the reforms of the state left to a considerable extent a policy and planning vacuum. The Thatcherite view was that the market mechanism could take over responsibility for economic development and the allocation of land use. Institutions of sub-national government, particularly local government, had other ideas, and in relation to economic development, transportation and land-use policy matters, sought to reconstruct regional planning mechanisms on a co-operative basis between themselves. In the early 1990s, Conservative governments, faced with the twin pressures of a shortage of land for housing and the 'not in my backyard' tendency of Conservative supporters, were reluctantly forced to recognise the need for some form of regional strategic land-use planning. As a result, they backed local authority activity at the sub-regional level to provide guidance for central decisions. The recognition that such functional policy requirements needed to be carried out at the regional level was a reflection of the fact that the planning philosophy, so influential in the 1960s in shaping the indicative planning era, was still of substantial importance in local government in the 1990s, and even had to be accepted, albeit reluctantly, by a reforming market-orientated government.

Second, functional pressures for the presence and enhancement of regional capacity came from the impact of state reform and European integration on the political economy of regionalism. In the 1970s the argument that Scotland and Wales should take greater charge of their economic fortunes was problematic because the link with the wider British economy was seen as crucial. In that devolution might affect adversely economic fortunes in the British context, either by discouraging market activity or reducing central government financial subsidy from London, then it was to be opposed. In particular, many jobs in Scotland and Wales were directly or indirectly dependent upon nationalised industries, and in turn upon government demand management and finance. After 1979, however, the economic context to regionalist debates substantially changed. Conservative state reforms in both Scotland and Wales created economies which were much less reliant on nationalised or other heavy industries dependent upon government contracts and financial assistance. Instead their economic development focus became more orientated towards attracting industry through inward investment, and selling the advantages of a well-trained and disciplined industrial workforce, a deregulated economy and easy access to the large European market. This occurred at the same time as developments such as the communications revolution encouraged a more global market-place, and European integration resulted in the pursuit of a Single European Market (SEM). As a consequence Scottish, Welsh and, indeed, many English regional economic interests, became not so exclusively dependent upon the British economy as they were in the 1970s. In many ways the domestic market became the SEM, necessitating the development of effective economic promotion in a European context. Given that after the late 1980s the pursuit of the SEM was accompanied by fiscal subsidies through the EU Structural Funds on a bigger scale than was the case in the past, it became necessary also to develop new regional capacities for effective lobbying for funds. This functional necessity for regional capacity was exacerbated by the fierce competition over place-marketing and accessing of EU funds which emerged across the EU from the late 1980s, a trend identified by many as consistent with the emergence of a neo-mercantilist political economy within the EU (see Campagni 1991; Cooke 1993; Cornett and Caporaso 1993). Indeed a new Scottish and Welsh economic nationalism and English economic regionalism reflected in the opening of representative offices in Brussels, was regarded as essential to compete with the other nations and regions of the EU which so vigorously sought to provide the governmental infrastructures and policy support necessary to operate effectively in the SEM. It is important to note that these phenomena remained firmly in line with the broader sentiments of local patriotism, in that the British state was still seen as a vehicle through which economic interests could be promoted, and that there were other purposes of membership of the British state. Rather, such an approach recognised that the British state could not alone successfully promote the economic interests of Wales, Scotland and the English regions, particularly if the political economy of government at Westminster was itself influenced more by values of the free market than by those of market intervention.

These domestic and European-related functional policy-making and promotional pressures led to the development of a regional level of governance during the 1990s, based on the networking and partnership activities of elected local government, often working with other key regionally located organisations such as the CBI, TUC, TECs and voluntary organisations. This worked at two levels. First, a regional level capacity developed in England based on the regional local authority associations, whose boundaries were defined by the standard regions. These were funded by their constituent local authorities and comprised assemblies of nominated elected members who received professional support from local authority staff, sometimes seconded on a full-time basis. Mostly dormant since the indicative planning experiment of the 1960s and 1970s, they steadily re-emerged as increasingly important regional institutions, dealing with a wide range of strategic policy, advocacy and implementation issues, such as regional planning, economic development and European funding. Second, a number of sub-regional and local partnerships arose to conduct various implementation tasks of both a statutory and non-statutory nature. For example, some arose as a result of the need to undertake structure planning and other strategic land-use issues; other partnerships arose in relation to accessing and managing EU programmes, and consisted of public and private agencies meeting together through committee arrangements. Alternatively more voluntaristic partnerships of public and private agencies developed out of a perceived need to work jointly to plan and implement such activities as inward investment, business development and bids for government and EU funding. Many of these networks were fostered or encouraged by government agencies, through such programmes as Business Links, the Single Regeneration Budget Challenge Fund, Rural Challenge, Regional Challenge and the Millennium Fund. Whilst this added to the complexity of the nature of regional governance, policy practitioners nevertheless had a clear appreciation of the inter-relationships between regional and sub-regional working. The chapters in this volume elaborate on the development of this regional governance primarily in England, but there was also much evidence of such regional networking and partnership development in Scotland and Wales, although plainly there was less functional necessity for such joint local authority working when development agencies and European offices were already provided to serve Scottish and Welsh interests. It was clear in the mid 1990s that this trend towards regional and sub-regional governance would almost certainly continue for some years to come, for many institutions had come to acknowledge that against the background of an increasingly fragmented public realm the development of collaborative networks would become a dominant mode of public administration. Clear notice of this future trend was given by the rapid development of regional associations in England in the mid 1990s, even in areas where there had previously been poor inter-institutional relationships. Hence it may be concluded that irrespective of whether or not the political pressures for constitutional change which developed in this period led to the creation of new elected assemblies, there was a substantive achievement for regionalism in the development of a regionalist policy-making capacity, with much potential for future development.

The development of regional governance in this period, however, did have potentially wider implications in that it cemented the territorial pressures for constitutional change. The councillors, local government officers and other agency professionals who participated in networks and partnerships all saw evident policy-making gains in these forms of inter-organisational management. But, as Roberts argues, there was evidence that the benefits of more formal democratic structures, with greater political authority, could prove even more effective. Comparison with other states in the EU indicated that a large number of regional level state territories had their own elected political structures at the apex of an administrative machinery specifically geared to the promotion of economic development within the SEM. In Scotland, Wales and the English regions it was not surprising, then, that there should have been renewed debate about what institutional framework would best serve their economies, with many coming out in support for the extension of regional level capacity in the form of a Scottish parliament, Welsh senedd and English regional chambers. This brought more members of the sub-national political and administrative elites into the emergent wider consensus on the need for constitutional change, though through a different route than those more directly politically engaged with the need for constitutional change.

The policy rationale for regional governance and the stimulus this gave to support for constitutional reform was particularly important in Wales, where politically based movements for home rule were less dramatic than those in Scotland, and in the English regions, where there was an even weaker political basis to regional reform movements. Jones' discussion of Wales shows how after economic reforms and the development of the SEM the British state had an obviously diminished influence, and hence there were functional grounds for entertaining new institutional structures to promote Welsh interests in the enlarged core market. It is interpretations such as these which led to increasing support amongst elite professional groups for devolution as a means of gaining more direct control over Wales' economic destiny within a wider European context. Mawson's discussion of England shows how the development of regional governance provided the Labour Party with a practical *raison d'être* for further proposals for reform which developed from existing practice. In the mid 1990s Labour developed proposals for indirectly elected regional chambers as a formalisation of the networks of regional governance, and showed how these might be turned into directly elected regional authorities. Even business engaged with the need for regional governmental capacity and became sympathetic to the notion of some form of regional representation in which business played a key role. These points add weight to the idea that peripheral elites moved towards entertaining devolution for positive regionalist reasons. In the early to mid 1990s functional policy requirements and neo-mercantilist logic became increasingly influential in Wales and England, so that it could no longer be claimed that the Labour Party's support for Welsh devolution and English regional reform was simply to provide a logical corollary to Scottish devolution.

It is clear, therefore, that developments in domestic state reform and European integration in the 1980s and early to mid 1990s inspired novel political pressures, economic changes and policy needs which had a significant impact upon the regional agenda. In assessing the precise impact, however, it is important to differentiate between the popular and elite level. For these regionalist pressures did not achieve any clear change in the popular political climate surrounding issues of home rule or regional reform. Indeed, in Scotland at a popular level there was actually little evidence of an intensification of support for some kind of home rule in the first half of the 1990s. Brand and Mitchell's research finding that there was strong majority support for home rule but that it was not seen as a matter of first importance was an outcome which would have been broadly true of any period since 1947. The consistently high level of support for home rule reflected the fact that it was primarily based upon a sense of Scottish identity and not upon any particular rational choice calculations; that home rule was not a matter of first importance reflected a feeling amongst a majority of Scots that they had both a Scottish and British identity, associating the former mainly with characteristics of language, landscape and culture and the latter with those of public and political institutions. Scottish identity in a political sense was routinely recorded by pollsters at relatively low levels. In the case of Wales, Jones suggests that at a popular level there was a high level of support for devolution throughout the early to mid 1990s, but a critical assessment of Welsh public feeling over the constitutional question would doubtless mirror Brand and Mitchell's findings on Scotland. Unfortunately, it is not possible to come to such a definitive conclusion due to lack of funded research, but it would appear reasonable to suggest that the lack of a strongly politicised national identity was if anything even more significant in Wales than in Scotland, and that generally the weaknesses in support that Brand and Mitchell identify in Scotland, were very similar only more so. In England popular political identity with regions remained very low.

Instead, the general theme which emerges from the chapters is that the most significant novel development in support for devolution occurred outside the SNP/Plaid Cymru constituency and amongst the non-Conservative institutional, professional and political elite. It was at this level that the more positive arguments for devolution on the basis of the political and policy pressures discussed above had their impact. As a result of the campaign for devolution and regional reform being waged more broadly by those who were in a position to shape public opinion, and the campaign being waged on the basis of arguments of a positive and substantive kind rather than simply on those focused around a desire to combat the separatist threat, the campaign did prove to be more robust in the cut and thrust of political debate in the short term. On this basis, it was also thought likely to remain more durable in the long run, even if the separatist threat declined.

The importance of apparent elite support within the regions for change, or at least for entertaining change in the structures of government and administration, and the pressures which inspired them in this period, should not, however, be accepted uncritically. There were several other issues which had to be faced up to and posed dilemmas for those at an elite level advocating a move to constitutional change. First, the political pressures for change still had the potential to prove problematic. The new nationalism, seen as positively promoting devolution in Scotland and Wales, could not be assumed to be a stable and unthreatening political form in the context of the contemporary British state. Gladstone proved to be wrong in perceiving Irish nationalism in the nineteenth century as a local patriotism. Similarly, it was possible that elites in Scotland and Wales could come to see devolution as the midwife of a separatist nationalism rather than as purely a decentralist project within the British state. In particular, from a Unionist perspective there were grounds for concern that the continuation of the relative decline of the British economy could push separatism more into mainstream politics; and that the potentially conflictual relations between Westminster and devolved assemblies could form the catalyst for a movement towards the break-up of Britain.

Second, the deterministic nature of arguments that functional demands would sustain support for devolved elected assemblies was also questionable. For example, the announcement in July 1996 of the commitment by the Korean firm, LG, to develop semi-conductor and monitor assembly plants near Newport in South Wales, with its enormous economic development implications, cast in a positive light the promotional capacity of existing regional development structures when allied with the financial resources of the Treasury. Labour Party arguments that LG had gone to Wales because of its expectations of the supportive framework of a Welsh senedd appeared rather hollow. Similarly Mawson's discussion indicates that there were participants in the regional debate in England who believed that the developing patterns of joint local authority working and public–private partnerships, perhaps reinforced by the move to some form of indirectly appointed regional chamber, would provide an adequate response to the functional requirements of contemporary regional development pressures. Hence there would be no need to move to elected regional government. Such points highlighted the fact that the impetus to devolution from this perspective may have hinged too much on central government neglect and weaknesses of the existing administrative machinery and inter-governmental relations. It could be argued that such neglect or organisational weakness could be remedied, thereby possibly converting elite actors or organisations back to support for the status quo, and leaving the continued advocates of governmental reform with a much stiffer task in convincing others of the need for change. Even if the economic rationale continued to provide a powerful case for devolved assemblies, it seemed likely that the prescriptions it led to for the development of assemblies would not coincide with those of the advocates of devolution for more explicitly political reasons. Whilst the former were more concerned with issues of economic development policy, machinery and organisational capacity, the latter were far more interested in constitutional issues, questions of democratic accountability and the securing of ever-more power.

Third, it was questionable as to how solidly rooted the elite consensus over devolution was anyway. In Scotland, as Brand and Mitchell show, key issues had to be ignored by the Scottish constitutional convention, in particular the relations between Westminster and the proposed parliament, because of Labour-Liberal Democrat differences. Cracks between the Labour Party and its partners in the Convention were also opened up by Labour's unilateral decision in 1996 to opt for a pre-legislative referendum as part of its proposals for devolution. The referendum decision also caused ructions within the Labour Party in Wales. Furthermore, in both Scotland and Wales business became in the mid 1990s at best indifferent to devolution, and in any referendum it was unlikely that business would come out in favour. The CBI in Scotland, for example, announced its official opposition to the devolution proposals of the Scottish constitutional convention in the autumn of 1996. In England, despite Mawson's and Goldsmith's portrayals of a rapidly developing local authority regionalism, all contributors on English regionalism acknowledge a varied picture of the extent of co-operation at the regional level between local authorities, and between them and other public and private bodies, and the extent of its success. Stewart provides a more sceptical perspective and John's case study of London and the South East reveals the problems which arise in the construction of what might be termed 'bottom-up' regional governance.

Fourth, there was, of course, nothing inevitable about the continuation of British regional responses to trends in state reform and European integration. For example, it was possible that Scotland and Wales could be persuaded of the rightness of conforming to a British norm; and the English regions could come to appreciate the role of Government Offices of the Regions (GORs) and back off from reform. Equally it was possible that the trends in state reform and European integration which so influenced British regionalism from the 1980s would not persist. As will be discussed in the next two sections, both the Conservative Party and Labour Party by the mid 1990s had embraced approaches to the role of the state which were contradictory, making prescriptions of how government policy might develop in future uncertain. Equally, there was nothing inexorable about the process of European integration. The European Community was planning for Economic and Monetary Union in the early 1970s, only to be hit by a long period of Eurosclerosis following the oil crisis and the return of protectionism. In the mid 1990s there were many prepared to say that the EU project might again be derailed and existing integration eroded as a result of external shocks, internal conflicts or the shifting views of national electorates.

Finally, even if elite support could be sustained and developed there remained the question of how popular opinion could be mobilised behind the movement for devolution both in supporting Labour electorally and in referenda. On Scotland, for example, as Brand and Mitchell emphasise, there was some cause for optimism in the case of the Scottish Labour vote. There was a hard core of Labour voters who did see home rule as a matter of first importance. The 1992 election survey, for example, showed that 20 per cent of Labour voters actually supported independence, an advance on the 8 per cent support of 1979. In addition, developments to firm up Labour's commitment to devolution had had some impact upon the possibility of mobilising wider popular opinion. The confirmation of Labour's commitment to devolution after 1979 made devolution a party identification issue, turning Labour supporters who otherwise may have been indifferent to devolution into supporters. Beyond this, Brand and Mitchell conclude that the capacity of the Scottish elite to whip up popular support for a Scottish parliament by politicising conceptions of Scottish identity, however, did depend upon context. Favourable contexts had been generally few and far between, but the community charge reform and water privatisation had both provided politicising opportunities and in the context of a government committed to market-based state reforms it would seem that there would be the potential for further opportunities to arise. A popular front for change was more rather than less likely than in the 1970s. The capacity to mobilise public opinion in favour of devolution in Wales was also greater than in the 1970s, but it remained more questionable as to whether it could be done conclusively. Scepticism arose from the view that a Welsh assembly would become a vehicle for promoting the Welsh language against an English-speaking majority, symptomatic of a broader distrust by the public of Cardiff-based pro-devolution elites, who were often perceived as just as, if not more, self-serving than London-based elites. It was clear that garnering public support in Wales would be a substantial challenge for the devolution movement. In England, even advocates of reform were realistic about the problems of getting public support for directly elected regional assemblies. This explains Labour's preference in their 1996 proposals for an indirectly elected regional chamber in the first instance, which might lead to fully fledged regional government only in the event of a considerable change in the climate of popular opinion.

British regionalism undoubtedly flourished in the supposedly barren years of the 1980s and early to mid 1990s, and the case for devolution right across Britain, including in England, was argued with a commitment which was both more principled and robust than was the case in the 1970s. Advocates, nevertheless, still faced hard questions, and, of course, they still had to contend with the problem of attaining their aims in a political system which remained highly centralised. We shall now turn to considering the attitudes that reformers faced from central government in the period prior to the 1997 election. What evidence was there of new trends here?

Conservative policy and the politics of executive regionalisation

During the 1980s and the first half of the 1990s as part of the approach to developing state reform and responding to European integration, Conservative policy on the government of Scotland, Wales and the English regions was notably different from hitherto. This section defines this novel model of regionalisation, explains and discusses its complexities, and considers its implications in terms of preserving an approach to the government of Britain within a traditional constitutional framework.

The distinctiveness of the Conservative approach can be seen if a direct comparison is made with the approach taken in the 1970s. In that era the Conservative approach to regionalisation involved a refurbishment of the upper tier of local government: reforming the counties in England and Wales; creating the regions in Scotland. By contrast, in the early to mid 1990s it involved to a very large extent the abolition of the upper tier and reduction of local government powers. These were replaced by the refurbishment of the central government administrative system, based on the Scottish and Welsh Offices and the GORs in the English regions, and the creation of a fragmented system of direct service providers of a public and semi-public sector character, all appointed from central government. Overall, this must be seen as a process of enhancing the centralised character of the British system of government and processes of policy delivery. The local government regionalisation of the 1970s, identified by Sharpe (1993), was replaced by an executive regionalisation in the 1990s. The question then remains as to the political approaches which determined how this central power was used, and may be developed in the future.

Within the existing literature it has become conventional to argue that executive regionalisation involved approaches to the government of Scotland, Wales and the English regions which departed from respect for the different traditions within the British constitution. Notably, it is suggested that Conservative administrations took all the logic of the unitary tradition and the capacity of centralised power, latent within British constitutional development, and exerted them to the fullest extent possible in order to achieve ideologically driven reforms of the state. This, it is argued, was to the detriment of respect for the union-state tradition in the government of Scotland and Wales, and the local autonomy tradition right across Britain. Cooper (1995), for example, reminds us that Mrs Thatcher responded to Scottish dissent in the late 1980s by saying that Scotland had obviously not had a high enough dose of Thatcherism, and by embarking upon a policy of using all the powers available through the Scottish Office to sell Thatcherism in Scotland. In both Wales and Scotland the growth of a centrally appointed quangocracy to ensure the delivery of Conservative policy on the ground also implied a blatant reluctance to accept the legitimacy of locally elected representatives. Indeed, it is frequently argued that Conservative reforms of local government were designed to undermine local government as the major potential focus of peripheral dissent and to diminish its direct powers in preference for centrally controlled quangos and market providers (Cochrane 1991). Furthermore, in seeking to counter the threat posed by the new British regionalism it could be argued that Conservative governments reacted with greater central control, and a negative attitude towards the involvement of local government in the formulation and implementation of European programmes at the regional level and in Brussels (Taylor 1991). From this perspective the Major government's reforms of local government across Britain and the introduction of the GORs in England, could be interpreted as efforts, in part at least, to reduce local government's participation in European issues and to stifle the emergence of countervailing political voices threatening to speak on behalf of Scotland, Wales and the English regions. This suggests that a priority was placed on the enforcement of market reforms against potential opponents in sub-national government, and on coercive territorial management of sub-national groupings and institutions which could potentially threaten central power both domestically and in a European context.

This is a seductive conventional wisdom which has much validity, but it does not reflect fully the complexity of Conservative Party leadership responses to state reform and European integration from the late 1980s, and the way in which these affected Conservative policy at the regional level. Evidence from essays in this volume would support the idea that there were two very influential schools of thought in the Conservative Party on how to develop state reform and respond to European integration, and hence on how to approach the regional level, rather than one. The first of these, the

Thatcherite school, sought to reduce the scope of the state, placing much of its day-to-day delivery role in the private sector or under market conditions, whilst strengthening the strategic management function at the centre. This underpinned approaches which sought to sustain uniform state reform across Britain, together with central control over a fragmented and marketised system of service delivery at the regional and local levels; both conducive to undermining the development of a relatively autonomous regional level in an EU context. The pursuit of this form of executive regionalisation was supported by a number of ministers, a fact made clear by John Redwood, the former Welsh Secretary, following his departure from the cabinet, as well as in the approach which a number of central government departments adopted towards the English GORs.

The second school of thought emerged from the alliance of Conservatives who removed Mrs Thatcher from the party leadership and the premiership. Leaving aside personal and electoral considerations, those MPs who voted against her in the leadership election of 1990 did so because of the unpopularity of her approach with their instincts of one-nation Toryism, which preferred government by consensus and reform of the state by making it work more efficiently and effectively rather than through root and branch privatisation. She also fell because of her unpopularity with those in the party who were more relaxed about the development of EU links by British public as well as private sector institutions, placing a higher premium on the economic and diplomatic advantages that might accrue from EU membership than on the national sovereignty considerations which so preoccupied Mrs Thatcher and her supporters. This school of Conservatism – the Tory modernisers – could trace its political philosophy of managing Britain out of relative decline back to the MacMillan and Heath era. Having lost the intellectual arguments within the Conservative Party during Mrs Thatcher's heyday, this faction appears to have made a substantial recovery, not only helping to oust her from power but also in influencing the Major governments in a number of ways. These included securing commitments to the maintenance of a state role in a number of key areas of social responsibility that the Thatcherites would have perhaps ended, and an approach to the EU which kept the door open to including Britain in further stages of European integration rather than slamming the door shut, which had been the intention of Mrs Thatcher.

The Tory moderniser strand of Conservatism, epitomised by senior ministers such as Peter Walker and subsequently Michael Heseltine and Kenneth Clarke, took the view that measures to improve the machinery of government and to embrace the stimulating benefits needed to be undertaken in such a way as to respect and, indeed, take advantage of the diverse interests and strengths of the British state. Hence in the 1970s the Tory modernisers under the Heath administration showed such respect for the union-state tradition in British politics as to be open to the idea of devolution. In the event, Peter Walker pursued the local government regionalisation approach as the means to improve the working of the state in the early 1970s. This still, however, presumed the need for regional strategic planning and co-ordination. It simply placed faith in elected local government representatives not only to be in the best position to know what needed to be done but also to carry out policy effectively. Subsequently, the Tory modernisers appear to have accepted the general Conservative policy drift towards executive regionalisation, but they nevertheless sought to influence its practice in rather different ways from the Thatcherites. The latter sought to deploy the Scottish and Welsh Offices and the GORs as agents of central government with the intent of implementing central policy in ways designed to minimise the direct role of the state, encouraging market mechanisms wherever possible, and disapproving of sub-national government – EU relations. By contrast the Tory modernisers placed a greater emphasis on the role of the territorial offices in reasserting unionism, on a role for the GORs as agents of policy co-ordination, encouraging local authorities to define the needs and priorities of their areas, and on facilitating good functional relations between the institutions of British government and the EU, irrespective of the implications for national sovereignty.

The essays in this volume contain evidence of the influence of both schools of thought on Conservative policy. First, it is clear that the Thatcherite school developed a clear approach towards the government of Britain during the 1980s, which continued to have a significant influence during the 1990s. On Scotland, Bradbury argues that the first two Thatcher governments were implicitly assimilationist in the sense that they tried to impose the same policy agenda as in England. Between 1987 and 1990, policy became explicitly assimilationist as every effort was made to try and persuade Scotland to accept Thatcherite policies and perspectives. Even under the more apparently consensually minded John Major the policy agenda pursued in Scotland continued to be in line with the aims of modern Conservative free market political economy and strong central control. Paddison's discussion of the case study of local government restructuring easily dismantles the credibility of the government's supposed rationale for this reform and paints a picture of a Scottish Office wishing to gain clearer control over local government in order to impose a uniform policy agenda. In Wales, too, Bradbury finds much evidence of such a perspective operating against the stated wishes of local territorial interests. It was at its peak during the tenure of John Redwood as Secretary of State, but vestiges of this approach were also present under the incumbency of William Hague. Where Redwood sought to use Wales as a laboratory for post-Thatcherite political economy as a bid for intellectual and political hegemony within the Conservative Party, Hague acted more perceptibly in line with the policy approaches of the second Major government. However, both proved remarkably unpopular with many of the elite interests in Wales, Labour Party-dominated or not. Barry Jones' discussion of the development of quangos, abuse of parliamentary conventions and reform of local government adds weight to the view of the centralising tendency of Conservative Party policy as applied in Wales.

Much of the analysis of central government activity in the English regions would also bear out this centralist perspective. Stewart conceptualises central policy under the Conservatives as a new mode of regulation designed to dilute the autonomy of local political forces, thereby preventing moves towards elected regional government and any sustenance of the idea of a Europe of the Regions which might in the long run undermine the autonomy of the nation-state. Such a perspective, it is contended, was also present in the development of the GORs' administration of the Single Regeneration Budget, which was used to impose a 'divide and rule' approach upon local authorities, and enabled the Treasury to gain a tighter and more detailed grip over public expenditure at the regional level. Stewart further argues that the restructuring of local government in England was a missed opportunity in terms of enhancing regional capacity, because the Local Government Commission interpreted regional planning as a central government preserve. Case studies of the interface between local government, central government and the Commission in the development and implementation of EU programmes lend some further credence to Stewart's analysis. Both Goldsmith and John provide evidence of how the GORs sought to impose a centralist agenda on the work of a number of local authority networks and sub-national partnerships. Finally, Roberts highlights the Major government's reticence to support regional level representation in EU decision-making structures, most starkly evident in the British presence on the Committee of the Regions. In this case greater emphasis was given to the issue of party representation than to that of regional representation.

Equally, however, there is evidence of the influence of the Tory moderniser approach on the Major governments; that they attempted to combine state reform with greater respect for traditional conventions of the constitutional framework. This was evident in the revival of the unionist strategy of actively celebrating the special benefits, particularly economic benefits, enjoyed by Scotland and Wales by being members of the United Kingdom, and developing the distinctive arrangements by which they were governed within the general parameters set by the Westminster parliament. Bradbury suggests that this policy of unionism was implicit in the approaches to the government of Scotland and Wales through much of the first two Thatcher governments, when the Prime Minister left the direction of Scottish Office policies very much in the hands of the Scottish party establishment; and was also evident in Peter Walker's tenure in Wales after 1987 when he was allowed to develop his own distinctive style. More importantly, however, Bradbury suggests that it was pursued explicitly in Scotland after 1992 and simultaneously in Scotland and Wales from 1995. In the latter period much emphasis was placed upon the development of the Scottish and Welsh Grand Committees as ways of giving special voice to Scottish and Welsh concerns, but within the framework of parliament rather than through the separate channels that would be provided by devolved assemblies. Whilst a policy agenda continued to be pursued with all the hallmarks of central government design, nevertheless the style of government did much to resurrect a show of respect for the union-state tradition, in order to alleviate dissent. Thus in the early to mid 1990s Conservative responses to the new regionalism bore the imprint of approaches towards territorial management of a much longer vintage than was often appreciated.

The Tory moderniser influence could also be discerned in the way in which executive regionalisation was pursued through a focus on policy co-ordination at the regional level; an approach which was particularly relevant in England. This development was consistent with the idea that the centre was seeking to occupy the regional space to an increasing extent, but with the emphasis as much on a managerial as upon the controlling imperative suggested by Stewart. Mawson and Spencer identify a number of pressures behind this trend, including the re-emergence of land development pressures, particularly in the more prosperous regions and the consequent need for strengthened Regional Planning Guidance; a functional requirement for co-ordination because of an increasingly fragmented and devolved central state apparatus; and recognition of the need to co-ordinate central action with a fragmented structure of regional and sub-regional governance. In particular, there was a concern to improve the co-ordination of European, economic development, regeneration and European regional policy programmes. All of these concerns informed the development of the GORs. Both Goldsmith and John add validity to the view that the GORs were a welcome facility for co-ordination in their first two years of operation by showing how they often improved dialogue with local authorities and other agencies in agreeing regional priorities and encouraging partnerships, and that in most regions GOR relationships with local authorities and other agencies were very good.

This trend reflected the extent to which Conservative government approaches in the English regions were still influenced to a degree by patrician views of state intervention that had their origins in the 1960s and 1970s, when Conservative governments supported a more *dirigiste* approach, involving commitments to regional development and strategic planning, and co-operation with elected local authorities in formulating priorities and policies for implementation, a heritage summarised by Sharpe. In the context of the 1990s this approach to the operational style of the GORs was in conflict with the imperatives of the Thatcherite school, and actually had considerable common ground with the proposals formulated by the Labour Party for regional reform. Mawson's discussion of the views of David Curry, Minister of State at the Department of the Environment, shows how Conservative policy, whilst being uniformly hostile to elected regional government, could equally accommodate itself to working at the regional level with regional chambers of elected local authority and other co-opted representatives. On this basis there were the makings of a cross-party consensus on how executive regionalisation could be co-ordinated with the development of a more bottom-up regional governance. Amidst the hyperbole that dominated political debate between the parties over devolution and regional reform this was always going to remain, however, a very quiet consensus.

Hence there is much evidence that following the fall of Mrs Thatcher as Prime Minister, Conservative policy at the regional level, whilst focused on a clear development of executive power, was informed by quite conflicting party ideals of how that power might be used. Whilst the Scottish and Welsh offices remained at the cutting edge of an agenda to reform the role of the state according to a free market political economy which theoretically displayed no particular concern for the distinctive demands of the territories concerned, they also promoted unionist strategies, in which the special benefits and distinctive governing arrangements that the territories enjoyed were highlighted and developed. Similarly, while the work of the GORs in England might have been derived partly from a pro-market and centralist approach operated by individual departments and ministers, it also clearly was influenced by a pro-regional co-ordination approach, championed by such ministers as Michael Heseltine and Kenneth Clarke. The presence of both Thatcherite and Tory moderniser strains of politics suggests that in relation to the government of Scotland, Wales and the English regions, as in many other areas of policy, notably Europe, the Major governments conducted policy with one eye on the issue of party management. Both Thatcherites and Tory modernisers were promoted in cabinet, and policies were pursued which bridged great divides within the party.

The implications of these developments for the ability of central policy-makers to govern without vocal opposition from territorial elites are hard to judge conclusively, but there would appear to be much to suggest that they were adverse. In the long term, the general shift to a model of executive regionalisation was almost certainly likely to be more problematic than the approach of local government regionalisation followed in the 1970s. Where the latter was able to incorporate territorial elites by giving them a share of power through service in local government, the practice of executive regionalisation plainly limited that access, excluding and alienating those who wished to participate in the government of their territories. This would feed any movement for devolution.

In the short term, it is clear also that the specific experience of strands of both Thatcherite- and Tory moderniser-influenced approaches did not lead to successful policy, either in terms of territorial management or policy development. First, Thatcherite attempts to employ all the powers of the unitary state to exert central control proved highly problematic. Bradbury's discussion of Scotland and Wales, for example, indicates that territorial dissent and pressure for constitutional reform were increased rather than diminished during the periods of most explicit assimilationism. Thatcher's Scottish policy excursion after the 1987 election achieved quite the reverse of her stated aims. Redwood's sojourn in Wales had the same effect when less explicitly assimilationist approaches pursued by previous Secretaries of State had ensured that territorial grievances, where they existed, simmered rather than boiled. At a case study level, Paddison and Jones both indicate the problems of the attempt to enhance central control through the mechanism of local government reform. In Scotland and Wales the Conservative presence in local government was subsequently diminished, and in Scotland the more implacably anti-Conservative left-wing elements of the Labour Party were actually strengthened.

For England, too, there is evidence that a centralising tendency backfired. Implicit to much of Mawson's analysis is an understanding of English local authority regionalism as a response to central control: to empower communities collectively against the imposition, for example, of the GORs, and to reconstruct governmental capabilities which central government had in the past sought to erode. John's assessment of partnerships as an important new form of sub-national politics and governance, and Mawson and Goldsmith's discussion of the rapid growth of regional networking even in areas with a history of limited regional co-operation, further emphasise the point that a centralising agenda did not have its way easily. One is reminded of Bulpitt's (1983) warning that central government does not have the organisational capacity and resources to ensure strong central control of the periphery.

Similarly, there is much evidence of the problematic nature of Tory moderniser-influenced policy. For in practice the mix of influences on government policy was asymmetrical. Thatcherite policy assimilationism dominated in the approaches to Scotland and Wales; and Stewart, Mawson and Spencer agree that in practice a Thatcherite centralism was the primary characteristic of the workings of the GOR initiative. This leads to a qualified endorsement of the view that a different approach was followed by Conservative governments under Thatcher and Major compared with the more balanced mix of government according to the unitary and union-state traditions which informed a traditional Conservative approach. More importantly, the obvious dominance of assimilationism and centralism undermined the aims of a compensating unionism in Scotland and Wales and policy co-ordination in the English regions to manage dissent. Bradbury, for example, is doubtful whether a renewed Conservative commitment to unionism, seen as largely cosmetic, could easily turn around a Scottish non-Conservative elite committed to home rule or make substantial inroads into public opinion. Given the potentially greater fragility of the Welsh push for constitutional change, it appeared that this approach might have rather better prospects for success in Wales than in Scotland, although nothing could be taken for granted. Similarly, Mawson and Spencer trace some of the major problems of the GORs back to a centralist political agenda allied with a departmental functionalist division of the machinery of government in Whitehall. However, as Paddison shows, the compromising of a purely centralist approach to government could also create problems the other way. For example, the attempt by Michael Forsyth at a consensual relationship with local government, part of the tilt towards a unionist style of government after the 1992 election, had the unfortunate consequence of creating tensions between the desire to be seen to allow the representation of local feeling and the Scottish Office objective to control as much as possible the substantive activities of local government.

Of course, there were potentially significant benefits for the Major governments in combining the political impulses of Thatcherism with a Tory moderniser approach, which had greater respect for more traditional conventions, in developing government at the regional level. In Scotland and Wales the mix of policy assimilationism and unionism could be seen as a deliberate approach, designed to maintain the modern Conservative agenda of state reform whilst reassuring a general public wary of a high-handed and ideologically driven political leadership. In England the mix of control, co-ordination and partnership, whilst less clearly an overt strategy, could be seen as helping to establish support for the role of the GORs, thereby enhancing regional capacity and respect for central government. The combination of approaches may also have been seen as helping to achieve the unity necessary to achieve electoral success for the Conservative Party. Some or all of these benefits may in the fullness of time come to pass. Whatever the case in the mid 1990s, it appeared that the modern Conservative Party would remain committed to a general model of executive regionalisation which invited the support of the electorate, if not territorial elites, for the substance of what it delivered in terms of policies. This strategy of appealing over the heads of territorial elites was potentially very risky in terms of maintaining the conventional constitutional framework. What was less certain was the way in which Conservative policy-makers would develop this approach, as ultimately approaches to regional government would be intimately related to the course which the Conservative Party chose to take with regard to domestic government and European integration. For the first half of the 1990s that choice was postponed, meaning that both Thatcherite and more traditional approaches to the development of Britain's territorial constitution and regional capacity had influence. It remained an open question as to whether this would stay the case in the future.

New Labour and the politics of devolution

While Conservative policy in the 1980s and 1990s developed a new model for addressing the regional agenda within the existing constitutional framework, in the first half of the 1990s the Labour Party returned to its advocacy of devolution and regional reform as part of its alternative project for reforming the constitution. There was much to suggest, however, that the Labour Party had returned to the issue with new momentum. After successive general election defeats the Labour Party leadership sought to make major adjustments to the party's image and proposed programme for government. This change of direction, encapsulated in the term 'New Labour', took account of the changes in British politics effected by the years of Conservative rule, notably on the role of the state, and faced up to the realities of a more globalised market-place, specifically the importance of membership of the EU to Britain. New Labour sought to promote the message that it would not repeat the mistakes of Old Labour. In respect of the regional agenda, the Labour Party's leadership's response to Conservative state reform and European integration embraced a renewed commitment to devolution, only this time with an apparent desire to deliver successfully what was so poorly conceived in the 1970s. This section will seek to examine the effect the advent of New Labour had on the policy agenda for devolution during the early to mid 1990s, and consider the implications of these developments for the successful adaptation of a devolution project within Britain's territorial constitution.

Much scepticism surrounded the Labour Party's attempts at devolution in the 1970s. There were doubts about the party's commitment, the constitutional logic of the reforms and the practicality of the proposals, all of which were seen as important contributors to the ultimate failure of devolution (see Chapter 1). Such scepticism was not easily shaken off. During the early to mid 1990s, however, some commentators placed more faith in the Labour Party's plans than hitherto. To begin with, it was argued that faced with far greater support for political autonomy in Scotland, focused on the Scottish Labour Party, the Labour leadership at Westminster had a greater commitment to the successful achievement of devolution than was the case in the 1970s. Equally, the growth in support for a Welsh senedd and for regional autonomy in the North of England further strengthened the case for a wider reform should Scottish devolution go ahead (Gamble 1993). A further argument related to Labour's electoral experience during the years of unbroken Conservative rule. Specifically, it became questionable whether it was in Labour's interests to leave the concentration of power at the centre when relatively they held it so much less often than the Conservatives and when they had a so much better electoral record in sub-national government (Keating and Jones 1995).

Second, there remained a view that devolution could be carried through in such a way as to make it constitutionally defensible and successful in practice if certain key issues were addressed. For example, it was possible to draw upon Bogdanor's (1979) critique of Labour's 1970s proposals in which a checklist of desirable improvements was provided (see Chapter 1). According to this account, any party seeking to pursue successfully a devolution project needed to establish clear and thought-through mechanisms of decentralisation and democratisation; clarity about relationships between Westminster and devolved assemblies; legitimisation of the devolved assemblies both to guard against later re-centralisation or against devolution leading to the break-up of Britain; and, if necessary, a clear defence of non-uniform or asymmetrical devolution. To achieve these aims Bogdanor argued that the assemblies needed to be given a wide legislative competence; the right to raise their own revenues; and a genuine autonomy such that they are free from Westminster override powers. They also needed to provide for broad party representation. In any referendum there would need to be a second question on independence in order to secure a convincing 'no' vote to forestall the threat of independence. Finally compensation needed to be provided for asymmetrical devolution or the approach would need to be defended aggressively against any critics. On this basis it was argued that devolution could be accomplished in a way which was constitutionally defensible and technically practicable. It was simply that the process of implementation needed to follow a set of rational guidelines.

Contributors to this book primarily focus on how the Labour Party within the various territories of the United Kingdom approached anew the issue of devolution. Such a focus is not unsurprising given the way in which most policy development on devolution was itself devolved to the Scottish and Welsh Labour Parties. Conclusions which may be drawn from such an analysis, however, also need to take account of the concerns of the party leadership at Westminster, which ultimately decides on priorities, proposals for legislation and future development. On this basis, a complex picture emerges concerning how far the Labour Party during the early to mid 1990s moved in its commitment to devolution; and on how well it gained a better grasp of the constitutional difficulties and developed a more coherent and practical framework setting out how a decentralised system of government would work in practice. Let us first look at the evidence which supports the case that there was a transformation in Labour's thinking, before looking at the evidence against such a movement.

We have already noted that from the late 1980s there was a growth in commitment to change at the grass roots level which compared favourably to commitment in the 1970s. It may also be argued that the party leadership also became more committed. Indeed, there are four points which need to be emphasised about the early development of New Labour, all of which resulted from the national leadership's need to respond to the challenge of Conservative state reforms, which suggested a changing approach. First, it is clear that New Labour sought to distance the Labour Party from the notion that it was the natural party of state intervention, that in office would seek to use all the direct levers of the state to manage the economy and to engineer social change. Labour's attachment in the past to a high level of intervention had been one of the key reasons why it wished to see an effective concentration of power at the centre. The abandonment of such a philosophy undermined the pressures for such centralisation, leaving open the scope for a more principled commitment to devolution. New Labour, in seeking to find an ideological identity which was anti-statist but also one which was not identified with the market individualism of the modern Conservative Party, sought to promote itself instead as the party of the community. It was a feature of New Labour's communitarian message that the party leadership began to argue that many contemporary social and economic problems could be addressed by devolving power not to atomised individuals solely within a market setting, but to citizens working together, pursuing common interests within strong communities. In this respect the advocacy of devolution and regional reform were key elements in New Labour's political vision, and hence became an increasingly central part of the debate between the political parties.

Second, from the perspective of the party leadership, devolution and regional reform were also seen as helpful policies in terms of the management of the party in respect of New Labour's changing approach to the state. In the short term, New Labour's anti-statist political economy proved to be profoundly worrying for some of its traditional supporters in Wales, Scotland and the English regions. Thus it could be argued that supporting New Labour in the drive for power at Westminster would be made more palatable if such a victory were followed by granting to the regions a degree of autonomy over key areas of domestic policy. The Labour Party leadership's consistent support for devolution in this respect could therefore be seen as very important in maintaining party unity. It could further be argued that the party leadership also saw obvious political benefits for a Labour government at Westminster in instilling a sense of realism amongst its natural supporters. For undoubtedly there would be enormous expectations in the Labour Party heartlands which a Labour government would find difficult to meet, given the Conservative's dismantling of much of the welfare state apparatus. Moreover, New Labour's anti-statist political economy would rule out meeting many of these expectations. In this context a cynical interpretation might be that a decentralisation programme was also embraced because it would release a Labour government from the obligation to respond to unrealistic expectations, whilst forcing territorial party elites and their supporters to face up to some of the practical difficulties of government. Finally, it might be said that the charges of over-centralisation and democratic deficit became central planks of New Labour's critique of the Conservative state reforms. Having set out the stall of regional reform, a failure to deliver on a measure so closely linked to core philosophy would open up the Labour Party to the charge of hypocrisy.

Third, it would also appear that the party leadership became more positively supportive of devolution and regional reform as a result of its changed attitude towards the EU and the forging of closer links with European Socialist parties. Specifically, the EU's commitment to measures of economic and social cohesion emphasised the importance of the regional dimension in the delivery of its Structural Fund policies. The development of the SEM and the widening of the EU through further enlargement brought home the importance of effective regional development structures. Moreover, the party leadership, in seeking to modernise the party, took note of the policies of some of the more successful Left-of-Centre parties in Europe. Enthusiasm for the moderate reformist movement of European social democracy meant acknowledging the emphasis placed on decentralisation and regional autonomy as mechanisms to promote economic development and democratisation. Such arguments taken together suggest that a greater level of commitment to devolution emerged as a consequence of more general policy shifts within the party to take account *inter alia* of state reform and European integration.

Specific policy prescriptions on devolution going into the 1997 general election also showed elements of change from the proposals of the 1970s, a fact that can be highlighted by reference to Bogdanor's model for improvement. None of these policy changes in the case of Scotland and Wales appeared to derive explicitly from the challenges of state reform and European integration, rather they reflected the influence of inter- and intra-party politics. As a result of compromises with other parties and interests worked out in the context of the Scottish constitutional convention, Labour's published proposals for a Scottish parliament included a number of changes from those of the 1970s. The legislative powers to be granted were primary powers and related to a wider range of functions than those proposed in the 1978 Scotland Act. The proposal that the parliament would be able to vary income tax by 3 pence in the pound meant that some financial devolution was now proposed. In addition, Labour became committed to the constitutional convention's compromise plan to adopt an additional member voting system, as well as seeking to achieve a gender balance in the parliament. These proposals provided for a clearer decentralisation and democratisation of government in Scotland than was provided for in the 1970s, and allowed a greater legitimisation of the parliament by ensuring its representation of the broad range of political interests in Scotland. There were far fewer significant changes in the proposals for Wales. But a key issue for debate was the voting system. Here, Tony Blair's insistence that the Welsh Labour Party considered the option of a proportional voting basis to the senedd ensured that the senedd would have a wider range of party representation.

With respect to England, Labour clearly made a rather more significant development of its reform proposals in comparison with those it formulated in the 1970s. Back then Labour promised full elected regional government when in Opposition, only to offer no regional decentralisation at all when in Government. In opposition in the 1990s Labour developed a more plausible staged approach to regional reform in England which was seen as pragmatic but achievable, in its first stage not necessarily requiring legislation. Clearly this was only made possible by the emergence of new forms of regional working and governance, which arose in large measure as a result of the pressures inspired by Conservative state reform and European integration. Labour's first stage proposals sought to formalise this tier of regional governance, and then to develop its powers, potentially in a final stage to involve elected regional government. Supporters saw that there was much to be gained by giving English regional chambers powers of appointment, scrutiny, consultation and oversight over quangos, agencies and the GORs, thereby facilitating decentralisation and greater policy co-ordination, and addressing the democratic deficit. Roberts highlights the possible parallels of Labour's approach with the French experience. In this case, functional decentralisation of policies to prefects led to the development of territorial collectives in which significant consultative roles were given to local authorities and other agencies, which in turn led to the establishment of directly elected regional authorities in 1982.

In reviewing Labour's devolution proposals as a whole there still remained significant differences in the proposals for Scotland and Wales and England. Even taking the broadest level of definition, the proposals for Scotland offered a form of legislative and fiscal devolution, whilst those for Wales and England offered different degrees of executive devolution. However, it would appear that the Labour Party had taken more care to defend the asymmetry of the package against accusations of unfairness or instability than was the case in the 1970s. The Labour Party leadership was adamant that there was nothing wrong with asymmetrical devolution, asserting that it was right that devolution should be consistent with the demands of each territory. In taking this position they drew strength from administrative and governmental reforms elsewhere in Europe which provided various models of successful regional devolution. The example of Spain was most frequently drawn upon and requires some attention here.

In Spain devolution had occurred on a varied basis, with each region having a major say in the extent and nature of its autonomy. This occurred without any significant debate about the case for comparable devolution in each region, or a reduction in representation in the national parliament for those regions which had achieved the greatest levels of devolution. Spain was portrayed in Labour Party discussion as a political culture in which it was accepted that particular territories may have greater autonomy by virtue of their special characteristics whilst all wished to remain an integral part of the state. Indeed, the view was taken that a failure to acknowledge such demands would lead to regional separatism and the break up of the state. Drawing on this comparative experience and upon other political arguments, Labour was able to rebut arguments that there should be a uniformity of treatment much more robustly than was the case in the 1970s. The view was taken that each region should have the form of devolution most appropriate to its circumstances, and it was hoped that English interests in particular would accept the varying forms of devolution for Wales and Scotland as a price worth paying to keep the British state intact.

Finally, on the matter of how Labour's proposals for devolved assemblies would work in practice, it can be argued that they offered a more well thought out and coherent package of proposals than was the case in the 1970s. In the 1970s Labour remained a party committed to nationalisation and state intervention, with an emphasis on central control. There were evidently some contradictions between that position and the rhetoric of decentralisation which accompanied proposals for devolution. In opposition in the 1990s, Labour's proposals were set out in the broader context of the distinctive communitarian vision of New Labour based upon different modes of state–society relations. New Labour's message emphasised decentralisation and democratisation, the delivery of government based on a spirit of pluralism between Westminster and the new assemblies, and the practice of decentralised government according to co-operative partnership principles. From this perspective devolution was to be seen as consistent with a general philosophy for government. On a more practical basis it was clear that this approach needed to work to ensure that the new assemblies were legitimised without on the one hand leading to further pressures for the break-up of Britain or on the other hand new pressures for the centralisation of power. Claims that such a strategy could work were, of course, bolstered by the experience of decentralised government in other EU states since the 1970s.

However, there remained potentially significant problems with Labour's approach to devolution, irrespective of its embrace of a new approach to the state and to Europe. First, despite the political salience of the project it remained to be seen how committed a Labour government would prove to be when faced with other competing policy priorities and the inevitable political difficulties. For example, the leadership decision to propose pre-legislative referenda in Scotland and Wales, including on the question of the tax-varying power of a Scottish parliament as a result of Michael Forsyth's campaign against the 'tartan tax', could be interpreted as revealing greater sensitivity to electoral pressures than to a deep-seated commitment to devolution. For whilst the referenda decision undoubtedly neutralised Conservative claims that the assemblies would be imposed upon an unwilling public, it did pose the threat of 'no' votes or unconvincing 'yes' votes which might derail the legislation altogether. It was clear that devolution would also undoubtedly take up a huge amount of the parliamentary timetable and the political resources of a Labour government. Against this background some critics (Keating and Jones 1995) suggested that once in power Labour might be tempted to stick rather more closely to its historic centralist/unitarist tradition. Several Labour MPs continued to question the need for devolution, some of whom represented Welsh and Scottish constituencies. There were concerns therefore that a Labour House of Commons majority, even with the support of Liberal Democrat MPs, might not prove sufficiently large to override Conservative opposition and Labour backbench dissent. In such circumstances it was feared the plans might be watered down or dropped altogether, or, as occurred in the 1970s, a Labour government might have to accept amendments to devolution bills which ultimately would lead to their downfall.

Second, whilst there were some grounds for arguing that Labour had developed a more coherent approach than was the case in the past, there remained potentially significant problems from a constitutional point of view, which were apparent when measured against Bogdanor's criteria for success. If one looks at the proposals for a Scottish parliament, it was envisaged that the majority of its finances would still be provided by block grant from London, and the Labour leadership signalled its concern about the parliament's tax-varying power by proposing a referendum on the issue and indicating that a Scottish parliament would not in practice raise income tax. Furthermore, Labour's proposals were silent on the issue of future relationships with Westminster, notably relating to the role of the Secretary of State. It could be argued that the proposals left scope for constitutional instability on three different fronts: with doubts concerning how compatible the decentralisation and democratisation measures would be when set against local demands; with concerns that there would be contested relations with Westminster; and the likelihood of continuing political debates about the case for independence.

Jones suggests that even less headway was made in respect of proposals for Wales than in the case of Scotland. Compared with the 1979 Wales Act, the Labour Party made only limited proposals for strengthening the legislative powers of a Welsh assembly. Moreover, they were secondary rather than primary powers, and there were no provisions for taxation powers. Decentralisation of power in practice was intended to be entirely dependent upon legislative and financial settlements made by Westminster. The precise form of relations with Westminster and the future role of the Secretary of State were also left unclear. Finally, it remained to be seen whether Labour's proposals would provide for the successful legitimisation of a Welsh assembly. Whilst the Labour leadership was in favour of the elected assembly based upon a proportional voting system, many inside the Welsh party were opposed to this approach. Legitimisation of the senedd was in any case problematic. It should be remembered that Labour's proposals were developed in-house, and not in the more consensus-forming framework of a constitutional convention.

Similarly, the proposals for English regional reform fell short of what was required to meet Bogdanor's ideal scheme for improvement. Whilst they involved a much greater advance on the proposals of the 1970s than was the case in either the Scottish or Welsh schemes and contributed substantially to the development of regional governance, in constitutional terms the devolution of executive powers envisaged was still much more limited even than that for a Welsh assembly, and there was no question of any legislative or fiscal autonomy in the event of going all the way to a directly elected assembly. Indeed, without any legislative back-up or strong cabinet backing, the political influence of the indirectly nominated regional chambers, created in the first stage of regional reform, was likely to prove limited in the event of government ministers and departments not placing a great priority on decentralisation. The nature of the relationship between Whitehall and the regions was not examined in any detail by Labour Party policy-makers. Indeed it could be argued that lack of commitment to a substantial measure of decentralisation was reflected in the fact that the future roles of the various Secretaries of State and central departments were not raised to the same extent as the roles of the Scottish Office and Welsh Office and their Secretaries of State were in relation to Scottish and Welsh devolution. Whilst it was apparent that the democratic legitimacy of elected regional authorities would be confirmed, especially given the expected requirement of support from regional referenda and the possibility of them being based on a proportional representation voting system, a similar legitimacy for regional chambers, which would be the experience of regions in the first instance and probably most regions even in the longer term, would not. Indeed there was a fear amongst some interested parties that it was possible to perceive such chambers merely as local government (instead of central government-based) quangos, stuffed with representatives of the dominant party within the region. Hence there were grounds for fearing that unless it was handled sensitively English regional reform would be faced with disputes over the extent of decentralisation and democratisation and the legitimacy of indirectly elected bodies and regional development agencies in the first stage of reform.

Finally, looking at the proposals as a whole, there remained much the same constitutional problems that afflicted devolution in the 1970s. For essentially, the variations in the proposals, which meant that devolution would be asymmetrical, still left the West Lothian question: should the MP for West Lothian, or indeed any other Scottish constituency, be able to vote on primary legislation for England whilst English MPs were not in the same position in regard to primary legislation for Scotland? The answer to this question logically was no, except if some form of compensation were given to English representation. The most frequently canvassed expedient solution was to reduce the numbers of Scottish and Welsh MPs in the House of Commons relative to those of English MPs. Brand and Mitchell point out that the Scottish Constitutional Convention had chosen not to address the issue at all.

However without a concession in this direction there was the danger of an English backlash in the House of Commons. Of course, some took the view that the West Lothian question need not be answered since the Spanish experience had shown that asymmetrical devolution was a practical possibility, and British constitutional history had provided precedents for flexibility, including an asymmetry, for example, in administrative devolution.

It has to be recognised that on closer inspection the Spanish and British cases are not directly comparable. Spain has a quasi-federal constitution which is capable of accommodating regional devolution as a dynamic process. Under this constitutional framework the regions have a right to exercise choice as to their level of autonomy, meaning that the question of national representation is less of an issue. Moreover, given recent Spanish history it is recognised that there needs to be a degree of tolerance on such constitutional issues if the stability of the state is to be maintained. This is evident in the support which has been forthcoming when some of the more prosperous regions have exercised the right to pursue greater autonomy (Hopkins 1996; Morata 1995). In contrast, Labour's approach in the mid 1990s continued to assume that Britain was primarily a unitary state, in which sovereignty was determined by the Westminster parliament. The desire not to be associated with a federal solution was understandable given the anti-federalist nature of Britain's political culture and Labour's poor electoral record. Only if Labour were to win a second term of office could the party leadership genuinely change the terms of debate. Given this context, regional devolution was presented as a one-off process in which regions were not offered the same opportunities for autonomy, otherwise this would have created an open-ended threat to the stability and credibility of the unitary state. In Scotland, Wales and England Labour offered varying forms of devolution depending on the degree and nature of demand, but it was an asymmetrical devolution which constitutionally would be fixed unless parliament decided otherwise. Decisions over the degree of autonomy would be much less a matter of regional choice, leaving one region's compensation for feelings of relative disadvantage *vis-á-vis* another only in calls for reform of the latter's representation at Westminster. Theoretically, therefore, British devolutionists were wrong to take such comfort from the Spanish example. Moreover, recent history has suggested that it would be unlikely that the English, or representatives of particular English regions, would be prepared to accept Scottish and Welsh devolution without some form of compensation to preserve the British state.

To placate constitutional and English concerns about asymmetrical devolution, Labour needed to have embraced a more uniform home rule project. Alternatively it needed to consider a reduction in the relative levels of Scottish and Welsh representation in the House of Commons or an equivalent increase in English representation (Mclean 1995) as some form of compensation. Labour showed no inclination to consider the first option, and appeared understandably reluctant to confront the latter for fear of presenting the Scottish and Welsh Labour Parties with a devolution 'menu with prices'. Increasing the number of English MPs was seen in some quarters as seriously diluting the political voice of Scotland and Wales in the House of Commons. Moreover, given Labour's traditional support in these areas there was a fear that it could have some long-term electoral consequences for Labour's parliamentary position. Yet it was recognised that no compensatory device was entirely painless. How Labour ultimately faced up to this issue was clearly an acid test of its commitment to devolution.

There were of course also constitutional issues to be addressed in relation to relationships with the EU. As Hebbert (1986) pointed out, most of the responsibility for implementing EC/EU legislation resides with the governments of member states. Hence the need to secure a single negotiating position in Brussels, and consistency of approach between the Westminster parliament and the devolved assemblies over the management of European affairs. Finally, it remained unclear as to how a Labour government would seek to encourage the role of devolved assemblies once they had been set up. The substance of New Labour's communitarian philosophy in regional terms had yet to be fully revealed by the time of the 1997 general election, and in practice the politics of partnership and pluralism at this level was a novel and developing experience. There were those in the Labour Party leadership who, whilst supporting decentralised government, wished to see a rather more interventionist economic and social strategy associated with the new assemblies and regional development agencies. Others, however, wanted a more cautious 'facilitative' supply-side role with a much greater degree of Whitehall departmental control over regional agencies and assemblies. This was a key issue which an incoming Labour administration would need to resolve. Specifically, it would be necessary to determine the precise role of the new RDAs, their relationship with chambers or assemblies and what remaining functions would be left with Whitehall departments and the Government Offices.

A key figure in this debate was the Deputy Leader of the Labour Party, John Prescott, whose enthusiasm for regional government during the early

1980s helped to keep the issue alive. His Alternative Regional Strategy of 1982 combined devolution with an interventionist 'bottom-up' approach to economic and social regeneration, drawing heavily on the role of local government and regional development agencies (Parliamentary Spokesman's Working Group, 1982). He remained committed to this approach, as reflected in his close identification with the report of the party's Regional Policy Commission in 1996. Yet he was also a key figure in facilitating the political compromise between the Left and Centre-Right of the party, which helped to give birth to New Labour. His support for successive party leaders in implementing internal party reform, first to reform the role of the trades unions, and second to reform clause IV of the party constitution, made him a key link between Old and New Labour. No single figure better encapsulated the tensions present between the different schools of thought within the Labour Party as to how Britain should be governed within a decentralised system of government. Such a problem mirrored that which the Conservative government had in developing its approach of executive regionalisation in the context of quite different schools of thought on how the apparatus of government should be used.

Overall it can be concluded that the Labour Party and its leadership developed a greater commitment to devolution in the early to mid 1990s than was the case some twenty years previously. Yet in the run up to the general election of 1997 there remained some key constitutional issues to be resolved. In many ways the problems were not of the same order of magnitude as those raised by the 1970s devolution proposals but they neverthless had to be faced up to in a clear and unambiguous manner. There were also questions over how the assemblies and the regional development agencies would operate in practice, which related in part to broader ideological arguments about the future direction of a Labour administration. Given Labour's greater commitment to reform it was clear that once in office legislation would be brought forward without delay with the likelihood of a strong use of the party whip and a persuasive presentation of the justification for asymmetrical devolution. However there remained the danger that the momentum would not be sustained once constitutional and political dilemmas began to be faced in the event of unsuccessful or less than wholehearted electoral support in one or more of the referenda and during the passage of legislation. In such circumstances commitment to reform might falter and the end result might be a piecemeal and unstable settlement. The reforms of lasting significance would then have been achieved by Conservative governments. As we enter the next millennium, not withstanding the development of regional governance, the dominant central model for the development of British government in Scotland, Wales and the English regions would instead be that of executive regionalisation.

A conclusion which posits the existence of novel trends with such equivocation is a reflection of the problems of analysing the near-past. This volume nevertheless provides some insights into an era in which there were substantial developments in how Britain was governed, and debate over how it should be governed, specifically over what forms of public policy and administration were appropriate at the regional level. The book reveals continuities but also significant changes in the pressures leading to the reconfiguration of government, and the responses of the political parties to such challenges. State reform and European integration had a substantial impact on debates about constitutional reform in the early to mid 1990s, and have inspired the development of a form of regional governance, which in turn inspired more robust arguments for devolution in Scotland and Wales and formal regional government in England. Conservative policy-making on regional issues was now made in the context of a fundamentally different approach to regionalisation than that adopted by Conservative governments in the 1970s. Executive regionalisation replaced local authority regionalisation, and the manner in which it was to be developed was also constrained by faultlines in the party over the role of the state and over Europe which simply did not impact on the regional debate in the 1970s. Finally, the Labour Party responded to structural change with the same broad agenda for devolution that it promoted in the 1970s, but there were some important changes in the Labour approach relating to commitment, the detailed provisions for devolution and the spirit in which it would be implemented. Labour's future development of devolution, were it to suceed in implementing legislation, could also be constrained by party faultlines over the role of the state and the nature and extent of decentralisation to the English regions.

In the late 1990s and beyond the reform of the state and European integration are likely to continue to be major concerns of politicians at Westminster and elsewhere in Europe. Indeed, Britain faces key political choices regarding how to develop the role of government in the continuing attempt to reverse Britain's relative economic decline, whether or not to join the European single currency and whether to co-operate in further political and economic integration in the EU. Even if the regional debate dies down in the immediate future, these key choices will certainly bring it to the fore again. For, if nothing else, the last decade has shown very clearly that developments in state reform and European integration, and trends in British regionalism and debates about devolution are intimately linked.

References

Birch, A. (1989) *Nationalism and National Integration.* London: Unwin Hyman.

Bogdanor, V. (1979) *Devolution.* Oxford: Oxford University Press.

Bulpitt, J. (1983) *Territory and Power in the United Kingdom: An Interpretation.* Manchester: Manchester University Press.

Bulpitt, J. (1989) 'Walking back to happiness? Conservative party governments and elected local authorities in the 1980s.' In C. Crouch and D. Marquand (eds) *The New Centralism, Britain out of Step in Europe?* Oxford: Basil Blackwell.

Campagni (1991) 'Europe's regional-urban features: conclusions, inferences and surmises.' In L. Rodwin and H. Sazanami (eds) *Industrial Change and Regional Economic Transformation.* London: United Nations and Harper Collins.

Cochrane, A. (1991) 'The changing state of local government: restructuring for the 1990s.' *Public Administration 69,* 281–302.

Cooke, P. (1993) 'Globalisation of economic organisation and the emergence of regional inter-state partnerships.' In C. Williams (ed) *The Political Geography of the New World Order.* London: Belhaven Press.

Cooper, J. (1995) 'The Scottish problem: English Conservatives and the union with Scotland in the Thatcher and Major eras.' In J. Lovenduski and J. Stanyer (eds) *Contemporary Political Studies.* York: Political Studies Association.

Cornett, L. and Corporaso, J. (1993) '"And still it moves." State interests and social forces in the European Community.' In J. Rosenau and E. Czempiel (eds) *Governance Without Government: Order and Change in World Politics.* Cambridge: Cambridge University Press.

Gamble, A. (1993) 'Territorial politics.' In P. Dunleavy, A. Gamble, I. Holliday and G. Peele *Developments in British Politics 4.* London: Macmillan.

Harvie, C. (1989) 'Thoughts on the union between law and opinion or Dicey's last stand.' In C. Crouch and D. Marquand (eds) *The New Centralism, Britain out of step in Europe?* Oxford: Basil Blackwell.

Hebbert, M. (1989), 'Britain in a Europe of regions' In P. Garside and M. Hebbert (eds) *British Regionalism 1900–2000.* London: Mansell.

Hopkins, J. (1996) 'Regional government in Western Europe.' In S. Tindale (ed) *The State and the Nations, the Politics of Devolution.* London: Institute of Public Policy Research.

Keating, M. and Jones, B. (1995) 'Nations, regions and Europe: the UK experience.' In B. Jones and M. Keating (eds) *The European Union and the Regions.* Oxford: Clarendon.

McCrone, D. (1993) 'Regionalism and constitutional change in Scotland.' *Regional Studies 27,* 6, 507–512.

Mclean, I. (1995) 'Are Scotland and Wales over-represented in the House of Commons?' *Political Quarterly 66,* 250–268.

Morata, F. (1995) 'Spanish regions in the European Community.' In B. Jones and M. Keating (eds) *The European Union and the Regions.* Oxford: Clarendon.

Parliamentary Spokesman's Working Group (1982) *Alternative Regional Strategy: A Framework for Discussion..* London: Labour Party.

Osmond, J. (ed) (1994) *A Parliament for Wales.* Llandysul: Gomer.

Osmond, J. (1995) *Welsh Europeans.* Bridgend: Seren.

Sharpe, L.J. (1993) 'The United Kingdom: the disjointed meso.' In L.J. Sharpe (ed) *The Rise of Meso Government in Europe.* London: Sage.

Taylor, P. (1991) 'The European Community and the State: assumptions, theories and propositions.' *Review of International Studies 17*, 109–125.

The Contributors

Jonathan Bradbury, Lecturer in Politics, University of Wales Swansea

Jack Brand, Senior Lecturer in Government, University of Strathclyde

Michael Goldsmith, Professor in Politics, European Studies Research Institute, University of Salford

Peter John, Lecturer in Politics, University of Southampton

Barry Jones, Director of Political Studies, University of Wales Cardiff

John Mawson, Professor of Town and Regional Planning, University of Dundee

James Mitchell, Senior Lecturer in Government, University of Strathclyde

Ronan Paddison, Senior Lecturer in Geography, University of Glasgow

Peter Roberts, Professor of European Strategic Planning, University of Dundee

L.J. Sharpe, Fellow in Politics, Nuffield College, Oxford

Ken Spencer, Professor of Local Policy, University of Birmingham

Murray Stewart, Professor of Urban and Regional Governance, University of the West of England

Glossary

ACC	Association of County Councils
ADC	Association of District Councils
AER	Assembly of European Regions
ALG	Association of London Government
AMA	Association of Metropolitan Authorities
AWC	Association of Welsh Counties
BARB	Broadcasting Audience Research Board
BOB	Buckinghamshire, Oxford and Berkshire
CBI	Confederation of British Industry
CLES	Centre for Local Economic Strategies
COR	Committee of the Regions
COSLA	Consortium of Scottish Local Authorities
CSA	Campaign for a Scottish Assembly
DE	Department of Employment
DES	Department of Education and Science
DFEE	Department for Education and Employment
DoE	Department of the Environment
DT	Department of Transport
DTI	Department of Trade and Industry
EC	European Community
EDR	Cabinet Committee for Economic Development and Regeneration
EP	European Parliament
EPC	Economic Planning Council
ERA	English Regional Association
ERDF	European Regional Development Fund
ESF	European Social Fund
ESRC	Economic and Social Research Council
EU	European Union
GDP	Gross Domestic Product
GOCU	Government Office Co-ordination Unit
GOL	Government Office for London
GOM	Government Office for Merseyside

GOR	Government Office of the Regions
GOSE	Government Office for the South East
HO	Home Office
IRO	Integrated Regional Office
LEL	Lancashire Enterprises Ltd
LGC	Local Government Commission
LPAC	London Planning Advisory Committee
NUTS	Nomenclature of Units for Territorial Statistics
PC	Plaid Cymru
RA	Regional Association
RDA	Regional Development Agency
RETI	Regions of Traditional Industry
SEM	Single European Market
SERPLAN	London South East Regional Planning Conference
SHRA	Scottish Home Rule Association
SNP	Scottish National Party
SPD	Single Programming Document
SRB	Single Regeneration Budget
SRD	Senior Regional Director
TEC	Training and Enterprise Council
TEED	Training Enterprise and Employment Division
TUC	Trades Union Congress
UDC	Urban Development Corporations
WDA	Welsh Development Agency
WDI	Welsh Development International
YHRA	Yorkshire and Humberside Regional Assembly

Subject Index

Reference titles in italic indicate figures or tables.

Author Index